4 Week Loan

This book is due for return on or before the last date shown below

Muslims and Media Images

Muslims and Media Images
News versus Views

edited by

Ather Farouqui

OXFORD
UNIVERSITY PRESS

OXFORD
UNIVERSITY PRESS

YMCA Library Building, Jai Singh Road, New Delhi 110 001

Oxford University Press is a department of the University of Oxford.
It furthers the University's objective of excellence in research, scholarship,
and education by publishing worldwide in

Oxford   New York
Auckland   Cape Town   Dar es Salaam   Hong Kong   Karachi
Kuala Lumpur   Madrid   Melbourne   Mexico City   Nairobi
New Delhi   Shanghai   Taipei   Toronto

With offices in
Argentina   Austria   Brazil   Chile   Czech Republic   France   Greece
Guatemala   Hungary   Italy   Japan   Poland   Portugal   Singapore
South Korea   Switzerland   Thailand   Turkey   Ukraine   Vietnam

Oxford is a registered trademark of Oxford University Press
in the UK and in certain other countries.

Published in India
by Oxford University Press, New Delhi

© Oxford University Press 2009

ISBN-13: 978-0-19-569495-6
ISBN-10: 0-19-569495-3

Typeset in Esprit Book 10/12.5
by Eleven Arts, Keshav Puram, Delhi 110 035
Printed in India by De-Unique, New Delhi 110 018
Published by Oxford University Press
YMCA Library Building, Jai Singh Road, New Delhi 110 001

For Imtiaz Ahmad, Fitrat Ansari,
and Comrade Saghir Ahmad

Contents

Tables

Acknowledgements

I daresay I have put in much more effort into this edited volume than perhaps, I would have into a volume of my own writings. This is particularly so because of its theme. One can find all kinds of misconceptions, even poetic ambiguities, in the so-called academic writings on Indian Muslims. The theme of media images of Indian Muslims was no exception. There was, and is, no writing available on the theme of the present volume. The situation was worse in 1993 when I began working on this volume, and it was really difficult to make contributors write articles in the absence of any substantive material, debate, or even a thought process on the subject. But the contributors triumphed over the obstacles. The volume could not be published at the time but the inordinately long delay has led to a lot of reworking and it is now coming out with substantive contemporary material. Most of the contributors who had contributed in 1993 revised their articles in 2002 when I overcame my laxity to finalize the manuscript. A lot more new articles were then added. But even after that I wasn't able to send the manuscript to press in spite of my best efforts. For my sake these distinguished contributors updated their articles for the third time when I finally submitted the manuscript to Oxford University Press. They did so for the fourth time on the advice of Oxford University Press after the typescript was evaluated. Finally, most of the contributors obliged Oxford University Press and read their articles after the copyediting for which they remained in touch with Oxford University Press while doing so. Some of them revised their contributions in the light of new material. I am grateful to all of them for their cooperation and extend my sincere apologies for the delays and for the demands made on their time.

Three of the essays in the volume—by Vinod Mehta, Chandan Mitra, and Siddharth Varadarajan—were transcribed by me and I worked for months to word the content in the spirit in which the authors had made them in their addresses. I must especially thank them who, despite their professional commitments, took out time to read their pieces and rework them once the edited copy was sent to them by Oxford University Press.

I owe a lot to Salman Khurshid as I have learnt much from him in life. I am truly grateful to him.

I would like to thank the management and editors for handling the project competently, particularly getting the final copy approved by the authors.

Gautam Siddharth, now with *The Times of India*, is an old friend. He has been writing for over a decade on, among other subjects, modern Hinduism—I should add, completely free from any angularities since anyone writing on Hinduism is often seen as communal. His writings in *The Pioneer* are impressionistic but he isn't a votary of the status quo; rather, he espouses change without which, he says, societies tend to stagnate, which is equally true of the Muslim world. His insights were very helpful.

I had long, pleasant discussions with Zia Abdullah Nadwi Sahib and spent months in his guesthouse or the outhouse of his plush villa at Jeddah while working on this book. The strength of our relationship is such that though he did not agree with me most of the time, we always discussed the theme and, in the light of our discussions, I thought on various aspects of the theme.

With this volume I have completed the project that I started fifteen years ago. I can now heave a huge sigh of relief as I will never be able to undertake such academic work which, though an edited volume, in terms of thought process and effort, has been much more than writing a book. Moreover, the passion for the theme is simply impossible to explain in words.

With a great sense of gratitude to everyone instrumental in helping me with this compilation of the present volume, I bow my head in all sincerity and humility.

I dedicate this book to my three mentors: scholar and legendary teacher Professor Imtiaz Ahmad, Dr Fitrat Ansari, and Comrade Saghir Ahmad.

Professor Ahmad did me the greatest possible favour that a teacher can do for his students: He made me think. This is the most crucial aspect in the life of a student and because of Professor Ahmad, I could shift my focus from Urdu literature to interdisciplinary aspects of language, particularly its sensibility and politics. When I did this, the scope of my work automatically expanded to various themes involving Muslims, such as their media images, the sociology of religion with reference to Islam, particularly in South Asia and more specifically in India, politics of media capitalism, and its relation to Muslims. The sociology of market forces in itself is a challenge for media capitalism and not even a Marx can predict with confidence how capitalism will dictate its terms to media in the days to come. Though I have not met Professor Ahmad for the past few years, his views continue to inspire me.

Dr Fitrat Ansari was my first mentor and it had it not been for him, I would perhaps have been nowhere in the academic field. He died in 1998.

Comrade Saghir, as we used to call him, brought me in contact with the Communist Party of India (CPI) when I was about 15. A district-level comrade, he dedicated his life for the party and remained unmarried. He was aware of the left-wing discourse (and polemic) throughout the world but decided to work at the district level to build the organization. At the same time, he kept fighting with the party's national leadership and was expelled many times. Comrade Saghir was brought back every time since the party could not have survived in Bulandshahar district without him. He did everything he could to make me his successor but somehow it did not work out. For the last three years, I haven't renewed my party membership and haven't met Comrade Saghir for the last twenty years nor do I have any idea about his activities. There is no apparent reason for both these acts but since I had not done anything in my life which has an apparent reason or rationale so I am now happy only for one thing: the fragrance of this attachment to him and his views remains.

Hopefully, this dedication will revive my spiritual relationship with all my mentors and will serve as very small *gurudakshina* for them. I have nothing else to offer them.

To the best of my knowledge, only the *Economic and Political Weekly*, Mumbai, has published the article by Robin Jeffrey included in this volume. I thank them for allowing me to include it.

MUSLIMS AND MEDIA IMAGES

Introduction

I

I wish to begin the customary introduction on a slightly personal note: I worked on this volume with a passion bordering on madness. Obviously, it has a lot to do with personal reasons: My Muslim identity, more specifically the Indian Muslim identity, for one. Like many other things in life, my Muslim identity was not of my choosing—as it is for most people adhering to the religion of their birth. Being born an Indian Muslim, I fit a definite stereotype, and against this background I can understand the dilemmas of Muslims in today's world.

In this post-9/11 (2001), post-Iraq invasion (2003), post-London blasts 7/7 (2005), post-Glasgow world 30/6 (2007), and following the serial blasts in local trains in Mumbai 7/11 (2006) and recently in many cities of India (2008), the topicality and relevance of the theme of Muslim identity are universal because of the aspect of pan-Islamic identity. If we discuss Muslims in India, most of the broader aspects are applicable to the rest of the world and vice versa. Being Muslim in today's world often means carrying a special burden of suspicion and prejudice on the one hand, and social, political, and religious conservatism on the other. The common Muslim is caught between the increasingly strident anti-Muslim propaganda of the West and the equally strident religious fervour of the 'jihadi' Muslims. Both sides are pushing the common Muslim towards making a clear choice between either being anti-Muslim or being pro-jihadi. However, this is not a choice that every Muslim wants to make. But it is a dilemma that has driven many Muslims to become followers of militant Islam. The situation is the same for Muslims in India and so is the impact of fringe extremism, though it is manifested differently because of a Hindu majority and the secular nature of the Indian Constitution; this makes the case of Muslims in India more complex.

While civil society is often suspicious and distrustful of Islam and Muslims, Muslims believe that non-Muslim society is overtly influenced by anti-Muslim propaganda. Therefore, there is no way out for a person who does not wish to belong to either party or subscribe to either point of view. His/her situation epitomizes the old saying: 'Those who are not with us are against us, and therefore our enemies.' Although most Muslims do not at all subscribe to the extremism of militant Muslim groups—that are growing alarmingly—I believe it is important to understand the reasons behind their formation and increasing aggression. This is the quest out of which the volume has emerged.

II

Throughout the world, there exist groups that subscribe to violence and advocate militant Islam in one way or the other in their search for an exclusive Muslim identity and supremacy for Islam. What is more alarming is that they are finding a growing constituency of adherents and supporters. What is ironic is that no one can define the Islamic culture for which these Muslims are supposedly fighting. This trend points to increasing Muslim dissatisfaction with their conditions. The sense of insecurity and the search for an assumed Islamic identity is the same everywhere and prevails in Islamic countries as well; it manifests itself as Muslims pitted against all other beliefs (unlike in medieval times when the enemy was specifically Christianity).

This ideology, besides being obviously destructive and suicidal, has plenty of contradictions. It aims at destruction, carnage, and upheaval in the modern world. These so-called Muslims want to destroy the modern civilized world—to the development of which they have contributed little, while enjoying its comforts—terming it anti-Islamic in justification of this aim. However, there has never been one sole model of Islam even in the past and there certainly is none in the modern pluralistic world. It is difficult to imagine that these militant Islamic groups are advocating a world compatible with a desert culture of 1,400 years ago. Even in those times Islam was already divided, resulting in the murder of three caliphs out of four immediately after the demise of Prophet Mohammad! Thus the cause of Muslim antagonism against all other groups—religious, cultural, and social—might be said to be based on ideological confusion among various sects and sub-sects—of which there are hundreds, if not thousands—of Muslims. There remain unresolved contradictions and conflicts within Muslim society from the very time of the advent of Islam.

It is apparent that no exclusivist culture, especially the 'Muslim' culture dreamt of by Islamists, would be able to survive in the free market economy that dictates contemporary geopolitics. Muslims are participating in and enjoying the fruits of global activity—social, cultural, economic—both IT- and diaspora-driven; yet they are often engaged in the quest for an exclusive Muslim society or culture with supposedly 'Islamic' characteristics and this defies logic. The entire civilized, cultured, affluent, and educated world is perceived to be in the hands of those whom militant Muslims consider their enemies, and these militants have nothing practical to offer as a constructive alternative to what they want to destroy.

III

In contrast to views in the West, the Indian perspective is somewhat different because Muslims form an intrinsic part of Indian society. After the advent of Islam in India and till the time of the British conquest, Muslims were the ruling community in many parts of the subcontinent. However, through conversion and inter-marriage, Islam did not remain confined to the upper echelons of society and permeated every stratum of Indian life and culture. The British conquest resulted in a cultural upheaval among the Hindus, termed as the Bengal renaissance. It, however, failed to bring about a similar change in the Muslim community. Thinkers and leaders amongst Muslims were unable to take a lead in this matter. The idea of Pakistan was popularized by feudal sections of Muslims in colonial India among the Muslim masses, and this resulted in large-scale sectarian violence. Military dictatorship and feudal lords and their dominance over the polity and power structure in Pakistan resulted in the creation of Bangladesh in 1971. In effect, it proved the complete failure of the two-nation theory. The fight for cultural hegemony is continuing among different cultural groups and ethnic entities in Pakistan, resulting in the destruction of civil society.

The growth of the Indian media is one of the biggest success stories in independent India. For many decades after independence, the English language media, with its largely Western orientation, monopolized the scene. Now, even after the decisive emergence of the regional language presses, the English language media continues to dominate; its orientation is still largely elitist, but not alien as was the case until the 1980s.

Present-day English language media in India frequently displays stereotypical image of Muslims and its analysis is often simplistic. There is no clash of civilizations between Hindus and Muslims, as Hindus and Muslims broadly operate in the same social domain—both societies are ridden with divisions along caste and regional lines. Despite the claims of Muslim religious theoreticians that Islam has no room for caste, the social ethos of Muslims and Hindus in India is similar, as it is bound to be. Interestingly, Hindus largely seem as sceptical of the Western way of life as Muslims. However, the Indian media, especially the English language media does reflect the ubiquitous international prejudice against Muslims, albeit with some domestic variations and flavour. While open hostility against Muslims is precluded by the nature of the Indian Constitution, Pakistan's persistent effort to disrupt harmony (particularly its support for militant movements on Indian soil including the separatist movement in Jammu and Kashmir) creates reasons for doubt in some quarters about the allegiance of Indian Muslims, and the media at times reflects this doubt. The political leadership is often seen to be playing on the sensibilities of the illiterate masses of both religions and has done little to ease the doubts and suspicions regarding each other.

IV

Many years ago in 1986, I began considering the question of 'the image of Muslims', especially Indian Muslims, in the media. In those days print media dominated the scene. I had just started my career as an Urdu journalist. As a young Muslim hailing from a small town of Uttar Pradesh, whose political understanding had been shaped by Urdu newspapers, I too believed that the media was by and large anti-Muslim, that it was out to distort the image of Muslims. Two years later, by 1988, I tried to look at things differently, analysing whether or not Indian Muslims are really a distinct entity. After much analysis, I reached the conclusion—perhaps simplistic—that in a way urban north Indian Muslims could be regarded as an entity because, among other things, Urdu (though not all speak Urdu and indeed most speak regional languages) is one of the most important elements in their political sensibility. However, so scattered is the wider Indian Muslim population—and economically, socially, and regionally so differentiated—that it probably never emerged as a distinct entity. Nevertheless, there does exist the political aspect of Muslim identity as a vote bank, which has made a considerable difference to the polity of the nation.

I have been writing periodically on this subject, mainly in Hindi. After the demolition of the Babri Masjid on 6 December 1992, which resulted in nationwide riots and a rising tide of hatred that took months to subside, a seminar on the subject 'Muslims and the Press' was organized in May 1993 in Sikandrabad, a small town in Bulandshahr district of Uttar Pradesh. The invitees for the seminar included people of different ideological persuasions, ranging from the Jama'at e Islami to the Rashtriya Swayamsevak Sangh (RSS), freelance journalists, intellectuals, and some clear-thinking Muslim friends as well as some independent Hindu journalists.

Subsequently, the late Rafiq Zakaria, in his book *The Widening Divide*, included an article, 'The Role of Media',[1] which contained details of the papers presented at the May seminar. Excerpts from my paper were published in many papers and journals across the world.[2] Later, the major part of my paper was published in *South Asia*,[3] a journal published by the South Asian Studies Association (SASA), Australia. Robin Jeffrey, professor of politics, La Trobe University, Australia, wrote a series on journalism in various Indian languages that appeared in the *Economic and Political Weekly*.[4] Apart from these two efforts, I am not aware of any substantive writing on Urdu journalism after independence. These two, along with a piece on the same subject by Arshad Amanullah, have been included in the present volume.

Urdu is important here for the simple reason that it has played a decisive role in setting the pace and direction of Muslim politics in India in the last 200 years. All the references and excerpts in my article are from Urdu periodicals, especially those from Delhi. I am still facing the repercussions, and the Urdu newspapers and journalists whose names I quoted (most of them are now with one or the other political dispensation as Muslim leaders) have still not forgiven me. A common complaint is that Urdu journalism is an internal matter of the Muslim community, and that by writing in English and pointing fingers at journalists and Urdu newspapers, I have exposed them to their enemies—that is to say non-Muslims.

There have been various attempts to present the 'Muslim' point of view in the English media. In 1989, an English weekly, *One Nation Chronicle*, funded by Muslims started publication in response to a widespread perception that issues related to the Muslim community either did not find space in the national press, or that the community's image was deliberately projected in a distorted manner. The main stated purpose of this weekly was to bring Muslim issues to the attention of English-speaking Muslims and, to some extent, of secular-minded Hindus. It was funded by prominent Muslims from every part of the world. *One Nation Chronicle* folded up within a year of its birth and was replaced by the fortnightly *Nation and the World*. Although the latter continues to be published, it has failed to make an impact among any section of Muslims, leave alone non-Muslims.

In January 2000 or thereabouts, English fortnightly, *The Milli Gazette*, made its appearance. Its readership consists mainly of English-speaking Muslims, which is a significant and fast-growing section of the populace all over the world. Since it presents only Muslim issues, with a Muslim or soberly articulated Islamist orientation, its readership has remained largely confined to Muslims. Its owner and editor Zafarul Islam Khan seems caught between the paradox of ideology of the Jama'at e Islami and the demands of the readership, which also has a base amongst the followers of his father, the famous Islamic scholar Maulana Wahiduddin Khan. The Maulana believes that Muslims in India should cooperate with Hindus and try to emulate their economic and social progress, and he is opposed to any religious clash between Muslims and Hindus. In the Babri Masjid controversy, he advocated that Muslims should give up their claim to the mosque in order to honour the sentiments of their Hindu brethren. Zafarul Islam Khan is also the president of one faction of the All-India Muslim Majlis-e-Mushawarat of which Syed Shahabuddin is the key player. The Mushawarat claims—or rather, aspires—to be the umbrella organization of all Muslim political parties. Zafarul Islam Khan is respected among the Muslims. Like his father, he is considered upright and honest.

The non-Muslim readership of *The Milli Gazette* comprises only those intellectuals and journalists who take an interest in Muslim issues. Muslim issues are wide-ranging—from educational empowerment to social emancipation—and the hold that religion has over secular activities of even broad-minded Muslims is sometimes puzzling to an outsider. It is not as if the failures and frailties of Muslim society have not been identified—the mainstream media does that with a vengeance. The Muslim press, on the other hand, often playing up to vested interests, chooses to justify these frailties. Thus, both end up giving a bad name to the community and it remains backward in its outlook as well as in economic terms.

In 1983, Syed Shahabuddin launched a monthly magazine namely *Muslim India*. Initially, it was published in Urdu and English. Later, the Urdu version was scrapped owing to reasons best known to the founder-editor. This was perhaps the only publication that made its presence felt in academic circles the world over for the simple reason that one could find in it some material on every Muslim issue in India. Of course the material published in *Muslim India* is edited with an ideology that suited best its editor's politics. After 20 years of publication, in 2003, *Muslim India* was handed over to the management of *The Milli Gazette*. But *The Milli Gazette* lacked the political orientation and theoretical basis of *Muslim India* under Syed Shahabuddin, and after coming out sporadically for about a year-and-a-half, it ceased publication.

Between 8 and 11 February 2002, the Zakir Husain Study Circle organized an international conference on the theme of minorities and minority languages, in which one session was devoted to the media images of Muslims, in particular Indian Muslims. The conference was attended by a host of eminent academics from across the globe, and this particular session was attended by noted Indian editors and journalists representing various schools of thought, including the likes of Siddharth Varadarajan and Vinod Mehta.

Varadarajan served for long with *The Times of India* in the transitional phase of the quota-permit raj hangover. *The Times of India* was then targeted by the intelligentsia—as serving the cause of rich families oiled by poor taxpayers' money, stigmatizing it as a newspaper which had only commercial concerns. Later, *The Times of India* proved that only a market-driven paper can lead the way in changing the Indian mindset. Now Varadarajan works with *The Hindu*, a widely respected daily with the maximum circulation in South India.

Also present were Chandan Mitra, a Bharatiya Janata Party (BJP) Member of Parliament (MP) and editor of *The Pioneer*, and Mohammed Afzal, also known as Meem Afzal, a Rajya Sabha MP during V.P. Singh's tenure and now the Indian Ambassador to Turkmenistan. All of them presented thought-provoking papers. Later, Vinod Mehta, editor of *Outlook*, published an abridged version of his paper in an issue of *Outlook*.[5] I wrote a rejoinder to it, a portion of which (edited by the magazine) appeared in a later issue of *Outlook*.[6] Vinod Mehta was invited to deliver the Zakir Husain Memorial Lecture on 8 February 2004 and he chose the same theme and delivered a very remarkable lecture, which is included in this volume along with his responses in the discussion that followed, as an extension of his views. (His earlier article of 2002 and my rejoinder are included as Appendix I and Appendix II.)

This conference was organized a few months after 11 September 2001, and just before the riots in Gujarat. The Western intellectuals who attended this seminar have written extensively on Muslim, especially north Indian Muslim, issues. The papers read in the conference were related to language politics and were published in the volume *Redefining Urdu Politics in India*.[7]

V

While assessing the Muslim relationship with the press, the issue of why Muslims have been misunderstood not just by Hindus but also by other religious minorities in India needs to be tackled with greater sensitivity and understanding. Even where Muslims have a sizeable presence, certain misunderstandings about them persist in the Hindu mind. But it is the Muslims who need to urgently ponder and address these issues, as they are the victims of this mindset. At the academic level, attitudes or positions that have led to this general distrust should be studied and identified very carefully and placed in perspective. However, Muslim studies have often received marginal and shabby treatment globally, and India is no exception. Since India is home to about 200 million Muslims, Muslim studies should be a serious academic pursuit, but the available writings on

Indian Muslim society, culture, psyche, and problems rarely reflect the complexities of issues involved.

The chapters in the present volume try to fill some of these lacunae. Almost all of them discuss the contemporary situation with special focus on 'Muslim South Asia', especially in the Indian context. They analyse the Muslim psyche that gave birth to the peculiar brand of modern Indian politics, particularly in north India, that projects the entire community as an entity that may eventually become part of a broader pan-Islamic world. Today, religious representatives and unscrupulous politicians are exploiting this notional pan-Islamism.

A discussion on how far this goal of pan-Islamism is part of popular Muslim consciousness, and what its consequences have been, would help us understand the media image of Muslims worldwide as well as in the Indian context, including a broader South Asian perspective. Needless to say, Muslims of India, Pakistan, and Bangladesh are generally educationally backward and economically deprived and hence easy targets of religious bigotry. All the chapters included in this volume have a continuity that deals with that reality.

In the Indian context the most important question is what the Indian Muslims' strategy should be in a situation where foreign money will sooner or later be given complete access to Indian media, and where Western media houses gain entry. What are the Muslims, and especially Indian Muslims, doing to change distorted media images, particularly in the changed international scenario? In the age of the free market economy, how do Indian Muslims approach this issue? How does the media view Muslims, especially after 9/11? The papers not only raise these questions, but also help us in trying to find answers to them. One point on which all writers, editors, and intellectuals agree is that, be it in the Indian context or at international levels, we need to ask whether it is Muslims who bear the sole responsibility for changing their media images. In India, especially now, when the free market economy has made a decisive impact, and Hindus themselves remain woefully divided on the question of caste, we find that Indian Muslims have to fight their own battles. It is, of course, difficult in the absence of intellectual leadership, a substantial and forward-looking middle-class, and general awareness on this issue.

But the issue that is again paramount is why the Indian Muslim middle-class is so shy of its identity and tends to dance to the tunes of Muslim fundamentalists. Why do educated Muslims in the whole of South Asia, including Pakistan (where there is a huge middle-class) often exhibit backward-looking attitudes? The media image of any community, whether distorted or glorified, plays a vital role in establishing its status in society. The distorted and negative image of Muslims in the international and Indian media must therefore be changed. But Muslims must themselves take the lead in this direction. The first step towards this must be introspection and self-reform.

VI

This volume is divided into four parts: English Media: Image and Depiction; Transcending Boundaries; Muslim Journalism: A Phenomenal Dichotomy; and Popular Images and the Story of Stereotypes. There is an inevitable overlapping of themes between articles so all those that are thematically interlinked follow each other in succession.

PART I

Vinod Mehta's essay entitled 'Muslims and Media Images: Where Things went Wrong' is an eye-opener with regard to Muslim expectations from non-Muslim journalists. The condition of Muslims in independent India is so abysmal that they expect all unbiased non-Muslims to promote the Muslim cause. As a successful editor, Mehta has had to deal with these hopes and he tries to explain why these hopes are misplaced. His perspective on Muslim media images is that of a seasoned English language journalist belonging to north India and fully conversant with the complications created by Partition. He does not apportion blame but maintains that there is a lack of understanding between Muslims and the Indian media. He explains the compulsions and challenges faced by the Indian media in its depiction of the Muslim community and the role of the media in society.

Muslim critics of the media, particularly in north India, should be aware of the constraints within which it has to operate: first and foremost, the media is a business that requires capital and which needs to generate profits for those who invest this capital, that is, the media house owners. Then there are the particular constraints and mindsets of the quota-permit days of which the media is only now breaking free; and last but not least is the absence of Muslim voices in public spaces because of a general lack of education. Mehta regrets that professional Muslim socialites dominate Muslim media and public space. He is critical of the media giving space to these Muslims as representative voices but warns that the situation is unlikely to change unless the common Muslim makes efforts to be heard. So, while the moderate Muslims' grouse that the media provides space only to Muslim socialites who are far removed from the problems of the common Indian Muslim or to fringe Muslim voices may be justified, they must remember that circulation, readership, and finances are the primary dharma of most newspapers. The same is the case with magazines that are perceived by Muslims as being fair—*Outlook*, for example. Fringe voices make for better copy; moderate voices therefore tend to be ignored unless they make special efforts. The onus is really on the Muslims themselves.

Rajni Kothari's article asserts that the politicization of the people of India before Independence was in two directions: homogenization and hegemonization. Unfortunately hegemonization and separatism have come to the fore in the post-Independence period, and in this Kothari feels that the role of the media has been negative. It has not provided enough space for minority opinions and has portrayed them negatively. He urges the Muslim leadership to work hand in hand with secular Hindu elements towards a realignment of forces that can rebuild India's democratic secularism. He is optimistic and believes that once this happens the press will have a very positive role in building constructive cooperative relationships.

Kuldip Nayar's article discusses changes in the attitude of the Urdu press in India after Partition. He states that strained post-Partition Hindu–Muslim relations have affected journalism as a whole; the role of the English language press is however more balanced, albeit subtly biased towards majority concerns. He does not agree that the national press is a puppet controlled by majoritarian communal forces, dismissing such claims by Muslims as product of fear psychosis. He agrees that there do exist irresponsible journalists but emphasizes that these are in a minority. He believes that the national press is, on the whole, balanced and fair. He concludes that the supposedly anti-minority approach of the press can be blamed on the lack of professionally trained Muslim journalists. He urges the

Muslim community to encourage their youth to come forward and represent the community in the national press.

Mrinal Pande provides a gender-centric viewpoint on the issue. She informs us that the press often fails in its role of a powerful social watchdog as far as women and minorities are concerned. International forces accord the English language media in India a place of pride at the cost of the vernacular media, which is the voice of the common people in India. Minorities and women lose out in this situation because male members of the majority community control media coverage and institutions. She laments that English language media wields disproportionate influence on policymakers. She goes on to say that the English language media segregates people more effectively than anything else. English language journalists are far removed from the realities of the majority of Indians and therefore report on issues related to common Indians in a clichéd and stereotypical manner. In the second half of her essay, she discusses the devastating role the press can play and the effect it has on the psyche of the community it targets. While male domination of the English language media is being challenged, the vernacular media is still, overwhelmingly, a male preserve and its chauvinism is evident in the quick politicization of issues concerning women belonging to the minority community. Pande concludes that integrity of the press can only come about through the efforts of professionally dedicated individuals who are not influenced by narrow sectarian and commercial interests.

Howard Brasted seeks to investigate how the Australian press understands Islam and what goes into reproduction of this understanding. Ambitiously enough, he has dug into archives of the last fifty years of selected media publications to build his narrative. In the process of exploring different aspects of the production of knowledge which feeds into the construction of media images of Islam in his country, he critically engages with Edward Said's thesis of Orientalism. He feels and also shows, as his arguments flow, that certain aspects of Said's thesis are 'ill-fitting and problematic' when applied to the texts and practices of the print media. In an attempt to underline 'other possible factors' responsible for shaping Western imagery, Brasted devotes a significant chunk of his piece to a socio-political account of the post-colonial world with special reference to events unfolding in the Arab region. Addition of the veil as a new signifier of Islam to the visual vocabulary of the Australian press symbolizes a perceptible change in the Australian portrayal of the religion and its adherents. It, in a way, suggests a shift in the post-Gulf War period, in the focus of media debate on both the internal dynamics and the outward form of Islam. Brasted, in conclusion, convincingly states that it is the challenge before the Muslim community to come up with an idiom of its representation, both textual and visual, if it is critical of what the Australian press has been doing for the last fifty years. A postscript, specifically written for this volume, updates the study by covering the ten-year period from 1998 to 2007. Brasted detects a more sensitive treatment of Islam early on, at least in quality press. With journalists themselves conceding that their image of Islam has been flawed, an attempt is made to get it right. But against the background of Taliban Afghanistan and the phenomenon of 'Islamic' terrorism, this proves to be difficult. Indeed, the standard associations of Islam with female servitude and radical militancy are reinforced. An unprecedented investigation into the causes of Islamic militancy is sparked by 9/11, but the search for answers uncovers two very different explanations, one attributing the blame entirely to a distorted form of Islam, the other in part to American foreign policy in the Middle East. Ultimately, as Brasted suggests, what may determine which interpretative account stands up and how the media may consequently portray Islam in the future will depend as much on the domestic as the international dimension of Islamism. So far the signs in Australia augur badly. In the last couple of years the government has not only targeted Muslims who fail to embrace 'Australian values' as Islamist, but has also questioned the very basis of Australia's multicultural future. The 'politics of stereotyping' is back in vogue.

In his contribution, 'The Print Media and Minority Images', Chandan Mitra begins by endorsing the view that the English language media of India does not project a positive picture of the Muslim community. Mitra is the articulate, modern face of the RSS. As a BJP-backed MP, he has for long espoused the RSS viewpoint. Mitra argues in erudite journalistic fashion that the generalization that the media is biased against Muslims is not true. As a journalist intrinsically involved with news distribution, he is aware of the constraints and ground realities. He reminds us that the Urdu media is also not interested in projecting a positive image of the community or in raising awareness among Muslims about social changes and developments that are affecting the rest of India. Mitra also tells us that in the English media two polarities exist, one patronizing and the other antagonistic. The former tends to understand the issues concerning Muslims and the latter believes that Muslims are prisoners of their own image. In conclusion, he maintains that there are biases existing in the media, but there are also dedicated people who go to great lengths to rectify such distortions.

Siddharth Varadarajan starts with an interesting historical perspective on the media in India. He tells us that journalism in India is a by-product of colonialism but the 'nation building' it did during the early part of the so-called Indian renaissance ended up deepening cultural and religious identities. In line with the emergence of 'national' consciousness, a 'national' media also emerged but a complete break with the notion of looking at Indians as 'Hindus', 'Muslims', 'Sikhs', etc., never took place. Although the mainstream media after Independence did not openly support communal forces, the press, in common with the ruling Congress, arguably gave undeserved prominence to the views of the mullahs, portraying them as the leaders of the Muslim community. With the emergence of more virulent communal politics from the 1970s onwards, the communal biases of a section of the print media became more pronounced, and this came into stark relief every time a major incident of communal violence occurred.

He then provides an insider's insight on riot reporting in the mainstream press and its invariable bias against Muslims, though veiled under a garb of impartiality. He bewails the fact that the compulsions of the market dictate that trivialities concerning celebrities get much more prominence than serious national issues. However, on an optimistic note, he assures us that all is not lost as there are dedicated people in the media with a mission 'to do the right thing'. He also notes the fact that he has the liberty bluntly to speak the truth about communalism in the media largely because he is a Hindu, and that a Muslim journalist or intellectual might not find this so easy to do.

PART II

In 'Muslims and the World Forum', K.M.A. Munim tells us that the plight of Muslims in general has its roots in the division of the pre-oil-wealth Muslim world. After World War I and before World War II, the Muslim world was in a sorry state. Politically bankrupt and economically pauperized, it was at this time that Muslims became non-entities in international geopolitics. Munim attributes the rise of Islamic fundamentalism to social and economic causes. He also talks about the international distrust of Muslims that exists among non-Muslims. To boost the image of Muslims, he feels that a powerful Muslim press is an essential tool, for which the spread of journalistic education and an awareness of the glorious heritage of Islam among Muslim youth are necessary. He, however, warns against basking in past glory and instead advocates working towards the regaining of lost self-confidence.

Sabya Sachi takes us on a journey through the composite cultural corridors of Bengal. He looks at the coexistence of Bangla-speaking Bengali Hindus and Muslims, and how their paths are gradually diverging from one another. As a cultural entity, both the communities of Bengal were and are one. Sachi notes the glaring difference between north Indian Muslims and their Bengali counterparts. He also tells us that, more than religion, it is regional identity that dominates the sensibilities of both communities in West Bengal. An interesting observation that he makes is that the trauma of Partition has affected Bengalis differently from how it has affected north Indians. He also talks about the distinction made by the government in the settlement of Bengali Hindu and Muslim refugees in Bengal and Delhi. While the former have been given civic space and facilities in upscale localities like Chittaranjan Park of south Delhi and spread comfortably all over West Bengal, the latter are living in subhuman conditions in jhuggi clusters in and around Delhi, which too are destroyed from time to time with an eye to consolidating the Hindu vote bank. Sachi also indicts the Bengali vernacular media for depicting negative Muslim images.

In his essay, Charles J. Borges examines the relationship between the Goan press and Goan Muslims. He supports his arguments with the help of several examples of reportage on local Muslim issues in the Goan press. He also discusses Muslim organizations operating in Goa for the benefit of the community.

Dagmar Markova discusses the Central European perception of Muslims, in particular Indian Muslims in the context of the Babri mosque controversy. She talks about the Czech experience of Muslims, and states that Czechs share the conceptions of other Europeans about Muslims. She examines the reportage about the Babri mosque controversy in the Czech press and notes its indifferent nature.

In 'Indian Muslims and the Free Press', Estelle Dryland examines the sorry state of the Muslim press in India and analyses the reasons for it. In the first part of her essay, she tackles the question of Urdu and Muslim identity; in the second she talks about the relationship of Muslims with the press in India; and in the third she throws light on reporting in the vernacular press on Muslim issues. In her well-researched paper, she analyses the concerns of Muslim identity and its representation in various public media including films. In her examination of Muslim journalism, she includes Pakistani media. She concludes that Muslim journalists are still living in the past and that this has negatively impacted media images of Muslims. She is optimistic, however, that once this obsession with the past is tackled, reporting on these issues will move forward.

In 'Islam and the West: Ominous Misunderstandings', Susan B. Maitra discusses the demonization of Muslims as enemies of civilization by the Western press. This propaganda, according to her, is gaining ground in the minds of Westerners and she blames this on their ignorance of Islamic culture. The Western press is a powerful policy-making tool in the hands of Western powers and they have cleverly employed it to further their geopolitical ambitions vis-à-vis Muslim nations. They have used the press to mobilize public opinion in favour of their designs on Muslim countries, and this is the reason for the negative projection of Muslims in the Western press. In order to counter this covert war on Muslims, she calls for a broad-based dialogue between different religions. She argues that geopolitics has reduced man to the level of a beast and to rid itself of this curse, mankind must call humanitarianism to the fore.

PART III

In 'Urdu Newspapers in India: Waiting for Citizen Kane?', Robin Jeffrey examines circulation figures of Urdu newspapers in India and concludes that under present circumstances their circulation is limited to a minuscule minority. He states that a careful study of the condition of Urdu language in India is a pointer to the way in which the state in league with capitalism can often influence the perceptions of its citizens. He concludes that the condition of this language in the country reflects that of its speakers.

In 'Urdu Press in India', I have looked at the role of Urdu journalism in helping the Muslim community in post-Independence India face up to the challenge of adjustment as a large minority group, and have argued that it has largely failed to perform this role. This failure is due in part to the nature of Urdu readership and in part to the political and economic interests and linkages of Urdu journalists. Thus Urdu journalism has been prone to reinforcing a sectarian and emotional outlook amongst readers. At any rate, Urdu journalism has often negatively shaped Muslim positions on substantive issues of concern to the community and the country at large by ignoring the emerging social realities within the community. Accordingly, this discussion of Urdu journalism in India is set against the changing position of Urdu and the socio-economic changes Muslims in India have experienced during the past sixty years.

In 'Muslims and the Press', Wahiduddin Khan states that the Muslim press is in no way comparable to the standards of the Western press, be it in terms of circulation or independence of reporting. It is overly dependent on the international press for news coverage. The international press has a large pool of professional journalists of high intellect, and this is sadly lacking in the Muslim press because Muslim intellectuals do not often consider it an attractive career option. The Muslim press is thus largely involved in 'lifting' news from the Western press. Moreover, it reflects the chronic protest mentality of Muslims in the international as well as national scenario. Muslims tend to blame their ills on external factors, and the Muslim press is enlisted in this cause. He concludes by suggesting certain measures to improve the standards of the Muslim press.

Arshad Amanullah's essay deals with the current state of Urdu journalism in India. He first talks of its decline, as is evident from most of the writings on the theme. He, however, feels that in the last decade it has witnessed some positive changes under the influence of the forces of liberalization, privatization, and globalization. While most experienced Muslim journalists are pessimistic about the future of Urdu journalism in India, others continue to venture into it because Urdu is an emotional issue for Muslims. Amanullah is optimistic that in the years to come Urdu journalism will attract the attention of all big media houses.

PART IV

Moinuddin Jinabade examines how the negative depiction of Muslims in Bollywood films influences the perceptions of viewers. He gives examples of several popular commercial hits from the Mumbai film industry, even by Muslim directors, in which either a villainous character or someone engaged in a lowly occupation bears a Muslim name. It is an oft-repeated cliché in Hindi films, and he argues that it is harmful for inter-community relations. On television too, Jinabade notes that commercials that are supposed to cater to all communities are lacking in Muslim representation. He warns us that this subtle brainwashing helps breed a phobia that is very harmful to the health of a composite society.

In his study of Indian parallel cinema, John W. Hood takes up aspects of Muslim issues that have been tackled in parallel cinema. He notes that this treatment has been meagre, and adds that both commercial and independent cinema have largely ignored issues of concern to Muslims—Partition, for example. He offers possible social and commercial reasons for this, noting the financial difficulties of independent film-makers as well as the social dangers inherent in dealing with minority concerns in India. In his examination of the more accomplished parallel cinema in Bengali and Malayalam, he notes some interesting and worthy efforts to give a positive portrayal of Muslim concerns, while ruing the fact that such efforts have been few and far between.

The contributions in this volume conclude that media depiction of Muslims is indeed negative all over the world and offer different causes and solutions for the phenomenon in different parts of the globe. They all feel that this is a matter of urgent necessity.

NOTES

1. Rafiq Zakaria, 'The Role of Media', in *The Widening Divide* (New Delhi: Viking, 1995), pp. 267–77.
2. Among others, in the *American Journal of Economics and Sociology*, 53(3), July 1994, pp. 360–2.

3. *South Asia* (*Journal of South Asian Studies*), New Series, 17(2), December 1995, pp. 91–103.
4. Robin Jeffrey, 'Urdu Press: Waiting for Citizen Kane', *Economic and Political Weekly*, 29 March 1997, pp. 631–6.
5. Vinod Mehta, 'Medium is the Image', *Outlook*, 44(43), 1 November 2002, p. 32.
6. Ather Farouqui, 'Who's the Real Muslim?', *Outlook*, 44(48), 6 December 2002, p. 64.
7. Ather Farouqui (ed.), *Redefining Urdu Politics in India* (New Delhi: Oxford University Press, 2006).

PART I
ENGLISH MEDIA
IMAGE AND DEPICTION

1

Muslims and Media Images
Where Things went Wrong

Vinod Mehta

Before I come to the subject matter of this essay, I must make a disclaimer, namely, that I do not bring to the issue an academic's or a specialist's perspective. All I can say is that I have been an English-language editor for more than twenty-five years, and in that period I certainly have a working experience and knowledge of some of the problems and some of the complaints of Muslims in this country in terms of their media representation, especially in the English-language section of the press.

We need to spend more time debating from the Muslim point of view the reasons why things have gone wrong for the Muslims with regard to the Indian media, particularly the relationship between the north Indian media and north Indian Muslims. I refer to north India and north Indian Muslims because in the arena of Indian politics this area and this community are thought to be representative of the entire Indian Muslim community.

Without seeking to apportion blame, we will begin by sketching one of the reasons for things having gone wrong. This reason is the lack of understanding among Muslims of the nature of the media in India, and where Muslims stand in the common civic space of India in 2006. This, again, is more important and relevant in the context of north Indian Muslims.

The next question is what the mandate and compulsions—or, rather, the challenges—of the Indian media are and what the role of the media is in society at large. Much of the problem begins because there is a lack of understanding on the part of common Muslims of the compulsions of Indian society. For a number of reasons, there is no forward movement in general amongst Muslims, again especially in north India, towards social transformation and modernization. Most north Indian Muslims, even educated ones, are unable to understand what the Indian media in the twenty-first century is, and should be. They are not ready to realize that life goes on and that time cannot be reversed.

Against this backdrop, let us examine the hypothesis that the media has a special responsibility to portray Muslims sensitively, to be balanced and fair, since Muslims are in a minority and are supposed to be the most backward community of India. Theoretically this may be true, but in the contemporary world, cut-throat competition is the driving force as much for the media as for any other business. However, it is argued that the Indian media should be more sympathetic and objective towards Muslims in comparison to other smaller minorities who are much better off, more educated, and modern in their outlook simply because of their economic condition. The media is, therefore, seen in very idealistic terms. It is also seen as almost having a special responsibility because Muslims are the largest religious minority in the country.

There is a politico-psychological angle to this. The impression and assurance given to Muslims at the time of Partition was that their interests and identity would be safeguarded in a democratic country, irrespective of the fact that India is a Hindu-majority nation. However, the harsh fact is that even for the majority of Hindus there are many constraints in life, and they will have to exert themselves to overcome them. I am not debunking the expectation, but we must also remember that the media is a business. The media would not exist, it would go bankrupt very quickly, if it did not take its business responsibilities seriously. While being a business does not mean it should be exclusively devoted to making money, it is not feasible for any such venture to be purely idealistic.

Another aspect to remember is that most media in this country are run by businessmen and business families who have little understanding of what the media's role vis-à-vis the Muslim community should be. They are interested only in making profits. When people talk of the commercialization of the media, which is a kind of catchphrase for all evils, what they are getting at is that the media are only interested in making profits and that their social responsibility has been diluted.

This is a somewhat facile view of the media, and a facile view of our responsibility. It is the job, within these challenges and constraints, of the editors and editorial teams to maintain a balance between editorial integrity and the reasonable assumption of making a profit, so as to ensure that these two things are not necessarily incompatible and inconsistent. It is possible at one and the same time to be a media house interested in making profits (though not solely dedicated to this) yet also fulfilling its social responsibilities. When people talk about commercialization of the media, it is accompanied by the assumption that commercialization necessarily means an erosion and downgrading of media standards.

As a working editor, I submit that there is, in the media, sometimes even more cut-throat competition than there is in other, more honestly commercial, ventures like selling soap and ice cream. The media operate today in one of the most competitive environments as far as the marketplace is concerned. In this country, besides, we have a problem of too much media. In New York or Washington, you will probably find one major English-language daily. Delhi has twelve broadsheets, without even counting the small ones. This is a good thing and I am not deriding it, but we have to understand that in India a great deal of media rivalry and competition exist. This marketplace competition has its own compulsions, and an editor or editorial team that pretends otherwise does so at its own peril. This must be the basic premise and everything else, including the media's presumed social responsibility towards Muslims or any other issue, must be seen in this context.

If you remove this context and see the media purely in terms of having a social responsibility, of not measuring up to the standards of the press during Gandhi and Nehru's time and of the *National Herald* and all those editors, you are looking at only half the picture. I think we had very eminent people and great newspapers in the times of Gandhi and Nehru. They did not, however, live in the current environment, with its competition, nor did they, as most editors do today, have to be constantly worried about the bottom-line. In these competitive times, if you are not worried about how well your paper is doing, you are held in low esteem as an editor, and your editorial policy is circumscribed in some ways by this constraint. There is, however, no fundamental incompatibility between making profits and social responsibility. Of course, standards can be lowered, some papers can sell out—as has indeed happened. But if you have a paper that is commercially successful you cannot assume that it automatically has poor editorial standards, nor does it automatically mean that a paper is going to lose money if a paper has very high editorial standards.

The question of whether the media has been fair to Muslims and where it has gone wrong has to be seen in his context. Keeping this in mind, we can now pose our questions. Have the Indian media been fair to Indian Muslims? Have we portrayed them with sensitivity and objectivity, keeping in view the problems they face? Have the media given undue prominence to the lunatic fringe? Have the media suppressed and ignored liberal or moderate voices? Have they paid too much attention to the *maulavi*s and *mullah*s? Have they given 200 million Muslims a bad press and painted them as rabid and fundamentalist?

These are very relevant questions, and I do not pretend to have answers to all of them. But from time to time, I have been confronted with some of these questions and complaints, and I must say that some of the criticism of the media in this regard is justified. I will not attempt an apology or defence here but will try to present some of the problems and compulsions of the media as a backdrop against which these complaints should be viewed.

One of the things that we should remember is that journalists are fundamentally extremely lazy people. The assumption that we are very industrious and will do a lot of groundwork for stories is an erroneous one. If a sound-byte is readily available from the Imam of the Jama Masjid, for example, why should the TV reporter go looking for the not-so-easily-available moderate voice, which anyway makes for dull copy?

But it is assumed, because of the special responsibility that has been thrust on us (or sought to be thrust on us), that we will go looking for that moderate voice and perhaps ignore the strident one. In a way, much the same charge is made by secular Hindus against the media— that too much space is given to people like Praveen Togadia. The reason we do so brings us to the other part of the criticism—that the rabid and fringe voice is strident and extreme, and is therefore more saleable. It makes for better television if you have two people shouting at and abusing each other than if you have two people having a reasoned and moderate debate. The lazy way out is to look for the strident voice that lends itself to a raucous debate. I think that if there is a defining complaint against the media from progressive and liberal Muslims, it is that we deliberately go out looking for these voices and ignore and suppress the more moderate and enlightened voices. But in all this there is a problem and I can tell you that I face exactly this problem as an editor: where is this moderate Muslim liberal voice and how are we going to access it?

Anyway, liberal Muslims have their own views on the issue. They argue that whenever some foolish person makes a reactionary or extraordinarily stupid statement they are expected to come up with a response. The same is not expected of liberal Hindus; why then should this always be expected of the liberal Muslim? Liberal Muslims feel that it is humiliating for them to be constantly pressurized by the media and other people to state what the alternate voice is. But, as some people have pointed out, do they have a choice? Maybe they do not have the luxury of keeping silent.

So what is this image of Muslims that an unfair media has created? According to this view, Indian Muslims are held captive by an extremely powerful but regressive religious leadership and a passive and backward-looking political leadership that is attuned to this religious leadership and therefore determined to resist change and modernity. Whether this image is correct or not, it exists. It is also true that, right or wrong, this image matters decisively in the contemporary world. (One encounters a state of denial here, exemplified by the statement that this is just a perception floated by a rather unfair media concerned with its own interests and profits. In my opinion that is simply not true.)

What has happened in the past is that there has been too much analysis of why this image exists. We have got into long historical debates that are quite irrelevant. Instead of confronting the challenge, we have spent a great deal of time in apportioning blame. A great deal of time has been wasted in examining the problem rather than solving it. Rather than run away from it or over-analyse it, it would be more useful to take up the challenge, accept the problem, and see what can be done to resolve it.

If the Muslim community itself introspects, this is a problem that can be solved. We need to get away from the sterile debate on who is responsible, and begin a new debate on correctives and a new strategy to redress the balance. How do we improve the image? How do we accelerate the process of modernization and social change among Muslims? We can be sure that dwelling on historical glories or the sense of the past will not help Muslims to face up to the challenges of contemporary life.

Who speaks for the Muslims in India? Of course, you can argue that there are at least 160 million Muslims in India, and they are not a monolith, so why should there be one or a few spokespersons? Let there then be a plurality of voices—the media would be delighted if there were many voices from which they could select different voices to interview on different days of the week. Unfortunately, that situation does not exist. So what does the time-pressed TV reporter or the print journalist with a deadline do when looking for a byte?

Much of the problem begins here. The conservative voice, ironically, is the most easily available. For instance, the All-India Muslim Personal Law Board that claims to be 'the true protector of Indian Muslims' and various other clerics who perpetuate Muslim stereotypes are the only ones easily available. These people are extremely media-savvy—they have websites, phone numbers, press conferences, press officers, public relations officers, and clout. In many ways, they understand the media much better than the Muslim middle-class and enlightened Muslims do, and they exploit the media much better and to the greatest possible extent. On the other hand, there are too few liberal Muslims who can be called upon to speak. So whenever there is a problem or debate, the media rounds up the usual suspects amongst the liberals. Sadly, of these some use the Muslim cause only for self-promotion. So you have to be very careful whether they are really interested in the problem or whether they are just interested in seeing their images on the television screen and in newspapers. You thus have a small pool of these voices to begin with, which is made even smaller if you try to discriminate too much between the genuine voices and the rent-a-voice that is available for every cause including that of Muslims.

What has happened as a result of this is that the so-called Muslim debate in this country has become a slanging match, a forum for abuse. You get a television studio, you lay out a few chairs and get a moderator—and then you get extremes, polarized views, and put them one against the other and goad them to call each other names. It is a dialogue of the deaf. But there is a feeling among television producers that this is what improves television ratings. So this is the only kind of 'debate' that occurs in India at the moment on these questions. It is completely counterproductive: for 20–5 minutes you are getting TV as a kind of entertainment sport; even in the print media, things are the same.

We need more sober, more meaningful debates that can chalk out an agenda for change. And here the liberal moderate voice, which is reticent, which is perhaps not sure whether it should speak out, has at the very least to meet the media halfway. It must come out of its self-imposed restraint. It must be accessible; it must be eager to be heard. The expectation that the media will go searching for it is unrealistic.

Of course the assumption here is that such voices do exist. Some time ago, we spoke to Muslims for a cover story, 'The Other Face of Indian Muslims', in *Outlook* (5 October 2004). We did not go to the modern jeans-clad sort of Muslims, but those from the Jama Masjid-like areas, and we got some very interesting voices of Muslim women and men who combined tradition and modernity so effortlessly. We assume that there is some kind of conflict between the two, but in the lives and professions of these ordinary Muslims they coalesce effortlessly. The Muslim question is very much a part of their psyche. The one thing that emerges, however, is what they want is to get on with their lives.

But this is only one part of the story, the pleasant part; it is not the whole truth of Muslim society. Later on we realized from the response of the readers that some of the families cited as examples in the story have no roots in the community and are thus not role models for the community. Besides, the number of such families is negligible. Moreover, there are also professional Muslim socialites who claim to be true representatives of the community simply because they live in the old-city area. They also sell themselves as progressives. No surprise then that, like other communities, there are also Muslim 'seminarist intellectuals' of the 'Walled City', who give wrong feedback to the media about Muslims. As I have already confessed, journalists are lazy, so the correspondent doing the story chose only those families that are socially prominent and in touch with professional intellectuals.

It seems that these days many a socialite is capitalizing on the exploitation done by the Imam of Jama Masjid and the institution of the Jama Masjid. There is no purpose behind frequent statements and press releases against the Imam by these socialites. I do not mean that I approve any kind of exploitation, religious or political, by the Imam of Jama Masjid; nor do I approve of governments in power or political parties that have been using the Imam's name or the institution of the Jama Masjid for political gains. But then there is hardly anything constructive in the approach of Muslims and various groups who are against the Imam except a desire for self-publicity. Muslims will have to fight both the socialites and the Imam—or, for that matter, all religious institutions who are exploiting them. Muslims will have to channelize all their stamina towards social and political empowerment. As an editor, even though I know that the Imam is exploiting the community to the core, I have to be careful not to give publicity to anti-Imam groups among Muslims. It would, in any case, not solve any of the problems faced by the community but only show it in poor light.

This is the age of publicity and propaganda and I want to emphasize once again that there is no point having good ideas and moderate views if you choose not to air them in a public forum. Good ideas need to be promoted, and you have to use all the tricks of modern media promotion. The liberal moderate Muslim voice appears to be somewhat uncomfortable with publicity.

But they have to break out of that trap—they have to use the media, and they have to learn how to use it. And if these progressive voices come from Muslim institutions, from Muslim associations and Muslim bodies, then they will carry much greater weight. We therefore need a new partnership between the media and the moderate forward-looking Muslim voice. We need to stop calling each other names and criticizing each other. We must forge a partnership, and we must forge an agenda for a partnership. Most of the media would be more than eager and willing to participate in this partnership but the moderate Muslim voice must be prepared to meet the media halfway.

It is also true that the Muslim problem is not the only problem as far as an editor's basket is concerned; there are hundreds of other national problems. So it must take its place, high up in the priority list, but as one among other issues nevertheless. This must be seen in the wider context, and the wider context is that the media is a huge business today. However, I believe that it is the only business today, and the only institution, through which all your complaints are going to be aired, and in which there is great growth and which enjoys great public credibility. Competition may foster biases and other unethical factors but, by and large, if you ask the common man how he knows something is true, he will say that he read it in the newspaper. And I think that we should cherish this: that the media does have this public credibility despite all its shortcomings. If the media were biased from day one, it would not have this credibility.

Let us take up the case of the English-language media in particular. In liberal and Muslim forums, the English-language media is often accused of being guilty of an anti-Muslim bias; in other forums it is often accused of just the opposite. In my understanding, the English-language media is not biased. We try and understand the problems of the community, but Muslims are not our only concern. Thus my plea to all concerned and to the Muslim liberal voice to meet us halfway—partly in response to the fact that we are lazy, but also because it is in the interest of all concerned. To wait for us to change, to expect us to operate with heightened social responsibility on the issue and to make greater efforts to find the liberal voice is not in the self-interest of Muslims. The media and Muslims are both engaged in the same project, both on the same side.

There is no doubt that not only are media images of Muslims generally projected in a distorted form, but that every debate on the subject is also sought to be derailed. The populists, among Muslims too—those who do not want it to be discussed with sincerity—raise non-issues with reference to the role of English as a language and by corollary the English-language media. Their main argument is that the English-language media has played the biggest role in this distortion of Muslim images simply because it knows virtually nothing about Muslims, most of whom live below the poverty line and are backward in most spheres of life. Besides, hardly 1 per cent of Muslims know English. Both facts may be correct, but the hypothesis rests on wrong assumptions about a populist approach and an oversimplification of a very complex situation.

I would like to examine both hypotheses to the best of my ability as an English-language editor who also belongs to north India. Of course it must be borne in mind that I am not a sociologist. I also do not know Persianized and hybrid Urdu—that is considered as part of the Muslim sensibility for political purposes, mainly after Partition. For that matter I do not even know hybrid Hindi, which has also been used for political purposes in the name of Hindu nationalism.

The problem is that, despite the fact that in the entire country there would not be more than 10 per cent of people who are well-versed in English, among the Muslims they are hardly 1 per cent. The English media is therefore only for the English-speaking people of India, and, English being a universal language, the English-language media of India becomes a window on India to the entire English-speaking world. Contrary to the wishes of Hindi nationalists, English is expanding its scope in India and, hence, the Indian English-language media becomes the showcase of India for the outside world. Hindi propagators underestimate the growing influence of English in every sphere of life, even in north India.

In the southern states, English has a sound base, yet there still is a real sense of pride for local culture and languages. But in north India, the political elite continue to play politics in the name of Hindi- and Urdu-medium education for the masses—while they send their children to institutions in India and abroad where there is hardly any scope even for Hindustani as a spoken language. However, north Indian politics in the name of language—especially Muslim politics, in the name of Urdu—is not the subject of discussion here; I only want to make the point that it has remained very powerful in shaping Muslim sensibilities over the last one hundred years. The same is true for Hindi and Hindu politics.

To conclude my discussion on distorted media images of Muslims and how they can be improved, I would say that only processes of modernization and social transformation within the Muslim society can alter the situation. It is the community that would have to work out a feasible strategy for this in a hostile situation of an indifferent, hypocritical, and mediocre leadership in a Hindu-majority, yet democratic and plural, society. In the context of language, I shall conclude that one should know either Urdu or Hindi to comprehend the problems of the community. What is needed is interaction with the community and an understanding of the issues and the socio-political backdrop. For that, any language of communication would suffice, because it is frank interaction that would bring out the hidden reality, the exact problems faced by the community.

It is true that a section of the English-language media (which is also not one homogeneous entity, and has many variations) has very little interaction with the members of the Muslim community. Those with whom it interacts are the elite, especially socialites among the community. This section of elite Muslims is itself cut off from the community and are professional 'contractors' of Muslims. Hence, they cannot in any way be the real representatives of the Muslim community.

A look at the Muslim community as a whole would also serve some purpose here. Lately, the community has awakened from a long slumber, and has started making some progress. The modern generation is going in for education based on a secular curriculum and, on this basis, they are entering the competitive market. But there is one negative aspect here. The educated class among the Muslims at once starts aspiring for a leadership role. The end result is that the transformation process among the Muslims becomes sluggish. The common educated Muslims in the common civic space have gradually disappeared; they do not take part in addressing problems that they face in common with the same socio-economic group among Hindus, or other smaller religious minorities.

It is true that, for various reasons, the government did nothing for the overall uplift and empowerment of Muslims. The Muslim leadership, just after Partition and till the 1980s or so, was mainly responsible for this. It was unable to handle the situation arising out of Partition. But my question is why Muslims remain confined to emotional issues, especially in north India. Apart from establishing the Aligarh Muslim University, they did nothing for the educational empowerment of common Muslims. Surely the process of empowerment starts with education. My question, which fortunately is subscribed to by many, is: why do Muslims only nurture the madrasas—half a million of them with 50 million full-time students—and not think about providing secular education on their own? Definitely, the elite need madrasas for their political survival. What is intriguing is that these very people do not send their children to madrasas. The interesting thing is that Muslims, including educated Muslims, wholeheartedly support the madrasas, perhaps because they are not interested in secular education for common Muslim children. The madrasas serve their ulterior motives of aspiring to leadership, which is only possible if the community remains backward.

2

Muslims and the Press
Some Reflections

Rajni Kothari

The longer one's experience of a relationship (such as between the Indian Muslims and the press), the deeper one's insight into its complexity and multifaceted reality. Four observations are in order with respect to the relationship between Indian Muslims and the press. First, there is an in-built limit to Indian society accepting extremist positions. The Sangh Parivar misunderstood this completely. Second, there are limits beyond which the press cannot be effective in moulding opinion and behaviour; this was shown clearly in Uttar Pradesh. Third, upper-caste Hindu communalism is not limited only to Muslims, Sikhs, and Christians only; it also extends itself to the minorities within the Hindu fold—the Dalits and the tribals in particular. Fourth— and this is where a relevant future strategy for the Muslims lies— there is a need to work out a common strategy for all minorities, including the minorities within the Hindu fold. The Muslims are by no means a minor force in Indian politics. They are a considerable power, provided they too view themselves not communally but socially, as part of a larger struggle for social justice, equity, and democracy— in society as a whole, and as a part thereof, in the internal functioning of Muslim society as well. Failing this, the impulse towards a communal Hindu backlash could well arise again.

Let me return to the theme of the national press and the Muslims. It seems to me that the Muslims care a lot about what is said about them in the influential media. This applies across the board and has no relationship with levels of literacy. Formal literacy has little to do with sense of social status and proximity to power and influence. In many ways Muslims are more of a civil and political community than are the diverse social strata known collectively as 'Hindus'; their levels of skill formation and professional and occupational self-consciousness are also higher. What the press says about the Muslims and the impact it has on them influences their states of consciousness, of trust and distrust, of response and withdrawal, of how to cope and, in relation to this, whom to believe in and about whom to be sceptical. Looked at it this way, it is not just an issue of what the national (or regional) press says about Muslims as a group or a community but also what it says about the situation in which Muslims find themselves, or are made to find themselves. This includes what it says about the state and its policies and postures, and about political parties, in and out of power.

There is also the issue of the political and intellectual profile that the press projects about Muslims. This relates to the way the community is perceived and how this perception affects attitudes and thinking; how different individuals and sections are encouraged to take divergent positions—some more accommodative, others more strident—together creating great confusion and uncertainty; and giving rise to a number of question: who represents the genuine Muslim reality? Who enjoys credibility among the masses? Who seeks to reinforce or change received perceptions? And in all this, what impact does this projection have in terms of national opinion formations, especially in areas like human rights and the rights of community? When, in the background of all these issues and responses thereto, there takes place a major event like the Shah Bano episode or the destruction of the Babri Masjid, how do things shift—through accentuation and hardening or through moderation and softening of existing attitudes? Crucial to all this is the big turnaround in perceptions of mutuality and common pursuit of practical tasks between people and communities. In normal times, there is less of a sense of differentiation as to who in a neighbourhood or occupation are Muslims and who are not, but suddenly as a result of a conflict they get isolated and targeted. How does this affect perceptions, not just of neighbours and co-workers but also of journalists? Do the media heighten differences and animosities or do they play them down?

The role of the press becomes relevant in all this, more so for Muslims, given their greater civic and political orientation, and also given their tendency to exaggerate the role of the media in mediating inter-community affairs and their tendency to either see matters dichotomously or buckle under pressure.

One good example of this, over time, has been the discussion of the economic condition of the Muslims, and the way this is perceived by others. Are the Muslims worse or better off compared to (a) others, (b) their own position 15 or 20 years ago? The reality is that, in this as in other matters, perceptions tend to override the actual state of affairs, with the former (the 'worse off' thesis) asserted by Muslim communalists and the latter (the 'better off thesis' and the complementary thesis of Muslims being 'pampered') by Hindu communalists. There is a need to see things in perspective—especially given the way the press (national, regional, and Urdu) plays up things— and examine the situation in terms of the complex social and political mosaic in which the Indian Muslims are placed.

It is necessary to realize—and to build on that realization— that India is remarkably, and in many ways uniquely, a plural society, with a diversity and plurality based on social history. This society, long sustained in that diversity and plurality, has been undergoing a process of transformation and change, mainly in the modern period, but also preceding it. Following Independence and adoption of electoral democracy and planned development, there has taken place a strong wave of politicization. This politicization has been moving in two directions: integrating both in the homogenizing and hegemonizing sense, and differentiating with a great deal of stress on diversity of identities and affiliations. During the 1980s (both a 'lost decade' in the sense of nation-building and a bloody decade in terms of violence and civil strife, assassinations and genocides) the integrative dimension turned hegemonic and homogenizing, while the differentiating dimension became separatist, intensely conflict-ridden and alienating vis-à-vis the relationship between the state and civil society and between sections within civil society. The press has both neglected all this and contributed to it.

As we move forward it will become necessary, both with regard to the overall communal situation and to the role of the press, to understand and develop deeper insights into the implications of rebuilding and restructuring a plural society out of the ruins in which it is currently. It will be necessary to insist that India is and must remain a multicultural and a multi-centred polity. Unique to the conceptions of pluralism in India, as it has been thought of ever since Independence, has been a special regard for minority communities in which the state and the law of the land have been assigned a positive and creative role. One cannot leave it to diverse groups to fend for themselves, either in terms of undertaking social change or in terms of seeking security and protection. This is the responsibility of the entire nation.

At the same time, we must also insist on pluralization within each major community. It is unrealistic and short-sighted to have a monolithic approach for the whole community (be it Muslim or any other). Though many will not agree with me, insistence on Urdu as a lingua franca for Muslims all over India is as unreal and dogmatic as is insistence on Sanskritized Hindi for the nation as a whole. There is already, and there will continue to be, more and more need for regional languages and dialects for the rural and the tribal folk, weaving it all into a mode of communication which has been uniquely Indian. The same should apply with the economy, culture, technologies, and forms of art and aesthetics.

The problem with the national press and the excessive importance it is given (as the Muslims tend to do) is that it undermines precisely the diversity and plurality that have allowed a multicultured, multi-centred polity to be built. In a way the apolitical Hindu is wont to ignore the way the press reports and ruminates about matters political (as compared to the politicized Muslims). Of course, being apolitical and ignorant about both history and history-in-the-making, they can be easily taken for a ride, sensitivities can be played upon and they can be blinded to the deeper nuances of culture and polity, as has happened under the Hindutva tirade. Fortunately for Hindu society, new and vibrant processes are under way, thanks to the politicization of the Dalits, sections of the tribals, and the Other Backward Classes. Hence the point is that, in the future that lies ahead, it should be the aim and strategy of the Muslim leadership to work towards new alignments of forces. In rebuilding India's democratic secularism, the minorities in particular have a major role to play—in close liaison with the democratic secular elements within the Hindu social fold. Once this happens on the ground, the press will follow suit and become more constructive. If a section thereof becomes an instrument of one or other variety of communal backlash, the rest of the press will put it right.

3

Muslims and the Indian Press

Kuldip Nayar

I began my journalistic career with a job in an Urdu paper, *Anjam*. I shall start from there because that may in some way tell the story of Muslims and the press. This was around October 1947 after the subcontinent's partition.

The *Anjam* office was located in the Ballimaran area of Delhi, a Muslim locality where a pall of tragedy hung in the atmosphere. Smells and sounds were no relief and the maze of lanes and by-lanes overlooked by the curtained windows were not even enigmatic. It was a spectacle that submerged personal tragedies and human sufferings but did not evoke hope.

The Muslims felt cheated because Partition only aggravated their problems. Fear was writ large on their faces. They were confused and rudderless. They wanted to turn over a new leaf. But the Muslim press—essentially meaning the Urdu papers owned by Muslims—was of little help; it had done a volte-face overnight, without giving any explanation or advice on why it had supported the demand for Pakistan and what they should do in the future. The Hindus were unforgiving and so was the dominant opinion of the general press, which wanted the Muslims to go Pakistan, the country they had demanded and created.

Probably the attitude of my Muslim colleagues towards me in the *Anjam* office reflected the feelings of the community and the Muslim press in those days. They treated me as if I were a privileged citizen and they a second-class lot. Their dependence on the generosity of the majority community was tragic; they behaved like somebody with a hat perpetually in hand. The Indian Muslim press criticized the beatings, killings, and forcible evictions of Indian refugee Muslims by the previously domiciled inhabitants of Pakistan. And with it the

Muslim press also regretted the promise of the Muslim League during the division-demand to make them 'free'. Regrettably they were now a hopeless minority in India. The Muslim press however opened a new chapter, to forget and forgive; little did it then realize that Pakistan was the cross which they and even their children would have to bear for the rest of their lives.

There were voices from some Muslim editors, and even some Hindu-owned newspapers, to remind the people about what Maulana Abdul Kalam Azad (the then education minster and a top leader of the Congress) had envisaged. Several years before Partition, he had told the Muslims why, as a Muslim, he opposed the demand for Pakistan. His warning was 'They [the Muslims] will waken overnight and discover that they have become aliens and foreigners in India after partition. Backward industrially, educationally and economically, they will be left to the mercies of what would then be called an unadulterated Hindu Raj.'[1] But this warning had only evoked jeers and abuse in the Muslim press, which ran him down as a show-boy of the Hindus.

Anjam was losing circulation rapidly but it was still the most read paper among the Muslims. The biggest embarrassment facing the paper was the two-nation theory. It had propagated Mohammad Ali Jinnah's line that the Muslims and the Hindus constituted two separate nations and should therefore live in two separate countries. The paper was inundated with letters from its readers, abusing it for the division it had created between them and the Hindus.

If the paper were to attack this thesis, which it had supported for years, it would affect the paper's credibility. That was why I twisted the meaning of nations in an editorial, identifying them as the haves and have-nots. That did not mollify the Muslims; there was a storm of abuse all over again and the circulation fell further.

Maulana Hasarat Mohani, a great Urdu poet, was still on the scene, living in a house near the *Anjam* office. We became friends, or, to put it in another way, he more or less considered me his son. He told me one day that I should quit Urdu journalism because it had no future in India. I followed his advice, which helped highlight two points: the uncertain future of the Urdu press and the assured place of the English press.

Events have proved that Hasarat Mohani was not wrong. The English press has over the years has come to dominate the journalistic field and has far more influence than the vernacular press, not to speak of the Urdu press. The Urdu press is pegged to a few areas and to a limited circulation. Its finances are mostly from government advertisements, which have strings attached to them. Its readership is confined primarily to Muslims, and it generally seeks to cater to Muslim minds considered to be attuned to the Islamic world. That may by one reason why the Urdu press devotes a lot of space and prominence to the events in the Arabic world and Pakistan.

This has trapped many Muslims in a vicious circle: they want to read about Muslims elsewhere and, since they want it, the Urdu press gives them more and more of it. This has also somewhat distanced the Muslims from the Indian mainstream. Essentially exposed to the happenings in the Islamic world, the Muslim readers have developed a kind of affinity that make them feel part of the *Ummah*. The fallout of this is the vicarious satisfaction of having far-reaching roots and a large brotherhood. But all this is of no avail to them in India because the Muslims are alone when it comes to suffering at hands of the Hindus.

Since Urdu has ceased to be the first language of the majority of Muslims, other languages have claimed them as their readers. Many Muslim papers now appear in Bengali, Kannada, Malayalam, Tamil, and Hindi. However the opinions expressed in these papers continue to be on the lines of what has been expressed by the Urdu press. The regional problems have come to figure in its print more than before. But essentially, the Muslim press is inward-looking and has a slant towards Muslim issues.

In the national press, the Muslims often get the wrong end of the stick. Their problems are oversimplified and interpreted more in terms of religious beliefs than economic considerations. All Muslims are tarred with the same brush. The impression spread by the national press is that Muslims initiate the trouble and consequently suffer because they are fewer in number. On the other hand, the Muslim press often argues that the rioting is now not between the Hindus and Muslims but between the Muslims and the police, which acts on behalf of the majority community.

The Hindi, Gujarati, and the Marathi press are particularly harsh on the Muslims. It has been noticed that the papers' response or the lack of it is in proportion to the influence the BJP, the Shiv Sena or the like enjoy in a particular area. There is some truth in the charge that the BJP, when in power in Himachal Pradesh, Madhya Pradesh, Rajasthan, and Uttar Pradesh, helped many journalists to find place in the newspapers appearing from those states. This was also said about L.K. Advani when he was the minister of information (1977–9) in the Janata government. Many reporters and sub-editors, alleged to have been placed by him, now occupy senior positions. Even otherwise, many Hindi journalists have been influenced by the BJP propaganda. Like many Hindu intellectuals, they too have been taken in by the argument that Indian nationalism is coterminus with Hindu nationalism.

The Muslims are at a loss because they respect the cultural side of Hinduism, although they have not identified themselves with it. But the religious aspect has deterred them and they are afraid of diluting, if not losing, their identity, even if they find the cultural aspect acceptable.

Wrong information or lack of it has created misunderstandings about Islam among the Hindus and Hinduism among the Muslims. The press eschews writings on religious subjects. The Urdu papers in the Hindi press do sometimes run articles on their own religion but there is very little done towards removing misunderstandings about one another's religions. The ignorance on both sides is colossal and the perceptions based on these have given the two religionists the role of adversaries.

The English press too does not say much on Islam but interprets this neglect in a way which is acceptable to Muslims. One editor of a leading English newspaper says, 'We would like to run articles on Islam, but see where even an indirect reference to Rushdie's book has landed some of the commentators.' He continues, 'Now that we have Taslima Nasreen's novel *Lajja*, no objective debate can take place when everything is seen in terms of danger to Islam.'

Still, the English press does come to the rescue of the Muslims, highlighting their pain and police brutalities against them. Two events that support this contention are the demolition of the Babri Masjid and the rioting in Bombay. The English press uniformly condemned the demolition of the disputed mosque, while the comments in the language press varied from lukewarm criticism to blatant support of the carnage. That also reflects the minds of most Hindus, because it is the vernacular press that represents the majority. It shows the bias and prejudice that has increased with the passage of the time.

In the reporting of the Bombay riots, the English press was vehement in condemnation. It cited examples of 'ethnic cleansing' and brought such acts to light by writing at length about the atrocities that the Muslim community had to face at the hands of the police. The vernacular papers again decided to underplay the excesses committed on the Muslims. Most journalists and newspapers of Maharashtra were afraid of the Shiv Sena, particularly its leader Bal Thackeray.

Here the Muslim press played the role of the injured party. It was justified in doing so because the Muslims were the victims. But it also exaggerated the accounts and even concocted a few stories. Disproportionate space was given to the reaction of the Muslim countries, once again reflecting the feeling that outside Muslim sympathy was a dependable support to the cause of Indian Muslims.

While the Babri Masjid controversy remained the single most important factor vitiating the communal atmosphere and occupying the attention of the Indian press, mainly in the northern heartland, there have been other major irritants on the communal front. These include the Muslim demand to offer *namaz* in the protected mosques under the control of the Archaeological Survey of India (ASI), communalization of politics, disputes over religious processions, playing of music before mosques, construction of religious places, etc., have remained the other major irritants on the communal front.

What it boils down to is that more space is allotted to those who are fomenting communalism. The mainstream newspapers also give a lot of space to communal organizations, creating fissures in the fabric of Indian society. Even when the newspapers show restraint, the space for secular news is shrinking.

I do not accept the allegation that the national press is a toy in the hands of Hindu communal forces or that it is engaged in a conspiracy against the Muslims. There are some irresponsible elements in the vernacular press, but that is not the pattern of the press as a whole. The stand of the English press has remained balanced and objective. Still, if some Muslims feel hurt about some writings, it is perhaps due to the misunderstandings of the writer about Islam and its followers.

For example, the case of Shah Bano by and large concerned the Muslim community alone and it was not necessary for the national press to make it an issue. Any move, if needed, should have been made from within the community. Most of the Muslims took the wide attention paid by the national press, including the language it used, as 'uncalled for interference in their personal law'.

In my view, the seemingly anti-minority community approach in the press is due to the scarcity of Muslim journalists. The press should encourage more participation from the minority community. Young Muslims should come forward and face the challenge with pragmatism and boldness.

Communal politicians and preachers have in reality never left the gullible common citizen alone. Seeds of distrust have been planted in the minds of the Muslims, while the Hindus have been told that they are unjustly coerced into making undue concessions to the Muslims in economic, social, and cultural fields. Exploiting the deep religious traditions of both the communities, differences in their perspectives are often shown as attempts to destroy the other. Thus, no lasting solutions have ever been found for such issues as playing of music before mosques, either during prayers or at any other time. Normally in civilized developing societies such problems should have been sorted out by the local communities themselves, taking into consideration the traditions and practices prevailing in such communities. It is not as if attempts have not been made by well-meaning people of both communities. Objective but sustained propaganda by interested parties and newspapers belonging to both communities has created an atmosphere in which permanent solutions are made to appropriate the impossible.

The present trend of Hindu majority communalism is, I believe, temporary and an aberration. It will subside, and when this happens the Indian press will once again be vigorous in its support to our secular polity. Till then the Muslims and the secular forces have to fight the communal onslaught relentlessly, pertinently, and tactfully.

NOTE

1. Maulana Abdul Kalam Azad, *India Wins Freedom* (New Delhi: Orient Longman, 1988), pp. 143–4.

4

Indian Press
The Vernacular and the Mainstream Babel

Mrinal Pande

As long as the Vajjins hold full, fearless and frequent public assemblies, so long may they be expected to grow and fight decline.

—Gautam Buddha to Anand

A full and free exchange of news and views has always played a vital role in sustaining the political economic, social, and cultural well-being of a democracy. In our times, an honest dissemination of diverse news and views about the day-to-day functioning of our democracy by the national press has certainly developed as an important antidote against sectarianism, communalism, and autocracy. By informing people about the policies and activities of both the government and public bodies, and also helping them form rationally sound opinions, the Indian media has often helped our young democracy cope with major confrontations and communal conflagrations. The threat of disintegration into a caste- and religion-based cluster of warring republics, however, persists. Because of this, it becomes necessary from time to time to do a bit of introspection and ask honestly whether the media is being fair, just, and objective to all sections of our very varied and complex society.

This article is a humble effort in that direction by a woman journalist. Women as feminists often say, are the largest minority in the world. As a woman I have had the (not always very pleasant) advantage of viewing the mainstream culture of both our media and national politics somewhat differently from the males in positions similar to mine. This has enabled me to reach conclusions which may not always be welcomed.

Like other fundamental freedoms, the freedom of the press is not absolute but subject to certain well-known exceptions acknowledged in public interest. The right to freedom of expression also carries with it an inherent obligation to exercise this right without injuring the rights of other fellow citizens of both genders, of both the majority and minority communities. The press may be a powerful watchdog, but vis-à-vis minorities and women it has at times shown an alarming propensity to overlook the truth and to abandon professional norms and natural laws of fair play. When that happens, the basic democratic ideals of liberty, equality, and fraternity are in great danger of disintegrating.

Philosophically, a communalized ethos may appear to be out of place in Indian democracy, sworn constitutionally to socialism and secularism. But the sad fact is that it is firmly anchored in both the history and geography of this sadly divided subcontinent of ours. The post-Partition events leading to the formation of an Islamic Pakistan and the strained relationships between the leadership of the two countries since then have led to deep misgivings among the majority community in India about Indian Muslims. The media, unwillingly, often becomes a pawn in the aggressive sabre-rattling game of politicians. And when that happens, an exaggerated fear about national security makes it view events not objectively, as professionals and humane citizens, but as Indian nationals threatened by a colossal tide of Islamic belligerence. The post-Partition generation is especially susceptible to such fears. It is a paradox that here the young are often more conservative and the old show a greater understanding and a more radical approach to the subject. Our senior journalists, who have been witness to the build-up of events that led to Partition, remember clearly the harmony and perfect understanding that existed among the Hindus and Muslims before politics intervened. They are, therefore, less likely to be carried away by the rhetoric of right-wing political groups, and are more sympathetic to the minorities.

Another important but equally neglected factor that results in under-reporting or mis-reporting of the status of Muslims is the disproportionate importance of the English language as the language of decision-making in post-Partition India. A lack of access to Hindi and Urdu fosters an ignorance about the situation of the majority of both Hindus and Muslims, to whom these are the only bridges of communication.

Most of our media is controlled by male members of the majority community. While our language media has a far larger readership, our bureaucrats and policy-makers swear by the English media. The English media walks away with a disproportionately large share of advertising revenue, while the language media often has to look to the government or political groups for funds. Money supply to all media is, moreover, being shaped by the global (read Western) market-ethos. Since Western priorities are white-male centric, the media ethos all over the world is also becoming pro-majority and xenophobic. This gives a sly sanction to the anti-Islam bias in Asia as well. It is no coincidence that opinions of columnists like Arun Shourie, Swapan Dasgupta, and M.V. Kamath, to whom a conservative Hindu India with a globalized market is the only viable option, are frequently cited by the Western media.

The English language in India today segregates people more firmly than class, caste, and community into haves and have-nots. Most English-language journalists and their readers have little understanding of the lives of majority of the poor and little or no contact with the languages the poor speak and worship in. So even when some of the more liberal and well-meaning of them discuss the Muslims and their status in India, they either use a sentimental approach or mouth clichés about secularism. When they come to complex issues such as the personal laws of the minorities or anti-Islamic writings of controversial authors, they get confused. Journalists writing in Indian languages on the other hand live in closer proximity to minorities and often share the same socio-economic background. But this very proximity also leads to a greater envy and fear of being overtaken by the minorities. Any visible rise in prosperity of Muslims (such as the opening up of job opportunities in the Gulf region), an induction of a number of Muslims in the government or the cabinet, a face-lift given to mosques, etc., can all lead to sneers, snide comments, and charges of 'appeasement'. Recently Muslim-baiters from within the Muslim community, such as Taslima Nasreen or Salman Rushdie, have been treated as heroes by right-wing papers such as *Panchjanya* and *Saamna*. However their reaction to Rushdie's Hindu-baiting in *The Moor's Last Sigh* revealed how shallow their respect for the freedom of expression is.

Interestingly, our English dailies, periodicals, and their reporters and commentators may have no direct truck with their counterparts in vernacular publications; yet when they all set-out to discuss Hindu–

Muslim issues, a family resemblance begins to emerge from all such reports and analytical editorial writings. Some salient features that mark all such biased reporting and analysis of events in our media are as follows:

1. *A rejection of all modernism.* This may be presented as a dislike for the Western way of life and thought, but eventually it always boils down to supporting conservative and narrow Hindu thought as the only correct one. *Jansatta's* astounding support even for the retrograde *sati* and its subsequent indictment of Sahmat's *Hum Sab Ayodhya* exhibition and its 'modern' interpretation of Hindu myths are traceable to this mindset.

2. *A constant consensus-seeking from the majority community while simultaneously fanning their fears of unknown and different minority cultures.* To this end it becomes imperative that the minorities and their reactions to national issues be always seen and presented as those of 'outsiders', and even their truly liberal and humane representatives, such as Maulana Wahiduddin Khan and Mother Teresa, be subjected to snide remarks and insinuations.

3. *A subtle and special appeal to the neo-rich urban professionals of the majority community to return to their 'roots'.* They know that this westernized class, which lacks a clear social identity and is being rocked by globalization today, can easily be made to fear political and economic rejection and/or humiliation at the hands of newly empowered out-groups, such as the lower castes, minorities and women. Thus, under the slogans of *swadeshi* and tradition, all liberal and progressive measures are sought to be stalled.

4. *A constant trivialization of all genuine intellectual activity that denies the cult of Aryan racial purity.* Intellect or intellectual argument is mocked as emasculating or artificial, and an overemphasis is given to Rambo-type action against 'the enemy'. The use of masculinity and virility are seen as the positive yardsticks in such right-wing writing. Left-wing historians who plead for an unbiased and objective reading of our medieval history and the contribution of Muslims to India's composite culture are attacked in a particularly nasty way.

5. *All pacifism and civilized exchange of views whether vis-à-vis communal or caste or gender problems rampant in our society, are seen as trafficking with the 'enemy'.* There is a marked predilection

for hawkish and pro-militaristic solutions. All incidents of communal violence and people's uprisings against harsh police and judicial measures are seen as anti-national.

It is clear by now that what we see in the media is a reflection of the complex reality of modern-day India. The media does not create these situations, but it publicizes them, and creates public reactions. Obviously then what is required is neither a mechanical increase in the number of news items and articles about the Muslims nor sentimental preaching about the brotherhood of man. What we need is a less exclusive media culture within both the English and the vernacular media. Since social discourse is a great influence on the media, Hindus and Muslims need to be exposed to and made more receptive to each others' ideas and dreams and fears, and the newspapers have to be more willing to debate them without partisan point-scoring.

The Hindi media, which services the single largest group of India's literate citizens, certainly has a special obligation. But a major problem for Hindi editors today is to locate good reporters and commentators in Hindi who specialize in particular subjects. Discussions with my Urdu-language colleagues confirm that nearly all the truly brilliant and well-informed intellectuals we have, from among both Hindus and Muslims—from Bipin Chandra to Irfan Habib, from Amartya Sen to Shahid Amin—have taken to writing exclusively in English, no matter what their mother tongue. In contrast to this, the right-wing parties have carefully cultivated the language press all along. They have even used their brief reigns in the Hindi belt to plant their men in crucial posts in the most influential Hindi dailies and periodicals, both as correspondents and as news editors. Thus, as soon as party leaders begin talking about the threats to Hindus and Hindutva, their men get activated and raise a mighty chorus in several wings of the print media, demanding political and constitutional changes that will restore the balance in favour of the majority. They translate Arun Shourie into Hindi and Dinanath Mishra into English as a matter of course. Thus they have developed a loyal readership of like-minded people of all classes. It is they who help circulate the right-wing ideologies from teashops to schools, deepening the feeling of outrage among secular Hindus and that of an unfair siege among the Muslims.

Communal thought in India is largely being transmitted in the vernacular. The state of Punjab in the north-west is one of the most communally sensitive areas in India. As a state that faced the brunt of the Partition in 1947 and then again a decade-long inner siege by militant groups, Punjab's media scene makes an interesting case study in how communalization of vernacular readers takes place. The Punjabi media has been dominated by three languages: Punjabi, Hindi, and Urdu. A study of the colossuses of the Jalandhar press— *Vir Pratap*, *Jagbani*, *Punjab Kesri*, and *Ajit*—reveals the strengths and weaknesses of all vernacular media in the communally volatile north. In Punjab, people of three faiths speak one language but write it in three different scripts. Culturally and anthropologically they have always shared one cultural heritage, but people of all three faiths (Sikhism, Islam, and Hinduism) perceive each other as rivals and have built little language cells for themselves to underscore and mark out their separate and independent cultural and religious identities. This marking of territories means marking out readerships too.

This phenomenon also sums up the approach of the Hindi–Urdu press to Hindu–Muslim issues in the volatile Hindi belt. Basically the language press here, as in Punjab, is a child of the 1940s that reached its adolescence and growth in the post-Partition years and has carried many communal chips—both real and imaginary—on its shoulders as a result. Professionalism and technical innovation along with commercialism are attributes this press acquired only in the late 1970s and thereafter.

Interestingly, the fire and venom, so evident in print, is conspicuous by its absence when editors and reporters from these papers get together to defend professional interests. They forget, however, that while they continue to interact with each other as intellectuals across communal and linguistic borders, they polarize perceptions by taking communal stand on vital issues. Their readers, who lap up everything they print by way of both news and views, have also come to nurse great hostility against the community their paper criticizes so vehemently in print. Just as the Jalandhar press has unwittingly contributed to the crisis in Punjab, the vernacular press (Hindi and Urdu) in the Hindi belt has often encouraged and deepened the Hindu–Muslim divide in the states of Uttar Pradesh (UP), Madhya Pradesh (MP), Rajasthan, Bihar, Himachal Pradesh, and Haryana, knowingly or otherwise.

In the last two decades, the Hindi press has grown both vertically and horizontally. Apart from *Navbharat* (The Times of India group),

Hindustan (Hindustan Times group), and *Jansatta* (The Indian Express group), *Amar Ujala* under Ashok Agrawal, *Dainik Jagran* under Narendra Mohan, and *Rajasthan Patrika* under Kulish are all growing exponentially in circulation, and are bringing out new editions thick and fast. However, the use of state-of-the-art technology by the vernacular press is not always accompanied by a similar sophistication and professionalism in gathering and presenting the news and views that they put out. Where reporting on minority communities, riots, and women is concerned, most of the regional papers have still not moved very far from the 1950s mindset in which a woman is a second-class being. The approach is that a Hindu is a Hindu and a Muslim is a Muslim, and at no point shall the good of the twain meet.

Reporting on riots and other communal conflagrations in the post-Ayodhya era may have become somewhat more restrained after the Press Council's severe indictment of several papers. But the latent communal biases of the majority community can still occasionally be seen where a slight altering of focus may create enormous misgivings on sensitive issues. Recently a major news agency put out a seemingly innocent news item about the phenomenal rise in the population of Muslims in the last decade in India. Most of us know how the BJP and its votaries have been whipping up in the majority community a fear of being overtaken by Muslims. So this report was certainly loaded with implications. The Census report for 1991 from which it was sourced was yet to release its final data. But the report was prominently published in most major English and Hindi newspapers. Only one woman journalist in an English paper (Kalpana Jain) did a follow-up story on how this census data did not include the data from several states. A week later this was followed by another report on an enormous rise in the Muslim population in the nation's capital. It is not difficult to see how in the absence of a logical rebuttal of half-truths in a pre-election year, the right-wing parties will capitalize on these reports to create a fear of a Muslim influx and the possible links to Pakistan and the Inter Services Intelligence (ISI).

Given such a complex scenario, it is imperative that a fine and sensitive monitoring of the vernacular papers be done, and any instances of communal biases in reporting and presentation of news items be speedily brought to book. This, one finds after perusal of many cases, seldom happens. For example, in a complaint by Syed Shahabuddin dated 20 February 1993, it was alleged that *Dainik*

Aaj of Lucknow had published a news item headlined 'The impregnable security net at Gyanvapi has written the black history at Kashi Varanasi', with a box headline 'Injured faith of the broken-hearted devotees remained sobbing within their homes'. The report, according to the complainant, castigated the government machinery for its efficiency and seemed to express sorrow over the fact that a potentially mischievous plan to commit desecration was thwarted.

There was no response from the respondent, the editor of *Dainik Aaj*. The case came up for consideration before an enquiry committee on 13 December 1993. There was no appearance from either side. The committee noted with regret that the editor of *Dainik Aaj* had not sent a written statement with reference to the Press Council's show-cause notice despite a reminder. Nor did the newspaper depute any representative to appear before the committee. The case was considered, therefore, only on basis of the complaint. The committee concluded that though the headlines were misleading, the body copy was not provocative and was not justified by the headlines. It recommended, therefore, that the Press Council dispose of the case with the observation that the headlines should have been more sober and in tune with the tenor and content of the body copy.

Such dissonance between the editorial position taken by important newspapers and the obviously mischievous choice of headlines and sub-headings reveals a structured ad-hocism that militates against the basic tenets of journalism. And since there is little or no in-house discussion on the position papers should take over specific issues of national concern, one often finds astounding contradictions in news pages and editorial comment. Many of our Hindi papers today carry columns by noted English-language columnists in Hindi translation. Here again there is a lack of a consistent approach. So one may find Nikhil Chakraborty's well-argued column on the Kashmir situation side by side with an opinionated editorial by the editor (who in many cases is also the owner) advising a repeal of Article 370 and an army crackdown. Such presentation does not signify a many-sided approach to the subject but a total lack of understanding of the importance of the issues involved, and does incalculable damage. It leaves the readers confused and in many cases they choose to return to their biases.

Character assassination and libellous writing is an important part of communally provocative journalism. In a complaint dated 8 May 1993 filed by Shakil-Ur-Rehman Shamsi, a journalist from

Pilibhit, against *Rashtriya Sahara*, it was alleged that the paper, in its New Delhi and Lucknow editions of 5 and 6 May 1993, had published a news item under the caption 'Dawood Ibrahim net extends upto Terai Area', alleging that the complainant was working for the gangster. The complainant said that a contradiction of this assertion by the superintendent of police, Pilibhit, was published in *Amar Ujala*, another Hindi daily, but when he wrote to the Lucknow edition of *Rashtriya Sahara* and asked them to contradict the news, there was no reply. A memorandum was submitted by Muslim citizens of Pilibhit to the district magistrate and superintendent of police, Pilibhit, objecting to the other insinuating references to the activities of Muslims of the area. The SP even held an enquiry into the matter and found that the allegations against Shamsi about his connections with Dawood Ibrahim were baseless. Show-cause notices to the editors of *Rashtriya Sahara*, Delhi and Lucknow, were issued on 23 August 1993, but the respondents did not file the requisite written statement, despite reminders to the Lucknow office.

The matter came up for consideration before the Inquiry Committee on 13 December 1993. There was again no appearance from either side. But a telephone call was received from Shamsi saying that he was hospitalized due to a heart attack. He requested that the case be adjourned. However, the Inquiry Committee decided not to do so. After going into the case the committee recommended to the Press Council that the complaint was to be upheld and the respondent newspaper was to be warned.

If the Hindi press goes berserk, can the Urdu press set an example in professional restraint? The answer, sadly enough, is 'No'. In two complaints dated 5 May 1992 and 31 May 1992 against *Azimabad Express*, an Urdu daily of Patna, the highly esteemed director of the famous Khuda Bakhsh Oriental Public Library of Patna, alleged that several false statements, editorials, comments, and mischievous allegations in vile and abusive language were published against him in several issues of the daily (which apparently prints only about a hundred copies). According to the director, the reason for this sustained onslaught on his character and the instigation in the name of region and religion was that he had refused to oblige certain local influential leaders by running the library not according to their diktats but along professional lines.

The respondent editor did not file a written statement with reference to the second complaint dated 31 May 1992 despite a show-cause notice and a reminder. He also did not file any written statement on the merits of the first complaint despite specific directions and a reminder. The complainant, Dr Bedar, appeared in person before the Inquiry Committee on 29 June 1993, but the respondent editor did not. Only a letter was received from him, counter-alleging that while his reports were not abusive or defamatory, the complainant did not have permission from the chairman and board of the library to sue him in the Press Council, and the case should therefore be adjourned. The Council, however, on consideration of the records of the case and the report of the Inquiry Committee decided to censure the newspaper.

Where Muslim women are concerned, the large influx of sensitive women reporters in the English media has helped. But the vernacular media is still by and large a preserve of males. A close perusal of the vernacular media shows that all incidents involving minority women are immediately politicized and used to settle scores. For one, it is events and personalities rather than processes which are mostly reported and commented on, more so if they are politically loaded against the image of Muslims. Such motivated reporting creates a predictable backlash, so eventually the serious, positive, and broad-based issues regarding Muslim women, their economic and political needs, their assimilation in the workforce, and their reactions to national events mostly go unreported, while select information that confirms the stereotype of Muslim women as illiterate and scared pawns in the hands of religious leaders is widely put out. In highlighting issues related to all Indian women such as work, health, their position in society, and experiences within families, our media has generally been unable to provide equally important space to Muslim women. For example, during the Shah Bano controversy, the editorial comment in most Hindi papers centred on the Muslim Women (Protection of Rights on Divorce) Bill or the political implications for the Congress of the resignation of Arif Mohammad Khan from Rajiv Gandhi's cabinet. The editorials largely pushed for the adoption of a uniform civil code with very misleading information about how comparatively liberal the Hindu Code Bill was. None of the editorials this writer read in the major Hindi dailies even hinted that vis-à-vis women there existed lacunae in the Hindu laws and that Shah Bano's plight should have become an occasion to sit down and seriously discuss how to raise the status of all Indian women, irrespective of their religion and marital status. Only a few editorial articles surfaced—all of them by women—which cried out for a sense of fair play and honesty in the discussion. They were largely ignored. The editor of *Manushi*, Madhu Kishwar was one of the few who mentioned that two previous Supreme Court judgements of 1979 and 1980 had also granted maintenance to Muslim women.[1] The crucial difference between Justice Chandrachud's judgement in the Shah Bano case and the earlier ones was that the earlier verdicts had not emphasized the fact of the complainant belonging to the Muslim community. The issue had been considered purely as the legal right to maintenance under the secular law. Kishwar wrote: 'By singling out Muslim men and Islam in this way, Justice Chandrachud converts what is essentially a women's rights issue into an occasion for a gratuitous attack upon a community.'

In the post-Shah-Bano, post-Babri Masjid, and post-Bombay blasts era, the Gandhi–Maulana Azad legacy of the vernacular press in India, a generally liberal and reform-oriented approach, has been getting less and less visible in Hindi dailies. In several cases a commitment to truth and justice may be articulated, but it is mostly superficial and sentimental rather than deep and rational. As in the case of actor Sanjay Dutt, after the initial tears have been shed, snide references to the doubtful credentials of his minority connections begin to flow thick and fast. There is a near-total refusal to present facts of the case and criticize the Terrorist and Disputive Activities Act (TADA) as a harsh discriminatory measure, in the light of actual data.

There is another factor which is seldom debated but has caused enormous harm to professional system of checks and balances within the media. Editorial authority in the Hindi press today is becoming a tenuous divided phenomenon, with more and more owners anointing themselves as editors and dispensing with the services of professionally groomed and disciplined teams of seasoned editors and accredited correspondents. Becoming owner-editors benefits them in two ways: it is a cost-cutting measure, and it brings them enormous political clout. However, this also means that news gathering, subbing, and editorializing work generally ends up in the hands of sycophantic lackeys of corruptible stringers and the owners' political patrons. This has generally coarsened the atmosphere in most newspaper offices, leading to a steady rise in corruption and dishonest practices, and ultimately to a near-total erosion of professional objectivity and a humane sense of justice. Some conscientious stringers, who may still risk life and limb to expose crime and injustice, end up like Aziz Qureshi of *Amar Ujala* and Umesh Dobhal of *Jansatta*, both of whom were killed by unknown assailants.

Liberty, democracy, and the workings of a secular society are all ultimately built on foundations far larger than self-interest and political bigotry. Within the press, as within nations, professional norms can be sustained only by professionally dedicated people whose sense of history stretches for beyond narrow sectarian and commercial interests. If we are all to survive as a democracy in the true sense, we must all pray together that their tribe should increase both within our polity and our media.

NOTE

1. *Manushi*, no. 32: 1986.

5

Contested Representations in Historical Perspective

Images of Islam and Australian Press, 1950–2000[1]

Howard Brasted

Over the last fifty years, newspapers have provided Australians with much of what they know, or rather apprehend, about Islam as a religious system and about Muslim culture in general. This stands to reason. On the one hand, very few non-Muslims would bother going to the length of consulting the Koran, the prime source of Islamic theology, to discover for themselves the prescriptions for life that it lays down and embodies. On the other hand, the press has long superseded all other forms of literature as the instrument of mass communication, a register of current national and international information, and the medium through which the world's changing landscape can be regularly viewed.

It follows that the popular conception of Islam, and things Islamic, is for the most part derived from journalistic coverage of events in the Muslim world as they unfold as news on a daily basis. Reports, feature articles, editorials, bold headlines, and the mandatory photograph, illustration, or cartoon[2] supply a montage of intelligence and imagery that collectively sum up Islam and all that it seems to stand for. The question is, what does Islam seem to stand for, based on the kind of reports it has been, and continues to be accorded by the Australian press?

The few Australian-based studies which have directly addressed this question paint a very unflattering picture.[3] All tell much the same story—that Islam has received a less than fair, and at times a farcical press; and that it has been encapsulated through a number of stereotypical images which have been simplistic and prejudicial. Mosques, bearded mullahs, menacing Muslim crowds, and *burqa*-clad women, which have collectively come to symbolize irrationality, fanaticism, intolerance, and discrimination on an almost medieval scale, are the most commonly projected images.

Writing in the early 1980s, Barry Lowe noted that the frequent association of Islam with violence, fanaticism, and militancy had aroused a degree of 'hysteria' in Australian newspapers. With every Muslim depicted as a potential Gaddafi or admirer of Khomeini, the press primed its readership to regard 'all Arabs' and even 'all Muslims' as the recognizable foe. However, it was the 'racism' embedded in the correspondence columns of local and district newspapers, particularly those circulating in areas with significant Muslim populations, which had especially caught Lowe's eye.[4] A decade later, during the period of the Gulf War and its immediate aftermath, Daryl Champion detected an intensification of the 'battering' Muslims were receiving in the 'mainstream media'. Quoting David Bowman, a former editor-in-chief of the *Sydney Morning Herald*, he laid the blame squarely on the anti-Muslim bias of Australian journalists, a 'cynical' breed who 'exploited people and situations for their own journalistic purposes', and who 'preferred to encourage conflict' and 'maximise division'.[5]

In a broad survey of newspaper images of Islam, covering the period 1980–96, Howard Brasted identified three salient features. First, Islam had been treated as if it were essentially monolithic. Thus Muslims, whether in Mecca, Madras, or Melbourne, were lumped together as an 'identikit' species, and Muslim states, regardless of cultural diversity or geographical location, were envisioned as sharing similar turbulent environments. Second, 'Muslimness' was invariably associated with what was happening in the Middle East—such as terrorist activity, war and oil embargoes—and was mostly defined by Middle Eastern patterns of Islamic culture. Third, there was a sameness and resilience about the graphic portrayal of Islam throughout the sixteen-year period under review. The equation of Islam with fundamentalism, religious regimes, Sharia punishments, and the inhuman treatment of women was mooted time and again.[6]

In a somewhat ironic development, journalists have themselves become self-critical, decrying this staple imagery of Islam as unbalanced and stating that it should cease. Some selected headlines will suffice to convey this message:

- 'Our image of Islam just too lopsided'—James Murray, *The Australian*, 9 November 1993.
- 'Islam bedevilled by cliches of the West'—Greg Sheridan, *The Australian*, 15 August 1994.
- 'The West is undoubtedly prejudiced against Islam'—*Daily Telegraph*, 13 August 1994.
- 'Perils of Islamic Stereotyping'—Paul Collins and Salahuddin Ahmed, *Sydney Morning Herald*, 14 October 1996.
- 'Muslims and Islam itself are not the enemy'—Chris McGillion, *Sydney Morning Herald*, 11 August 1998.

While Greg Sheridan's essay[7] was written to counter the controversial, if largely derided, hypothesis of Samuel Huntington, that the West and an Islamic coalition were the likely protagonists in World War III,[8] other commentators had the press firmly in their sights for its reductionist treatment of Islam. In an article entitled 'Beyond fundamentalism', Peter Fray, the religious affairs writer for the *Sydney Morning Herald*, conceded that Islam was misunderstood in a way that other religions were not. And he was in no doubt who was responsible: '... virtually every day the media reinforces the idea that Islam is somehow different, difficult, even dangerous'.[9]

However, if the Australian press was directly implicated, it was not alone. Similar criticisms levelled at mainstream newspapers in Britain, Canada, Europe, and the United States suggest that this attitude to Islam was widely shared, and that its creation of stereotypical imagery was universally Western.[10] This can, in part, be traced to the practice of syndicated reporting in which selected feature articles from *The Times*, the *Guardian*, the *Washington Post*, and *The New York Times*—to name the most prominent—are not infrequently reprinted in Australian and other Western newspapers. That news agencies like Reuters, AAP, AFP, and UPI regularly supply field report copy to the entire Western press is also an important standardizing factor. Exasperated by such levelling coverage, Muslim communities have sought to counter it. In Britain an Islamic Awareness Week (IAW) has been launched principally to challenge the ways journalists have represented Islam,[11] while in Australia a Media Watch Committee was established in 1998.[12] All this rather begs the question why the Western press, whether in Australia, America, or elsewhere, has not only commonly purveyed negative images of Islam and Muslims in the first place, but has continued to perpetuate them.

The conventional reference point for cross-cultural study and the standard explanation for Western representations of Islam is Edward Said's 'Orientalist' thesis.[13] Said put the case that as far back as classical times, and in particular throughout the nineteenth and twentieth centuries, Western scholars, novelists, commentators, and agencies of the state had constructed an idea or theory of the 'Orient' that effectively misrepresented it. What they had produced, he argued, was not value-neutral knowledge but a disfiguring discourse—Orientalism—which portrayed the East as uncivilized in comparison with Europe and alien by every criterion. Over time, an imagined 'Other'—a caricature of binary difference—has emerged to colour the West's perception of Islam and to influence the way it interpreted and categorized Islamic culture, as much in the present as in the past. Especially as an 'academic inheritance', Orientalism has been bequeathed as 'truth' to each succeeding generation.[14]

The issue Said raised is critical to this study, concerning as it does the nature of knowledge, the processes involved in its production, and the form in which it is conveyed. In reviewing the Australian press's treatment of Islam over a much longer period than has been attempted to date—from 1950 to 2000—this discussion proposes not only to engage with these issues historically but also to confront a number of related questions. For example,

- How fabricated has been the 'knowledge' of Islam and Muslim culture offered through the columns of most of the newspapers during this period?
- Have Australian journalists collectively succumbed to the 'Orientalist' understanding of the Muslim world that Said outlined and regularly sustained it?
- Have there been particular aspects of Islamic life and activities involving Muslims which may be said to have informed the press's stereotypical explanation of them?
- Have the changing circumstances of the post-colonial world made no impact on the way the press has viewed Islam?

Due to the length of the study and the limits on space, only the leading metropolitan dailies and the quality weeklies—*The Sydney Morning Herald*, *The Age* (Melbourne), *The Australian*, and *The Bulletin*—were monitored in any systematic or regular way. Local and district newspapers have been excluded, partly because they are too numerous, and partly because their journalists encounter an

Islam of suburban skirmishes[15] which does not readily translate into the 'international' Islam that is predominantly featured and imagined in the metropolitan press.

THE ORIENTALIST THESIS REVISITED

In accounting for the way the mainstream Australian, and indeed it would seem the entire Western, press has reported events associated with Muslims, Orientalism has become the standard, but this is arguably not a sufficient explanation. A range of other factors, such as the mechanics and milieu of news production, the nature and evidential basis of the news making the headlines, the attitude of the reading public, and its understanding or ignorance of what is being reported also need to be taken into consideration.

There are a number of aspects of Said's Orientalist case for the West's portrayal of Islam in literature which are ill-fitting and problematic when applied to journalism. For example, the underlying assumption of the West's continuous inheritance and absorption of Orientalist values and perspectives has been seriously questioned. There may be little scholarly disagreement that the Western literature on the Orient which Said investigates is full of the overt biases he discusses. But as Albert Hourani and others have posited,[16] Orientalism was a historically based knowledge which should be placed in its own historical context. The kind of thought Said defined as 'Orientalist' belonged specifically to the particular age that had produced it. That age was the age of European empires when much of the Muslim world fell under the colonial hegemony of Britain and France in particular. In an unequal encounter,[17] Islamic society came to be depicted in European literature as a civilization in marked decline: militarily, economically, culturally, and morally. The imagery of a defenceless, bankrupt, illiberal, easily compromised Orient in need of European governance and rational reconstruction reflected the imperialist rationale of that era.

In the post-colonial setting, however, a completely new typology of images emerged to categorize Islam in a way that is altogether different—aggressively militant, intrinsically fundamentalist, ideologically anti-modern, and socially repressive. Today, the focus is very much on Islam as an assertive, reviving civilization, a civilization to be once again taken seriously rather than scorned. Now that Muslims seem variously engaged in attempts to 'Islamize' their states and restore them to former greatness, a quite different Islam has begun to be projected.

A further refinement on this theme is the image conjured up in 1993 by Samuel Huntington, of an Islam primed for the ultimate jihad against the type of civilization exhibited by the West: secular, materialistic, and largely Godless. In this doomsday scenario, Islam manifests as a frightening, formidable, religious force, a match for the West in contesting the shape and thrust of the ultimate world order. Although encountering ridicule and rejection from scholars, Huntington's 'Clash of Civilizations?' thesis continues to receive pictorial and literary reinforcement. *The Economist* recently provided an outstanding example of this in a special 'Survey of Islam'. While its analysis was conducted in Huntingtonesque terms, the cover illustration depicted not a modern war but a Crusades rematch with Richard the Lionheart and the legendary Saladin in deadly confrontation.[18]

That such diametrically opposite constructions of the Islamic 'Other' can be equally attributed to Orientalist invention exemplifies part of the trouble. Paradoxically, the major problem of the Orientalist thesis is that it has acquired—particularly in the fields of cultural and literary studies—the status and qualities of a paradigm, an analytical model which when applied carries an underpinning, assumed, authority. But as an omnibus explanation for all Western commentary on Islam and activities involving Muslims, Orientalism effectively shuts the window on the other possible factors shaping Western imagery. It does this by totally discounting the possibility of any Muslim agency. For Said has been emphatic on this point: that Europeans were ontologically incapable of producing other than an inherently fabricated and flawed knowledge of non-Europe.

All this raises the critical question of whether a 'true representation of anything' is possible and whether Muslims are any more capable of producing it than Europeans, Americans, or, for that matter, Australians. A number of scholars have denied that Orientalism was and remains an exclusively Western phenomenon,[19] suggesting that it has its Eastern counterpart—'Occidentalism'.[20] What this indicates is the rather obvious fact that people unavoidably view the outside world through the perspective of their own cultural experiences, no matter what is being studied or who is doing the studying. Cultural relativism aside, V.G. Kiernan and Roger Owen have subtly raised doubts about the assumption that there was an ideological, not an empirical, basis to Orientalist images of the Muslim 'Other'.

OVERVIEW OF A CHANGING IMAGERY

Taking all these qualifications into consideration, how does the Australian press measure up? What kind of Islamic landscape have several generations of journalists—the supposed 'new wave' of Orientalists[21]—travelled through and mapped over half a century? Three or four different styles of imaging Islam and tracking Muslimness are discernible between 1950 and 2000. For the most part, all these styles are derived from a passing parade of eye-catching international events involving Muslims. However, since the 1990s, an Australian dimension has added a more parochial, less detached perspective. Journalistic stereotyping abounds, but the extent to which any of the resulting images are the product of an Orientalist mindset is uncertain. Journalists do fit the first of Said's definitions of Orientalism, but this definition is so elastic that anyone 'who teaches, writes about, or researches the Orient ... either in its specific or in its general aspects' is classified as an Orientalist. The two remaining definitions: a conditioned centuries-old mentality essentializing the distinction between East and West, and a corporate 'Western style' for gaining mastery over the Orient, are not obviously applicable to journalism.[22]

1950–67: FROM SUEZ TO THE SIX-DAY WAR

Two momentous conflicts in the Middle East which captured the attention of the world press were the Suez Canal crisis of 1956–7 and the Six-Day War of 1967. In neither case was the Australian press commentary extensive. Gamal Abdel Nasser's seizure of the Suez Canal tended to be explained in terms of outright brigandage;[23] legitimate decolonization did not figure as the more logical explanation. Israel's defeat of an Arab force was seen more as a victory for military daring than as any vindication of its right to exist in Palestine.

More instructive were the pictorial messages emerging from this history. They appear to indicate that 1950–67 was a period of transition in Australian attitudes to the Middle East and to Muslims at large. Many of the cartoons in *The Bulletin*, to take the most outstanding example, came very close to the type of historical caricature that Said emphasized. They reflected the Arab world through a picture-postcard portrayal of a fabled, but not yet feared, Orient: its magical side, its sleazy side, and its oil-rich 'Arabian Nights' side, consisting of harems, polygamy, and petrodollar wealth. A Molnar cartoon capturing Robert Menzies' ultimately unsuccessful dash to Egypt to broker a peace settlement over Suez was classically Orientalist. It depicted a starchy prime minister being lewdly offered some 'feelthy Suez canal shares', by a grotesque street trader, against a mirage-like background of distant pyramids, a camel balancing several bales of cotton as well as its rider on a single pointed hump, and a *chador*-clad woman carrying a pitcher of water on her head.

Complementing this view were early glimpses of a different, more volatile, more formidable Orient in the making. As profiled at the time, Nasser was almost the prototype of later Arab adversaries of the West: a 'tinpot Hitler' with an 'inferiority complex'. Nasser emerged as a 'dictator' to be taken seriously, if not, of course, to be respected.[24] Add unspecified quantities of 'oil' and 'Islam' to fanatical leadership and you have the core ingredients of the mix of Western perceptions of the Middle East which were to persist to the close of the twentieth century and beyond. Control of the 'fabulous oil riches' of Arabia was deemed to be Nasser's objective and the greatest threat Nasser posed to Western security. 'Oil', as *The Bulletin* read the situation, was what Suez was mostly about.[25]

However, for *The Sydney Morning Herald's* correspondent, Islam loomed potentially large in the wings. The Muslim Brotherhood's support of Nasser was considered an ominous sign, and the threat by the leader of the Baath Socialist party to unleash a 'Holy War', should force be used against Egypt, seemed to confirm the danger of escalation.[26] For the first time, perhaps, although not the last, one headline was couched in symbolic Islamic overlay: 'Veil of fear over Suez'.[27] More presciently, the possibility was envisaged of Islam mobilizing around the world, not only to end colonialism, as in the case of Suez, but also to build on a growing sense of 'solidarity' and the 'idea of kinship' which had 'always been inherent in Islam'.[28]

At this stage, while the Muslim 'Orient' was treated with unease, there was little evidence of any wide journalistic appreciation of Islam as a rising or revivalist influence in the region. Typifying the overall approach of detached interest, and often total bemusement, was a cartoon which 'sent up' reports of an 'Islamic bomb', under manufacture in Pakistan, as a rocket shaped like a minaret.[29]

1970–80: ARAB TERRORISM AND OIL DIPLOMACY

Disinterest rapidly gave way to concern in the 1970s as the West was rocked, and for a time completely unnerved, first by the emergence of Arab terrorism and then by the application of Arab 'oil diplomacy'. The hijacking of international airlines was perceived as a kind of terrifying pandemic against which there initially appeared to be no defence and no remedy. Colonel Gaddafi of Libya and Yasser Arafat, leader of the Palestinian Liberation Organization, became household names and were instantly recognizable—but as the ringmasters of incomprehensible violence. Assassinations, suicide bombings, another Arab-Israeli war in 1973, and the disintegration of Lebanon did draw attention to the plight of Palestinians. However, surrounding issues remained obscure and little obvious attempt was made to clarify them. Despite Yasser Arafat's symbolic address to the United Nations on 13 November 1974, and the United Nations General Assembly equating Zionism with racism a year later, rehabilitation as a legitimate freedom fighter continued to elude him.[30] Once again the spotlight fell mainly on 'oil', this time as the most effective weapon the Arab states seemed able to employ.

In 1973, two events came close to bringing the world to its knees: the total oil embargo imposed on the USA and to a lesser extent on Japan and Europe by the Persian Gulf states, including Saudi Arabia, on 17 October 1973; and the fourfold increase in the price of oil announced by the Organization of Petroleum Exporting Countries (OPEC) on 23 December 1973. As inflation soared, along with interest rates, and petrol rationing was imposed, recession stalked Australia as well. The Middle East no longer seemed so far away. Indeed, the cash-strapped Whitlam government's clandestine dealings with Tirath Khemlani, a 'Pakistani international commodities dealer', proved to be one of the triggers of Australia's 1975 constitutional crisis.[31]

As yet there was no strong indication of journalistic attempts to put Islam under the microscope or to link any of this turmoil to Islamic religious culture. That OPEC had the world 'over a barrel', as *The Bulletin* put it, was a 'political' issue—namely, an attempt to force Israel to the negotiating table.[32] Even Gaddafi was pictured as one of the controlling group of oil-producing 'Sheikhs'. Louay Safi has rightly nominated the 1970s as a 'turning point' in the global media's interest in Islam, with the phenomenon of 'Islamic resurgence' capturing its attention,[33] as Muslim terrorism had done at the 1972 Munich

Olympics. However, it was really towards the end of the decade that this turning point occurred. Arguably the dominant, and certainly lasting, image of the 1970s belonged to the face of an Arab terrorist. As graphically depicted in 1992 this face menacingly glared out of the page as subhuman, simian, and merciless, with uneven chiselled teeth ready to pull the pin on a hand-grenade. The image emblazoned on this apparition's lapel was of an airliner exploding mid-flight.[34]

1979–92: IRANIAN REVOLUTION, AND THE EMERGENCE OF AN ISLAMIC DOMINO THEORY

In 1979 the Iranian Revolution dramatically shifted the focus to Islam as a 'fundamentalist' religion. To the initial amazement of Western (including Australian) onlookers, the seemingly strong, secular regime of Muhammad Reza Pahlavi collapsed under the force of religious denunciation and was replaced by an Islamic republic led by an aged cleric, Ayatollah Ruhollah Khomeini. Returning from exile in Paris, Khomeini proclaimed the message that Iran, like the Islamic world at large, had been the victim of Western imperialism and secular corruption. The solution lay in the restoration of Islamic government and the Islamic way of life to undo the 'Westoxification' of the nation.

The prescription was simple and it proved seductive. An Islamic republic was voted in by popular referendum in March 1979 and Khomeini was installed as Head of State and Chief Justice. Acquiring dictatorial ascendancy as the supreme interpreter of Islamic law, Khomeini launched an unrelenting drive to Islamize society. This was despite waging a destructive, economically draining war with Iraq which dragged on from September 1980 until August 1988. During this time, civil, commercial, and criminal law were brought into line with the Sharia, education was reformed—universities and colleges being shut down for two-and-a-half years while a new curriculum was prepared—and a new moral code was legislated through parliament. Women were compelled to adopt Islamic dress, adultery was punishable by public flogging or execution, and homosexuality was similarly discouraged. Everything Khomeini considered un-Islamic, such as alcohol, gambling, prostitution, and even mixed-sex schooling, was banned. The old ruling elite was replaced by a new clerical order. The proclaimed objective was the establishment of a divinely ordained system of rule under which Iranians could function as a religious community.[35]

As this history unfolded from afar—not far enough according to an Emeric cartoon[36]—the Australian press was a fascinated observer. The initial concentration was on Ayatollah Khomeini, proclaimed by *The Bulletin* as the 'Man of 1979': 'The year that chaos ruled the world'.[37] Appearing always as an austere, imposing figure in a black robe and black turban, bearded, with a prominent brow and scowling gaze, Khomeini was the stuff satirists dream about. He received some very rough treatment, some of the roughest coming from an American female journalist who had interviewed Khomeini in Paris on the eve of his historic flight to Iran. Her syndicated appraisal published in the *Los Angeles Times* offered readers a comic choice of characterizations: an 'avenging angel from the Old Testament'; a 'geriatric genie' with a 'complex and conniving personality'; a 'satanic madman' living in a world of 'Kafkaesque' nightmares; and a 'carnival swami' who was 'making the most powerful nations jump at his whim'.[38]

Even when more sober commentary prevailed, Khomeini was never portrayed as a benevolently inspired leader. He continued to attract opprobrium with reports of harsh punishments, restrictions on free speech—the most notorious being the fatwa of death against Salman Rushdie, author of *The Satanic Verses*—and the terrorist campaign that he seemed to be orchestrating against the United States as the 'Great Satan'. In the year of Khomeini's death, a Moir cartoon under the caption 'Free Thought' summed up the mood of journalistic distaste and disenchantment. It depicted a grizzled Ayatollah pontifically laying down the law. 'I may not agree with what you say. But I'll fight to the end for ... my right to kill you?'[39] Fundamentalism, bigotry, and violence seemed to go together. In effect, throughout his ten-year rule, Ayatollah Khomeini was a larger-than-life symbol, who came to typify the worst, rather than the best, features of revivalist Islam in its Shiite form.

Seeking to explain why Islam was 'on the march again', analysis in the press initially showed some balance. It was variously acknowledged that Islam was not monolithic but a diverse religion; that the Sunni, not the Shia sect constituted the dominant expression of Islam around the world; that the balance between modernists, traditionalists, and Islamists by no means favoured the latter; that only a small minority of Muslims aspired to forgo the advances of history and return their societies to the time of Muhammad; and that the rejection of capitalist and communist models and their replacement by moral society lay at the heart of the reformist drive. An interim report on the position of women in Iran and the issue of veiling also reserved judgement on whether the chador confirmed the 'inferior status' of women in Islam, or whether it conferred on them a considerable measure of 'freedom' and 'security'.[40]

Nevertheless, progressively throughout the 1980s, the images inspired by Iran began to merge with images of Islam in general. Despite an awareness that Shiite Iran could hardly present a model for all other Muslim societies, the spectre repeatedly conjured up in newspaper headlines, archival photographs, and cartoons was that of fanatic Muslims poised not only to 'cleanse' their own societies and restore their Islamic basis but also to ultimately 'Islamize' the world along the lines established in Iran. 'Islamization' was deemed to presage the installation of religious rule at the political level, full re-introduction of the Sharia, reconfirmation of patriarchal tradition, the seclusion of women, and rejection of Western liberal-democratic, secular, society. This prospect, which appeared frighteningly medieval, was not easily laughed off or dispelled, although some of the press might have tried to do so with headlines such as: 'The Muslims are Coming', 'Mahomet Down Under', and 'Holy War in Car Plant'.[41] Australia's inherent fearfulness of Indonesia was never far from the surface.

Based on reports of rising Islamic insurgency in both the Middle East and Asia, an apparent Islamic 'domino effect' began to be glimpsed as early as the year 1980, gathering shape and some currency throughout the 1980s. Under the domino effect, it was assumed that Muslim communities would succumb one by one to fundamentalist revolution. 'With Iran opening up a strain of Muslim religious fervour, we've by no means seen the last of Islam,' a visiting expert in religious studies was prominently reported as saying.[42] The danger of Iranian style contagion was considered greatest at Australia's back door. In southern Philippines, the Moro National Liberation Front, which had been fighting for independence for five million Muslims, was reported to be financed by Gaddafi's Libya. Signs of burgeoning Islamist unrest in Indonesia and Malaysia were also considered ominous.[43] Numerous articles regularly predicted that Indonesia, the largest Muslim domino about to fall, was tottering 'on the edge'.[44] The separatist conflict in Aceh, the murderous Christian–Muslim confrontation in Ambon, and Christmas Eve attacks on churches in Jakarta had the potential to give fresh impetus to the domino concept.

It was an easy step for the rhetoric of the Cold War to be dusted down and recycled in an anti-Islamic form. According to John Esposito, with the collapse of the Communist system in the Soviet Union, fundamentalist Islam stepped into the void as a green, rather than red, menace to threaten the so-called free world.[45] Article 154 of Iran's Islamic Constitution, which enshrined the concept of exporting revolution, seemed proof enough of this sinister intent. However, just how seriously the press and its readers took an Islamic threat to Australia of this magnitude is difficult to measure. Neither the 'Sword of Islam', which had been sighted in 1979 and again in 1992,[46] nor the 'Holy War',[47] reported to be 'heading' in Australia's direction, actually arrived. However, the Iranian 'sword', did manage to slash a lucrative trading venture with an Australian company in 1979.[48] A cartoon in the *Southern District Times* had the 'Minto Islamic Centre' taken over by an Ayatollah Khomeini look-alike and set up as a heavily armed and fortified military headquarters in 1985. In 1994 a headline in *The Sydney Morning Herald* proclaimed Australia as 'The Jewel in the Crown of Islam'.[49] The possibility that Australia would be placed sooner or later in the firing line was a recurring theme.

1991–2000: THE GULF WAR, THE TALIBAN, AND AN ISLAMIC WORLD ORDER: MOVING 'BEYOND FUNDAMENTALISM'

In 1991 the Gulf War—another cataclysmic event involving Muslims—inaugurated a new, more investigative phase in the way the Australian press perceived and imaged Islam. However, this did not become clear until well after the 'Desert Storm' campaign, which forcibly ejected Iraq from Kuwait. Initially, the Gulf War gave powerful reinforcement to the, by now, stock view that the Middle East was a dangerously irrational place led astray by an array of unstable leaders including Nasser, Gaddafi, Arafat, and Khomeini, who represented the different faces of Muslim assertiveness. Saddam Hussein was just the latest to 'go off the rails': a dictator straight out of Nasser's mould, although mad and far more brutal, who also aspired to lead the Arab world.[50] What was thought to lie behind his claim to Kuwait was again oil—Saudi Arabia's as well Kuwait's—and the immense strategic power this would confer on whoever controlled its supply.[51] It was only with Iraq's back to the wall that Saddam invoked the rhetoric of jihad, launched scud missiles on Israel, proclaiming he was defending Islam from Western attack. Little of this rang true for the press, who depicted

Saddam as a 'monster' willing to sacrifice, if necessary, the 'last drop' of Iraqi blood for his own dubious ends.[52] It certainly did not see him as a potential 'caliph' or a legitimate spokesman for Islam.[53] Despite his 'Houdini-like' survival, in the eyes of the press Saddam was confirmed as a psychotic despot who might still unleash on the West those weapons of mass destruction believed to have escaped detection by the UN.[54] 'A decade on', according to Richard Butler head of the UN Special Commission to disarm Iraq, 'Saddam remains a danger to the world.'[55]

What effectively prevented any different opinion from surfacing was Australia's own involvement in the war, if only in a largely support capacity. This placed a premium on Australian national sentiment and effectively stifled serious debate. Those who did summon up the courage to question Australia's role were subjected to accusations of disloyalty, un-Australian behaviour, and even treason. This was the fate of Robert Springborg, for instance, who as a regular expert commentator on the war adopted a persistent anti-war line.[56] The Australian Broadcasting Commission was itself placed under scrutiny and was pressured by the Labour government and Prime Minister Bob Hawke to conduct an inquiry into its perceived 'bias', a charge which the inquiry subsequently rejected.[57]

The opinions of Australia's Muslim community were discounted altogether, the clear insinuation being that, as Arabs, they were all ethnically related to the enemy and thus a potential fifth column. Giving some reinforcement to this notion were reports that the New South Wales government had set up a Gulf Crisis Committee to meet under the chairmanship of the Premier 'in the event of a serious terrorist incident'. In addition, it was reported that Australian Security Intelligence Agency (ASIO) and the New South Wales Special Branch were 'monitoring' Sydney's Muslims closely.[58] Headlines such as those furnished by the Imam of the Lakemba Mosque[59]—'I'm for the Iraqi people'—and the defacement of the Arncliffe RSL building with the slogan 'Long live Saddam' were grist to the mill. Calls for all Muslims to be interned or repatriated became frequent on Sydney radio. Bruce Ruxton of the Returned Service League proclaimed, 'It's high time the Western world took on the Arabs. They are nothing more than a tribe of ratbags?'[60] A telling and symbolic turn of events was the abuse which began to be heaped on Muslim women wearing the veil.[61]

While the image of Islamic violence remained largely intact, the press began progressively to replace it with the image of the veil as the more fashionable signifier of Islam. Since the Gulf War, and to an extent arising out of it, there had been a perceptible shift in the focus of journalism to both the internal dynamics and the outward form of Islam. The fact that Australia's 250,000-plus Muslims suddenly emerged from relative obscurity during the conflict to become highly visible for the first time played a part.[62] The old refrain that the Muslims 'were coming' was rendered suddenly inapt; they were in Australia already and in growing numbers.

The Gulf War had been elevated by US President George Bush into a contest for a lasting and just 'world order'. To judge from the appearance of the Huntington thesis two years later, that contest had been indecisive. Certainly, Islam has not been vanquished as a dynamic, and possibly rival, religio-cultural system. Tongue in cheek or not, Huntington advised the West that the battle lines of the future would be drawn up at the 'civilizational' level, and that it should get to know its future enemy better before it was too late.[63] Despite the widespread criticism of his general thesis,[64] the press did take up the challenge. For the first time a sustained quest to discover the basic tenets and beliefs of Islam and to locate the core cultural differences it promoted was launched. Thus a series of articles began to appear on such issues as the role and rights of women in Islamic society; the Islamic approach to human rights;[65] Sharia punishments such as stoning, lashing, and lopping off limbs;[66] the connection, if any, between Islam and customary practices like 'female circumcision' in Muslim North Africa;[67] and 'honour killings' in Jordan and Pakistan.[68] In each category, however, Islam tended to be portrayed as failing the tests of civilized society.

Once again, the emergence of international models partly determined this negative view. A convenient and contemporaneous point of reference was the ideal society that the Taliban had installed in Afghanistan following a destructive internecine war. Unfortunately, fundamentalist Afghanistan proved a poor advertisement for what an Islamic world order might look like. Indeed its regime was patriarchal, brutal, dogmatic, and repressive. War-torn Afghanistan fed the press with a ready supply of tragic images, mostly relating to the life ordained for women by the Taliban. Invariably, what these images captured were scenes redolent of subordination and servitude.

Whether walking down Kabul's devastated streets or caught in front of ruined dwellings, women were pictured in the confining burqa, not even their eyes visible behind a grille of coarse fabric. The inference of imprisonment and oppression was tangible. As far as the press was concerned, this was symptomatic of no brave new Islamic world, but a return to the 'Dark Ages'. 'Year 2000', as *The Weekend Australian Magazine* described the Taliban's project, suggested a society built, not on utopian, but primitive foundations.[69] A 'Veil of Tears' was the verdict of Kim Willsher, who travelled to Kabul to discover the situation for herself. Photographed peering cautiously out of a burqa, minus the thick mesh, she supported the view that it was better to be a dog than a woman in the new Afghanistan:

Its true; the mangy animals which roam the streets foraging for scraps in the gutters at least have their liberty and a grudging acceptance of their right to exist. The women of this troubled city have neither.

She had observed women, considered to be inappropriately attired, receiving 'summary lashings' or a 'rifle butt in the face', and had incurred a warning herself from soldiers for not having her eyes covered. For Willsher, the burqa was 'an obvious, and odious, symbol of women's slavery'.[70] Other journalistic exposés carried much the same message. While Blanche d'Alpuget reported that *purdah* was not always hated, she confirmed that 'to be female was to suffer?'[71] Chistopher Kremmer in an article headlined 'Life is finished as Taliban force women out of sight', described Afghanistan as a 'smouldering fuse of reaction' where women continued to be killed as witches and were now cut off from education.[72] The burqa might hide women, but it could not mask the 'terror' which was imagined to reside behind it.[73]

Despite the fact that none of these investigative reports identified any of the Taliban's actions as specifically Islamic, there has been little attempt to de-link the implied association. Concessions that the burqa represented a 'corrupted brand' of Islam, that the Taliban's policies were expressions of a 'unique' cultural tradition,[74] and that 'spooky clothes' had been a common feature throughout the entire 'Judeo-Christian-Islamic world'[75] were hidden in bodies of text and thus easily missed. In no article was the veil in its various forms put into a Koranic context as a sign of modesty and devoutness rather than subjugation or menace. The fact that the white *hijab* (or head shawl) was more common than the black chador in most Muslim societies, or that many Muslim women chose not to veil themselves at all, were distinctions seldom highlighted.

The 'veil' has become the new all-encompassing metaphor for Islam itself—a kind of shorthand for every negative perception about Islam from excessive virtuousness to endemic violence. Indicative of its Islamic signification, the term routinely features in newspaper headlines such as 'Net and the Veil an Uneasy Mix'[76]— a story about how the internet is crossing the 'final frontier' of Saudi Arabia. The standard reference to a 'Veiled Threat' refers to practically any Muslim news item. These examples illustrate the noticeable gap which has begun to appear between headlines and the reports they introduce.[77] In a way that does not apply to other religions, Islam has come to be judged by the status accorded to women in Muslim societies—particularly where that position is seen as low, unequal, and discriminatory. That Muslim women have for the most part been photographed collectively and anonymously as crowds, rather than as distinct individuals, has facilitated this practice.

As time went by and press reports from Afghanistan under the Taliban became less sensational, the imagery depicting the experience of Muslim women lost a little of its harsh edge. Panning away from Afghan women in the 'war' zone,[78] as one headline put it, to Muslim women in situations of 'peace' elsewhere—including Australia— the press lightened up its hitherto unremittingly dark portrayal of their lives. A series of in-depth articles published in *The Sydney Morning Herald*, on the theme 'Beyond Fundamentalism', arguably set a new standard.[79] The series focused on the meaning of Islam— particularly for Australian Muslims—and received front-page billing and editorial comment. According to Peter Fray, who spent two weeks studying Sydney's Islamic community, Islam meant a 'New Dawn' for the 90,000 or more Muslims from 67 countries who had settled in Sydney. They were able to 'reclaim their Qur'anic heritage', by establishing their own schools in an Australia that was becoming more tolerant, despite its 'ingrained prejudice'. A subsequent softening in the portraiture of Muslim women followed, showing them in relaxed poses, both veiled and unveiled.[80]

A report on the children of Muslim immigrants embracing the religion their parents had abandoned turned the stereotype of the enslaving veil completely on its head. Under the rather poignant heading 'OZLAM', it featured a Muslim university student adopting the hijab as a 'liberating' experience'. She found everything that non-Muslims had said about Islam to be wrong:

When you actually go in and find out, Islam expects you to be intelligent and to educate yourself. It gives you such an incredible status as a woman that no other faith, no other belief has given women at all, and this is 1400 years ago.[81]

In yet another corrective article, Sian Powell suggests that Islam, far from being a religion 'stuck in time', was 'facing up to the new Millennium'. Again this interpretation centred on the relationship between Muslim women and the veil. A photograph of a gathering of young Muslims in white chadors was captioned: 'Free to choose. Modern Muslim women say their veils and robes force men to appreciate their intellect, not their appearance'.[82]

Against this, however, might be juxtaposed articles stating that nothing much had changed overseas and that Iranian women had achieved only minor gains in the 'battle' to restore the rights taken from them in 1979.[83] 'If you need direction, do the women a favour and ask a man', was advice offered to tourists planning to visit Iran.[84] A small item in the The Advertiser (Adelaide) about an Iranian transsexual wanting to become a man again—because of the 'restrictions' making her new life 'unbearable'—was bizarre but suggestive.[85] Also intriguing were photographs of groups of women in black chadors, on the one hand apparently filing submissively in line,[86] and, on the other, photographs of the same women reaching their destination—a parade ground where they were transformed into a regiment of fearsome warriors. The incongruity of their fighting to the death for a system that the West declared was oppressing them did not draw comment.[87]

Less ambiguous, more familiar stories of Muslim ferment have never been absent for long. The Sydney Morning Herald's Asia Editor, David Jenkins, reported that Indonesia was becoming Islam's 'New Bastion'. In a 'trend not likely to be reversed', he noted that Islam was 'on the march, to the beating of Mosque drums and the waving of green flags'. Adherents in their millions were dancing to this tune in 'mushrooming urban centres'.[88] In the Moluccas 'angry' Muslims were reported to be hell bent on 'holy war',[89] and in Pakistan an endless crowd of veiled Muslim women was depicted parading behind a banner celebrating the 'Islamic Bomb'.[90] American embassies continued to be bombed and in Osama bin Laden yet another Muslim has become the new Public Enemy Number One. Reports of 'honour killings' in both Melbourne and Sydney, drive-by shootings in Lakemba, and battles fought out in local councils over what were termed '24-hour Mosques' in Hume and Bankstown[91] could easily reinforce the fear that violence was seldom far removed from Muslim culture, even in Australia.[92] On the basis of all that the press had reported about Muslim activity around the world over five decades, the conclusion might logically be drawn that Islam offered a world not of order but of prevailing disorder.

CONCLUSIONS

There is much to contest about the way the mainstream Australian press has imaged Islam through its investigative lenses over the last half-century. Having focused on a narrow segment of Muslim activity, it has constructed, from a piecemeal knowledge of the Muslim world, a version of that world which is dominated by recurrent ferment and fervour. Very rarely has this narrow view been balanced against the larger perspective of the normal, stable, social existence experienced by the vast majority of Muslims. In effect, Islam has been captured in a series of single snapshots of its episodic history, which have spotlighted only the conflicts, charismatic leaders, and the more contentious aspects of revivalist Islam. It is these snapshots which have captured world attention.

A stereotypical representation of Islam has resulted based on mental and material images of Muslims at war and under challenge: as Arabs, as terrorists, as mullahs, as veiled and veiling women, as passive and proselytizing communities of believers. But this representation has been a changing one. The image of violence in both nationalist and terrorist forms prevailed throughout the 1960s and 1970s. This was replaced by the image of fundamentalist revolution and insurgency in the 1980s, personified in the dominant figure of Ayatollah Khomeini. During this period no account of Iran or analysis of Islam was complete without the mandatory photograph or life-sized placard of Khomeini held aloft by chanting supporters.[93] In the 1990s the image of the veil has emerged as the symbol of Islam, as Islam has come to be judged in terms of women's position in Muslim society. However, there is a good deal of overlap and some degree of contradiction within this imagery. That women could be simultaneously presented as forlorn and submissive crowds and as fearsome warriors is testament to this.

A more sympathetic image of Muslims may be beginning to emerge as Muslim Bosnians and Kosovars have attracted attention as victims of non-Muslim aggression and 'ethnic cleansing' in the 'killing fields' of the Balkans.[94] Even the Palestinians have received a better press as the images emerging from the latest conflict with Israel have revealed an unequal contest with stone-throwing Palestinian youths pitted against heavily armoured Israeli tanks, and tragic scenes of Palestinian death and bereavement.[95] The traditional pro-Israel stance of the Australian press is less pronounced than it has been at any time. A cartoon by Moir, captioned 'Lasting Peace is in Sight' and showing the 'last' Palestinian and the 'last' Israeli left standing to fight, bleakly reflects this newfound even-handedness.[96]

While much of this imagery might seem to be reminiscent of an Orientalist perspective, it is more immediately related to journalistic methods and the marketing requirements of newspapers. Journalists do not construct news as the surviving custodians of the Orientalist tradition. According to Rodney Tiffen in his analysis of the print media,[97] journalists now present news to conform to the time and space constraints of newspapers and the marketing imperatives of a highly competitive environment. What sells best is material that is dramatic, shocking, and eye-catching. This limits the kind of stories that are selected for coverage, and it restricts the way they are covered. The more sensational stories are given priority, with the most seductive piece of information positioned in the headline. Like a 'reversed pyramid', the news is processed as a selection of the 'highlights of highlights'.[98] Often the headline is relied on to tell the whole story. Such 'active winnowing', as Tiffen puts it, results in a fragmented, one-sided, view of the world—generally as a place of drama and tragedy—and in the reproduction of a 'repertory of images' that convey this limited representation.[99]

In view of this, newspaper coverage of Islam in Australia, which has formed the subject of this study, could not seriously be considered as a 'mirror of reality'. However, this is also true of the treatment of any subject investigated by the press. Just as the Muslim world has been compressed rather than covered in news reports featuring bits and pieces of reality, so has the world at large been treated in much the same manner. Akbar Ahmed has tacitly conceded this point in suggesting that 'Occidentalist' images of Western civilization have been shaped by its selective coverage in the Western press itself.[100] Political crises, social problems, crime in various forms, sexual exploitation, and sport have constituted the staple diet of even the mainstream newspapers. In this regard, the overall outlook of the press might be considered 'Worldist', rather than 'Orientalist'.

Even so, the news served up by the press cannot be totally cast aside as a complete fabrication. As Tiffen has stated, it is 'rare' to find stories which are 'sheer invention' or which have 'no substantial basis'.[101] There can be little doubt that the events the Australian press reported in the Middle East and in Muslim Asia in the period 1950–2000 actually took place. It is also certain that these reports predominantly consisted of 'bland', 'nuts and bolts' information that was factual, not analytical. It has been the attribution of such events to Islam in less frequently occurring news commentary that is much more contestable. Nonetheless, it has proved difficult to divorce Islam absolutely from this history, when substantial parts of it have been undertaken in the name of Islam, and when Islam itself draws no distinction between faith and life, the temporal and the spiritual. That certain customs might not be considered authentically Islamic does not diminish their Islamic status for those Muslims who have religiously observed them as normative.[102]

In the end, the challenge facing Muslim communities in the future is that of describing and defining the world of Islam more accurately than the Australian and Western press might have managed to do. For it is unlikely that the non-Muslim press will report or interpret the world—including the Muslim world—in a more understanding or low-key way than it has in the past. In a series of lectures in Australia, the Imam of New York, Siraj Wahhaj offered this blunt message: if Muslims want Islam to be promoted as a religion of tolerance, not terrorism, they will need to demonstrate this by their own actions.[103]

Notes

1. This research was made possible by an Australian Research Council grant and with the help of Andrew Messner who undertook some of the basic research on newspaper files. A sizeable archive of press reports covering the theme of Islam has been collected since 1979.

2. Since I have tended to concentrate on textual images, examples of visual imagery have not been included. However, a sample of these may be viewed by accessing Howard V. Brasted, 'The Politics of Stereotyping. Western Images of Islam', *Manushi*, 98: January–February 1997, pp. 6–16, which is also available at: www.freespeech.org/manushi/98/islam.html.

3. Barry Lowe, 'Islam and the Media', in New South Wales Anti-Discrimination Board (ed.), *Islam in Australia* (Sydney: NSW Anti-Discrimination Board, 1985), pp. 55–62; Daryl Champion, 'Muslims and the Media in Australia', *Journal of Arabic, Islamic and Middle East Studies*, 1(2), 1994, pp. 8–24; and Brasted, 'Western Images of Islam'.

4. Trenchant opposition to the establishment of a Muslim school at Greenacre and the building of a mosque at Bass Hill, both Sydney suburbs, are two examples he provides of such racism. Lowe, 'Islam and the Media', pp. 55–8. Racism of this kind has also been sighted by Michael Humphrey. See M. Humphrey, 'Islam, Immigration and the State: Religion in Australia', in Alan W. Black (ed.), *Religion in Australia. Sociological Perspectives* (Sydney, Allen & Unwin, 1991), pp. 176, 191; and 'Is this a Mosque Free Zone? Islam and the State in Australia', *Migration Monitor*, 12: June 1989, p. 12.

5. Champion, 'Muslims and the Media in Australia', pp. 10–11.

6. Brasted, 'Western Images of Islam', pp. 10–11.

7. Greg Sheridan is Asia Editor of the *The Australian*.

8. S.P. Huntington, 'The Clash of Civilizations?', *Foreign Affairs*, 72(3), 1993.

9. 'Beyond Fundamentalism: Islam in Australia', *The Sydney Morning Herald*, 15–16 May 1995.

10. Narmeen El-Farra, 'Arabs and the Media', *Journal of Media Psychology*, 1(2), 1996; James A. Reilly, 'The Distorted Images of Islam', *Ottawa Citizen*, 7 September 1998; Charles Glass, 'A Prejudice as American as Apple Pie', *New Statesman*, 127(2), November 1998; Neil MacMaster and Toni Lewis, 'Orientalism: From Veiling to Hyperveiling', *Journal of European Studies*, 28(1–2), 1998; and J.A. Progler, 'The Utility of Islamic Imagery in the West. An American case study', available at: www.themodernreligion.com/assault/imagery.html.

11. 'Muslims Seek to Counter Prejudice', *BBC Online*, 6 November 2000.

12. *Australian Muslim News*, 8 September 1998.

13. E.W. Said, *Orientalism: Western Conceptions of the Orient* (London: Penguin, 1991).

14. Said, *Orientalism*, p. 2. See also E.W. Said, *Covering Islam* (London: Routledge, 1981), in which journalists are more directly implicated as the modern transmitters of the Orientalist tradition.

15. For example, over building regulatory, noise abatement, and related environmental concerns.

16. A. Hourani, *Islam in European Thought*, (Cambridge: Cambridge University Press, 1991), pp. 38, 57–8; see also P. Mansfield, *The Arabs* (London: Penguin, 1992), ch. 29, pp. 479–87.

17. Akbar Ahmed, 'Islam. The Roots of Misperception', *History Today*, 41, April 1991, pp. 201–2.

18. 'Not again, for heaven's sake', *The Economist*, 6 August 1994. See some of these images in Brasted, 'Western Images of Islam', pp. 11–12.

19. Sheldon Pollock, for example, discovers evidence of Orientalism in Sanskrit texts, and Gyanendra Pandey attests to the demonizaton of Muslims in recent Hindu fundamentalist writing. See Sheldon Pollock, 'Deep Orientalism?', in Carol A. Breckenridge and Peter van der Veer (eds), *Orientalism and Post-Colonial Perspectives in South Asia* (Philadelphia: University of Pennsylvania Press, 1993), pp. 76–133; and Gyanendra Pandey, 'The New Hindu History', *South Asia*, Special Issue, 17: 1994, pp. 97–112.

20. According to both Akbar Ahmed and Aijaz Ahmad, Muslims 'routinely' draw essentialist distinctions about the West. See Akbar Ahmed, 'The Roots of Misperception', p. 36; and Aijaz Ahmad, *Theory, Classes, Nations, Literatures* (London: Verso, 1992), ch: 5, p. 183.

21. See, for instance, Ahmad Shboul quoted in Hanifa Deen, *Caravanserai: Journey among Australian Muslims* (Sydney: Allen and Unwin, 1995), p. 167.

22. Said, *Orientalism*, pp. 2–3.

23. *The Sydney Morning Herald*, 10 August 1956.

24. *Sun Herald*, 12 and 19 August 1956.

25. *The Bulletin* (8 and 22 August 1956; 5 and 26 September 1956; 7 and 28 November 1956; 16 January; and 4 September 1957). See especially cartoon representations.

26. *The Sydney Morning Herald*, 7 and 9 August 1956.

27. *Sun Herald*, 12 August 1956.

28. *The Sydney Morning Herald*, 9 August 1956.

29. From *The Bulletin circa* 1960, but have been unable to retrieve specific reference.

30. *The Sydney Morning Herald,* 12 and 13 November 1975; *The Australian,* 12 and 14 November 1975. Australia, along with most of Western bloc, voted against the resolution.

31. The Labour party also unsuccessfully attempted to secure a donation from Iraq. See Ross McMullin, *The Light on the Hill: The Australian Labor Party 1891–1991* (Oxford: Oxford University Press, 1991), pp. 357ff, 377–80.

32. *The Bulletin,* 24 November 1973.

33. Louay M. Safi, 'Distortion of the Image of Islam by the Global Media', *Australian Muslim News,* 1(2), 1996, p. 9.

34. See cartoon accompanying the article, 'The Secret World of Abu Nidal: A Young Volunteer's Chilling Story of the Arab Death Squads', *The Weekend Australian,* 23–4 May 1992.

35. 'No Exceptions to the Iron-clad Will of Allah', *The Australian,* 25 September 1980.

36. *The Sydney Morning Herald,* 14 February 1979.

37. *The Bulletin,* 8 January 1980.

38. *The Bulletin,* 11 December 1979. Against this see Ian Murray's much more moderate assessment, 'Battle for Iran's Soul', *The Age,* 19 January 1979.

39. *The Sydney Morning Herald,* 7 March 1989.

40. *The Bulletin,* 29 May 1979.

41. Cited in A.W. Ata, 'Moslem Arab Portrayal in the Australian Press and in School Textbooks', *Australian Journal of Social Issues,* 19(3), 1984, p. 213.

42. *The Australian,* 25 September 1980. See interview with Professor Ninlan Stuart.

43. *The Bulletin,* 8 January 1980.

44. *The Sydney Morning Herald,* 27 January 1981, 27 April 1998; *The Weekend Australian,* 8–9 October 1994.

45. John L. Esposito, 'Political Islam: Beyond the Green Menace', *Current History,* January 1994.

46. Ata, 'Moslem Arab Portrayal', p. 213; and *The Times* (Australia), 15 June 1992.

47. *Reader's Digest* (Australia), January 1995.

48. *The Bulletin,* 13 February 1979.

49. *The Sydney Morning Herald,* 12 April 1994.

50. *The Weekend Australian,* 2 and 3 February 1991.

51. *The Sydney Morning Herald*, 25 January 1991.
52. *The Australian*, 22 January 1991; *The Sydney Morning Herald*, 23 January 1991. See also 'The Sins of the Father', *The Weekend Australian*, 21–2 February 1998.
53. *The Sydney Morning Herald*, 11 January 1991.
54. *The Sydney Morning Herald*, 8 November 1997; 'Saddam Hussein's Houdini Act', *The Weekend Australian*, 13–14 January 1996.
55. 'Despot has to be Disarmed', *The Australian*, 17 January 2001.
56. *The Sydney Morning Herald*, 25 January, 2 February 1991, and 13 March 1993.
57. *The Sydney Morning Herald*, 22 January, 1, 2, and 8 February 1991.
58. *The Sydney Morning Herald*, 25 January 1991. That such surveillance had much to do with ensuring the safety of the Muslim community was not made clear. A Molotov cocktail had been thrown at the mosque at Rooty Hill, for instance, forcing its imam to live 'in a virtual state of siege'.
59. Sheikh Taj Eldine al Hilali.
60. David Bowman, 'Crisis in the Gulf, and Another Veil Slips', *Australian Society*, December 1990, pp. 16–18.
61. *The Sydney Morning Herald*, 14 January 1991.
62. The establishment of the *Australian Muslim Times* on 10 January 1991, giving a formal voice to Australia's various Muslim communities, was also a landmark development. See 'A New Sign of the Times for Muslims', *The Sydney Morning Herald*, 11 January 1991.
63. Huntington, 'Clash of Civilizations?', pp. 45, 49; and S.P. Huntington, 'If not Civilizations, What?', *Foreign Affairs*, 75(5), 1993, pp. 134–8.
64. For example, symposium on thesis in *ASAA Review*, 18(1), July 1994.
65. 'Veil of Tears', *Sunday Telegraph*, 17 November 1996; 'Muslim Women Fight for Rights', *The Australian*, 10 March 1998; 'Little Progress on Women's Rights: Amnesty', *Canberra Times*, 8 March 2000.
66. *The Australian*, 8 September 1993; *Sunday Telegraph*, 8 October 1995.
67. *The Sydney Morning Herald*, 4 October 1994.
68. *The Australian*, 28 July 1999; and ABC documentaries on 18 September 2000 and 2 October 2000.
69. *The Weekend Australian Magazine*, 8–9 March 1997.
70. 'Veil of Tears', *Sunday Telegraph*, 17 November 1996.
71. *The Weekend Australian Magazine*, 18–19 June 1994.
72. *The Sydney Morning Herald*, 7 June 1997.
73. *The Sydney Morning Herald*, 13 April 1996.

74. *The Sydney Morning Herald*, 7 June 1997, 24 December 1999.
75. *The Weekend Australian Magazine*, 18–19 June 1994.
76. *The Sydney Morning Herald*, 24 March 1998.
77. *The Sydney Morning Herald*, 2 November 1998; 'The Veiled Threat', *The Weekend Australian*, 6–7 March 1999. See also as an example 'Veiled Threat', *The Weekend Australian*, 19–20 June 1999, which refers to Wan Azizah's taking up the cause of her embattled husband, Anwar Ibrahim.
78. *The Weekend Australian Magazine*, 27–28 June 1998.
79. *The Sydney Morning Herald*, 15–16 May 1995.
80. *The Sunday Telegraph*, 26 November; 3 December 2000; *The Sydney Morning Herald*, 27 January 1998; 24 November 2000.
81. *The Weekend Australian*, 30 September–1 October 2000.
82. *The Australian*, 29 November 2000.
83. *The Weekend Australian*, 6–7 March 1999.
84. 'The Iranian Cover Up', *The Weekend Australian*, 17–18 January 1998.
85. *The Advertiser* (Adelaide), 16 June 2000.
86. 'Behind the Holy Veil', *The Weekend Australian Magazine*, 25–6 February 1995.
87. *The Australian*, 24 September 1997; 'The Veiled Threat', *The Weekend Australian*, 6–7 March 1999; See contrasting images in Brasted, 'Western Images of Islam', pp. 7, 12.
88. *The Sydney Morning Herald*, 10 January 1998.
89. *The Sydney Morning Herald*, 8 January 2000.
90. *The Weekend Australian*, 30–1 May 1998.
91. *The Weekend Australian*, 13–14 February 1999; *The Sydney Morning Herald*, 29 October 1999.
92. *The Weekend Australian Magazine*, 3–4 September 1994; *The Australian*, 28 July 1999.
93. See, for example, the photograph in Brasted, 'Western Images of Islam', p. 6.
94. *The Australian*, 9 June 1998, 9 March 1999; *The Weekend Australian*, 7–8 March 1998. Against this, see article on media bias on Bosnia in *Australian Muslim Times*, 10 December 1993.
95. 'A Tragedy in Gaza', *The Sydney Morning Herald*, 3 October 2000; 'Palestinian Children Caught in the Ritual of Death', *The Sydney Morning Herald*, 9 October 2000; 'Middle East Tragedy', *The Sydney Morning Herald*, 10 October 2000.
96. *The Sydney Morning Herald*, 27 December 2000.

97. Rodney Tiffen, *News and Power* (Sydney: Allen & Unwin, 1989), esp. pp. 1–80; and 'The Press', in Stuart Cunningham and Graeme Turner (eds), *The Media in Australia* (Sydney: Allen & Unwin, 1997), pp. 191–200.

98. Graeme Turner, 'Media Texts and Messages', in Stuart Cunningham and Graeme Turner (eds), *The Media in Australia* (Sydney: Allen & Unwin, 1997), pp. 339–46.

99. Tiffen, *News and Power*, pp. 65–6,

100. Akbar Ahmed, 'The Roots of Misperception', p. 205.

101. Tiffen, 'The Press', p. 199.

102. For a discussion on local custom-based syncretistic Islam, see Asim Roy and H.V. Brasted, 'Islam in History and Politics: A South Asian Perspective', in *South Asia*, Special Issue on 'Islam in History and Politics', 22, 1999, pp. 1–12.

103. 'Imam on Mission to Clear Away Fear', *The Sydney Morning Herald*, 16 May 2000.

POSTSCRIPT[1]

Since the above article was published, the stereotypical associations of Islam with holy war and hostage taking, with radical mullahs and militant leaders, and with honour killing and female subordination continue to be drawn. It was never likely that the tabloids and television stations, which thrived on sensationalizing the news they purveyed, were going to de-link them totally and retail the kind of 'truth' about Islam that Edward Said might have approved of. Indeed, the image of the veil as a signifier of all that was wrong with the world order Islam proclaimed has if anything been reinforced. Despite the overthrow of the Taliban in late 2001, following Al Qaeda's attack on the World Trade Center in New York, Afghanistan has continued to feed the world press with an endless supply of tragic images of burqa clad women and their female children in various familiar poses suggestive of oppression, misery, and servitude. Pictures of veiled Muslim women continue to illustrate article after article on Islam. Typical of the recent genre is the photograph of the courageous, if manifestly vulnerable, Afghan politician, Malalai Joya, with an armed bodyguard, and the accompanying message that her mission, or 'One Woman's War', to improve the plight of women in post-Taliban Afghanistan is fraught with imminent physical danger.[2]

The earth shattering events of 9 September 2001 have served to reconfirm the connection between Islam and violence as well, though to an extent a strategic shift in the media's approach to Islam can also be observed. First, despite 9/11—and subsequent suicide attacks against tourists in Bali and 'rush hour' commuters in central Madrid and London—journalists, radio commentators, and television reporters generally resisted the temptation to attribute these atrocities to Islam per se and to inculpate all Muslims as a result. The repeated calls for calm assessment by Western governments anxious to avoid any backlash against their own Muslim communities no doubt played a part in this. But the ready accessibility of the media to academics, terrorist experts, and Muslim watchers to discuss these events and derive sense from them allowed the whole complex issue of causation to be opened up on an unprecedented scale.

Since 9/11, the search for answers has widened the framework of explanation, if it has also divided it. While sharing the conciliatory view that most Muslims are politically moderate and abhor terrorism of any kind, two contending narratives of the Islamist phenomenon have emerged, parting company over the underlying causes of the terrorist attack on the World Trade Center and the attribution of responsibility. Even before the dust had settled on the site of the twin towers, the simple line adopted by the administration of George W. Bush and its neo-conservative supporters, that Al Qaeda had targeted the United States because 'they hate its freedoms', their leaders are deluded and deranged, and their followers are the fanatical products of madrasa-style indoctrination, provided one version.[3] Accordingly, the condemnatory spotlight falls on a radical minority of Islamists and their teachings that portray America as an evil force in the world that must be combated and ultimately destroyed. Blame is attached to a perverted form of Islam.

An alternative reading, that Islamic terrorism was the by-product of US foreign policy in the Middle East, appeared shortly after in a series of articles carried in such influential journals as the *Christian Science Monitor*,[4] *Newsweek*,[5] and *The Nation*.[6] Turning the focus around these pointed out that what had engendered anti-Americanism amongst Muslims everywhere and mobilized groups of militant radicals to embark on a campaign of terrorist activity against American targets had been the constabulary role that the US had exercised for over sixty years. By underwriting the establishment and expansion of Israel at the expense of Palestinians, propping up despotic rather than democratic regimes in Arabia, North Africa, and the Gulf, and acting against any state that it could not control, the US had enforced a law and order on the region that had seriously destabilized it. Islamism was, in effect, a form of 'blowback' for US military and political intervention.[7] In this scenario, the US stands out as less a benevolent than a belligerent and bullying force.

Of the two, the latter narrative has acquired more momentum. In a very measured, almost disarming way, it received authoritative backing from the National Commission on Terrorist Attacks—the 9/11 Commission—when it reported its findings on 22 July 2004. What it found was that while Osama bin Laden may have tapped into a 'long tradition of extreme intolerance' from a stream of Islam stretching back to Ibn Taimiyya (1263–1328), American foreign policy 'choices', particularly over Israel and Iraq, had been more immediately 'consequential' in fuelling Muslim antipathy to the

West. The Commission urged the US government that, if the 'next generation of terrorists' was to be 'stopped', it needed to 'treat people humanely', 'abide by the rule of law', and 'be generous and caring to our neighbours'. That it had done none of these things is clearly implied in its report.[8]

For the time being at least the storyline favoured by the Bush administration is encountering widespread scepticism, certainly in Australia. The ineffectualness of the current American strategy of eliminating terrorism by taking out terrorists is one reason. With the exception of Osama bin Laden and Ayman al Zawahiri, who would rank among the most recognizable people in the world today— so often do pictures of them appear in the press and on television— terrorists are not easily identified and tracked down. The revelations that the US and the 'coalition of the willing' invaded Iraq on false pretences, discovered no weapons of mass destruction (WMDs) there and belatedly embraced the cause of liberal democracy to justify their actions have also not helped. Of course this could all change depending on the turn of events overseas and how the public perceives them. As Peter Manning, a former head of news and current affairs at ABC TV and the Seven Network has shown, using a computer study of some 12,000 articles that appeared in the *The Sydney Morning Herald* and the *The Daily Telegraph* a year either side of 9/11, Australians are fed on a large diet of American and European representations of Arabs and Muslims that collectively convey a 'deep and sustained fear'.[9] Residing just below the surface that fear is very easily tapped into.

Ultimately, however, it is the domestic, as much as the international dimension of terrorism that may determine not only what narrative will come to stand the test of time, but also how this will impact on the way Islam will be portrayed in the media. Following the suicide bombings on the London transport system on 7 July 2005, the cue given by the then Australian government in addressing the threat of 'home grown' Islamist terrorism developing in Australia, as it had done in the United Kingdom, has been nothing short of confrontational and belligerent. One after another the Prime Minister John Howard, the then Education Minister Brendon Nelson, and the Federal Treasurer Peter Costello issued challenges to migrants in general, but Muslims in particular, to embrace 'Australian values' and teach them in their schools. Otherwise they would 'face the prospect' of being stripped of their Australian citizenship and 'kicked out' of the country. There was especially no place for Islamists who 'wanted to live under sharia law', refused to integrate with mainstream Australian society, and gave 'comfort to terrorism'. They could 'clear off' immediately.[10] From 15 October 2007 all migrants, except those from New Zealand, are required to affirm their primary commitment to Australia and their knowledge of Australianness courtesy of a purpose built manual, *Life in Australia*,[11] which they must familiarize. Arguably the introduction of a loyalty test, which this procedure entails, was designed with Muslims specifically in mind.

Whether the questioning of Muslimness was generated by the Howard government as a way of distancing itself from Australia's long standing commitment to multiculturalism—at least of what it calls the 'mushy misguided' kind[12]—or defending its continuing military involvement in Iraq and Afghanistan, is difficult to say. Whatever the reason, the juxtaposing of Muslim and Australian values is resonant of the 'them versus us' mentality that characterized orientalist discourse. Islam and violence is a motif that simply won't go away.

Echoes of it permeate journalistic comment on the Cronulla riots of December 2005, for example, when thousands of Australian and Lebanese youths invaded Sydney's beach suburb in racially motivated confrontation. Muslims have also been the only victims of Australia's anti-terrorist laws.[13] The case of the Indian physician Mohamed Haneef, who had his visa revoked and was detained on the very flimsy grounds that he was related to two of the terrorists involved in the attack on Glasgow airport, is the most notorious. Another, involving a medical student, Ishar ul–Haque, has just been thrown out in the New South Wales (NSW) Supreme Court because of the illegal, 'sledgehammer' tactics of the ASIO, which reminded the presiding judge of Franz Kafka's *The Trial*.[14] In the opinion of the convenor of the Islamic Sydney website things could not get much worse: 'The media's portrayal of Muslims has been so bad for so long that we just don't care anymore. There is a siege mentality and it's justifiable in my opinion.'[15]

Eight years on, one is left to reflect whether anything has really changed. While historical contexts change, the politics of stereotyping continue in one form or another.

NOTES

1. This postscript draws on Howard Brasted, 'A New World Disorder in the Making? An Historical Assessment [hereafter 'New World Disorder'], in Fethi Mansouri and Shahram Akbarzadeh (eds), *Political Islam and Human Security* (Newcastle: Cambridge Scholars Press, 2006), pp. 15–31.

2. Glyn Strong, 'One Woman's War', *Good Weekend, The Sydney Morning Herald*, 3 November 2007, pp. 37–40. Another example is the front cover of *The Economist*, which draws attention to a special report on Iran and the 'riddle' of its confrontation with the West, *The Economist*, 21–7 July 2007, pp. 20–5. See also, 'Brides of the Drug Lords', *The Weekend Australian Magazine*, 5–6 June 2004.

3. See Victor David Hanson, *An Autumn of War: What America Learned from September 11 and the War on Terrorism* (New York: Anchor Books, 2002).

4. Peter Ford 'Why do they hate us?', *Christian Science Monitor*, 27 September 2001.

5. Fareed Zakaria, 'The Politics of Rage: Why do they Hate Us?', *Newsweek*, 15 October 2001, http://www.fareedzakaria.com/ARTICLES/newsweek/101501_why.html

6. Chalmers Johnson, 'Blowback', *The Nation*, 15 October 2001 http://www.thenation.com/doc/20011015/johnson

7. See new Introduction in Chalmers Johnson, *Blowback. The Cost and Consequences of American Empire*, 2nd edn (New York: Henry Holt, 2004).

8. Brasted, 'New World Disorder', pp. 23–4; *9/11 Commission Report*, pp. 362, 375–6, http://www.9/11commission.gov/report/911Report.htm

9. Peter Manning, *Dog Whistle Politics and Journalism: Reporting Arabic and Muslim People in Sydney Newspapers* (Sydney: University of Technology, 2004), pp. 15, 45. See also Manning, 'Australians Imaging Islam', in Elizabeth Poole and John E. Richardson (eds), *Muslims and the News Media* (London & New York: I.B. Taurus, 2006), pp.128–41; and *Us and Them: A Journalist's Investigations of Media, Muslims and the Middle East* (Sydney: Random House, 2006).

10. See 'Our Values or Go Home: Costello' by Josh Gordon and Jewell Topsfield, *The Age*, 24 February 2006, http://www.theage.com.au/news/national/our-values-or-go-home-costello/2006/02/23/

1140670207642.html and 'Accept Australian values or get out', by
Michelle Grattan, *The Age*, 25 August 2005, http://www.theage.com.au/
news/war-on-terror/accept-australian-values-or-get-out/2005/08/24/
1124562921555.html]

11. See http://www.immi.gov.au/living-in-australia/values/book/
    index.htm

12. 'Our Values or Go home', *The Age*, 24 February 2006.

13. See 'Mob violence envelops Cronulla, *The Sydney Morning Herald*,
    11 December 2005, http://www.smh.com.au/news/national/mob-
    violence-envelops-cronulla/2005/12/11/1134235936223.html, and
    David Marr, 'Alan Jones. I'm the person that's led this charge', *The
    Age*, 13 December 2005, http://www.theage.com.au/news/national/
    alan-jones-im-the-person-thats-led-this-charge/2005/12/12/
    1134236003153.html

14. Tom Allard, 'Spies in the eyes of others', *The Sydney Morning Herald*,
    17–18 November 2007, p. 28.

15. Quoted in Tom Allard, 'Under siege: Muslims blame the media', *The
    Sydney Morning Herald*, 3 May 2007.

6

The Print Media and Minority Images

Chandan Mitra

It is a general view among Muslims in India that the English-language media does not project a true and positive picture of the community. They also believe that there is a bias in the international media against Muslims in general. This, of course, is an over-simplified analysis of an otherwise complicated situation, portraying the image of Muslims as the largest religious minority in India, as well as that of a stereotyped monolithic community living in a Hindu-majority country. The reality is that the image of Indian Muslims projected by the Indian media varies vastly, but the expectations among Muslims are unfair in the given circumstances. My point of reference is the English-language media, for the simple reason that, being an insider, I am closely aware of the reality and the limitations.

Though I do not fully agree with the perception of Indian Muslims as far as their media image is concerned, I will not directly contest their perception. I would rather go into details of the features of this psyche along with the problems of the media. Only for this reason, I shall also speak about the Urdu press in India; as it is, the Urdu press run by Muslims that has done more damage to the Muslim image in India than any other language media. In this analysis, I shall not include such Urdu newspapers as *Pratap*, *Milap*, and *Hind Samachar*, as they are neither run by Muslim establishments nor is their readership Muslim. Their professional concerns and editorial orientations are altogether different. The Urdu media, especially in north India—and more specifically in Delhi—is negative and least interested in propagating and encouraging positive Muslim images in a plural society such as India. There is a perception among scholars, and even among Muslim readers, that Urdu newspapers are not interested in playing the role of making Muslims a part of the social changes and modernization that is rapidly taking place in India. Ather Farouqui sums this up aptly:

.... the prospects remain that Urdu journalism will continue the traditional game of arousing Muslim sentiments through provocative writing, and render them susceptible to the influence of the communal leadership with which a good many Urdu journalists are themselves aligned due to their own ambitions for political prominence and professional clout ...[1]

It is also true that, other than Delhi, the English media and the regional-language media (other than the Hindi print media of north India, which is a different story altogether with a complicated political sociology) in respective regions see Muslims as part of the regional culture and local politics. Except for north Indian Muslims, the Muslims of the entire country whose mother tongue is other than Urdu or Hindi have fully assimilated themselves with the regional cultural ethos to the extent that they cannot be counted as one entity with the Muslims of northern India. Farouqui further says:

Without doubt the Muslims of South India and West Bengal never recognized Urdu as their language and a symbol of their religious identity. In the changed political milieu too, Urdu was never their language and in the past they were greatly distanced from the Muslims of North India. Culturally, north Indian Muslims always considered themselves different from Muslims in the rest of the country. They are also the victims of a pronounced sense of superiority. Cultural distance and the strong sense of superiority on the part of north Indian Muslims become a great hurdle in linking them with the South Indian Muslims. This factor also prevented the movement for Pakistan from reaching South India except for a few big cities such as Hyderabad. Migration to Pakistan from the South was limited precisely because of the hold of north Indian Muslims over the Muslim League, particularly by the *Ashraf* (gentry). Linguistic and cultural conflicts have arisen there even after the formation of Pakistan; thus the subsequent establishment of Bangladesh and the remarkable rise of the Muhajir Qaumi Movement (MQM). The strife in the refugee-dominated urban areas of Sindh province is ample proof of this. Muslim politics in contemporary India are not particularly different from what they were in the past. The hold of north Indian Muslims on Muslim political campaigns even after independence has been strong. This prompted the presumption that the north Indian Muslim leadership would also be successful in the South.

However the humiliating defeat of Syed Shahabuddin, a self-designated vocal spokesman of South Indian Muslims, in Bangalore during the 1989 general elections made the North Indian Muslim leadership acutely aware of its real standing in the South.[2]

In north India, not only Muslims but Hindus too are a unique socio-political phenomenon. Broadly speaking, north India is itself such a strange political phenomenon that understanding its psychology has never been easy, even for sociologists. The Hindu–Muslim context of north India is different from that of the rest of India. The imbroglio called 'Hindi versus Urdu' is therefore not only the politics of language but also has the gamut of political complexities at its forefront. The Urdu–Hindi controversy of the nineteenth century was the reflection of this politico-cultural conundrum. Even today the situation has not changed much. Howsoever complicated the reality may be because of its variations, in the eyes of the world the images that are projected by the English media of India, especially Delhi, are the images of India, irrespective of being Muslim or Hindu.

As far as Muslims are concerned, Muslim intellectuals in Delhi are deemed the sole representatives of the entire community for the simple reason that their being in Delhi gives the media easy access to them. To what extent are Muslim intellectuals working in universities and retired bureaucrats active within media circles genuinely concerned about the sociology of Indian Muslims? Very clearly, the members of the English-speaking Muslim elite in Delhi neither have an understanding of the problems of common Muslims nor do they have any interest in the matter. This is perhaps the reason why the common educated Muslim is not only unfamiliar with these so-called intellectuals but, if they know of them, even hate them.

To an extent, Urdu newspapers of Delhi, working as a single entity, could be said to have an understanding of north Indian Muslims' psyche, but they have only played a negative role in their lives. As far as the electronic media is concerned, some Urdu TV channels use the spoken language and focus on the Muslim middle-class that is still almost negligible in proportion to the entire Muslim population. But these channels too give way to misunderstanding about Muslims. As such, viewers of Urdu TV channels are mostly those who do not know English. It seems that there is no respite for common Muslims.

Despite being a single entity, the speed with which Urdu newspapers form north India, especially weekly newspapers of Delhi, are heading towards decay is rather on expected and anticipated lines. I shall not talk here about official circulation figures of Urdu newspapers that merely serve the purpose of the government to show that Urdu is flourishing. In the government files, of course, Urdu journalism is making steady progress, simply because the government officials are assigned the role of issuing misleading statements highlighting the progress made in case of the promotion of Urdu, particularly by a certain central government organization: the National Council for Promotion of Urdu Language.

The question of the progress of Urdu journalism is concerned with the system of Urdu education in common schools with secular curricula. The issue of script has now arisen in the context of the *dini madaris*. If children whose mother tongue is Urdu get an opportunity to study Urdu within their school curricula, the entire sociology of the dini madaris will undergo a sea change; it would mark their decisive decline. Until there is no arrangement for teaching Urdu in the secular curriculum, the population wanting to learn Urdu would remain confined to the dini madaris, and, the Urdu newspapers even though unwillingly, would print only what the madrasa-educated people would like to read. We all know what the madrasa-educated people want to read, and we are also aware of how a person educated in a religious institution views a pluralistic society, and how the religious person himself is viewed by the pluralistic society.

Unfortunately, after Partition, Urdu has not been included by the Congress leadership in the secular curriculum, especially in the north Indian states. Consequently, the madrasas kept growing. With the passage of time, they replaced school education among Muslims and established a parallel system dangerous not only for the nation but even more so for Muslims themselves. One reason for the survival and growth of the madrasas is the economic backwardness of the common Muslims. But when Muslim children did not go to school, both economic but social transformation stopped among Muslims. Without doubt, the increase in the number of madrasas is also an example of the failure of our national education policy and the constitutional obligation to treat Muslims at par in education too. Obviously, an economically backward section of society, such as Muslims, cannot develop an educational system parallel to the state-sponsored educational apparatus. Sooner or later, society will have to provide Muslims with secular education at par with other religious groups, mainly Hindus, so that they are made part of mainstream education and occupy a common civic space. It is for us to think how to stop the growth and spread of the dini madaris, whose network comprises half-a-million madrasas with 50 million full-time students. (These are authentic and undisputed figures known to all, issued by the government, and which were not challenged.) We should also not forget that because of being religious educational institutions, madrasas are much more organized and influential than the secular-curriculum schools run by the government.

The English media in India is an elite media, an offshoot of the baggage of history. As a large majority of Muslims in India are economically deprived and do not live in big cities, there is a tendency in the English language media to ignore issues that concern Muslims. The English media, however, plays an important role in shaping perceptions in the minds of India as whole. Although read by just 2–3 per cent (and really understood by hardly 1 per cent) of the Indian population, the images that the English media builds and creates are reflected decisively in the international scene as well as within India. These images enhance a political balance. The English media provides the pan-Indian picture for the regional language media unaware of north Indian languages, such as Hindi (which is already considered as biased as the Urdu media is overzealous in its presentation of Muslim issues). The English-language media is said to provide a common ground between these conflicting positions and is, in a certain sense, a moderator or a melting-pot among the various sections of India. There are also allegations from Muslims against the English media that are true, but the whole English media does not behave so irresponsibly.

It is true that the English media often picks up wrong Muslim voices that do not represent the community; this is counter productive. For example, we have Shabana Azmi, who always gets space because of being associated with Bollywood. She is easily accessible and knows the English idiom of discourse. But she does not represent anybody but herself, and due to the glamour element attached, her views get highlighted much more than those of various other more representative people. It is the duty of the media to search for the right voice, and the media has certainly been lazy in that matter.

Certain stereotypes in the media also condition issues. For instance, there is a widespread misconception in the media about the role of the Dar-ul Uloom, Deoband. The general feeling is that it is a place where one can get the 'fundamentalist Muslims' very easily. Certainly this perception is wrong, but Muslims did nothing substantive to remove this misconception. They just blame the media but cannot request the ulema not to issue fatwas that makes a mockery of the entire community. After 11 September 2001, there has been a lot of coverage of Deoband and its activities, on assumed lines based more on imagination than field work and visits to the prestigious Islamic university. To the great disappointment of correspondents from the electronic media, who occasionally happen to actually visit Deoband, they found that Deoband was not what they had actually visualized.

But all said and done, one is at a loss to realize that if half a million madrasas exist in India, where 50 million full-time students are enrolled, it is naturally a matter of great concern. These 50 million students do not include part-time students who attend the madrasas. There are lots of Muslim students who go to regular schools and attend the madrasas part-time to study the Koran and Islamic tenets. So instead of blaming Deoband, we should suggest something that can enable Muslim educational empowerment. I would not comment on the practical joke of a government which, in the name of the madrasa modernization scheme, proposed to spend Rs 20 crore. A break-up of this money would show that on an average it comes to Rs 0.40 per student. One can easily understand the Congress's logic or the whole logic of the modernization of madrasas scheme initiated by Rajiv Gandhi.

There are two strands in the media, particularly in the English media. One is patronizing, the other antagonistic. The patronizing strand recognizes that a wrong has been done to the Muslims, and one has to go out of the way to support them and advise them on what they should and should not do. This strand is growing among a section of the Hindu intelligentsia and the media. There is another well-known antagonistic strand mainly propounded by Vinod Mehta, which says that Muslims are a prisoner of these images. This strand does not reach out for any kind of dialogue or understanding and has created stereotyped images of which everybody has become a prisoner.

Siddharth Varadarajan, a senior editor with *The Hindu*, was scathing in his criticism of the media for long. I do not think that there is a conscious communal basis, at least in the English media, but I agree with the view that most of the people working with the English media, including Muslims, do not know Muslim society at large. They know only the elite Muslims and at the most, the upper-middle-class Muslim strata. The bias, if any, is a product of ignorance. It is time for common Muslims to come out of the paranoid feeling that the media has been consciously seeking to victimize or portray them as villains in Indian society. There are people with a communal viewpoint, who would not in acceptable parlance be called secular. Though they do have space in the English media, they belong to various communities (including Muslims). By and large, the media has tended to be responsible even in cases related to reporting on riots. The English-language media has persisted in trying to bring the guilty to book on a number of issues—whether it was during the 1984 anti-Sikh massacre, in Maliana, or Hashimpura, or Meerut, or Bhagalpur, or in the 2002 Gujarat carnage. The reporting of these incidents by the English press shocked the entire nation. The English press pursued these incidents relentlessly, and reporters have gone back to the spot on every anniversary of these riots to bring home the point that the guilty persons are running scot-free, and that the state has not taken any action to bring them to book. Siddharth Varadarajan is correct that there were lapses during the initial reporting because of newspaper reliance on the police version (which is often communally biased), the high financial cost of newsgathering, reliance on unprofessional stringers, and the bias of the news desk. But the media does thereafter take up in a systematic manner cases of human rights violations, police atrocities, and the tardy process of inquiries.

I do not agree with the view that the media is insensitive to the issues of the Muslims. It has, in fact, been responsible and responsive— to what extent is another issue. Instead of tarring the entire media with the same brush, one needs to differentiate and expand the space where there is a greater concern and sensitivity, rather than saying that the whole media is the same. The Muslim intelligentsia should not shut themselves away from the English media; rather, they have to enhance their space within it.

The painting of images is not only in terms of terrorism or madrasas. There are other issues with wider social ramifications that we must consider. Take the issue of the triple *talaq* in one sitting, for instance, on which reams have been written in the English media in the last ten or twelve years, ever since the Shah Bano issue. I am not saying these should not be discussed, but the disproportionate amount of space and time that goes into the over-simplified analysis intensifies stereotypes. Most of the nonsense becomes possible because of publicity-hungry ulema. We have to look beyond this, rather than just point to improper riot reporting or inherent biases. We have to highlight issues that will bring about fundamental changes: issues of the Muslims' socio-economic growth, progress, and educational empowerment and achievements. The reality is that issues that are not really germane to the genuine problems of the Muslim community get undue attention from the media as well as from Muslim writers. There are other issues that are of greater relevance. For example, how many Muslim students go to primary schools? What is the drop-out ratio of Muslim students after secondary and senior secondary examinations? How many Muslims have been inducted into the police force at the level of sepoy and sub-inspectors? How many get entry through the administrative services examinations conducted by the subordinate staff selection commissions in the states? If the proportion of Muslims is low, why is it so? These are real issues that the Muslim themselves do not get to read or reflect upon, debate, or discuss.

If we discuss Muslim education, we discuss it only through the English medium, which is just utopian. If we can discuss Muslim representation in government services, we just talk of civil services, an impossible thing for first-generation learners, whether Hindus or Muslims. Needless to say that this entire elite phenomenon will not work to improve the socio-economic conditions of common Muslims in India. In the world of entertainment, there is a great deal of Muslim participation, but again it is an elite phenomenon. I think this is where we are all collectively guilty: these issues do not get discussed.

Is there a bias that is causing the decline in Muslim representation in the government services? Why, for instance, has the Muslim middle-class, which was such a critical factor in the pre-Partition years, declined and dwindled in comparison to the Hindu middle-class? Arguably, it is true that a very large section of the Muslim middle-class did migrate to Pakistan between 1947 and 1950, but why did it not grow? We never discussed the complexity of the issue that the Muslim middle-class voice is not really the voice of the entire Muslim community.

The new Muslim middle-class is also the newborn psychological version of the aristocratic Muslim elite of pre-partition India. In the Hindu community, the Hindu middle-classes got education in state-run schools where regional language and not English was the medium. Now the Hindu middle-class dictates and determines the socio-political agenda and sets the tone for dialogue and discourse at the international level too. These issues, I emphasize again, need to be reflected in the media, debated, and discussed again and again. The media is the only forum for interaction and greater participation, both for intra-community dialogue within the Muslim community and inter-community dialogue between all communities that together can lead to a better, prosperous, and cohesive India. The media has to correct itself, but we also have to look beyond the media, as the myopic vision that we have at present will not solve the problem. The two communities have lived together for hundreds of years, and they will continue to live together. Biases have to be corrected, but unfortunately they have intensified. What do we do about that? I think that is what we have to focus on, and I hope that there will be more writers, more commentators, and more Muslims joining and contributing to the media. The media is today getting increasingly effective and powerful, and greater Muslim participation is needed in it.

Biases do exist everywhere. But just as there are biases, there are also people who go out of the way to try and correct them. These are both part of the fractured Indian reality that we should recognize, and try to widen the space, widen Muslim participation in the media, and have more people talking about real Muslim issues, going beyond those issues that unfortunately help intensify stereotypes.

NOTES

1. Ather Farouqui, 'Emerging Dilemma of the Urdu Press in India', *South Asia*, New Series, XVIII (2), pp. 91–103.
2. Ibid., p. 93.

7

Minority Images in the Indian Print Media*

Siddharth Varadarajan

When we speak of 'Minority Images in the Indian Print Media', there are two broad issues that need to be addressed. The first is the coverage in print—and images on television and the electronic media—of minorities and how these images have contributed to a process that has strengthened negative stereotypes of Indian Muslims, poisoned relations between religious communities (particularly Hindus and Muslims), acted as a mechanism to downgrade the level of political discourse in India, and helped political parties evade responsibility in a democratic polity. The second issue is that of representation, or workplace diversity, that is, the presence of Muslims in the media.

If you look at the state of the Indian news media today, it is hard to describe it as operating as a part of the public sphere or belonging to the realm of rational discourse in society. This is true not only of media coverage of religious or communal matters but of a variety of issues—political, economic, and social. Since we are focusing on the question of minorities in relation to communalism, I would like to draw on a study that I did a couple of years ago[1] and look a little bit at the history of the Indian print media, and how, unlike what Ben Anderson and others have analysed as the role of 'print capitalism' in the creation of a public sphere (or an 'imagined community' such as the nation), our history has been a little different.

In India, the print media was a product of colonialism and was as implicated in the nation-destroying project of colonialism as was active colonialism itself. In the early nineteenth century, one finds

*Transcript of talk delivered at an international conference on the theme of minorities and minority languages held on 8–11 February 2002.

the emergence of newspapers essentially as a vehicle for the articulation of community-centric grievances or concerns, sometimes in a benign way—centred on religious reform, for example—but often in a manner that posited communities as antithetical, opposed to each other. Of course, there were moments when the Indian print media tried to transcend the religious divide and strive for the elaboration of an Indian identity. One such moment in the history of Indian journalism arguably occurred in 1857, when Delhi had a very active Urdu press. In the context of the insurgency, otherwise known as the First Indian War of Independence, attempts were made to appeal to Indians as Indians, and for Hindus and Muslims to sink their differences. A number of publications played a prominent role at that time, including the *Sayyed-ul Akhbar* and *Delhi Urdu Akhbar*. The latter published propagandist sheets and was edited by Maulvi Muhammad Baqar, father of the famous Urdu literary historian Muhammad Husain Azad. Maulvi Muhammad Baqar was finally shot dead by Hodson after Delhi was recaptured. In the annals of Indian journalism, he was perhaps the first editor who paid with his life for advocating a vision of an India that was based on the unity of people, not simply on the elaboration of sectarian interests.

From the 1880s onwards, with the emergence of the Congress and of Muslim politics, and again from the early twentieth century, the print media in north India got fully implicated in all the different trends in operation at the political level and picked up (and amplified) all the communal biases that were prevalent in the political arena.

After Independence, the print media in India continued to mirror the political biases of mainstream politics and closely followed the imperatives of leading political parties. The attitude of political parties toward minorities in the post-Independence period was problematic. They relied primarily on the identification of so-called community leaders—either at the local or the national level—and brought them into the main political fold as representatives of their particular communities. More often than not, these representatives were as backward in their approach to the socio-economic problems of the country and of their community itself as were their mainstream political mentors. What this led to was a kind of unhealthy, unenlightened political culture, and the media itself faithfully reflected this.

The mainstream media at that time did not openly espouse communal ideologies or views. Instead, one had what I call 'low-intensity communalism'—the neat identification of Muslims as a community with particular leaders, so that every utterance of those leaders then got transmitted as the belief of the 'community'. Unfortunately, most Muslim leaders in post-Partition India were either from the aristocratic elite of yesteryears or were religious leaders. Both kinds of leadership—political and religious—belonged to the Congress party and worked to further the party's interest. Some prominent religious organizations such as Jamiat-e Ulema-e-Hind had been working virtually as Congress outfits. The maulavis, as 'leaders' of the Muslims, were of course backward-looking, and their backward views were (mis)represented by the media as being the view of the Muslims as a whole.

Of course, this 'low-intensity communalism' in the media could easily get transformed into something more virulent whenever a ruling party decided to indulge in openly communal tactics. During the 1980s, communal killings were organized in Moradabad, Meerut, Hashimpura, Malliana, and Bhagalpur, and especially against the Sikhs in November 1984. These incidents were engineered by the Congress for different political purposes. During these communal riots, one could see open biases on display in the media, and especially in the vernacular press. In general, one could argue that the same political parties which engineer the riots are also responsible for motivating this bias. This type of influence is easier to apply at a local level but the national media can also succumb to it. As a test case, let us look at the way in which the Sikhs, as a minority community, were demonized by the Indian media in the 1980s in the context of the Punjab agitation. If you actually read some of the writings of the newspapers and their identification of Sikhs with extremism and terrorism, it is clear that provocative material was being written on the community in 1984. Especially before and after Operation Bluestar, and in the run-up to the Delhi massacres after the assassination of Indira Gandhi by her two Sikh bodyguards, the role of the print media was shameful. The media was then reflecting the biases and the political imperatives of the Congress, the party in power, which for reasons of its own was committed to pursuing certain policies vis-à-vis Punjab and the Sikhs; the media reflected this and was complicit in it.

Unfortunately, the media readily tends to reflect whatever issue the big political parties project as the dominant news agenda. Today every political party—particularly the BJP and the Congress—has a well-structured media-briefing process in the form of party spokespersons. The Congress is perhaps less aggressive, simply because its media departments are less organized and lack conviction. But the BJP is extremely particular about this, as its organization and propaganda brigade is well organized almost everywhere, from small towns to villages. The RSS volunteers are trained in sensational propaganda-mongering and it is they who help the BJP in canvassing their agenda through the media. The end result of the RSS's organizational backing is that an agenda that the BJP sets in its evening news conference and decides to float then generates a lot of news coverage precisely due to the efficiency of this transmission mechanism.

The notion of Muslims as a so-called 'appeased community' is a product of this kind of concerted, effective projection by the RSS in the 1980s.[2] The Ram Janmabhoomi issue was very skilfully managed by the BJP through the use of media-friendly events that were also structured to capture the electronic media's need for visuals. The BJP understood this well and was able to come up with and stage 'media events'. They were able to set the terms of debate with a set of issues that perhaps were not the most important, nor the most relevant, as far as citizens were concerned but which nevertheless got top billing. And the media was happy to go along with them. Another example one can give in which the BJP was particularly successful was the issue of Bangladeshi (read Muslim) immigration into India. Bengali Hindus who came from Bangladesh were rehabilitated in West Bengal and Delhi quite gracefully in the same fashion as Punjabi Hindus were settled after Partition. But the press describes as 'infiltrators' those Muslim immigrants from Bangladesh who come here to work. This is a term that the BJP helped to popularize in the late 1980s. I had a running battle with people in my newsroom, where, innocuously and without thinking, a report could come from the Press Trust of India (PTI) or some other news agency in which a Muslim Bangladeshi immigrant is referred to as an infiltrator, suggesting that a person has come not for economic reasons but for something sinister or nefarious. Needless to say, this label of 'infiltrator' is applied when the immigrant concerned is a Muslim; a Bangladeshi Hindu migrant is called a 'refugee'. These terms have become current, and you will find references such as these in everyday discourse, and people unthinkingly use these terms without realizing their problems, meanings, and significance.

Another recent example is in the context of some of the terrorist attacks that have taken place in India. A number of newspapers have begun to speak about 'illegal madrasas' as being dens of terror, sabotage, and subversion. L.K. Advani, as home minister, called for a debate on the role of madrasas, saying that if General Musharraf could regulate these in his country, surely India should also be looking in that direction. But nobody points out that in an Islamic state such as Pakistan, the government has a right within its constitutional framework to make all kinds of pronouncements for regulating madrasas—specifying what they should and should not teach. In a society and polity such as India, which is constitutionally secular, madrasas exist to impart religious education and are run by the community. The government should not interfere as it cannot provide religious education at public expense. If children turn to madrasas for another kind of education, then it is more of a comment on the failure of the state educational system. Proper schools are not available in areas with a concentration of Muslims, and, as Syed Shahabuddin once said, the government is more willing to open a police post than a school in the vicinity of Muslims. So in the absence of schools, every debate on madrasas and their modernization is a romantic notion tinged with minority phobia and apathy.

Somehow the media has allowed itself to become a theatre or a platform where this kind of issue is debated in an insidious manner that has nothing to do with constitutional realities. If a madrasa is involved in illegal activities, or if its funds are coming in an unregulated fashion, you have the Foreign Exchange Regulation Act (FERA) that regulates conditions under which any charitable organization registered by the government can receive money from abroad and what kind of use it can put to it. Somehow, the problem of madrasas is never looked into seriously in order to discuss all relevant dimensions. They are always viewed through the lens of subversion, terrorism, or token academic activism. All these buzzwords keep cropping up, and to a large extent this is a reflection of a very effective manipulation and management of the electronic and print media by the BJP and its allies.

I want to turn now to the question of reporting on riots that sporadically break out in various parts of the country. These are the most important moments when media biases come to the fore. The damage that the media can inflict on community relations can have a long-term effect. I want to draw upon a study I published four years ago, and which might be quite helpful in terms of pointing out exactly what I mean.

Those who have studied the Indian press coverage of riots are aware of the rather quaint code of conduct that newspapers follow, which generally prohibits the identification of the communities involved in communal disturbances. For example, you can have a cryptic report that in an incident in Rajasthan members of one community attacked members of another community, leading to two deaths. At a certain level, one can rationalize this: if you are not identifying the communities involved then maybe you are not inciting people to react in a negative way. I can see the logic as to why one might choose to be 'coy', but we need to study how these kinds of 'coy' reports are actually decoded by an ordinary reader. Often, the coyness is itself defeated by various kinds of insidious markers of the community which are put into the news report. Consider an example that was reported in the Delhi papers a few years ago. The headline was a harmless one: 'Sacrilege at Place of Worship'. But the report read:

An incident took place at a place of worship in Lajpatnagar, where pieces of flesh were found in an envelope along with a letter threatening a particular community and their place of worship. The priest, Maya Ram, reportedly told the police that he saw a young woman wearing a '*shalwar qameez*' with a '*chadar*' enter. Later, they found the envelope containing the flesh pieces.[3]

Nowhere in this story are the two communities named, yet it is clear from the naming of the priest and the description of the young woman's clothes that the reader is being encouraged to assume that we are talking about Hindus and Muslims. In fact, reports of this kind are particularly insidious. Whenever the victim of an outrage is a Hindu and the perpetrator a Muslim, helpful clues such as names, dress, and type of facial hair are often supplied, even if the fiction of not naming the communities is maintained. But when a Muslim is the victim, more often than not the news report will be terse and lacking in nomenclature or other clues.

The media strategy of providing selective markers leads to an extremely distorted picture of communal violence. Even though a majority of victims in riots tend to be Muslims, the fact that their names are not reported, while the names of the few Hindu victims are, can create a false and dangerous impression of Muslim aggressiveness and Hindu victimhood. Let me cite another incident that occurred in Hapur a few years ago: 'More than a dozen shops were burnt in a night's incident. According to the Police Inspector of Hapur, the police have arrested a rioter called Sikander.'[4]

Despite overwhelming evidence that Muslims are the main victims of communal violence, why is it that the standard riot narrative as propounded by the bulk of the media continues to revolve around the alleged aggressiveness of the Muslims? Having worked in a newspaper during incidents of communal violence, I can think of four broad reasons. The first is the average newspaper's over-reliance on the police for news and information, given the communal bias of the police force. This is also well documented in a dissertation, *Communal Conflicts: Perceptions of Police Neutrality during Hindu-Muslim Riots in India*, by Vibhuti Narain Rai,[5] a senior Indian Police Service (IPS) officer, who has studied the pervasiveness of communal biases in the police force during riots. Given this bias, it is dangerous for a newspaper to rely on police handouts for information on riots, or on the sequence of events, when these kinds of incidents happen. Time and again, we see that during moments of riots the police often become the main source of information. Given that curfew is usually clamped, making movement difficult, it is tough for journalists to find others sources of information. But, insofar as we tend to rely excessively on the police, this is one place where this kind of bias creeps in. Since, in the bulk of riots, the majority of people killed in police firing tend to be Muslim civilians, the police narrative often tends to be aimed at sanitizing the role of the police and painting a portrait of Muslims as aggressors in order to justify whatever the police does.

The second reason why the standard narrative in the media tends to get biased in this way is because of the high financial and logistical costs of gathering news. Many newspapers, especially the smaller ones, cannot afford to have news bureaux all over the country, and cannot afford to send reporters to reach a particular spot soon enough. Often, they rely on a large roster of underpaid stringers. In *mofussil* towns, the stringer, who is a local representative of a daily paper, is usually a very prestigious person; while some of them are conscientious, others use the status essentially to get close to local bigwigs. This means that the integrity of the news gathering process at the local area could get compromised. In a situation of a communal riot where, more often than not, it is the local bigwig who is involved in the machinations behind the local riot, local stringers and local underpaid staffers perhaps do not find it easy to send across the real story, either because of blandishments by these forces or because of threats.

The third reason why riot reporting can be biased against Muslims is the prevalence of biases and unprofessionalism within the news-desks of newspapers. Unfortunately, this is not so infrequent. The reporter may be biased, or the person at the news-desk who is actually editing the story or putting it together may choose to highlight something on the basis of his or her personal bias. This is a major factor, to the extent of being decisive. Finally, there is the pressure of space and deadlines—in other words, the technique and the technology of news dissemination can also lead to communal stereotyping. Mukul Sharma and Charu Gupta, in an important study on media and communalism published a few years ago, observed that

if both journalists and a majority of readers associate Muslims with threats, then reporters and editors pressured by deadlines and constrained by the little space available may simply treat the news about riots in a way that conforms to this. In other words what they are doing is to present unfamiliar events in familiar and easily digestible fashion as quickly as possible. This leads to obvious distortion and also the tendency to neglect background context. Riots are likely to appear as sudden, dramatic and unexplained, or as having a direct or immediate cause. The underlying state of affairs is ignored and easy assumptions and instinctive associations are upheld.[6]

Stanley Tambiah has also looked at the problem of ethnic violence in South Asia. There are two terms that he uses—'focalization' and 'transvaluation'—as key processes in terms of the development and 'normalization' of riots. What Tambiah calls 'focalization' occurs when local incidents, which could be a property dispute or a fight between neighbours, get progressively denuded of their local context. 'Transvaluation' is a parallel process of assimilating particulars to a larger, more enduring focus, and therefore, beyond contextual causes or interests.

Thus, local incidents and physical disputes can be cumulatively built up to larger and larger clashes between growing numbers of antagonists who are indirectly or peripherally involved in the original disputes. Central to this process is propaganda that aims at distorting and inflating the substantive nature of micro-events, stripping them of their local context and translating them into countless and unchanging principles of communal identity interests and entitlements.[7]

It is this role that a substantial section of the media in India attempts to play before, during, and after a given incident of communal violence.

I cannot also help but think that the major problem of media coverage of communal riots and stereotypes of Muslims has to do with the very discourse on 'communal riots'. The term 'communal riots' is an infelicitous term to describe what is essentially organized and targeted violence in which the law enforcement machinery is fully implicated, either through omission or commission. Consider the riots in Delhi in 1984, in which the Sikhs were targeted and in which Congress activists were fully involved. Some of the accused individuals, who had been MPs and ministers in Congress governments, were exonerated as the victims of the riot could not follow the long and tedious legal battle. In turn, the police and the prosecution helped the accused go free because of their political affiliations.

To what extent can you call the 1984 incidents 'communal riots'? Was it a case of ordinary Hindus killing ordinary Sikhs, or was it a case of a political party using the state machinery to massacre a section of citizens? Can we describe as a communal riot the Bombay riots of 1993, in which the Shiv Sena, the state apparatus, and different sections of the ruling Congress party were involved? Was it a case of Hindus killing Muslims? Or was it a case where the political parties were fully involved in the selective targeting of a community? My contention is that the very discourse and notion of the communal riot is problematic because it posits one community fighting against another. And once you present a riot in that manner, with that language, media reports are invariably going to be biased one way or the other.

Typically the reports tend to be biased, giving the impression that Muslims are killing Hindus. This is not to say that if you have a narrative saying that Hindus are killing Muslims it would be better or more accurate. With regard to the coyness in identifying communities, a case can be made for identifying the victims because there is no ambiguity as to the fact that the victim is targeted because of his or her religion. But, I am wary of saying that 'Hindus' were the ones who were killing Sikhs in Delhi in 1984, because rather than 'Hindus' as a collectivity, it was essentially the police and the ruling political party, the Congress (I), that were involved. So the judgement I would make in the newsroom would be to always name the victim community because the community has been victimized for political reasons; but since the person or the group doing the killing is not really a 'community' but invariably a political party or a faction or the police, there is no point in blaming an entire community. The state machinery is involved, and there is no need to get into the whole language of riots, saying it is Hindus versus Muslims or the Hindus against the Christians. Of course, this means the 'riot' narrative has to be complex, and it can be complex only if newspapers devote sufficient resources and do not rely on police handouts or statements of political parties to get to the truth.

The second theme I want to stress is the issue of representation or workplace diversity. In one of his Republic Day speeches, K.R. Narayanan (then president of India) spoke about the need for Indian companies to emulate US-style diversity policies. He was drawing upon the Bhopal declaration drafted by the Dalit Conference at Bhopal. What he said was in the context of the Scheduled Castes and Scheduled Tribes. The logic was that the state sector as a means of economic empowerment has perhaps run its course in this era of privatization, where the state would not be the provider of jobs, and perhaps it is time for Indian companies to take a leaf out of the book of their US counterparts, which practise employee diversity only because the government forces them to do so. If you want to do any business with the US government, you have got to include some level of minority participation in your company. The president threw up the suggestion that perhaps it is time for Indian companies to do the same thing. This got us thinking in the newsroom. In *The Pioneer*, there was once a very interesting column written by B.N. Unniyal, in which he went through the list of journalists accredited to the Press Information Bureau and concluded that there was not a single Dalit in it. Similarly, if one were to count the number of Muslims involved in the 'mainstream English media', a case can be made for our newspapers to look seriously at the question of diversity in the newsroom. This is not to say that a larger number of Muslim and Dalit journalists would necessarily alter the way in which news is covered; the discourse of news is far too well structured to be undermined or changed easily. But certainly, if we are looking at images of minorities in the press, this is something to be looked at seriously. It is time for major newspapers and news media organizations in India to look inward and ask themselves whether it is in our interest to have greater diversity in our newsroom so that there are more reporters who are Muslims and more reporters who are from Scheduled Castes and Scheduled Tribes, so that the newsroom itself becomes diverse and news coverage becomes richer, if not more balanced and more objective.

RESPONSE TO THE DISCUSSION

In the English print media, bias against Muslims is not intentional, but exists as a result of the concerted efforts of the RSS as well as because of residual biases journalists may bring with themselves. Some newspapers were funded by the BJP during its rule, and many English journalists and editors officially joined the party or flirted with it, so their bias can be understood. Nevertheless, if you look carefully and compare the English-language media to the language media, the record of the former is by and large better in terms of the reporting of communalism and communal riots. Of course, because of stereotypical images, the coverage is certainly anti-Muslim at times. It is also true that the English media does not always pursue and investigate most cases related to Muslims. So the need for raising one's voice is most pressing when a riot takes place. During the riots in Delhi from 31 October to 10 November 1984, if the English mainstream newspapers had reported the matter objectively and published the truth about political complicity on the first or the second day on their front pages, maybe the Congress would have changed course much earlier and the brutality may have been stopped. What the PUCL-PUDR (People's Union for Civil Liberties–People's Union for Democratic Rights) report highlighted twenty days later— about the role of Congress MPs like H.K.L. Bhagat, Sajjan Kumar, Jagdish Tytler, and other leading Congress leaders in connivance with the police—should have been in our newspapers while the killings were going on. That might have made all the difference.

We can give the same argument for the Bombay riots or other riots. Detailed, truthful reports are required most when the violence is at its peak. The subtle show of disregard towards the plight of Muslims exposes the weakness of the English media. We cannot say that this is always a conscious bias, but often it is. My own experience in *The Times of India* was that editors did not have an anti-minority bias, but the stereotypical images they had of communities had their own negative and decisive impact in respect of Muslims. Sadly, the problem of Muslim stereotypical images is everywhere, as the RSS has been doing its bit quite vigorously for more than 80 years, and secular Indians have not done much to counter this propaganda.

If anything, most editors recognize and are conscious of the policies of discrimination against the minorities and want to reverse them. The problem is that, because of the technique of newsgathering and dissemination of news and the reliance on police reports and lack of objective sources, bias creeps into the reporting. One may also ask whether there is any political control and interference in our newspapers. Political leaders do try to put pressure on the management of newspapers, but if there is an element of self-consciousness prevailing in the newsroom, political pressures can be resisted. But this is not possible all the time and everywhere—for example, a correspondent in Kashmir may think twice before writing the truth about some human rights violation for fear that he could be dubbed an anti-national on the ISI payroll. In case that correspondent happens to be a Muslim, the pressure of self-censorship may be trebled. It is my view that had I been a Muslim, it may not have been possible for me to say and write whatever I have been these past few years on communalism because there are pressures which operate. This is especially true after 9/11, where those who wanted to criticize the American reaction were equated with Osama bin Laden's Al Qaida or its sympathizers.

In this context I must mention an incident which is quite relevant. In Malegaon, Maharashtra, some leaflets were distributed after 9/11 entitled 'Be Indian, Buy Indian' in which Indians were asked not to buy goods from companies belonging to countries that were waging war against Afghanistan. They called for a boycott of Coca Cola and other companies. The police put a forcible stop to these leaflets, and some people died in the firing. When this news reached Delhi and Mumbai from Malegaon, it was simply reported that 'pro-Osama bin Laden' leaflets had been distributed.

I don't quite agree with those who argue that it is the duty of the Muslims to raise a voice against all incidents of violence by Muslims. The well-known economic historian, Dharma Kumar, who rarely raised her voice or was active on any political issue, got very angry over one particular issue in 1984. This was in reaction to an article written by the editor of *The Times of India* during the 1984 riots, in which he questioned why 'the Sikhs' did not condemn Indira Gandhi's assassination. Dharma Kumar wrote back to the editor: 'As a Hindu I do not feel obliged to condemn or to speak out every time one of my co-religionists does something terrible.'[8] She added, with her characteristic wit, that if she did that she would perhaps be doing nothing else! So many incidents take place everywhere and what has to be condemned should be condemned—and is condemned—by many, but I do not at all agree with this pressure on Muslims every time.

It is the duty of the media to properly investigate and put issues in perspective. If Osama bin Laden does something or if Parliament is attacked this will be condemned by those who normally condemn such things—politicians, journalists, or writers to newspapers—but you cannot expect those who normally do not make public statements to be pressurized to issue a statement.

One last point: newspapers are run on market principles. That is definitely a constraint. There is more coverage of a film star's clothes than of the problems of education. We have to accept that reality, because we do not have a solution for now. But one should not write-off the newspapers as totally biased against the Muslims or some other community, because there are still many, many people in the media who are professional, honest, and sensitive, and who are trying to highlight genuine problems by taking up vital issues that concern the general populace. And they require the support of all thinking people in their endeavour to do the right thing.

NOTES

1. Siddharth Varadarajan, 'The Ink Link: Media, Communalism and the Evasion of Politics', in K.N. Pannikar (ed.), *A Concerned Indian's Guide to Communalism* (Delhi: Viking, 1999).

2. This section draws on Charu Gupta and Mukul Sharma, *Print Media and Communalism* (Delhi, 1990, published by Mukul Sharma).

3. *Hindustan Times*, 12 March 1987.

4. *Jansatta*, 2 November 1990. Cited in Charu Gupta and Mukul Sharma, 'The Muslim and the News', *Mainstream*, 13 February 1993, pp. 15–19.

5. Vibhuti Narain Rai, *Communal Conflicts: Perceptions of Police Neutrality during Hindu–Muslim Riots in India* (New Delhi: Renaissance Publications, 1998).
6. Gupta and Sharma, *Print Media and Communalism*.
7. Stanley Jayaraja Tambiah, a noted social anthropologist, has explored dynamics of violence in the region of South Asia, with special reference to civil war in Sri Lanka in his last two works: 1) *Buddhism Betrayed? Religion, Politics and Violence in Sri Lanka* (Chicago: University of Chicago Press, 1992); 2) *Leveling Crowds: Ethnonationalist Conflicts and Collective Violence in South Asia* (Berkeley: University of California Press, 1996).
8. Dharma Kumar, 'A Voice from "Rest of India" ', op-ed article published in *The Times of India*; reproduced in Patwant Singh and Harji Malik (eds), *Punjab: The Fatal Miscalculation* (New Delhi: Patwant Singh, 1985), pp. 162–3.

PART II
TRANSCENDING BOUNDARIES

8

Muslims and the World Forum

K.M.A. Munim

The modified theme of the seminar—'Muslims and the Press'—organized between 8–11 February 2002 is a logical follow-up to the 30 May 1993 seminar on 'Indian Muslims and Indian Press', broadening the perspective from national to international. Important as the May seminar theme was in the domestic context, bearing on the problems of the Muslims of India and their place in the national media, the seminar fits not only into the wider context of the contemporary press world but also the much wider history of Muslims. In fact that is where Muslims belong. Geography, with its boundaries set, was a later growth for Islam and Muslims, after its days of power and achievement. That is where geography came to overshadow history, with consequences that are common knowledge. This geographical division of the world of Islam was, however, inevitable over time in a world in which new politico-territorial concepts developed. But in its wake came conflicts and rivalries between the nation-states, eclipsing, almost wholly, the sustaining, unifying spirit of Islam.

The poverty and distress of the period, before the windfall of oil and wealth in the Arabian region, as well as other historical factors accounting for the spiralling decline under the foreign imperial rule of more than two centuries and the demoralization and brutalization that went with it, turned history on its head for Muslims. This resulted not only in the marginalization of Muslims and their cause and problems but their respectability or eligibility for a place of honour in the contemporary frame of things and in world opinion also sank to the nadir. This happened, roughly, over the period from the end of World War I through World War II.

Politically powerless, economically pauperized, educationally and culturally on the decline, Muslims in the best part of Asia and Africa were reduced to a state of little or no importance as far as the sophisticated world in the West and parts of the East were concerned. They came to exist well outside the intellectual mainstream of the world of education, of the growing public media, of learned and cultured debates—nearly all of which were limited to, and dominated by, those who had had the advantage of acquiring and assimilating the knowledge and culture that went hand in hand with the political and economic advantages already gained. This was true not only of the Muslims in the Indian subcontinent but also generally of Muslims across the Afro-Asian world.

Banal as these details of Muslim history may appear, they constitute the bitter and disenchanting truth about Muslims over the historical period ranging roughly from the late 1920s to the late 1960s. If you cut out of your thinking or deliberation this part of the history of Muslims, which is an inseparable part of world history, you will miss the perspective in which to find an answer to your theme, 'Muslims and the Press'. The answer is a simple one: Muslims have long since lost their importance generally, and have therefore been lost to the international forum or press, in the greater sense of having a place in the world press.

Consider also the amount of historical loathing created for Islam, its prophet, and Muslims in general, by non-Muslim writers in the press as well as by Western historians. The learned editors of newspapers, well-read in such literature of hate and prejudice, must have struggled not a little with the intellectual difficulty of sorting out the truth from the lies, because, ideally (and for the best standards of journalism) the truth and the press go, and have to go, hand in hand.

Consider also the vacuity in the intellectual resources of Muslims, the resources needed to establish a powerful press of their own, to push their cause nationally, regionally, or internationally. If, as a result, Muslims the world over have come to receive little more than peripheral attention from the international media, no-one need wonder. There, however, has been a relatively recent spurt of interest taken by the Western press in Muslims, an interest not so much in their problems as in them seen as a menace emerging on the regional and international scenario. This is in response to the growing spate of Islamic fundamentalism and deserves some specific treatment in what purports to be a discussion of Muslims vis-à-vis the international or Western press.

Outside the world of Muslim fundamentalism, Muslims have been treated by the international press more as news, particularly as what could be called hot news. Some Asian and African countries have been a rich source for such news with their wars (Iran, Iraq, Afghanistan, Sudan, and so on), their factional fights, terror and violence inside them or across their borders (Israel–Lebanon, Pakistan–India), and trouble and turmoil (for example, in the Israel-occupied Arab territories which the recent Israel-PLO (Palestine Liberation Organization) mutual recognition and agreement on self-rule in Jericho and the Gaza strip have seemingly ended). But, for our purposes, the simple news value of Muslims is of little importance.

A whole community's place in public media, regional or international, is quite another thing. How far the same media is interested in the ordinary and specific values cherished by the community, in studying them and presenting them in seriously written editorials or in articles contributed by specialists and learned scholars, is the principal measure of its representation. The leading newspapers or journals of the West seem to focus more on occasional comments in leaders or news stories which are mostly topical, rather than anything of more abiding interest to Muslims, barring events calling for immediate editorials or other kinds of specific treatment, such as the Bosnian war. Maybe the lack of interest, as some are inclined to believe, is due to temporary suspension of the civilized good sense—why else the ethnic cleansing and what very much looked like an abetment of it by the West in this enlightened twentieth century?

Incidentally, with apologies to the great journalists in this gathering, may I point out two major failures of the press, international and regional: one in stopping the slaughter in Bosnia and the other in forestalling the destruction on 6 December 1992, of the Babri Masjid in India. The former, Bosnia, was a horror for the Western press to rise against, saying, with one voice, that it be stopped. The latter was a case for journalistic courage and vision. For India and the Indian press it was the greatest challenge to its political principles and philosophy that was worth the most the national press could do to protect it. All the leading newspapers of India: *The Statesman, The Times of India, Hindustan Times,* and

The Hindu ran editorials denouncing the incident. The need for them was to be wise before the event, not after.

Outshining this twilight of interest is the seriousness with which the Western press has taken Islamic fundamentalism. It has figured in the articles in leading journals and also in the commentaries by specialists on the socio-political affairs of the Islamic world. The treatment of this issue in the Western press mainly shows the concern it feels over its spread as a chief obstacle to the spread of democracy.

From Algeria to Iran and Egypt, Muslim fundamentalists are active enough to bring on them the increasing wrath of the governments concerned. Algeria and Egypt are, currently, very special cases in point. Looking upon it more as a bogey and a source of terror and violence which is met by equal severity from the police and government security forces, the national and Western press seems only to have helped compound fundamentalist violence and terror, not ended it.

This is the uniform policy followed by the British, American, French, and German dailies and weeklies. What exactly the Western media needs to guard against is bashing the genuine growth of Islam in some Islamic societies, now enjoying better advantages of education and research. Some Muslim analysts tend to think that the Western press is using fundamentalist terror as a stalking horse to target Islam in the main.

It is easy to see that the increasing interest shown by the Western press in fundamentalism will earn it more and more attention. Since force (police or military) used by governments is not succeeding in curbing fundamentalism, the need is for some in-depth examination of this new socio-religious phenomenon in parts of the Islamic world. The regional and international media have a very important role to play in dealing with this new problem. The concerned governments (aided by the press, world and national), with the experience so far of having failed to wipe out fundamentalists by use of force, perhaps need to think in terms of a political solution.

Algeria, for instance, may now be regretting having not allowed the fundamentalists, who had won the national elections, to form the government. Inducting the fundamentalists into the political process might have weaned them away from the violence which they now use with no sense of accountability and that an elected government of their own would have imposed on them. In the absence of such democratic restraint, what is now happening in Algeria is that hundreds have since been killed, including high-ranking government officials.

There is another viewpoint from which the rise of Islamic fundamentalism in Muslim countries could be seen: the socio-cultural-religious causes behind the growth of fundamentalism, specially in Islamic societies. Incidentally, fundamentalism is spreading increasingly to larger areas in the Islamic world. A close look at the fundamentalists and at the causes motivating them to adopt extreme means of enforcing certain values will show they are an angry, aggrieved lot, wanting some traditional moral and religious sets of values to be re-established in society.

Consider first the fact that Islamic societies now facing the problem of fundamentalism had maintained, and still maintain in most cases, a traditional set of values based on the rules of conduct and ethics provided by the Koran and Hadith; the former is the word of God and the latter the sayings of the prophet. Both are an integral part of the Islamic faith. Islamic fundamentalism seems to be a counter-force to secularism carried to extreme limits; one seems as extreme a stance as the other. Here is a subject for social scientists and the media to study more closely in the light of action and reaction on which is based the entire structure of values in society.

The fact about Islam is that, contrary to Western and Muslim modernist views, it is the most secular of cultures: witness the level of secular power and prosperity it attained in the heydays of its rule from Medina to Damascus to Baghdad to Cordova. Islam, properly studied, is a tremendous historical event. The rise and spread of Islam with its historic record of tolerance and as a sound ethical code of life—a conscientiously developed secular way of life, embracing all right means of earning and managing social relations— is a remarkable thing. Socio-culturally it fosters a decent lifestyle and justice-based human relations, and it is intellectually an endlessly searching and researching process. Islam's claim to these distinctive qualities needs to be objectively examined by the modern media before rejecting or underrating it from half-knowledge or ignorance. Governments now menaced by fundamentalism can do one thing, perhaps with more satisfying results: instead of sending troops or contingents of police to shoot the fundamentalists down, let them launch a missionary campaign through the public media (which is now so well-developed) to rein in the ultra-secularists and the excesses of secularism that serve as a provocation to fundamentalists, and give them a cause to fight and martyr themselves for.

The excesses of secularism appear in various forms, including obscenities in the print or visual media. The case for decent and refined values of life, mostly based on tradition, needs to be made with more force, at both the government and media level. Such a campaign, conducted with patience and persuasion, will in time succeed in removing the cause or causes which lead fundamentalists to fight. Both the national and the international press can help substantially in this educative effort.

As for the peripheral representation of the Muslim's problems in the international media, it is due to the relative ignorance of Islam and the prejudice against Islam. One would exonerate the leading newspapers and their top journalists, in the West or elsewhere, of such lapses. But that they also need to know Islam better can be safely said. I repeat, Islam is worth all pains one can take to understand it better. Almost the whole of the Western world including a section of intellectuals, historians, and others need to know Islam much better than they do now, and develop a more cosmopolitan outlook based on tolerance and mutual respect.

The Muslim press in Muslim countries ought to try and promote such an awareness among those in the national or international press. The sad fact about the Muslim press vis-à-vis the local or international readership is that, generally speaking, it is a weak media. This is chiefly due to the lack of properly educated and trained senior journalists. Most newspapers in the Arab world employ foreigners, non-Muslims, to edit or manage national newspapers because they are more educated and have higher professional efficiency. They cannot, however, be expected to emotionally identify themselves with the deeper Muslim interests or social, cultural, and other issues. Without emotional participation in it, any cause big enough to involve a whole community or society, is impossible to pursue effectively. Editing or writing for a newspaper is not wholly a mechanical or commercial exercise, or a pure professional performance, but much more than that.

For Muslims and the Muslim press, this lack is a huge gap. This also is a question of lack of language skills. One thing that has long been at a discount among Muslims is proficiency in the English language. We in Bangladesh know what loss the nation has incurred from a legislative measure adopted in 1982 to abolish English from the university degree's syllabus. This has been compounded by the lack of efficient English-language teachers for our schools. So education—and the best standard of English-based education at that—has to be the centrepiece of the school, college, or university curriculum in Muslim countries. Administration in Islamic countries has to be guided by similar motivations to promote the teaching of English so that the present generation develops an interest to learn the language. Special stress has to be laid on this simple but absolutely necessary intellectual aid for Muslims, to find a place not only in the international press but also in today's world of growing knowledge and ideas. All said and done, the need for Muslims today is to close the intellectual gap that now exists between their world and the world outside. The question is not one of the world press giving a place, and that too a prestigious one; it is a question of earning it by one's developed intellectual culture. One could even gatecrash into it provided one has the capability to do so. And capability will have to be acquired by intense application under special state policies formulated by governments.

Please note that outstanding Muslim journalists in Muslim or non-Muslim countries with large Muslim minorities (India, for example) can be counted on one's fingers. That is a pity. This is where Muslims have to cultivate and raise a new, promising crop. Here are some pragmatic means by which to do it:

1. A powerful Muslim press—national, regional, and international—with the purpose of moulding national, regional, and international opinion and educating it in the role Islam has played in history, convincing the readership of the Islamic potential for providing an answer to the problems faced by the world of today.

2. A world news service, other than or alongside national news services, along the lines of BBC, VOA, and CNN, has to be developed and run.

3. Specific emphasis, in journalism or mass communication departments in national universities, on grooming students in the use of English as a tool in effective and persuasive journalism.

4. The existing and proposed Muslim press at all levels would lay emphasis on a thorough acquisition of the knowledge of science and technology, with as much application and dedication as our forefathers did in Baghdad, Cordova, Cairo, and other centres of knowledge in their time.

5.   A revamped publicity media as well as the proposed new
       world one will design their social and cultural programmes so
       as to revive in the minds of the new generation of the Muslim
       youth a historical sense, awareness of Islam's heritage in the
       intellectual field, embracing nearly all areas of modern science,
       technology, and philosophy, and the transplantation carried out
       by Muslims of the entire Greek heritage from the ancient world
       to modern Europe to make possible the European explosion of
       knowledge and ideas, known as the European Renaissance.

Such a historical community can pull itself out of its history only at
a great cost to itself. It is not about basking in past glory, it is a matter
of that spiritual sustenance without which no community with a
history of its own can be born again. I can see Muslims on the edge of
such a rebirth, though with one caveat: they have to regain their lost
self-confidence, caused chiefly by the ignorance of their history and
their slipping away from the mainstream of knowledge which was
and is the only base of power for individuals and communities.

9

Of Fish and Beef, the New Recipe of the Muslim Identity
A Journey through the Cultural Prism of West Bengal

Sabya Sachi

6 December 1992: I have vivid memories of this day, not as someone affected by the misdoings of the RSS-inspired carnage but as a mere bystander. In fact I was too young then to feel anything adverse, but I did sense a foreboding futility to this entire rigmarole. I was in Class VIII and had come home for the winter vacation, and was busy enjoying the free time with my friends. In those days of change in Bengal, one often met processions on the street. Some people (those who joined Communist Party of India (Marxist) [CPI(M)]-led possessions) were there to protest against the evils perpetrated by the Narasimha Rao government and the others (those who joined Mamta Banerjee-led processions) were there because Jyoti Basu was selling Bengal for the benefit of his son. The Bengali hangover of the erstwhile Soviet Union was still strong. The tea-stall intellectuals and the listeners at their *adda*s were prophesizing the fall of the Yeltsin government and discussing the winds of change. In some parts of Bengal, especially in urban areas, college students were busy collecting erasers and pencils from the students to be donated to the embargo-affected impoverished students in Cuba. Life just went on as usual. In the midst of all this, the politically righteous Bengalis cursed American imperialism but maintained the stance that Saddam Hussain and his aggression over Kuwait was wrong (though strong enough to take on the might of the US). Then of course there was this distant rumour of privatization and the harm it would bring to our cocooned society. All discussions in tea stalls and in the local addas (the proverbial conversations over cigarettes, *bidi*s and tea that can encompass every topic which exists on the face of this earth and in outer space) pertained to this. Before the Bengali mind could come to a decision on whether the distant talk of privatization as inspired by American capitalism was good for government employees and the proletariat, they were faced with one more event that divided their sensibilities. The destruction of the Babri Masjid divided the secular minds of the ever-inquisitive Bengalis, Hindus and Muslims alike. For once, the lament over the fall of the Soviet Union was shelved. The fall of the disputed mosque is one story that the Bengali mind still struggles with today, unable to comprehend the logic of it all.

I remember on that day I was with my friends in a place called Kazipara, about 2 kilometres from my home at Chapadalimore in Barasat. As the name Kazipara suggests, this locality is overwhelmingly Muslim, with a small number of Hindus living on the fringes of the locality. I was in the home of my friend Safiqul Islam and we were busy arranging masalas and fanning the open oven in his back garden to cook beef and rice. My friends at that picnic were a mixture of Hindus and Muslims. In order to break norms, beef was the choice of meat which was arranged, along with the hidden bottle of whiskey. I remember that towards the evening Safiqul's brother coming and telling us about the events in Ayodhya. At that moment the news felt so insignificant that we didn't even flinch. All my friends, including Safiqul of course, were busy gulping the contents of the bottle with mouthfuls of spiced beef. Late at night, when we were returning home, we saw a few gatherings of local Muslim boys on street corners, but nothing appeared menacing about them. In fact, in our minds we felt no fear of a repercussion or backlash on few drunken defenceless Hindu boys passing through a Muslim locality in the dead of night. The thought of danger, if one can put it that way, did not come up in our minds. The next day there appeared in the media—print and TV alike—the reports of this outrage, and the entire Bengali press, hand in hand with their English counterparts, decried this event and bayed for the blood of Advani and Kalyan Singh, the then chief minister of Uttar Pradesh, who resigned the same evening on 6 December.

Back home, things were as usual, apart from a certain amount of bitterness that tinged our minds. My father was at first sceptical about the lull that covered most of Bengal. He had very concrete reasons for this. My father was, and still is, in the fishing business. His fisheries are staffed primarily by Muslims and all his fisheries are in the Muslim areas of the fishery belt of Bengal (Haroah, Kanmari, and Sandeskhali). That morning a contingent of fish was to come to the local auction market (*aroth*) of Barasat. He feared, and rightly so, the disruption of his business, and wanted to leave immediately for his fisheries to see that things were all right. But he didn't have to worry for long. The manager of his Haroah fishery came as usual with the fish and sold them at the morning auction. (The manager was a Muslim, Ali Hussain by name, who I address as Ali Hussain Da.) He reported that there was nothing to get alarmed about and things were normal. Meanwhile the rest of the country, especially north India, faced riots. The leftist government of Bengal must be given kudos in their efforts to curb those few sporadic incidents of 'would-be communal riots' in Bengal.

The point I want to make is about the conduct of Muslims of Bengal after the fateful day of 6 December that disrupted the whole world. The fishery business is very risky because civil rules of conduct do not apply here. Most of my father's staff are either illiterate goons or petty criminals employed to protect the tiger prawns from robbers. But surprising as it was, my father's fears about his fisheries being looted at the hands of his Muslim employees came to naught. He went to his fisheries as usual, and his employees greeted him respectfully, going about their usual tasks as if nothing had happened. If one feels that it was the fear of repercussions by the law that prevented these Muslim staffs from looting the fishery, I would like to clarify that the fishery belt of Bengal is a lawless area and the nearest police station, and in fact the nearest sign of civilization like electricity and telephones, are miles away (the cellular phone service did not exist then). Believe me, a prawn fishery is a scary place for city dwellers, as every now and then one gets to hear of various murders committed and bodies of murdered victims found on the muddy banks of the Biddadhari river when it is at low tide (this river is the main supplier of saline water to the fisheries for the cultivation of exportable tiger prawns).

Keeping the above context in mind I think I need to elaborate something about the ethos of Bengali Muslims. For one, they are completely different from their brethren in north India and also from the north Indian Muslims (mainly from Bihar) who are settled in West Bengal, especially in Calcutta. I believe that Bengali Muslims do not consider the Muslims of Bihar as their brethren. It is true that in some areas there are some distinguishable features of Muslim life, but that is within the Bengali cultural ethos. Somehow I am as closely connected to the Bengali Muslims as to the Bengali Hindus. Some of my relatives are Muslims: my mother's younger sister is married to a Bengali Muslim and my adopted elder brother is a Muslim, Sahajan Biswas by name. My ancestral village of Chandpur is surrounded by the three Muslim villages of Panapukur, Mobarakpur, and Hatkhola, and the way of life of these villagers and ours is not alien to each other. On the other hand my in-laws are north Indian Hindus and I have no cultural affinity with their day-to-day traditions, despite sharing the same religion.

The difference that marks the Bengali Muslims as different from the north Indian Muslims is not subtle; it stands out and makes the Bengali Muslims a separate entity from the concept of pan-Islamism that the Jamaat-e-Islami advocates and the Tablighi Jamat preaches with full vigour. The Jamaat-e-Islami did not appeal to Bengali Muslims, and the same is true of the Tablighi Jamat. Both are confined to the north Indian Muslims of Calcutta, who claim Urdu, rather than Bengali, as their language. The difference here is that of the Bengali culture, which is cherished by Hindus and Muslims alike. Except for a few pockets of Bihari Muslims that live in the Muslim ghettoes of Kolkata—like Rajabazar, Matiaburuz, Park Circus, and the Khiddirpur dock area—the rural Bengali Muslims hardly stand out as different from their rural Hindu counterparts. They speak only Bengali (here I must mention the existence of the descendants of the Afghan settlers in the rural areas of Murshidabad district, who speak a distinctive dialect of Urdu/Hindi mixed with Bengali called *Khotta*, but they have no script of their own and identify themselves as Bengali Muslims). Among Bengali Muslims at large there exists no difference in the choice of mother tongue. The dress code of the rural Hindus and Muslims in West Bengal is mostly a lungi and a vest while working in the fields, and saris for women. Muslim married women can sometimes be differentiated from Hindu married women by the absence of the red-coral and white-shell bangles and the *sindoor*. There also exists a mild form of purdah among some sections of Bengali women, called *ghomta*: the burqa is only worn by the wives of few maulavis and ultra-conservative sections of Muslims and of course those under north Indian influence. But it is a rare sight in towns and rarer in rural areas. Food habits are similar (fish curry and rice, except for the occasional choice of meat), as is the desire for education and free interaction during Durga Puja in autumn. In short, the Bengali-speaking Muslims and Hindus are culturally one entity.

As far as north Indian influence in Bengal is concerned, there is the problem of Hindu ghettoization. North Indian Hindus, including Marwaris, have a ghetto mindset as they remain far from Bengali culture and language. In Calcutta they are spread out almost everywhere, but are mainly concentrated in the major business centre of Barrabazar and Esplanade, and in the posh locality of New Alipur. The educated Bengali urban Muslims (that is, non-Urdu-speaking) are more similar to their Bengali Hindu neighbours. The concept of elite Hindus and Muslims that is prevalent in Urdu/Hindi-speaking areas of India is alien to the Bengali mind. Elite in the Bengali sense is the idea of the diabetic *bhadralok* (the quintessential Bengali gentleman, educated, government-employed, and a bit of a sissy). By elite I do not mean the upper crust of Bengali society, as they cannot be easily categorized as separate from the crème de la crème the pan-Indian upper-class. The Bengali bhadralok exists in a class of its own within the middle-class fold; their idea of civility is handed down from colonial clerks, with a few modifications here and there to suit the times. And this typicality of existence has inspired a whole lifestyle that is quite unique and noteworthy. As it is with the Bengali mindset of the bhadralok culture, Rabindranath Tagore and Nazrul Islam are household names in urban and rural homes, elevated to the status of holy cows. I must mention that Nazrul was married to a Hindu girl (Promila Sengupta). He was initially educated in a *maktab* and was for a brief period attached to a Muslim shrine as its mullah, but he did not convert his wife to Islam, and so is the case with his children, who are Bengalis. Being born a Muslim did not make any difference to Nazrul's Bengali ethos.

Getting back to the discussion I must say that without the minimal knowledge of these two poets (Rabindranath and Nazrul), no Bengali can be called a bhadralok, be he a Muslim or a Hindu. Bengali Muslims and Hindus do not see these two personalities through the eyes of religion. The songs and dances of Rabindra Sangeet and Nazrul Geeti are taught to girls and boys in urban and semi-urban homes of Hindus and Muslims alike (one Rabindra Sangeet is in fact the national anthem of Muslim-dominated Bangladesh: 'Amar Sonar Bangla'). Even in the choice of a career, a middle-class Bengali Muslim and a middle-class Bengali Hindu will aspire primarily for a secure government job, a clerical or a teaching post. The ambitious ones aspire to the post of a West Bengal Civil Service officer. In north India there is a prevalent idea that tailors, barbers, quilt makers, potters, butchers, etc., belong to the Muslim community, but no such stereotype is found in Bengal. These types of jobs are rather caste-based and Hindu lower castes are involved in these professions. The rural Muslims of West Bengal are predominantly farmers and in riverside areas they are fishermen. In the town of Barasat there are about fifteen butchers and only four of them are Muslims. All Muslim butchers who have opened shop in the last five years or so are Biharis. Before Bihari Muslim butchers settled in Barasat, the Muslims populace bought meat from Hindu butchers. Hindu butchers have ceramic picture tiles of Kali in their shops, which is how one can make out the difference. The concept of halal, which is so strong among the Muslims of north India, is not so pronounced in West Bengal. The butchers who sell beef are all Muslims and they have their shops in Kazipara, the place I had earlier mentioned. Unlike some north Indian states, slaughtering of cows is not banned in West Bengal. Even though most Hindu Bengalis do not eat beef, they are not as averse to cow flesh as north Indian Hindus.

Education is a determining factor that separates the Bengali Muslims from their north Indian counterparts. Preference is mostly given to the secular curriculum among Bengali Muslims, and the middle-class households make no compromise. There is also the Madrasa Board of Higher Secondary Education, where subjects like science, mathematics, geography, and history are taught alongside the usual Koranic verses. Here the medium of instruction is Bengali, unlike in north India where Urdu is the medium of instruction in dini madaris. The irony here is in the ideological belief of the CPI (M), which claims to be secular to the core—yet, for the sake of populist votes they have constituted this unconstitutional and of course non-secular mode of education as a way of giving state patronage to religious educational institutes at public expense. We should not forget that after Urdu it is Bengali which is the biggest treasure of Islamic literature in the subcontinent. But somehow it was the Bengali ethos that could not create a rift in the name of religion, as did Urdu, mainly after

Independence and through the dini madaris. Urdu could never replace Bengali as the language of Islam in Bengali-speaking areas including Bangladesh. At the time of the formation of Bangladesh, the Pakistani rulers tried to use the north Indian ulema to exploit the religious sentiments of Bengali Muslims of then East Pakistan in the name of Islamic brotherhood. In their efforts, they stressed the common legacy of Urdu, whose alphabet is similar to the Koranic script. But Bengali-speaking Muslims of East Pakistan did not consider this view and the movement called Tahreek-e-Haroo ul-Qoran could not stop the Mukti Joddhas (the name given to the Bangladeshi freedom fighters) and the common people from declaring independence.

Getting back to the educational aspects of the Bengali Muslims of West Bengal; most Muslim parents generally prefer government-sponsored elementary and secondary schools, which are there in almost all big Muslim villages. Bengali is the sole medium of instruction in these institutions.

A queer phenomenon that perhaps exists only in Bengal is the fanfare that surrounds the annual Durga Puja, which ironically does away with one's sense of religion. In local puja pandals, especially in rural areas, these five days of festivities are thronged by people from all walks of life. People visit the pandals not to pray but to marvel at the craftsmanship of the idols that local puja committees put up. Muslims come from faraway places and spend nights walking from one pandal to another, comparing the artistry of the idols. I was personally associated with my club's Durga Puja Committee (Jubak Sangha, Chapadalimore, Barasat). Three years in a row (1997–2000), Rahman Ghazi, a local Muslim businessman, was the president of the committee. The club has a considerable number of Muslims as members, who are under no obligations to collect funds (*chanda*) for the event, yet do so without thinking that idol worship and its encouragement is contrary to the principles of Islam. In fact, without the slightest thought of religion, Hindu and Muslim boys alike sit in front of the pandals, all in the naughty hope of some 'quality girl watching'. A common complaint my Muslim friends have is that the Muslim festival of Id (both Id-ul Zuha and Id-ul Fitr) is rather stark in comparison to the Durga Puja or Kali Puja. In recent years I have noticed a new trend developing among the Muslims of our locality: the putting up of grand pandals during Id, and placing some chairs in them to while away the festival evening over loud Hindi music accompanied by liquor and dance.

Not everything is utopian in Bengal. There are extreme voices too, Hindus and Muslims alike. And this is where the craftiness of the media is at work. We all know that sensation sells more than any mundane act of reporting. Perhaps it all started with the reporting of RSS training camps in Nadia district and the subsequent Rath Yatra of Advani which culminated in the demolition of the Babri Masjid. I remember distinctly that in the winter of 1991, I had gone to see one such RSS camp in Ghosh Para (this place is famous for the annual Baul Mela, as many foreigners attend this festival of traditional Bengali minstrels called Bauls near Boro Jagulia in Nadia District). In Boro Jagulia we had a fish hatchery, an extension of my father's business. I was taken to the RSS training camp of Ghosh Para by an over-enthusiastic labourer called Rabon. I was in Class VII then and had no idea what the RSS stood for. All I saw were rows of puffed-up funny-looking khaki half-pants and bamboo staves. There I heard 'Vande Mataram' being chanted with enormous zeal. At first I was of the opinion that this gathering was a Congress rally (the official slogan of the Congress is 'Vande Mataram', the CPI (M) cadres never raise this slogan). In our school we also sang this song, Hindus and Muslims together, and its implications made no difference to me then.

I remember very clearly the media's follow-up of Advani's Rath Yatra on a day-to-day basis. In the Boro Jajulia hatchery where I loved to be during my holidays, I found that the tribal staff we had (about five Bunos including Rabon; the irony of his name I realized only later, Rabon being Ravan, the prodigious adversary of Rama) all of a sudden becoming more 'Hindu', applying a saffron *tilak* on their forehead and discussing Advani over the daily *Ananda Bazar Patrika*, my father's choice of newspaper. For this I will blame the media, which had brought about this transformation in the minds of simple folks. The media then laid too much emphasis on sensation by giving excessive front-page coverage to Advani and his retinue in their progress towards Ayodhya. Much later I realized through observation of national and international news reporting, that it is the media that makes a perfectly normal man a fanatic: one who offends sensibilities of others through open propaganda and violence in the name of rectifying historical wrongs, and then defends the offence, applying the same methods. And the media does its job in the name of reporting impartially. I fail to understand the nuances between impartiality and propaganda for the majority's cause. But I do understand that the press is the voice of society, and the voice that screams the loudest is heard the most. For in the incessant reportings of such events, however impartial, the reader does take sides; after all, we are the product of a culture that is always prevented from being separated from the pugnacious influence of religion. One does not require the acumen of a poet or philosopher to realize that sensibilities get clouded by experience, and experience guides the understanding of things and events. It is just this type of 'impartial' reporting that will perhaps change the sensibility of my friend Safiqul to give up drinking, as if repenting past sins. Who knows that tomorrow, in case of some other incident like an Advani inspired Rath Yatra or a Muslim massacre in Gujarat, he will further abandon his shaken belief in Indian secularism by sprouting a goatee and visiting the mosque five times a day!

It was only after the demolition of the mosque that the BJP gained a foothold in Bengal. Cable TV was just becoming popular and many did not have access to Zee TV's sensational stories on Advani, Joshi, and Vajpayee. Newspapers had all of a sudden started reporting on the rights of the Hindus and the historical wrongs done to them, mentioning the existence of various other disputed sites in an erudite style that never abandoned journalistic honour in the name of sensationalism. In the parliamentary election a few years after the demolition of the Babri Masjid, Tapan Sikdar of the BJP, in alliance with the Trinamool Congress, won the Dumdum parliamentary seat, becoming the first BJP Member of Parliament from West Bengal. Here one can note that Bengalis' convictions as to personal choice and to the choice of society are very different. Had this not been the case, the BJP would have overwhelmed the capitalist-baiting-yet-conferring CPI (M) in the electoral polls of 1998. The BJP had to form an alliance with the Trinamool Congress of Mamta Banerjee to pit itself against the party in power, as Mamta Banerjee's party comprises both the vote-banks, Muslims and Hindus.

One more point to note is the way Bengalis look at religion. Here I must emphasize the exclusion of the domiciled north Indian Hindus and Muslims in Bengal. Religion for the Bengali is something personal. I have hardly come across any young Bengali Muslim who diligently prays five times a day. A Bengali takes as much pride in his heritage as his religion. Worshipping Bengali Hindus are as much into religion as anybody else, but the gods and goddesses that they worship are different from the prevalent deities of north India. No doubt, both are Hindu and the object of worship is from the Hindu pantheon, but female divinities predominate in Bengal, whereas male divinities predominate in north India. Vegetarianism, however trivial it may sound, is also one factor that affects the way Bengalis look at religion, as opposed to their north Indian brethren. North Indian Hindus like to call themselves 'vegetarians'; though most eat meat, they prefer not to cook it at home, and almost all abhor beef. It is commonly said in north India that '*mussalman hote hain masahari, hindu sakahari*' (a Muslim is a meat eater, a Hindu is a vegetarian). The concept of vegetarianism is rather rare in common Bengali households; the Vaishanavs, a strict sect of the Krishna cult, are vegetarians, yet they eat fish. A Bengali Brahmin gladly eats the flesh of animals like chicken and goat; fish is his main diet, whereas his north Indian cousin will abhor such food. And in the general household, meat is a regular part of the diet, the sought-after weekend feast. This 'regular' part of a Bengali's diet is not so regular in north India. Similarly the consumption of beef by the young generation is not a big deal, and the number of Hindu beef-eaters in Bengal is quite large, even though the older generation considers it unhealthy, physically rather than 'spiritually' (old and invalid drought animals are disposed off as consumable protein). Hindu business classes of north India, the Banias, are strict vegetarians. Their roots lie in north India and they are the main source of funds to Hindu parties.

Hindu communal parties are not as visible in West Bengal as in north India. There is a presence of the fund-rich Marwari community in Bengal, as in north India, but they limit themselves to Kolkata. The really rich Marwari-owned business houses are open friends of the CPI (M); yet they are the ones who fund Hindutva protagonists in the name of Hindi literary activities, which have a direct link with fascist politics in Kolkata. What is interesting is that Hindi litterateurs, who are the backbone of the RSS, do not abandon opportunities available through the CPI (M). The silver lining is that the religio-political beliefs of these Marwaris remain within their settlements, not directly affecting the rest of Bengal.

Let me state very candidly that it is not the motivation of religion that stirs the Bengali masses, but something loosely described as ideology, fashioned in the queerest form. In rural Bengal, from where the bulk of the CPI (M) cadres come, the party has such a stronghold over their lives that they individually are not at liberty to change sides. East Bengal immigrants from among them may be the most rabid Muslim haters, yet they dare not go beyond the party line. In a way their personal belief remains personal. In municipal areas one can notice a difference, as these towns are generally the stronghold of the BJP–Trinamool Congress alliance.

While reading articles on Muslim issues I have often come across the question of Partition and the plight of the common Muslims (those who stayed back) in north India. Bengal has her share of the woes of Partition too, but this does not affect the psyche of the Bengali Muslims as much as it does their north Indian cousins. Not many Muslims from the Indian side, meaning West Bengal, migrated in 1947 to East Pakistan. The Hindus from East Bengal, on the other hand, have moved over not only during the time of Partition in 1947 but in another major wave in 1971, and they continue to do so till now. The absence of security that they feel as citizens of Bangladesh makes them leave their ancestral homes. It is quite obvious that with their sorrows they bring along a hatred for the Muslim community, and it seemingly ends there. The CPI (M) provides them security and ration cards in return for a sure vote, and these refugees become one with the rest of the pliant Bengalis. In fact there exists subtle animosity between the Bangals and the Ghotis (East Bengal immigrants are called Bangals, and the residing Bengali Hindus are called Ghotis). The cause is economic; there has been an unprecedented demographic change due to this unchecked crossover as jobs and economic opportunities have become scarce due to a sudden increase in the population. Bengal is now the most populated state in proportion to its land mass in the Indian Union.

The settlement politics that is prevalent in Bengal is reversed in Delhi. In Delhi, on the banks of the Yamuna and in sporadic slums that are found in different pockets in Delhi and Noida, about one million Bengalis reside. (Here I exclude the Bengali residents of Chittranjan Park in Delhi who got the land as compensation for their lost houses in Bangladesh; almost all of them are Hindus and the colony is considered an upmarket colony.) These slum dwellers are mainly Bengali Muslims eking out a meagre livelihood as domestic help and rickshaw pullers. They are generally called infiltrators, while the same class of Hindus slum dwellers is called refugees. The Muslims refute this by claiming Malda and West Dinajpur district as their place of origin. The politics played with them is one of settling and displacing them as per the whims of the political party in power. They are collectively termed illegal immigrants of Bangladeshi origin. In this play of politics, if, say, 500 Muslim immigrants are deported from Delhi, the political party doing this consolidates its Hindu vote-bank; whereas in Bengal, in settling Hindu immigrants from across the border, a solid chunk of votes is garnered for the sympathetic political party. Both ways this farce is the handiwork of opportunistic politicians of Delhi and Bengal. They totally disregard the plight of the people being ousted and those who are being encroached upon. In Delhi the most unfortunate part of the 'infiltrator' politics is frequent fires in the jhuggis of Bengali Muslims. The police always claim that these are due to short circuits, and the affluent classes blame these 'infiltrators' for not using electricity the proper way!

Coming back to the Bengali cultural prism, one can rightly state that Bengalis are very media-savvy. As 'media savvy' their everyday greetings reflect this: *khobor ki* (what is the news)? Though people do not notice this, it is the result of the impact of print over the subconscious mind translating itself as the urge to know, the urge to start an adda. The origin of this popular greeting can be traced back to the heydays of print journalism in Bengal as part of the renaissance. Then it was considered fashionable to read the newspaper and a knowledgeable person in tune with the views of his colonial master was praiseworthy in the eyes of his friends. The common Bengalis, Hindus and Muslims alike, trust print and the written word. To elaborate on this I will cite an incident that involved the mystery of Subhash Chandra Bose's death. Some years ago, it was reported by a Bengali daily *Bartaman* that Subhash Chandra Bose was not killed in the plane crash over Taiwan as believed; instead he languished in Stalin's jails. This piece of news created such a stir that West Bengal nearly came to a halt. The Forward Bloc, the party that Subash Chandra Bose founded, and which is now in alliance with the ruling CPI (M), created havoc on the streets of Kolkata. Everybody joined in, irrespective of their political or religious affiliations.

In a similar manner, if explosions are less on paper, they are less in the minds of normal Bengalis. In line with the pan-Indian English press, the vernacular media of Bengal, which is extremely strong, also parrots views expressed on Muslim issues in its own queer way. There is one strange and obscure issue that I think the general press could have left alone instead of flashing it as a matter of grave concern. That issue is the case of the Waqf Board properties of the Bengali Muslims. Till date I do not understand why the entire media all of a sudden decided to train their guns at the malfunctioning of the Waqf Board in and around Kolkata. True, the Waqf Board is a corrupt organization and owns lot of property everywhere, but my question is of what concern is this to the common Bengali, and why was so much print wasted on so trivial a matter? What I garner from all this is that the vernacular media of Bengal wanted to do something original in finding a new Muslim bogeyman; after all, they were just repeating what the 'national' media was projecting. Almost everyday news of the Waqf board appeared in print.

Cable TV is now very widespread in Bengal and has almost replaced Doordarshan. There are several Bengali Cable TV channels (Akash Bangla, ETV Bangla, CTVN, etc.) and some channels are in partnership with Bangladeshi media houses. The news reporting of these channels is so pathetic that it makes one sick to the stomach just to watch them. The idea of quality journalism is non-existent and sensationalism rules the roost. Non-issues and nonsense are telecast everyday. The worst part is the way they project unnecessary tales configured as news, makes a thinking person lose his faith in the integrity of journalistic creed. Muslim culprits of petty crimes are invariably found, and the reporters of those channels go to the extent of researching their background, psychology, and everything possible, and then lay them bare in front of the camera. These channels have turned the viewing public sadistic.

Some years ago the government, in order to appease Muslims, launched an Urdu Samachar telecast. Urdu news telecast over a Bengali news channel is like a tumour, meaningless and short-sighted. This divided sentiments further, the Bengali Hindus seeing it as politically motivated and the Bengali Muslims being pushed towards the idea of pan-Islamization as preached by north Indian Muslims. On the other hand, Hindu propaganda machines have launched Bengali versions of religious programmes, in line with the north Indian godman culture. So far Bengali Muslims of West Bengal have not launched any religious channels of their own; they remain contented with Islamic broadcasts from Bangladesh.

If one is sensitive, then one will notice that the Bengali psyche is being slowly brainwashed. Gone are mainstream quality movies and instead one views sleaze. Here too the Muslim is reflected as the mirror image of the Bollywod version: criminals or extremely righteous Islamic self-sacrificing do-gooder; mechanics, barbers, tailors, and all sorts of shoddy characters. Mainstream Bengali movies never reflect the reality of the Bengali Muslim's existence. One movie did break away from the norm, but the movie was not in Bengali. Since the cast and crew of *Mr and Mrs Iyer*, directed by Aparna Sen, are Bengalis, I have taken the liberty of mentioning that the protagonist's role played by Rahul Bose was that of a Bengali Muslim photographer caught in a Hindu–Muslim riot situation. Apart from this movie, I have never come across any normal depiction of a Bengali Muslim character who is not caricatured in the north Indian fashion.

The subtle changes that I have noticed has come within the span of a decade: 1992–2002. In my observations of the Bengali Muslims over the past two years (2005–7) I have noticed changes that only puzzle me. I believe that change which comes from within takes time, but rapid transformations can only be attributed to external forces. The only force that is instrumental in doing this is the media. The new phenomenon of 'Islamization' that has come among Bengali Muslims today is very conspicuous to one who has lived with them for years. The most noticeable difference that one can make out is by listening to conversations. The usage of various Urdu words, as in Bangladesh, is being adopted in the common parlance of a Bengali Muslim's Bengali. Some of the noticeable Urdu words are *waqt* instead of *somoy* (meaning time), *nashta* instead of *jol-khabar* (breakfast), *kamiz* instead of *kapor* (dress), *ghosol* instead of *snan* (bath), etc. There has been a marked increase in the pilgrimage traffic of Bengali Muslims to Ajmer, Nizamuddin, and other *mazaar*s. The influence of the Jamaat-e-Islami is increasing, though slowly and so is that of the Tablighi Jamat. With the growing influence of the two different models of Wahabi Islam, an obvious clash of interests is also growing amongst the followers of these two sub-sects in Bengal, as their modus operandi differs.

Similarly, an increase in the pilgrimage traffic is also noticed among the Bengali Hindus, their destinations being Vaishno Devi, Deogarh, Tarakeshwar, and the Baba Loknath temples. Bengali Muslims in turn have given prominence to the establishment of the

Nakhoda Masjid as the primary mosque of Bengal; this is exactly what north Indian Muslims have done to the Jama Masjid of Delhi. In this an attitude towards centralization of Bengali Muslims is noticed. Looking at the present religious zeal of both communities, one often gets the feeling that Bengalis were dormant monoliths and now they are somehow atoning for their past lack of religiosity.

My observation is that the recent phenomenon of pan-Islamism is also influencing Bengali Muslims, who are in turn betraying the sensibilities of their Bengali cultural heritage. With the increase in the rate of unemployment and the subsequent frustration that the feeling of uselessness festers in the volatile minds of the youth, they seem to lose their sense of identity as Bengalis. Instead, they search for an abstract promise that cannot be fulfilled. I am firm in the belief that this is the result of the defence mechanism working in the subconscious mind of Bengali Muslims, who now feel perpetually under attack. After the Babri Masjid demolition, 9/11, the Gujarat carnage of 2002, and the continuous propaganda of shoddy Muslim images by the media, the common Bengali Muslims, who had so far stayed away from the ideology of pan-Islamism, are now trying to find what they were never looking for: their identity. The only saving grace is that they are not clear about the identity model. By identity, north Indian Muslims mean the Wahabi school of Islam. This puritanism is gradually being imposed on the minds of Bengali Muslims through the deeds of both communal and pseudo-secular forces and the populist policies of the CPI (M) in league with the ever-righteous media behemoth. Let us see what the future holds for the state of Bengal.

10

Issues of Goan Muslims as Seen in the Goan Press*

Charles J. Borges

According to the 2001 census, the population of Goa was 1.4 million and comprised 65.79 per cent Hindus, 26.68 per cent Catholics, 6.84 per cent Muslims, and 0.69 per cent Sikhs, Buddhists, Jains, and other smaller religious groups. Though Muslims constitute a comparatively small group in Goa, it is important to study the various situations they find themselves in and the problems they face. One can study their issues from various sources, but in this paper I intend to refer to them as they have been portrayed in the Goan press. I refer largely to accounts that have appeared in the English dailies like the *Navhind Times*, *Herald*, *Goa Tribune*, and *Gomantak Times*, and the monthly *Goa Today* during the last two decades. Some of the issues dealt with are the Federation of Goa Muslim Associations and Jamats (FGMAJ), anti-Muslim incidents, inter-religious meetings, Muslim education, Urdu teaching and Waqf matters, the Muslim Personal Law, and the uniform civil code.

FEDERATION OF GOA MUSLIM ASSOCIATIONS AND JAMATS

The FGMAJ has been one forum that has, under the dynamic leadership of Ashraf Agha, spoken out in the press through press notes and letters to the editors on matters that touch the lives of Muslims in Goa. The federation called upon social, educational, and cultural associations of Muslims in Goa desirous of being affiliated with it to send in their written requests along with the names of two of their representatives for membership of its managing committee.

---

* I would like to thank Ashraf Agha, President, FGMAJ, Panaji, for making available to me his well-documented notes and references for this paper.

The federation planned to broad-base its organization, the only one of its kind for Muslims, and to spread its activities at different levels in the state.

It planned to submit a memorandum containing the grievances of Muslims to the government and to seek the intervention of the then Speaker of the Goa Assembly, Haji Shaikh Hasan Haroon. The federation had urged the government to appoint Urdu translators at the state legislature, to constitute an Urdu academy, and to appoint a Muslim nominee to the recruitment and promotion committees. It wanted to organize a state-level convention after a survey of the Muslim population and air the many problems pending for redress since the liberation of Goa in 1961. The Muslim youth, it believed, would hopefully find a place of pride and responsibility in the new organizational set-up of the federation. It decided to launch a special drive and sustained campaign against social evils like drugs, alcoholism, dowry, etc., through posters, songs, and short plays.[1]

The FGMAJ had consistently reacted as a Muslim body to events of national importance. It condemned the Delhi blasts and said that they were a reminder to the people to stand united to face the onslaught and challenge of subversion and terrorism. While expressing grief, it suggested the setting up of people's vigilance committees.[2] It regretted the permission granted by the Supreme Court for symbolic *kar seva* at Ayodhya. It welcomed, however, the decision of the Vishwa Hindu Parishad (VHP) to carry out the kar seva on 6 December 1995 in a symbolic way without raising any structure or changing the character of the acquired land around the Babri Masjid. It believed that national controversies ought to be tackled and resolved with unanimity of spirit and a give-and-take attitude keeping in view the need to maintain solidarity and unity of the country.[3]

The federation deplored the package proposed by the Centre for solving the Ayodhya tangle as it would be counter-productive and unacceptable. It urged Muslim ministers at the Centre to resign in protest against the proposed package and to build up pressure on the government to withdraw it for a better solution.[4] It also welcomed the verdict of the Allahabad High Court declaring the notification of acquisition of 277 acres of disputed land at Ayodhya by the BJP government as *ultra vires* and perverse to the entire process of law. The federation decided to launch a Qaumi Ekta (communal unity) movement to strengthen secularism in the country. It declared that it would cooperate with all agencies, government or private, working for peace and communal harmony.[5]

The FGMAJ met the then Vice-President of India, K.R. Narayanan, and submitted a memorandum highlighting the grievances of the Muslim community. It asked for a Muslim nominee on both departmental selection and departmental promotion committees, and the setting up of a financial corporation and an Urdu academy. It asked for his help in obtaining 10,000 sq. m. of land for setting up an institute for job-oriented vocational courses and technical trade short-term courses for the backward classes, and grant-in-aid to Arabic madrasas and Arabic educational institutes on par with other educational institutes. It sought his intervention for the proper maintenance of the Safa Shahaputi mosque at Ponda and the beautification of its surrounding areas by the Archaeological Survey of India.

ANTI-MUSLIM INCIDENTS

Muslims in Goa have sometimes found themselves under attack or suspicion. They denied that clandestine Jamaat-e-Islami meetings took place in a Vasco mosque as was reported in a local daily. The Jamat-ul-Muslimin Madina Masjid vice-president, Shaikh Abdul Azim Mohidin, denied reports published by *Tarun Bharat* in November 1992 (a local Marathi daily) that the Vasco Masjid president and his two sons were conducting secret meetings at night at the Masjid. The report had alleged that they enjoyed political patronage. A meeting was held at the Masjid to condemn the demolition of the Babri Masjid and to appeal to the Muslim community to maintain peace with all communities. Another meeting was held to welcome the government decision to rebuild the masjid. The Jamat-ul-Muslimin stated that it is a religious body in charge of the Madina Masjid and the Arabic schools at Vasco, and that it did not permit any activities in the masjid premises that were detrimental to communal harmony.[6]

The FGMAJ condemned the news report, terming it irresponsible, distortive, provocative, inflammatory, explosive in intent and content, tinted with character assassination, and tantamount to an attempt to browbeat the Muslim minority. It wondered how the paper could flout the directions of the Press Council of India to exercise restraint in publishing news which could lead to communal disharmony. It brought the news along with the clarification to the notice of the

Press Council of India, to the home minister, and the president of The Editors' Guild in Goa.

One writer found fault with another writer for his piece entitled 'Shun Un-Islamic practices'[7] and believed that all original native Sunni Muslims of Goa were faithful and had never deviated from the traditions of Islam. He felt that to accuse any Goan Sunni Muslim of deviation was an injustice.[8]

There had been reactions to the presence of a large number of Kashmiris in Goa. The central home ministry had informed the Goa government that Kashmiris who lived in Goa should not be allowed to build a mosque in the Baga-Calangute area as they had planned. There were over 10,000 Kashmiri migrants settled in Calangute and Colva, and around 25 migrants arrived in Goa each week. The Goa police and the Central Bureau of Investigation (CBI) were concerned over this influx and about the plan of the Calangute-based Goa Kashmir Youth Organization (GKYO) to build a mosque. There were differences on the question of language and religious rituals between the Goa Muslims and the Kashmiri Muslims, leading the Kashmiri immigrants to attempt to build a new mosque for themselves in March 1992. Their attempts were however thwarted due to the opposition by the locals of Calangute and Baga. During August 1992, the GKYO once again made attempts to buy land for the mosque at Baga, and were again opposed by the local residents.

One of the papers (*Gomantak Times*, 4 October 1992) had earlier reported the possibility of terrorist infiltration among the migrant Kashmiris, and this suspicion was later backed up by the local police and the CBI. The chief minister of Goa had stated that terrorist infiltration was one of the reasons for the promulgation of TADA in Goa. GKYO had 220 members in June 1992, which went up to 516 by 15 September. The leader of GKYO had told the Goa police that there were around 8,000 to 10,000 more Kashmiri migrants in Goa. The locals of Calangute and Colva had expressed serious concern over the activities of Kashmiris, suspecting them of underhand dealings, and the Colva panchayat resolved to oust Kashmiris from the area.[9]

The FGMAJ was quick to see the announcement about the non-supply of electricity in Goa on 22 May, which was Bakri Id, as an anti-Muslim act, and spoke out against it saying that it would cause hardship to the people and spoil the festive mood. The non-supply, it said, would cause the decay of perishable sweetmeats and eatables and the aggravated heat would negate the festivity. In a secular country the festivals of minorities ought to be celebrated without withholding public and essential services like electricity, it added.[10]

Hindu–Muslim relations have by and large been excellent in Goa and have often been hailed as a lesson for the rest of the country. It was with utter shock that the state witnessed disturbances between the two communities on 3 March 2006 in the mining regions of Sanvordem-Curchorem. Rumours were quick to appear that armed 'outsiders' belonging to the Muslim community had arrived from faraway places with plans to attack the Hindu community in order to take revenge for the demolition of a Muslim place of worship. A report in the press soon after the disturbances of 3 March 2006 stated: 'Whether these rumors were deliberately planted and consciously propagated by some anti-social elements with nefarious intent is a matter of conjecture at this stage, since nothing was brought on record during the magisterial inquiry to point conclusively at any particular person(s) or group or organization.' Hindus were accused by the Muslims of having resorted to selective loot and arson of the shops/houses and properties of their community in the area.

A magisterial inquiry[11] had this to say in its submission:

It is quite clear that some sort of pernicious instigation and insidious motivation was provided to the crowd to engage in the senseless and selective destruction of property of the Muslims. The report has also said that no efforts were made by the village panchayat to resolve the issue of the alleged illegal structure, which had serious religious overtones, by using conciliatory and consultative mechanism. Besides the panchayat failed to elicit the co-operation and assistance of the mamlatdar/deputy collector's office with respect to the sensitive matter. The police inspector also failed to engage the leaders of both the communities in regular and constructive dialogue, due to which, the tension and mistrust between communities continued to rise, as there was no platform to discuss and deliberate the issues. After the demolition of the illegal structure at Guddemol village, the local police were able to arrest only 7 of the 12 accused persons and the arrested persons had managed to obtain bail the very next morning. The immediate release of the accused served to further bolster the mistrust in the minority community and also buttressed the hands of the violators.[12]

There was an incident in the south Goan village of Chinchinim with reference to a place of worship of the Muslims. The district magistrate discharged an injunction order against the activities of the Al-Gulshan-e-Sunni Muslim Association, Chinchinim. He directed the association to maintain status quo on the so-called illegal construction activities in their prayer house stating that the panchayat was the right authority to decide on the matter. His order followed the Chinchinim-Deusa panchayat, Chinchinim Villagers Action Committee, and Chinchinim Citizens Committee informing the district magistrate about the activities carried out by the Muslim body. They had charged the Muslim body of illegally converting a residential house into a prayer house. Consequently, he passed an injunction order banning the Muslim body from conducting any illegal activities.[13]

INTER-RELIGIOUS MEETINGS

The holding of inter-religious meetings has been a welcome activity of the FGMAJ. It congratulated Father Filipe Neri Ferrao on his ordination as the auxiliary bishop of the archdiocese of Goa and hailed his episcopal motto 'May they all be one', hoping it would kindle the torch of universal and emotional harmony.[14] The auxiliary bishop, speaking as chief guest at the celebration of the birth anniversary of the Prophet Mohammad reiterated this motto. He emphasized the need for such occasions to promote fraternal feelings, communal harmony, and better understanding among people of different religions. There were well-known Hindu speakers too at the meeting.[15]

Communal amity has often been evident in Goa. At the north Goa village of Arambol the Muslim festival of Urus held in February each year brings Hindus and Muslims together. A Hindu family is traditionally responsible for making certain arrangements for the occasion. This tradition is common even at the dargahs at Priol, Ponda, and Cuncolim. Being predominantly Hindu localities, the Hindu community helps in arrangements at the Urus, even providing sweets on the occasion.[16]

Vishvacho Neto and *Jivit Morna Uprant*[17] were published by the Konkani Shanti Publication (Mapusa) with many Muslims in attendance at the release function, showing that Konkani is accepted and adopted by Muslims who do not use Konkani but Urdu at home. Two books, written in Urdu on Islamic thought and philosophy by the founder of the Jamat-e-Islami Hindi Maulana, Sayyad Abdul Ala Maududi, have been rendered into Konkani by Shridhar Naik and Shashikant Korgonkar. A plan was afoot to publish about seven books every year, including translations of the traditions of the Koran

(Hadith) and the life of the Prophet Mohammad. Works such as these would bring out the truth about Islam and would remove misunderstandings. Syed Haeeb, Abadullah Khan, Yusuf Khan, Samiulla Belwadi, and Shaikh Tajuddin were singled out for praise for the work of translation and publication of the work.[18]

One writer believed that the communal virus was alien to the culture of Goa and was entirely the creation of opportunistic politicians and sections of the media. Sons and daughters of some of the seniormost politicians in Goa, he informed us, had taken the lead in maintaining and reinforcing communal harmony. Sheikh Hassan's daughter is married to a Catholic boy. One of the leading builders of Panjim, Sajjid of Esar Builders, whose family has a glass business, is married to a Catholic. The well-known cartoonist Mario Miranda is married to a Muslim, Habiba.[19]

In a show of unity that could set an example for people in other parts of India, a group of Hindus, Catholics, and Muslims had gone on hunger strike to press for a Muslim *kabrastan* (graveyard) at Margao. Thirteen people from these communities sat outside the office of the South Goa collector to push their case forward. For several years, the Muslims had been demanding a kabrastan in south Goa. Their efforts to identify a couple of places had failed. The president of the protest committee on hunger strike, Urfan Mulla, had said that proper land for burial is a fundamental right. He alleged that all political parties had failed in fulfilling the genuine demand of the Muslims of Margao and surrounding areas.[20]

The Public Works Department (PWD) Minister Churchill Alemao assured the Muslims of Davorlim that he would pursue the issue of the kabrastan with the Goa government. He gave this promise when he visited Davorlim Masjid after the Ramzan prayers, when local Muslims asked for his stand on the sensitive issue of burial grounds for their community. He told them that he would find a solution which would be acceptable to all. When a local Muslim leader said that politicians had only given them empty promises in the past, he said he would do his best to fulfil their long pending demand.[21]

Inclusion in Other Backward Classes List

One writer in a local paper mentioned that Muslims ought to be included in the backward class list with immediate effect since most of them are largely illiterate and do not get higher posts in government service. They are usually not to be found in the Class I or II lists of the administrative cadre of the government but only in Class III and IV. Many of them have to work as drivers, cleaners, painters, blacksmiths, peons, watchmen, and unskilled labourers, he went on to add.[22]

The FGMAJ submitted a memorandum to the Chairman of the Backward Classes Committee urging him to include Muslims in the list of backward classes for Goa, as was done in Karnataka and Kerala, mentioning that Muslims are backward socially, educationally, and economically, both before and after the liberation of Goa. Their educational backwardness results in dropouts at the primary and secondary levels.[23]

MUSLIM EDUCATION

The FGMAJ welcomed the central government scheme under which madrasas and maktabs imparting Islamic learning and wanting to take up modern learning and teaching of subjects like English, mathematics, and science would receive financial assistance. The government intended to identify blocks where Muslims suffer from illiteracy. Yet, the federation felt, what was noticeable was that the state government, due to its traditional antipathy towards the Muslim community, opted not to take any concrete steps in the matter.

Muslim students were informed in the local press about scholarships to be had from the Student Islamic Trust if they had passed intermediate or equivalent examinations and were desirous of studying in a recognized university or college in the field of medicine, pharmacy, engineering, agriculture, fisheries, forestry, food technology, or computer science.[24]

A writer to a local paper referred to another writer's letter[25] regarding the charter of ten demands given to the government by Imam Bukhari on behalf of Muslims for reservations and proportional representation. The Rehman Khan Committee on Muslims in Karnataka had pointed out that 80 per cent of Muslim students abandon school after Class VIII.

The writer suggests one visit the Gandhi Market in south Goa where 95 per cent of the vendors are Muslims from Karnataka and Kerala. Muslim children do not go to school unlike those of other communities, he wrote. The reservation policy did not help if one had no educational background. He urged the FGMAJ to build more schools of higher learning and use its funds to give free education for Muslim women for education stimulates inquiry which is instrumental in demolishing 'the citadels of ignorance on which mullahs and imams preside over to teach religious obscurantism'.[26]

The FGMAJ had organized a function to felicitate Sadia Razak for being the first Muslim girl to secure first place in Goa in the BSc examination with specialization in textiles and clothing. It called upon Muslim girls to emulate her example and to make advancement in education on par with girls of other communities.[27] It also congratulated Sheikh Hassan Haroon, the then speaker of the Goa Assembly on being conferred with the award of Vikas Ratna by the International Friendship Society of India.

The press mentioned the annual function of the Al-Berooni Educational and Social Association which celebrated its founders' day during which Muslim students from the Senior School Certificate (SSC) to the doctorate levels were felicitated. Parents were assured of material and financial support for their children. The Al-Berooni Academy of Goa was opened to look into the problems of Urdu and Muslim education in Goa.[28]

A local monthly carried the success story of the Mohidin family in Goa. Originally from Karwar, the family has resided at Vasco for over a century. It deals in business related to mining, petroleum, travel, and estate development, and helped in setting up the Anjuman Islam High School at Baina in the 1960s, an institution which imparts education in Urdu and English. Another successful Muslim migrant, Akbar Rangila, came to Goa three years ago and runs a shopping centre at Panjim called Gulf Super Market.[29]

There was often mention in the papers about the case of a minor student Majdoline Habib. She was estranged from her parents, Venus Habib and her Lebanese husband Latif. The case took a curious twist when she was said to have left home and married a Cian D'Souza, a maid friend of hers. She was kept at the government Bal Bhavan and refused to speak with her parents.[30]

URDU TEACHING AND WAQF MATTERS

In a letter to the Director of Education, A.S. Kazi drew his attention to the appointment of the Urdu inspector to inspect the functioning of Urdu schools. These schools (both government and private) had not been inspected for seven years. Urdu school teachers treated their duties lightly, resulting in the closure of many government primary and middle schools. Some parents had stopped sending their children to Urdu schools since teachers were not trained in new methods. There was no one to check the teaching, and Urdu teachers once appointed were not sent for any orientation courses conducted by the board. During the Board of Studies language meetings there was no one to represent the grievances and problems faced by Urdu teachers with respect to Urdu textbooks, workbooks, and stationery. Urdu language, he reminded the director, had been deprived its rightful place, though it played a key role in the post-Independence era and is today in the mainstream of national integration.[31]

The FGMAJ submitted a memorandum to the chief minister of Goa urging him to redress the long-standing grievances of the Muslims for the establishment of an Urdu Academy and for the appointment of official translators for Urdu and Arabic. The government had earlier appointed sub-committees to finalize the draft of the bye-laws for the proposed academy, but thereafter the matter had been shelved. The federation had earlier submitted a similar memorandum regarding the Waqf Board.

The FGMAJ has demanded the extension of the Waqf Act to Goa and the constitution of Waqf Board. It had made pleas about this same to the then President of India Fakhruddin Ali Ahmed during his visit to Goa and then to every government, but the grievances had not been addressed although there had been a Muslim minister in the cabinet for a long time. It called upon the Goa government to allow mosques and religious institutions in Goa to benefit from the annual grant being given by the central government to the state Waqf board. The federation had urged the government to constitute Waqf boards immediately through its social welfare department, failing which it would be presumed that it was not interested in the welfare of Muslim minorities of Goa. The group would contact all authorities, submit memoranda, launch a signature campaign, and stage token hunger strikes in support of their demands.[32]

The then speaker of the Goa Assembly, Haji Sheikh Hassan, also added his voice and demanded the extension of the Waqf Act to Goa in order to streamline the functioning of religious institutions and places of worship. He met the minister for social welfare and the governor. Hassan felt that in the absence of the Act, religious places were being managed haphazardly since, unlike other states, there was no board to monitor the functioning.[33]

In 2007, the All Goa Urdu Teachers' Association had submitted a memorandum to the government to fulfil their long pending demands, including the filling up of two posts of Urdu Inspector, appointment of a Grade-I teacher to teach Urdu at a higher secondary school, and an increase in the number of teachers. Urfan Mulla, the president of the association, stated that the government must bring about uniformity in all government-aided Urdu schools in the state, adding that the seniormost teacher in the government primary schools should be asked to maintain accountability. He also stated that Urdu books should be provided in the village panchayat libraries wherever there is a Muslim population, and that there should be at least one Muslim headmaster in a school run by the minority community, considering the fact that there are four Urdu high schools in the state. Mulla said that any delay in fulfilling these demands would add to the hardships faced by the community at primary, secondary, and higher secondary levels and reflect on academic performances.[34]

The division bench of the Bombay High Court had dismissed the writ petition filed by Mohammad Badruduza against the state government for non-establishment of the Waqf Tribunal. Appearing on behalf of the petitioner, S. Lotlikar had alleged inaction and failure of the state government to establish a Waqf Tribunal for adjudicating the disputes relating to Waqf properties or other matters connected thereto under Section 83 of the Waqf Act 1995. On the other hand, Subodh Kantak, the advocate-general for the state, informed the bench that the state government had already established a Waqf Tribunal and contended that the petition ought to be dismissed. In his plea the petitioner pointed out that the Waqf Act 1995 came into force in 1996 and Section 83 made it mandatory for the state to constitute as many tribunals as it may think fit for the determination of any dispute, question, or other matter relating to Waqf or Waqf property, and define local limits of jurisdiction. The petitioner further stated that he was deprived from initiating proceedings under the Act against Mutawalli of Madina Masjid at Vasco as there was no forum for him to redress his grievance. The petitioner alleged that the Mutawalli had granted illegal lease of the tenements of the mosque for a period exceeding one year for consideration and had declined to take action against the defaulter tenants. He also apprehended that the records would be tampered as they were in the Mutawalli's possession, and he had therefore approached the court.[35]

Family Courts

The FGMAJ had submitted a memorandum to the chief minister regretting the government's refusal to set up family courts under the Family Courts Act. The government had earlier refused a central government offer to set up family courts on the grounds that the state was too small and that the customary laws and institutions were adequate. The federation claimed that Muslims who practise their age-old customs of *Nikah* and *Talaq-e-Sharia,* at variance with the other communities, would be deprived of the benefits available under the family courts. It believed that the existing laws were not based on customary practices of different religions but were canonical laws originating from the ecclesiastical order during the Portuguese regime.[36]

Writing in one of the local dailies, A. Agha mentioned that in the case of family matters there was a need to have specially constituted family courts under the Family Courts Act. The ordinary courts with their technical and legalistic approach were unsuited to administer family law and to deal with the delicate and intricate problems involved therein. The judges too were not competent to deal with family controversies alone and unaided. There was need for an attached cell of trained social workers and counsellors. The courts attempted to impose legal control on the stability of marriages without seeking reasons for its failure when it occurred. The constitution of family courts was imperative in the existing social order due to different customary laws and practices and changing values of different religious denominations.[37]

Portuguese Civil Code, Muslim Personal Law, and Uniform Civil Code

The FGMAJ had all along spearheaded a campaign for the extension of Muslim Personal Law to Goa and deplored any attempt for the compulsory imposition of the uniform civil code in the rest of the country, recalling the assurance given by Babasaheb Ambedkar that the Civil Code would not be imposed on Muslims against their wishes. Parliament would enact a law to the effect, Ambedkar had gone on to add, and the uniform civil code would cover only those who would make declarations about their willingness to accept it. Thus the compulsory imposition of a uniform civil code was contrary to the right to freedom to preach, profess, and practise the religion of one's own choice guaranteed under Article 25 of the Indian Constitution. The FGMAJ announced its denouncement of the imposition of the uniform civil code on Muslims and the enactment of the Criminal Law (Amendments) Act 1995 as being excessive and oppressive in nature.[38] It did, however, hail the positive statement of the prime minister that the code would not be imposed on any community.

The FGMAJ had on a number of occasions brought important issues to the notice of the Muslim population. It had urged its constituents and affiliate units to send the names of five representatives for its central committee, which would then meet to discuss issues like the uniform civil code, extension of the Central Waqf Act to Goa, inclusion of Muslims as other backward classes, and other economic and social problems. It decided to launch educational projects with the assistance of the central government and to constitute village-, taluka-, and district-level committees. It condemned the moves of the BJP to introduce the uniform civil code and other legislation against polygamy, terming it an utter disregard of religious tenets, customs, and usages prevalent among different religious denominations.[39]

The FGMAJ regretted the statement of the then minister of state for law in the Lok Sabha that no religious minority in Goa had made any representation to scrap the Portuguese Civil Code (*Codigo Civil Portuguesa*), terming the statement a distortion of facts. In response to strong Muslim resentment against the civil code, the government of Goa had constituted a Personal Law Committee to study whether the code ought to be retained or replaced by personal laws of different religious denominations. The agitation of the Muslims demanding applications of Shariat Act in place of the code grew in strength. The FGMAJ decided to commence its agitation and urged the government to honour and respect the religious sentiments of the Muslim minority. The code has undergone tremendous amendments in Portugal itself, hence its repeal or scrapping in Goa would be justified and appropriate since Muslims in the rest of the country were governed by their own personal law, it said.

A meeting was held as part of the Shariat Protection Week held throughout the country on the call given by All India Muslim Personal Law Board. One of the speakers deplored the move of the Maharashtra government to enact the Adoption Act banning bigamy and dis-entitling from poll contests any person having more than two children, terming all this as interference in the Muslim Personal Law. He emphasized the need to reform Muslim society by removing social evils like dowry and extravagance in marriage expenses, etc. He exhorted the Muslims to keep a vigil on the onslaught of the Muslim Personal Law. The FGMAJ planned to form a Shariat Protection Committee on the lines of similar committees formed in the rest of India and decided to convene state level groups for the protection of Shariat laws. It believed the government's latest promise of non-interference in religious matters. The assurance of the central government to implement a 15-point programme for Muslims was seen as a vote-catching device.[40]

The need for a civil code, however, was felt by many. One writer mentioned that there was a long-felt need for a civil code for India embodying human rights and values of life and guaranteeing to the citizens full freedom of personality and enjoyment of life in harmony with the world.[41] The Portuguese Civil Code is an extensive and pervasive document dealing with all civil rights regarding persons and things, such as civil status, citizenship, original rights, acquisition of rights, contracts and obligation, property rights, law of torts, and donations or gifts. It came into force in Goa, Daman and Diu on 1 July 1870. It was not binding on all. Amended in 1910, it was applicable to all those who did not opt for their own personal codes. The codes in use were *Codigo de usos e costumes de gentions Hindus de Goa* dated 16 December 1880; *Codigo de usos e costumes de habitantes não-cristãos de Damão* dated 30 June 1894; and the *Codigo de usos e costumes de habitantes não-cristãos de Diu* dated 10 January 1894. For the Muslims of Goa it was stated in the said code for Hindus that the non-Catholic inhabitants of Goa could observe the provisions of the present law, which would be applicable to them insofar as it was not contrary to their religious rites. Any Hindu or Muslim or any other non-Christian of Daman and Diu could opt for the civil code or for the provisions of their respective codes. Goa was now a state and Muslims would like to replace the civil code with Shariat personal laws. But a uniform civil code, however, could become a forum for social and cultural integration in the country.[42]

There had been demands, said another report, from certain quarters that the Portuguese civil code be replaced by the Indian Muslim Personal Law and that an official committee be appointed to examine the proposal. This sparked off a heated debate among the

Muslims in Goa. The government appointed a committee to consider the extension of the Muslim Personal Law to Goa. The majority of the Muslims were agitated over the possibility of the Portuguese Civil Code being replaced by the Indian Muslim Personal Law against their wishes. A committee was set up in 1968 to study Portuguese laws in Goa and to recommend which of them ought to be repealed. This divided Muslims in Goa into those who wished to have the Indian Muslim Personal Law and those who preferred the Portuguese Civil Code. Differences were raised at the Muslim Youth Welfare Association meeting on 15 August 1992. They formed the Muslim Personal Law Action Committee. There were then the All Goa Personal Law Protection Committee and the Muslim Personal Law Women's Association on the one hand and the Muslim Youth Welfare Association, the Margao Muslim Action Committee and the Goa Muslim Welfare Association on the other.[43]

One feminist in the forefront of the struggle was Rashida Muzawar, the then president of the Goa Muslim Women's Association. She stated, 'Let Shariat law in its true form be implemented and we will have no complaints.' As a law student, her concern was aroused when in the course of her social work she had met victims of the law from south India and elsewhere. These women had fled their homes on being divorced and were forced to fend for themselves and their children. Not able to make a living in their own home states, they found themselves in the red-light areas of Goa. To Muzawar, the implications of the personal law if extended to Goa were clear. She launched a door-to-door campaign to educate people about the dangers of Muslim law. She said that almost every Muslim she and her colleagues had met wanted the Portuguese common civil code retained and, surprisingly, the uneducated and elderly women were against a change. She said that one woman from Margao threatened to use her chappals on anyone who wanted the Personal Law extended to Goa. Another discovery Muzawar made was that Muslims in neighbouring states preferred to see their daughters married to Goan Muslims and under the Goan law. The Portuguese code gave a woman security and status, according to Muzawar. Support for the Indian Muslim Personal Law came mainly from Muslims of non-Goan origin. The *jamaat* of a mosque in Margao, she pointed out, was dominated by such Muslims. In Vasco, too, where the major segment of the non-Goan population is concentrated, feelings were for the

Muslim Personal Law. Her campaign attracted the wrath of the votaries of the Muslim Personal Law. She had been described as a Kabir, as anti-Islamic, and as one who knew nothing of Koranic law.

One maulavi in a Margao mosque forbade his congregation from attending a meeting to be addressed by her. He also suggested that when she came into town she be physically assaulted and driven away. Speaking at a seminar on Muslim Personal Law organized by Citizens for Civil Liberties and Democratic Rights, she said, 'One of these Muslim godmen once told me "Women are the chappals of our feet." If women are indeed chappals for them then these men must seriously reconsider where they have come from!' She believed that women in Goa were more equal to men than women elsewhere in the country, probably because Goa retained the Portuguese law, which gives a woman the same rights as a man. She was grateful for being a Muslim and a Goan because Muslim women under Muslim Personal Law in the rest of India were very oppressed and had a small say on crucial matters. Muslim women in Goa were much better-off. They were not bound by the Muslim personal laws and hence had a good deal of freedom and a chance to come up in life. For a long time women, and especially Muslim women, had been kept down. But now they were getting more aware of everything and were beginning to think differently, wanting to be able to support themselves and their children should their husbands die or divorce them. They wanted to be educated so that they could have something to fall back upon. Women still had a long way to go but were slowly getting there.[44]

CONCLUSION

Before the coming of the Portuguese colonizers to Goa in 1510, the state had a strong Muslim flavour and personality about it. Being an important maritime outpost of the Bahamani kingdom for around two hundred years, Muslim commerce, architecture, and lifestyle had then made a deep impression on Goan life. Much of that was wiped away after the arrival of the Iberian colonial power. Muslims today represent a mere 6 per cent of the Goan population. As the letters to the editors in some of the papers have stated, they are not in the forefront of Goan commercial and educational life. Will the continuing plans to include some of them in the other backward classes list help? Thankfully, there are groups, most notably like the FGMAJ, that reflect on issues aloud and make Muslims socially and educationally conscious. Yet there is no strong movement of Muslims in Goa which tackles some of the issues mentioned above or which helps the poorer sections of the community rise to positions of pride and sufficiency.

From time to time, calls have been given to Muslims to trust in their own traditions and to find redress for their problems therein. Recently, a renowned Islamic scholar, Moulana Qassim Qureshi, appealed to the Muslims in Goa to emulate the teachings of Prophet Mohammad and of the Koran to rid themselves of the nagging problems of the day. Speaking at a massive two-day annual Tablighi Ijtima (Islamic congregation) near Merces, he said, 'Take refuge in Sunnah of the prophet as a solution for all problems in life and life after death lies in it.' But should the Muslims in Goa really not do more and despite their small numbers in the state stake their rightful claim for a more prominent place in state politics and activities?[45]

NOTES

1. *Navhind Times*, 24 August 1991.
2. *Navhind Times*, 14 September 1993.
3. *Navhind Times*, 4 December 1995.
4. *Herald*, 15 January 1993.
5. *Navhind Times*, 16 December 1992.
6. *Gomantak Times*, 17 December 1992.
7. Abdul Khalif, *Navhind Times*, 12 August 1994.
8. Gaus Khan Usman Faroque of Canacona, *Navhind Times*, 7 March 1994.
9. *Gomantak Times*, 4 October 1992.
10. *Navhind Times*, 20 May 1994.
11. The magisterial inquiry was headed by the North Goa District Magistrate Nikhil Kumar. The report and its findings were submitted on 20 March 2007 and its details were mentioned in the *Navhind Times* the following day.
12. *Navhind Times*, 21 March 2007.
13. *Navhind Times*, 14 September 2007.
14. *Navhind Times*, 12 April 1994.
15. *Goa Tribune*, 24 August 1994.
16. Joel D'Souza, 'A Common Faith', *Goa Today*, p. 18.
17. *Vishvacho Neto* and *Jivit Morna Uprant* were translated from Urdu to Konkani and published in Goa in 1995.
18. *Navhind Times*, 20 November 1995.

19. Rajan Narayan, 'Communal Politics No Bar to Love Marriages', *Herald*, 12 April, 1997.
20. *Navhind Times*, 17 March 2007.
21. *Herald*, 23 September 2007.
22. Sayad Irfan of Cuncolim, *Navhind Times*, 20 August 1994.
23. *Navhind Times*, 3 August 1994.
24. *Herald*, 29 September, 1994.
25. 10 October 1995.
26. The letter referred to is the *Navhind Times*, 10 October 1995. Ashraf Ali refers to this letter and writes to the *Navhind Times* on 25 October 1995.
27. *Navhind Times*, 7 July 1995.
28. *Navhind Times*, 7 October 1995.
29. 'The Influx', *Goa Today*, August 1991, p. 22.
30. Devika Sequeira, 'A Convoluted Affair', *Goa Today*, April 1994, pp. 24–31.
31. A.S. Kazi of Sanquelim, *Navhind Times*, 18 March 1994.
32. Ashraf Agha, *Navhind Times*, 24 June 1995.
33. *Navhind Times*, 20 June 1995.
34. *Navhind Times*, 23 September 2007.
35. *Navhind Times*, 21 June 2007.
36. *Herald*, 8 September 1994.
37. Ashraf Agha, 'Need for Family Courts', *Navhind Times*, 23 November 1994.
38. *Navhind Times*, 25 May 1995.
39. *Navhind Times*, 1 August 1995.
40. *Navhind Times*, 3 December 1995; *Gomantak Times*, 23 November 1995.
41. Robert de Souza, 'Civil Code and Religious Laws', *Navhind Times*, 2 September 1991.
42. Rajaram Hede, 'Uniform Civil Code', *Navhind Times*, 19 February 1991.
43. Linken Fernandes, 'For Better or for Worse?', *Goa Today*, September 1984, pp. 10–13.
44. 'Are Goan Women Really Equal?', *Goa Today*, July 1983, p. 10.
45. *Navhind Times*, 13 March 2007.

11

The Ayodhya Controversy in the Czech Press of the 1990s

Dagmar Markova

To begin with, it is necessary to say a few words on the general notion of Muslims which has been prevailing in former Czechoslovakia and in the Czech Republic. At present, the number of Muslims in the Czech Republic is estimated at 13,000. Out of them, about 10,000 are Muslims from Arabic countries, Iran, and some other countries where Islam prevails. About 3,000 are Czechs. The number of Indian Muslims is insignificant. There are some Pakistanis but their number is difficult to establish because most of them are businessmen who come and go. The co-existence of all of them with the local population is throughout peaceful, though there are some apprehensions on the part of the Czechs.

These apprehensions can be explained by two different factors. The country has had a bad historical experience with the Turks, originating from the medieval period when eastern parts the country were frequently threatened by the Turks. The Turks were generally identified with the Muslims. There are many folk songs about somebody's beloved who was captured by the Turks and about young boys who were sent to fight against them and never came back; there are pejorative sayings and proverbs such as 'A neo-Turk is worse than a Turk', equivalent to the 'Naya musalman chhe baar namaz padta hai' (a neo-Muslim prays six times a day, that is, the converted are more fervent than the convertors), but the Czech saying has a pejorative tinge. People were scared of the Turks, and thus they were scared of the Muslims. The general image of the Muslim world was associated with the harems, where hundreds of women were allegedly imprisoned. Later on, folk songs with rather ironical undertones appeared, originating from the times when Czech lands were a part of the Austrian monarchy and Czech boys would be sent to war for the interests of the Austrian ruling dynasty, which were not identical with the interests of the Czechs. There is a folk song very popular even in our times which says: 'Under the slope, there are Mohammedans hidden. The Mohammedans are pagans, they have tattered trousers and no shirts. Our Great Emperor does not want them to be in Herzegovina'.

All this has been presented here just to illustrate the image of the Muslims prevailing in the Czech lands in the past. The folk song just mentioned has to be understood in the topical context. In the song, there is already a recognizable shift to the view that the Muslims are perhaps not that bad, if the Great Emperor who was far from being loved by the Czechs does not want them to be in Herzegovina. Meanwhile, among the educated, another image of the Muslims developed. That was associated with the 'Thousand and One Nights', that is, with the romanticized Arab world.

At present, the press, of course, reports on what is going on in the world, and the word 'Muslim' appears on its pages very frequently in various contexts, with various tinges. Those who follow the news and who ponder on what they have read and heard generally regard Islam as the most immediate ideology of the contemporary world, an ideology which, unlike so many other ideologies, has by no means yet become a thing of the past, and has been neither discredited nor defeated. Naturally, the Czech public feel the deepest pity for the suffering Muslims of Bosnia, but at the same time they are afraid of the terrorists of some Muslim countries. The latter feeling results in misapprehensions and fear of Muslims in general. The fears are nourished by more and more news coming in, for example, from Algeria. The old xenophobia against Muslims is prone to reawaken. Sometimes it is difficult to discern between dangers as they actually exist and those that are magnified. Here I would like to recall the apt words of Madhu Kishwar in the context of an analysis of the anti-Muslim politics of the Sangh Parivar:

After the collapse of the Soviet Union, the political perceptions of the US and other western powers have swung dramatically in a different direction. Now that Pakistan and certain other Muslim countries are not needed as buffers against communism, the West has created a new bogey. The very same Islamic fundamentalism that the US and its allies kept fanning and supporting in Pakistan, Afghanistan, Saudi Arabia, Iraq as a counter to communism, is now being projected as the new evil to be fought and kept under check. Western intellectuals and politicians are now busy convincing the world that the genie of Muslim fundamentalism has become the chief threat to world security as was communism at one time.[1]

To some extent, the Czech public, too, is influenced by this projection of the Islamic fundamentalism as the main evil.

Now Indian Muslims do not fit into this picture. Nobody in the Czech Republic seems to be afraid of them, because India is not a Muslim country. The perception of danger coming from Muslim countries is more acute, and, besides, it must be said that all these problems are overshadowed there by other problems, typically by Central European problems which are more urgent. In fact, not much is known about the Muslims in India. 'The Great Mughal' has, truly, always been a well-known figure, but little is known how there are so many Muslims in India. Little is known about the realities of life of the Indian Muslims—for example, people are not able to differentiate between Hindu and Muslim names. It is generally known that in 1947 British India was divided into India and Pakistan. Quite frequently, however, as late as the 1970s, we had to correct formulations appearing in the press that British India had been divided into Hindu India and Muslim Pakistan. Again and again, we had to point out that India is a secular state where there are some minorities.

In Czech lands, people have always been very interested in India. But, in general, their image of India has been identical with the image presented in the translations of ancient Indian Sanskrit literature and the works of Rabindranath Tagore. This image has partly lasted till now, though since the 1950s a number of works of contemporary literature have been translated from various Indian languages. As to Urdu literature, in the 1970s a very beautiful anthology of Ghalib's poetry was published, called *Hostage of Love*. Later, an anthology of Iqbal's poetry was published. Earlier, in the 1950s, when one-sided stress on what was called progressive literature was laid, an anthology of Krishan Chandar's short stories was published in Czech and a great number of his works in Slovak. Czech Indologists dealt with the so-called Muslim period of Indian history in a number of books, but little with the contemporary situations of Indian Muslims.

Those Czechs who have visited India, and their number has increased very much during recent years, admire, of course, the Taj Mahal, Red Fort, Qutub Minar, etc., but most of them do not reflect much on the Islamic tradition as it lives in contemporary India. They realize that these are monuments of Islamic architecture, and that they are somehow different from the others; that is all.

As to Urdu, there is not much known about what type of language Urdu is. People usually know that the official language of India is Hindi, though they sometimes say 'Hindu' instead of Hindi. People usually know that there is a language called Hindustani. All this is not intended to denigrate the level of the general knowledge among the Czech public. It is a distant country full of its own problems, and, after all, how many people in other parts of the world know something about the difference between Czechs and Slovaks? How many people know that there is not any 'Czechoslovak' language and that the Slovaks have their own well-developed language, similar to Czech, yet different?

All this was stated just to outline the situation. Now back to Urdu. In the 1950s, students of Hindi were told that Urdu is merely a style of Hindi. Our Hindi teacher was well versed in both Hindi and Urdu, and so both were studied. The students also learned to write in both scripts and to differentiate between the so-called styles. That was very useful, as though the subject studied was called Hindi, both languages and both literatures were included. Later on, Urdu disappeared from the curriculum and it was only a few years ago that it was revived. Now there are some students of Urdu and it is being taught as a regular subject, separately from Hindi.

Now, when people ask what Urdu is, and when we answer that the language is close to Hindi, yet different, then the next question is usually whether the difference is similar to the difference between Czech and Slovak. Then it becomes difficult to explain to them that the difference is of another kind, not like that between Czech and Slovak. The difference between Hindi and Urdu is really unique; therefore it is rather difficult to be comprehended in a distant part of the world where the situation is totally different. And when people are told that the difference between the two is based on the vocabulary and that most of the Urdu vocabulary originates from the Islamic cultural background, then they easily draw the conclusion that Urdu must be the language of Indian Muslims. And then, again, it becomes necessary to point out that the question is not that simple.

Now, coming to the Indian Muslims in the Czech press: under the Communist regime, little was published on matters of religion in general. Not that Czech mass media paid little attention to India; that was not the case. There were, however, two main trends. Firstly, quite a lot was written and published on the general development of the Indian economy, education, health services, etc., and on socio-economic and political conflicts in India. That was a part of the general tendency to put the problems of religion in the shade. True, this tendency diminished in the 1980s. When it was realized that religion is a powerful force, attention began to be given to the problems of religion in society. After November 1989, when the system changed, many things changed. All that was banned or almost banned in the totalitarian system came to the fore. Many books on religion have been published but they are concerned with the doctrines, not with the question of how the religion operates in everyday life. Insofar as these books are written by specialists, they really widen the horizons of the reading public. However, the book market has been swamped on the one hand with so-called spiritual Indian literature, which unfortunately many people regard as Indian philosophy, and on the other with ancient Indian erotica of the type of the Kama Sutra. This is an understandable reaction to all the bans of the recent past. Unfortunately, actually existing contemporary problems of India have been rather cast into the shade in this fashion, at least as the book market is concerned.

Partly, this gap is filled by the magazine *New Orient*, published by the Oriental Institute, where articles written by people specializing in the respective countries are published. The magazine is, however, a monthly, devoted to history, culture, and the contemporary situation of Asian and African countries. As it is a monthly, covering a large territory and a large scope of topics, it is unfortunately not able to always react promptly on every topical problem. There was, anyway, an article published in 1990 under the title 'Babur's Mosque or Rama's Birthplace?',[2] elucidating the situation of Ayodhya, by coincidence shortly before the situation became stormy. This magazine, however, is not issued on a mass scale and is read mostly by those who are interested in eastern countries anyway. A few years ago, articles on

Indian Muslims began to appear regularly in the magazine, each of them dealing with a phenomenon from history, closely linked with a phenomenon of the present. This was taken as a novelty by those who are interested.[3]

Apart from *New Orient*, reporting on Indian Muslims in the Czech press is usually rather accidental. One topic, however, appeared in the press of the 1990s again and again, and that was the Ayodhya problem. It must be admitted that most of the newspapers just reported what happened. In some cases, it was obvious that the reports were written by journalists who did not know much about the subject. In the Czech Republic people are generally not very religious-minded. Most of them simply are not able to relate to the situation. However, it could be sensed from most of the articles published in the Czech press that the case in point is more than a mosque or a temple. In most of the press articles, the contemporary situation, with more or fewer details of the politics, was briefly described and a short history of the Babri mosque was presented. It was usually pointed out that India is a secular state, but 'the old problem persists: the Hindus or the Muslims?'[4]

Most of the articles were written by journalists who tried to give some details of the present situation as well as of the history. However, a wider context was usually missing. It was up to the Indologists to fill this gap. That was done in the press organ of the Trade Union by the beginning of 1991 in the article 'Allah or Rama?' with the subtitle 'There is not necessarily peace if there is no war'.[5] The article was not a mere report on what had happened and what was going on, but a brief outline of how Islam came to India and that there is a Muslim minority there. Some details of Muslim life and customs were given, resulting in an explanation of why the Muslims stand out in India. In this article, as well as in a long article written by another Indologist for the illustrated weekly *Reflex*,[6] it was pointed out that the conflict was in fact based on politics, on misusing religious feelings of the people, and on creating differences between Hindus and Muslims for political purposes. It appears that some details for some later articles in other newspapers were drawn from both these articles.

It is quite interesting to note what the journalists put in inverted commas, implying that they were citing the opinion of somebody else. That was, for example, labelling the Muslims as 'Muslim invaders' who should 'assimilate with the mainstream'.[7] Characteristically, a photograph of a weeping Muslim woman was attached to the article concerned. That article was written at the time when the violence in Ayodhya culminated and when the Babri mosque was destroyed. In those days, all significant Czech newspapers reported on the event. The rightist *Czech Daily* strove for a careful impartiality, yet it mentioned 'the rampage of the Hindu fanatics'; after all, the title of the article itself was 'Rampage of Fanatics'.[8] Very similar was the tone of the country daily *Agrarian Newspaper*.[9] The Catholic daily, *People's Democracy* mentioned 'a rampaging mob of Hindu fanatics' and it even, rather too emotionally, called the Babri Masjid 'a symbol of love and understanding that should be brought by faith.'[10] In an article written by an Indologist in the then centrist *People's Newspaper*, it was pointed out that 'the wave of Hindu revivalism got a deadly tinge when politicians had started misusing it.'[11] In an article in the former organ of the Communist Party, now an independent opposition daily, the event was called 'an act of unparalleled fanaticism'; 'a rampaging mob of Hindus' was mentioned in the same manner as in the rightist *Czech Daily*; and the Babri mosque was, with much exaggeration, even called 'one of the most beautiful and one of the greatest mosques of the country.'[12] The most critical towards the Muslims is an article in the popular youth weekly *Young World*. It was written by a young Sinologist deeply interested in India who mentioned 'a strong minority complex' of many Indian Muslims 'dreaming of a past Mughal glory',[13] who was the only one to mention the Jamaat-e-Islami as 'a competent twin of the Hindu fundamentalists' and who was again the only one who stated that after the event Muslim mob went out into the streets first. However, she, too, reported much more on 'the saffron-robed fanatics'.

By the beginning of 1993, when the riots spread to Bombay, a number of articles appeared again. Most critical of Indian Muslims was the article in the Trade Union daily where it was stated that 'Indian Muslims assume that the government policy as a whole serves, above all, the interests of the Hindus.'[14] Even in this article, however, it was stated that 'the wave of barbarity in the name of a religion which strongly prohibits to hurt anybody was unleashed when the Babri mosque at Ayodhya was demolished in December.' Almost the same formulation appeared two weeks later in the *Business Newspaper*, which is otherwise, as a rule, merely concerned with business. It was stated that the riots in Bombay had been started by the Hindu fanatics.[15] Finally, there appeared an article in the *Agrarian Newspaper* under the title 'Fear sways over Bombay' with the subtitle 'Pakistan regarded as a terrorist state'. The author of the article wanted to know the real aim of the bomb attacks and added: 'If until recently the local Muslims have been feeling threatened by the Hindu fundamentalists, now they feel threatened by state reprisals as well.'[16]

In sum, it can be stated that no newspaper from the Right to the Left, whatever their internal differences may be, saw any reason why both places of worship could not co-exist side by side. However, none of them blamed the Muslims for the Ayodhya disaster. None of them cast discredit upon the right of the mosque to exist, though most of them mentioned the tradition of Rama which is older than the mosque. It is true that some details of the newspaper articles were drawn from the articles written by Indologists, but, unfortunately, not always are the Indologists' views taken as seriously as in this case.

Now, the question arises as to why it is like this, even though, in fact, not much is known about the Muslims of India, and when there is, in addition, a latent xenophobia against Muslims in general and when there is no particular reason to champion Indian Muslims? Why not remain absolutely neutral in a problem which, after all, is almost beyond the comprehension of the local public?

The question can be answered quite simply. The Czech Republic is a small country in the middle of Central Europe, having a bad historical experience with those who are bigger and stronger and who act from the position of power. Sympathies are easily created with those who are in a minority. Thus, as soon as a situation similar to Ayodhya is created anywhere in the world, the Czechs usually become very critical of the majority and very prone to suspect the majority of acting from the position of power. After all, the suspicion is usually correct. A bad historical experience helps a nation to develop a sense of justice. After all, this is all about human rights. And what are human rights? The right to have a roof over one's head. The right to earn one's livelihood. The right to feel safe. To profess one's religion, to pursue one's interests, in short, to be oneself. The bulk of people in the Czech Republic might not be able to feel themselves into the problem of 'mosque or temple'. They, however, understand quite well that the Ayodhya problem is just one facet of a problem which is much more than the issue of a mosque or a temple.

NOTES

1. Madhu Kishwar, 'Religion at the Service of Nationalism', *Manushi,* New Delhi, no. 76, May–June 1993, p. 14.

2. Dagmar Markova, 'Baburova mesita nebo Ramovo rodiste?' *Novy Orient,* Praha, April 1990.

3. Dagmar Markova, 'Patecni mesita a jeji lide' (Friday Mosque and its People), *Novy Orient,* October 1989; 'Pout za sultanou Razijou' (A Pilgrimage to Sultana Razia), *Novy Orient,* January 1990; 'Setkani ve Firozove pevnosti' (An Encounter in the Firoz Fort), *Novy Orient,* February 1990; 'Mughalsky princ vulickach stareho Dilli' (A Mughal Prince in the Lanes of Old Delhi), *Novy Orient,* June 1990; etc.

4. Vilem Buchert, 'Hinduiste, nebo muslimove?' (The Hindus or the Muslims?), *Mlada Fronta,* Praha, z.11.1990.

5. Dagmar Markova. 'Allah nebo Rama? Na miste, kde se nevalci, nemusi byt vzdy klid' *Prace,* Praha, 5 January 1991.

6. Jan Filipsky, 'Urny' (Urns), *Reflex,* Praha, 33, 1991.

7. Ladislav Kryzanek, 'Ve jmenu Ramy' (In the Name of Rama), *Respekt,* Praha, 50, 1992.

8. 'Radeni fanatiku', *Cesky Denik,* Praha, 8 December 1992.

9. 'Ceke Indii dalsi deleni?' (Is another Partition in Store for India?), *Zemedelske Noviny,* Praha, 8 December 1992.

10. Monika Vrablikova, 'Symbol porozumeni znicila nenavist' (Symbol of Understanding Destroyed by Hate), *Lidova Demokracie,* Praha, 9 December 1992.

11. Stanislav Mundil, 'Vybuch v Ajodhji' (Explosion at Ayodhya), *Lidove Noviny,* 10 December 1992.

12. Milan Madr, 'Fanatismus v Ajodhji hrozi konfliktem' (Fanaticism at Ayodhya is on the Point of a Conflict), *Rude Prevo,* Praha, 8 December 1992.

13. Libuse Polivkova, 'Jriskra a polar' (A Spark and a Conflagration), *Mlady Svet,* Praha, 2, 1993, p. 17.

14. Oldrich Pospisil, 'Vybusna smes' (An Explosive Mixture), *Prace,* 13 January 1993.

15. Martin Jankovec, 'Bombajske varovani' (Bombay Warning), *Hospodarske Noviny,* Praha, 27 January 1993.

16. Milan Frydrysek, 'V Bombaji vladne starch', *Zemedelske Noviny,* 21 January 1991.

12

Indian Muslims and the Free Press*

Estelle Dryland

Faiz writes: '... some language enthusiasts among us today have made it a part of their credo that to prove your love for Punjabi, you must detest Urdu as the handmaiden of decadent courts and to demonstrate your loyalty to Urdu, Punjabi must be despised as the gobbledegook of illiterate yokels. This approach obviously stems from petit bourgeois linguistic jingoism—although it is frequently veneered with progressive terminology.'

—Khalid Hasan (1988)[1]

The aim of this paper is to explore the underlying reasons for a perceived lack of representation of Muslim Indian writers in India's free press. To this end I have examined a selection of publications from 1948 to the present day in an attempt to ascertain if Muslim writers are indeed under-represented and, if so, why? This paper is in three sections. The first deals with the Urdu language and Muslim identity, the second with Indian Muslims and the free press, and the third with Indian Muslims, the vernacular press, writing and modernity.

How have the contributors to India's free press addressed Muslim issues throughout this period? Have Indian Muslim writers been given a fair and equipollent voice? The readers will be more able than I to distinguish (by name) between Muslim and 'other' writers whose contributions are examined in this paper. Again, the paper will seek to establish whether more 'others' are writing more on Muslim/Islamic issues more than Muslims themselves.

*I would like to offer my sincere thanks to my colleague Sabine Hoffmann for her meticulous editing of this version of the paper.

THE URDU LANGUAGE AND MUSLIM IDENTITY

The Urdu language, although as yet under-lexified, may be regarded as one of the most developed of the major modern languages of India/Pakistan. According to my research conducted among Muslim informants, following the Partition of India in 1947, the incoming Congress government started to purge the Urdu language from the north Indian central administration and from the education system on the grounds that Urdu was the language of Pakistan, and, by extension the language of Muslims. It was to be considered an alien language, having been brought into India centuries before by foreign invading forces. Detailed examination of the disputed origins of the Urdu language is not critical to this paper; however, suffice to say that pre-Urdu made its appearance in the early tenth century, shortly after the Ghaznavids travelled the historic Khyber Pass route from Afghanistan and established themselves in the Lahore region. Urdu may have been the result of the grafting of a comprehensive Persian and Arabic vocabulary, along with certain grammatical rules, onto the grammatical stem and basic stock words of Khari Boli, a western Hindi dialect spoken in the Delhi area.

There is an assumption that all Indian Muslims identify passionately with what they perceive to be the repository of their (possibly imagined?) ancestral cultural and literary heritage—the Urdu language. To this end, the learning of Urdu is seen as vital to the perpetuation of Indo-Muslim culture, a premise supported by M. Mujeeb who holds that '... the survival of Indian Muslims in a culturally recognizable form is generally linked ... with Urdu [which is] considered synonymous with [the] Urdu script.'[2] However, can the widely held notion that the Urdu language is the mother tongue of all of India's Muslims, along with the suggestion that there is an intrinsic relationship between the Urdu language and Islam, be deemed correct?

The cultural mosaic of India's Muslims has multiple traditions drawn from the Arabs (evident in Sindh, Pakistan, and on the west coast of India), the Turks, the Iranis, from Tadjiks, Uzbeks, and Afghans (north India), but mostly from India itself, remembering that the majority of India's Muslims converted from other faiths to Islam.[3] Evidence of the exquisite nature of this heritage may be found, for example, in a volume entitled *Muslims in India* edited by Ratna Sahai, featuring reproductions of sixteenth and seventeenth century

Mughal paintings, calligraphy, and motifs. However, according to Mohammed Peer, Urdu's rich literary heritage is the result of the combined efforts of Muslim and Hindu scholars.[4]

The Partition of India became the division of Indian Muslims, though not all of country's Muslims supported the Pakistan movement. According to my research, many residents of Pakistan today admit to having become 'Pakistanis' by default. In 1983, the following statement, in which the Karachi-domiciled Urdu poet Sarshar Siddiqi expressed his feelings of separation from his motherland of India, appeared in Pakistan's *Morning News:*

It is an undisputed natural instinct that every man loves his birthplace. I also loved my motherland [of] Kanpur as my mother. I still cherish the same love. That city gave me the consciousness of life and bestowed upon me the courage to live. My dear ones are buried in that soil. That city is my past; it is the architect of my future. I never decided to leave my ancestral home for good, and take abode in the ideological land on the grounds that my ideology, my honour or my livelihood were in danger. I left my motherland because my countrymen had started to express doubts regarding my patriotism. Had my old parents not been alarmed by the deteriorating situation, perhaps then that weak moment would not have entered my life which uprooted me like the green leaves and deprived me of the roots of my land.[5]

According to Michael Brecher, Pandit Jawaharlal Nehru, in a letter to one of his Muslim nationalist friends, stated: 'For mysterious reasons, Urdu is supposed to be the hallmark of Muslims. With all due deference, I am not prepared to admit this. I consider Urdu as my language, which I have spoken since my childhood.'[6] S.K. Zaidi writes that Nehru made the following emphatic and impassioned comment at a press conference held at Vigyan Bhavan: 'Urdu is an Indian language, it is a language of our country, and even if there is not a single Muslim in India, Urdu will remain our cherished language.'[7] In a further statement, Nehru observed: 'I regard it essential for Hindi to cultivate closer contacts with Urdu. This will make Hindi stronger. Similarly, if Urdu is to progress, it is essential for it to acquaint itself with Hindi and to cultivate close relations with it. The difference between Hindi and Urdu is not much; the difference lies in the script.'[8] However, Nehru did not live to see the changing linguistic forms/ attitudes of recent decades.

So a number of questions may be raised. Are the Urdu language and its Arabo-Persian script synonymous with the Indian Muslim? Are India's Muslims lending themselves to a type of religio-linguistic social mobilization, a phenomenon known as 'elite closure', whereby persons attempt to establish and maintain their powers and privileges via linguistic choices? (See the case of the Mohajirs and Urdu in Karachi, for example, where the Mohajirs, in an environment marked by uncertainty, hostility, and driving ambition, in fact made the Urdu language their ideological 'homeland'.) Here I pose one question: to what degree do Indian Muslims also claim Urdu as part of their true (or perhaps imagined) Arabo-Persian cultural heritage?

S. Irtiza Husain suggests that four major influences have contributed to the psyche of the Indian Muslims:
1.   Islam ... which invokes the deepest responses in life,
2.   The Iranian language, literature, mysticism, and the routine matters of everyday life,
3.   The local [Indian] environment, its music, colourful life, customs, sensitivities, and prejudices, and,
4.   Western technology, political thought, institutions, and science.[9]
In the first part of the next section of this paper I explore examples of the free press in India in an attempt to determine if and how these influences are reflected in the writings of Indian Muslims. I will also consider the frequency, content, and standard of Muslim literary contributions to the English language press, and attempt to examine the press attitudes towards, and space allocated to, events that impact the social, religious, and political *soorat-e-haal* (state of affairs) of India's Muslims.[10]

INDIAN MUSLIMS AND THE FREE PRESS

According to Thierry diConstanza, the first modern Muslim paper to appear in colonial India was *The Star of India* (established in 1932). (By 1942, many of its journalists had opted to transfer to Delhi to launch the enduring English language newspaper *Dawn*). This four-page publication was discontinued shortly after the events of 1947. 'The Indian Press prior to Independence had a theme and a goal; i.e., to assist in the objective of gaining freedom for India. Having gained freedom in 1947, the press, at least for a while, was at a loss for [a] goal'.[11] Issues regarding freedom of the press were among the first priorities to be settled. P.N. Malhan suggested: '[T]he freedom of the

Press is the corner-stone of democracy. Every citizen should be able to express his views freely, and for that he/she must have access to all the facts, not only those [deemed] convenient for the government to disseminate.'[12]

In 1948, the year immediately following Partition, questions of provincial languages appeared in the *Bombay Chronicle*. In an editorial titled 'Untenable Objections', one member of the House suggested: 'In India, all the major languages should be spoken in the House, and, that soon, by weight of numbers, Hindi would predominate.' 'It should be obvious,' he added, 'that whether Hindi or Hindustani is chosen as the national language, the other languages *and even Urdu* (emphasis added) will have to be permitted. For the three languages differ, not in kind but in degree, in the number of classical words used from Sanskrit or Persian or Arabic'.[13]

In *The Times of India*, on 10 July 1948, the government of Bombay instructed the District School Boards that they should continue instruction in all schools in the Marathi, Kannada, and Gujarati. Detailed instructions were also to be issued to schools imparting instruction through Urdu. On 30 September the same year this newspaper reported that the Bihar Legislative Assembly had adopted amendments to the assembly rules to the effect that proceedings of the house should be conducted in Hindi and the Devanagari script, provided that the speaker could call upon or permit any member to speak in any other language in the interests of the debate on special occasions.[14]

On 6 October 1948, prominent Muslim Nawaz Manzoor Jung hosted a party in Hyderabad at which high-ranking Muslims and Hindus freely mingled. Swami Ramanand Tirth, Hyderabad State Congress President, asked Muslims to shed their fears and to make common cause with the State Congress with a view to restoring law and order. In *The Times of India*, October 1949, an article appeared advising that: 'the possibility of adopting Sanskrit in a simplified form as India's national language [was to] be discussed at the 15th session of the All-India Oriental Conference, to be held in Bombay from November 5–7.[15] Another important question raised for consideration was the compilation of a 'scientific dictionary'. P.V. Kane, vice-chancellor of the University of Bombay, noted that the only dictionary of Sanskrit currently available at the time had been compiled some eighty years earlier by two German scholars.

On 6 November 1948, a lengthy and interesting article appeared in the *Bombay Chronicle,* the content of which I will paraphrase. A conference titled the Hindustani Convention was convened at which the participants supported the propagation of the Hindustani language as the national language of India. The initial item on the programme was the reading of an after-prayer speech by Mahatma Gandhi. The audience stood in hushed silence during the reading. In a subsequent speech, S. Lahuti stressed that he deplored the fact that 'certain people' had introduced religious bias into the language controversy, and that language was the cultural and not the religious heritage of the people.

Khwaja Ahmad Abbas, who also attended the conference, stated that the most widely circulated papers of the Hindu Mahasabha were published in Urdu. He claimed that the government-controlled radio had compiled a list of words that could not be used over All-India Radio (AIR). But when Sardar Patel broadcast over AIR on the occasion of Independence, he used 37 of the 'prohibited' words. Abbas observed: 'Again, it is a strange country where the victims of Pakistan [presumably the Hindus and those Muslims who 'stayed on'] were doing their best to propagate Urdu by establishing Urdu publishing houses in every part of India.'[16] With reference to the script, Abbas conceded that he was personally in favour of the discontinuation of the Persian script. Syed Sulaiman Nadvi, who was also present, stated: 'If there can be one national language for the whole country, it is Hindustani written in both scripts as a cultural heritage, for it is Hindustani alone which can serve the purpose of a *lingua franca* in a country of diverse races and languages.'[17]

Some days prior to the publication of this article, there appeared in the *Bombay Chronicle* the report of a resolution calling upon the Constituent Assembly to recognize Hindi as the lingua franca of India with Devanagari as the official script. Raja Bahadur Govindlal stated: 'Hindi was undoubtedly most suitable because both Urdu and English were of foreign origin.'[18] In the same issue, AIR (Bombay) advertised a programme on Muharram, the Shiite period of mourning, in Urdu on page 3.

On 10 November 1948, the Directorate of Publicity, Government of Bombay, placed an advertisement on page 2 of the *Bombay Chronicle* for the position of Film Officer. A sound knowledge of Marathi, Gujarati, Kannada, or Urdu was required. On 15 November, Bombay radio broadcast a 'Programme of Special Interest to Women' in both Urdu and Hindustani.[19] On the same day a paragraph appeared in the *Bombay Chronicle* titled 'Linguistic provinces issue subjudice', in which N.G. Ranga, an advocate for democracy, suggested that he 'was not in favour of reservation of seats for Muslims or for the second chambers which in the past had acted as a check on the country's progress.'[20] The point here is that in 1948 the topic of Urdu language still found a place in the press in India.

In the *Bombay Chronicle* again, on 11 November 1948, reference was made to the observance of Muharram. 'Muharram, by age-old tradition, is generally observed by Hindus equally with Muslims in India; and when Muslims would take out processions to dip the *tazia*s,[21] Hindus used to join in the processions'.[22] However, it appears that by 1948 this practice had to some extent been discontinued.

In the same newspaper, in October 1949, a small announcement appeared to the effect that Bombay's Muslims would celebrate Bakr-Id (Idu'l Azha—the term *Bakr* meaning goat, many of which are slaughtered along with other animals on the occasion). Raja Maharaj Singh, the governor of Bombay, stated that he was very glad that the Muslim Social Workers' Group was holding an inter-communal gathering to celebrate the festival, as he was and had been a great believer in communal harmony. At no time had this been more desirable or essential than at the present, he commented.

In Calcutta, on 30 September 1950, Purushottamdas Tandon, Congress President, spoke at a reception given in his honour by the Muslims of Calcutta. In his speech, Tandon stated (paraphrased): 'We do not take lessons from Pakistan on Hindu–Muslim relations for we are determined to regard Muslims as our equals.' He went on to say that he had always believed in Hindu–Muslim unity and drew the audience's attention to the causes of Partition. Were they political? No, Muslims sought Partition on the grounds that they are a separate nation. Tandon continued:

I have always said it is a mistake to think that Muslims and Hindus have separate cultures. Religion is something other than culture ... I want to tell you now that our culture is Indian culture. It is wrong to suppose that by adopting Indian culture you become a Hindu. The Hindu religion is something quite different from Indian culture.[23]

In *The Times of India*, 2 October 1950, in a paragraph headed 'U.P. & Partition', Sri Prakasa stated: '[T]he U.P. was greatly responsible for the partition of the country. If ... Uttar Pradesh had not helped the partition movement they would have not witnessed the tragic scenes caused by the division of the country.' He added that the maintenance of peace and goodwill between the two countries was ultimately the responsibility of the people.

Exploring the topic of journalism in the *March of India* (for the period 1952–63), by now one finds a plethora of Hindu writings on such topics as radioactive isotopes, the railways, atomic reactors, decimal coinage, pottery, arts and crafts, water and power research, sculpture, flora, jewellery, Indian botanic gardens, the Qutub Minar, Muslim architecture in the Deccan, and, of course, cricket. During the same period I found only five articles written either by Muslim writers or on Muslim-related topics. 'Muslim Wedding', by S. Farhat Hussain,[24] appeared in the July–August 1953 issue. I have selected the following excerpts from Hussain's account of the wedding: 'The shrieking of happy children and the shouting of the maids fills the house with a maddening din'; 'The girls then give the [bridegroom] pieces of crystallized sugar and paan in such quick succession that he is unable to keep pace with their haste and is greeted with roars of laughter'; and, 'with a dramatic suddenness the scene now changes from rejoicing to a sort of mourning. The bridegroom lifts up his precious burden' (presumably the bride, who may not, in fact, have thought of herself as a 'burden' in the literal sense). She 'mourns' the loss of her family as she moves to the home of her husband.

C.J. Chacko, Head of the Department of Political Science at Delhi University in 1953, noted in an article entitled 'India: A Living Democracy' that not all Indians share the same religion, nor do they belong to the same class, colour, climate, or culture. He further stated that the '... vast majority of our population would, and indeed should, proudly look to the Sanskrit language and literature as the matrix of [India's] culture and civilization.' He commented: 'If only everyone would utilize [the] Devnagari or Sanskrit scripts [to preserve] the great wealth of the common cultural and literary heritage we already possess in our different languages.'[25] This appears to be a contradiction in terms, because Chacko then went on to say that the fundamental principle of democracy is the recognition of, and respect for, the personality of the individual.

S. Ranganathan wrote to the editor, *The Times of India,* on 14 November 1957, drawing the latter's attention to the fact that the new transmitter in Madras should be used for broadcasting not only Hindustani programmes but for programmes on both Hindustani and Carnatic music on an equitable basis. The problem of the acceptance of Hindi was also active in Madras in 1957. 'Some people in Madras have come to look upon Hindi as an instrument with which the north wants to dominate the south.'[26] An additional problem appeared to be that although eight out of every ten students in Madras were taking Hindi as an optional subject, the teaching of Hindi presented difficulties because the language was not spoken at home.

With focus still upon 1957, *The Times of India News Service* carried the following item: 'Recognition of Urdu as a regional language in Delhi and Hindi as the official language [has] been unanimously recommended by the Language Committee of the former Delhi State.'[27] The home minister suggested that an admixture of Hindi and Urdu should be evolved. However, B.N. Datar, Minister of State, said that prior to the reorganization of the States some representations had been received from the *Anjuman-e-Taraqqi-e-Urdu* for the recognition of Urdu as one of the regional languages of Uttar Pradesh, Bihar, and Rajasthan. Pandit Pant added that the draft order sent by the Andhra government also dealt with safeguards to the services of the former Hyderabad State and the use of Urdu in official work. Meanwhile, in the same year, antagonism towards Hindi found voice in the Punjab and the *razai* (quilt makers) of Lucknow made headlines in *The Times of India.*

In the cultural sphere, the vice-chancellor of the University of Jammu and Kashmir, A.A.A. Fyzee, presented to the Bombay University Library a collection of 160 Arabic manuscripts dealing with the law, history, and philosophy of the Mustalian Ismailis.[28] The peculiar value of the manuscripts lay in the fact that they were deemed to be highly secret and were never allowed into the hands of non-members of the sect. Fyzee's two goals were to make Kashmir University a unique institution and to develop it as a centre for Kashmiri language. Still on the topic of universities (1957), Rashid Ahmad Siddiqui stated in an address at Jamia Millia Islamia that the government should resist interference in the working of the universities because it stifled the growth of free thought.

In November 1957, *The Times of India* announced the winners of the best literary contributions of the era. *Mir Taqi Mir*, written by Khwaja Ahmed Farouqi, was considered the most outstanding book published in Urdu in the years 1954 to 1956. The author was awarded the Sahitya Akademi prize of Rs 5,000. The decision was taken under the presidency of Jawaharlal Nehru.[29] On the 27th day of the same month, the results of the competitions for poems written on the topic of the freedom struggle were announced by the High Level Committee for the Centenary Celebrations of the 1857 War of Independence. There were cash awards for the four best poems in Gujarati, Hindi, Marathi, and Urdu. The Urdu-medium winners were (first) Ejaz Siddiqui for *Hamari Jung Azadi*, (second) Imran Ansari for *Jang-e-Azadi*, (third) Zafar Gorakhpuri for *Man ke Lal*, and (fourth) Fauq Jami for *Tarikh-e-Azadi*.[30] So, clearly ten years after the event, the Muslim Urdu poets' focus remained firmly fixed on the 'War of Independence'. It may be that this proclivity to 'look back' is part of the problem for today's Indian Muslim writers. However, this is not peculiar to Muslims alone. Hindus too, among other ethnic groups worldwide, tend to reflect on a 'glorious past'.

Again in November 1957 *The Times of India* published an article by Tara A. Chandavarkar, the title of which was 'Strictly Purdah'. Acknowledging that it may have demonstrated a particular brand of humour, I have chosen to reproduce a small section of it only in the interests of cultural sensitivity. Chandavarkar wrote:

In the days when the university classrooms had a curtained-off section for lady students, a bewildered professor was once confronted by an impatient young thing who boldly stalked out to discuss a subtle nuance in one of Shelley's lyrics. [The professor] solemnly turned his back on the class and refused to proceed until the fair interpellant has resumed her seat behind the purdah.[31]

He, however, was more fortunate than his colleague who, during a college strike, lectured away at the curtained enclosure for the best part of an hour before he discovered that its 'fair denizens' had vanished. The author's use of English was so extravagant that I (the writer of this paper) had to consult the English dictionary myself for definitions on more than one occasion (and I'm still not convinced regarding the terminology). In the same newspaper in 1957, an article appeared which referred to the question of the medium of instruction in universities. Shriman Narayan, Congress General Secretary, stated:

I am sorry to know that Osmania University [has] switched over from an Indian language [the name of which was omitted] to a foreign language. I am of the firm opinion that the national language and the regional languages should come into their own. For some years to come, English might be continued in the case of technical subjects. So far as technical terms are concerned, I suggest a common terminology should be formulated for all Indian languages.[32]

On 24 November 1957 Narayan maintained that India 'should get rid of the English complex.'

We are not against the English language as such. But I see no reason why English should continue to be the official language of the Indian Union without any serious attempts being made for the introduction of Hindi. Hindi is now the official language of the Indian Union. A national language is highly essential for bringing about [the] emotional and psychological integration of the people.[33]

At the risk of chronological disruption I would like to quote here from *India Today*, 28 February 1995. Sudeep Chakravarti writes:

What are Indian video-jockeys all about? They keep talking in a mix of English and Hindi. One accepts the fact that an all-English Veejay brings abysmal ratings, while an all-vernacular Veejay isn't hip enough for a country that generally worships English—Hinglish, Guljish, Punjlish, and Tamlish. Anythinglish![34]

Chakravarti is, of course, referring to code-switching, a linguistic strategy employed when one may not have a total grasp of a specific language and feels relaxed slipping in and out of the two (or more) languages familiar to and spoken by both 'speaker' and 'recipient'.

An article appeared in the June 1959 issue of *India Today*, the author of which opted to remain anonymous. It read as follows: 'The Constitution guarantees the citizen equality before law, prohibits discrimination on the grounds of religion, caste, gender, and place of birth. It secures equality of opportunity in matters of public employment'. (Review of Indian newspapers in the period immediately following Partition did not identify any expression of religious preference by employers advertising in the 'Situations Vacant' columns. This may have been due to India's declared secular policies. However, whether or not applicants were subject to discrimination at the time of the job interview was unclear.)

In *March of India* September 1959, an article appeared titled 'Urdu Literature'. This article was based jointly upon a talk broadcast on AIR by S. Ehteshan Husain and on an article by Khwaja Ahmad Faruqi, which appeared in the 'Contemporary Literature of India' published by Sahitya Akademi, Delhi. The article made reference to poets/writers Khwaja Mir Dard, Sauda, Mir Taqi Mir, Baba Fareed Ganj Shakar, the Lucknow School, the Delhi School, and the poetic form known as the *ghazal*. It included such lines as 'poets have written songs in graceful Urdu which have the fragrance of intimate domestic life', followed by 'the letters of Niaz are like soap-bubbles, too wonderful to be touched'.[35]

In October 1962, Inderjit Lal published an article in *March of India* on Amir Khusrau. The following year, in January 1963, an article written by journalist Kidar Nath appeared under the title of 'Masters of the Urdu Ghazal'. Again reference was made to Khwaja Mir Dard, Sauda, Mir Taqi Mir, Zauq, and Ghalib.[36] In September 1963, an article by Inderjit Lal appeared titled 'Khwaja Mir Dard— Famous Sufi Poet of Urdu'. Once again, the writer dealt with Dard, Mir Taqi Mir, and Amir Khusrau.[37] It would seem that some fifteen years after Partition, Muslim writers were still 'looking back', clinging—perhaps for emotional security—to the perceived exclusivity of a romantic Arabo-Persian cultural heritage. This does not in any way deny the Indian Muslim's Central Asian cultural heritage.

An article of some interest appeared in the same publication in July 1963. Its author chose to remain anonymous: the topic was 'Aligarh Muslim University'. The writer claimed that the university 'brought out' a journal in Urdu and a bulletin in English, and that the university, which was regarded as a symbol of India's secularism by millions all over the country, was cherished and generously aided by the government.[38] A further unsigned article published in 1959 and titled 'Muslims in India' stressed the conditions laid down by the Constitution, of equality, prohibition of discrimination on the grounds of caste, gender, and birthplace, and that equality of opportunity in the workplace was secured under the Constitution. These terms had resulted not only in unity and goodwill among India's various religious groups but also '... in the return of a large number of Muslims who, influenced by fake propaganda and uncertain conditions created by the division of the country in 1947, had been persuaded to leave for Pakistan. Already over a million have come back and hundreds more are coming every year.'[39] This article went on to laud the impressive part played by Muslims in the uplifting of the country since Independence. 'There are Muslim Judges in the Supreme Court and the High Courts of the States. Muslims hold many key positions in the Defense forces'. The article emphasized that there were Muslims in key public service positions working together with other citizens for the uplifting of the masses and toward the eradication of poverty. 'Handsome grants were given to educational institutes run by Muslims. Aligarh Muslim University, Jamia Millia, Dar-ul Uloom (Deoband) are all flourishing'. No mention of language was made in these articles. For the first time (according to my research), lengthy and interesting articles appeared in *The Times of India* on the topic of Muslims and India in 1968. But were they all written by Muslim writers? One such article, written by Hamid Dalwai and titled 'Muslims and India', questioned the attitude of Maulana Maudoodi[40] toward the creation of Pakistan, the opposition of the Jamiat-e-Islami and the Khaksar Party to Partition, aspects of the Jamiat e Ulema e Hind, the Ahrar[41] Party, and information regarding President Ayub Khan of Pakistan. The debate centred round the type of society these various groups envisaged for Pakistan and Muslim India.[42] Maulana Maudoodi had made clear that nationalism had no place in Islam, favouring instead 'Islamic (or Muslim) nationalism'.

A further article, which appeared one week later, similarly titled 'Muslims in India', took the form of a reply by M.A. Karandikar to Dalwai's piece. According to Karandikar, Maulana Maudoodi 'ridiculed the Muslim League's theory of Muslim nationalism and opposed the demand for Pakistan on the grounds that it would restrict Muslim activity and dominance within the geographical frontiers of Pakistan.'[43] In this instance, it seems that freedom of the press had given each party the right to express opposing views.

By the late 1960s, job advertisements required applicants to have a sound knowledge of English. AIR played ghazals (over Delhi, Patna, Jullunder, Jaipur, Bhopal, Srinagar, and Jammu radios, but not Calcutta). Patna radio featured a play in Urdu, while Jammu broadcast a Hindi play. In October 1968 the governments of Bihar, Andhra Pradesh, West Bengal, and Maharashtra, and the Delhi administration launched prosecutions against several newspapers and weeklies for publishing articles with intent to incite communal feelings and passions. These included English, Urdu, and Bengali dailies and periodicals owned by persons belonging to various communities.[44]

A further lengthy article appeared on 29 October 1968, under the heading 'Persecution Bogey' in which the problems of minority communities, and specifically Muslims, were addressed. Although grievances were acknowledged, the deliberate perpetuation by the majority [Hindu] community of a sense of fear and economic dependence was denied. 'Even the Brahmins regard themselves as a persecuted minority in some States, particularly in Madras, Mysore and Kashmir.'[45] The article suggested that the minorities should also think in terms of self-help:

Though more and more Harijans (today's Dalits) are joining the services, both at the Centre and in the States, the same cannot be said of the Muslims. Allegations of communal discrimination in recruitment should be fully investigated and the guilty officials punished. Muslims should be admitted to the special coaching classes started by State governments. Little has been done to tap the wealth of *wakfs* (religious endowments for the benefit of the community). The funds could be used to promote technical education and provide scholarships.[46]

Badshah Abdul Ghaffar Khan, popularly known as 'Frontier Gandhi', received considerable publicity in *The Hindu* during 1969. In Wardha on 6 November, he spoke of the Gandhian era when slogans suggested that Hindus and Muslims were 'brothers and sisters'. He supported family planning; he also supported a scheme which would unite India, Pakistan, Burma, Ceylon [Sri Lanka], and Tibet [China] in a confederation. From Ahmedabad he said that it was unfortunate that Muslims did not have the proper leadership to guide them. Khan further stated that communal trouble would not arise if Hindu and Muslim leaders worked jointly for the welfare of both communities. Again from Ahmedabad, this time addressing Muslim youths, he declared that Pakistan was created solely to please the British and not in the interests of Muslims. He commented: 'Hindu leaders who went to jail and suffered at the hands of the British were more patriotic.

But Muslim League leaders never underwent any suffering and were "servants" of the British.'[47] It was reported (Khan is remembered for, among other things, his frugality), that he finally agreed to have his feet measured for a new pair of shoes!

The same year *The Hindu* ran an editorial titled 'Communalism in Politics'. At a meeting of the National Integration Council (founded in 1961), Gajendragadhkar was reported as having said that the roots of communalism were to be found in illiteracy and obscurantism. A Western reporter recounted a conversation with a Muslim driver who said:

My village in Uttar Pradesh has a Muslim majority. We always lived on the best of terms with our Hindu neighbours. We have never had communal riots, not even in 1947. That is because we show each other consideration; for example, we never kill cows. The Hindus arrange their processions so that they never pass before our mosque. We have a Muslim headman. He is very important, he gets votes, the MLA who is a Hindu always consults him. It is this readiness to participate in politics not as Muslims but merely as citizens that distinguishes the non-communalist from the communalist.[48]

Also in *The Hindu* there appeared the report of a meeting of the 13th Rashtrabhasha Prachar Sammelan at which V.K. Rao stated: 'Hindi should have more and more words of other Indian languages so that non-Hindi-speaking people would feel that it belonged to them also.' He was sure that if the work of teaching Hindi was done with sympathy and patience, the day would come when people in non-Hindi areas would love Hindi more than their regional language.[49]

In 1973, *Indian Horizons* published a comment by L.M. Khubchandani directed toward the 'Language Situation in India'. The author stated: 'In a land populated by 550 million speakers, scores of small speech groups consisting of a few thousand people still maintain their mother tongues in everyday life in various multilingual pockets—including Urdu in Mysore and Madras.'[50]

In 1974, Saliha Abid Husain wrote on 'Women Writers and Urdu Literature', and, in the same issue of *Indian Horizons,* S.L. Ghosh wrote on 'Indian Nationalism—Some Surviving Problems'. Ghosh noted:

The quest for a national identity has since its beginning faced some inherent conflicts. Its main protagonists were from the new English-educated elite. The Muslim elite, comprised of the displaced governing class, sullenly clung to its medieval culture and resented the preponderance in the public life of the Hindus who [had] been the subject community during the preceding centuries.[51]

In 1978, Chandrakant Bakshi published an article on the Gujaratis of Pakistan in *The Times of India* in which he claimed: [52] 'During Partition, many Muslims from Gujarat opted to go to Pakistan. Today after thirty years, the Gujarati language still flourishes there.' Zulfikar Ali Bhutto once complained that half of the 22 families[53] who had a stranglehold over the economy of Pakistan, were Gujaratis. But on Pakistan TV and radio, Gujaratis were presented as semi-educated capitalists who spoke 'funny' Urdu. While some Gujaratis in Pakistan considered Gujarati to be a Hindu language, a large majority was keen not to lose its identity. 'There is much official support for Urdu in India,' wrote Bakshi, 'but very little for Gujarati in Pakistan. During the 1958 Martial Law, Gujarati was eliminated from schools but ten years later it was reinstated. Journalists, writers and stage artists have kept the language alive in Karachi and Memoni Gujarati dramas enjoy longer runs than Urdu plays'.[54]

In September 1978, the Imam of Delhi 'warned the Janata government that unless it took the minorities' commission seriously, it would be alienating the sympathy and support of these people'.[55] The Imam especially pinpointed the problems of minorities in Andhra Pradesh in his writings. Also in September, *The Times of India* reported the visit of the acclaimed Punjabi Urdu socialist poet Faiz Ahmad Faiz. In reply to the question 'Is it true that the regional languages in Pakistan are becoming more prominent and, if so, can it endanger the future of Urdu in Pakistan?' Faiz replied: 'This is natural. The regional languages must also get recognition. However, Urdu is a link language and has an importance of its own. As such it does not face any danger. Despite whatever is being written in other languages, Urdu retains its significance as an official and academic language.'[56]

Throughout 1978, Delhi radio listed programmes including the artists and instrumentalists Afeez Ahmad Khan, Fayyaz Khan, Mukhtar Ahmad, and Yaqub A. Khan. Ghazals were broadcast continuously throughout the period from Partition onwards, the news in Urdu was broadcast from Srinagar, and mushairas (poetic symposiums) were screened on Delhi and Amritsar TV.

In October of the same year, Lucknow's political leaders condemned the confiscation of copies of *The Times of India* and the *Navbharat Times* by the district administration of Aligarh. Ram Saran Das, general secretary of the Janata Party, stated: 'I am for freedom of the Press and I severely condemn the Aligarh district administration's action in confiscating copies of *The Times of India*, a paper which is outstanding for [its] responsible journalism.'[57] It appears that previously a similar attempt to stifle the press occurred at Jalandhar. In a separate article, P.C. Chunder commented in Kota that 'Hindi is the language of the masses, but it should not be forced on anyone.'[58] In Jaipur, at a three-day national Sanskrit educational conference, a message from the prime minister stated: 'Sanskrit [is] the treasure house of India's tradition, art and culture. It [is] being ignored and neglected but in the interests of the country's glorious past and present, it [has] to be revitalized.' [59] In Patna, the chief minister and the CPI (M) leader 'expressed their support for the bid for the promotion of Urdu language.' The function had been organized by the state unit of the *Anjuman-e-Taraqqi-e-Urdu.* Takur said he would do everything possible for the promotion of Urdu, while Satya Narain Singh openly denounced 'those who paid "lip sympathy" to the cause of Urdu.' He advised members of the *Anjuman* to resort to 'revolutionary tactics if they wanted to achieve their object[ive]'.[60]

It should now become clear that by 1978—31 years after Partition   references to India's Muslims and their viewpoints find more press coverage than in the years immediately following Partition. However, once again, who is actually writing on these topics—Muslims or 'others'?

Ten years later (1988), in the 'Letters to the Editor' column of *The Times of India,* Z. A. Ansari wrote: 'As the 80s draw to a close, one notices some trends emerging in the political culture of India. While linguistic chauvinism is on the rise, value-based politics are in the decline. Hindu, Muslim and Sikh communalism is becoming militant by the year.'[61]

The 'Salman Rushdie Affair' (my description) finds headlines in *The Times of India* under the banner 'Banning of a Book'.[62] The 'Letters to the Editor' column gives considerable space on 10 October to a lengthy debate between professors Saiyed, Hasan, Ali, and Khan and Zafarul-Islam Khan on the topic of Aligarh versus Jamia.

To paraphrase: The group of four acknowledged that Urdu had suffered years of neglect at Jamia despite provisions in the regulations. The decline in Islamic studies they felt should be revived by the collective will of scholars rather than by official patronage. The professors supported the Jamia bill (despite certain undemocratic provisions) because of its secular thrust and because it 'will strengthen the already secular ethos of Jamia.' Z.I. Khan suggested that the Aligarh school of thought maintained that the Muslim minority would be dominated by the majority community after Independence and that its plight would be worse than under colonial rule. Jamia's complacency and cooperation with the central government had resulted in the obliteration of the unique characteristics of their institution.[63] These letters were followed by yet another on this topic written by Syed Shahabuddin, MP, who stated: 'What Ashraf has said about the educational backwardness of the Muslim community applies to the whole country. Muslim youth have equal claim to all the universities in the country but they have a preferential claim on the facilities in universities established by the Muslim community— the Aligarh Muslim University and the Jamia Millia Islamia.' (Space is given to these debates to emphasize an increased Muslim media voice that becomes evident by 1988.)

In October 1992, *The Sunday Times of India* published a seemingly outspoken article by S. Prasannarajan, pointing out that writers, including Rushdie, Saadawi, and Haider, who have questioned developments in the Islamic world, find themselves living in exile.[64] On the same day, Shams Ahsan discussed A.R. Bedar's controversial book *Seema ki Talash*. The following day, 5 October, an article appeared in *The Times of India,* which considers a search by Pakistani intellectuals for a historical identity for their country.[65]

Also in 1992, various Hindustani music recitals were held, including the Barsi Dhrupad Festival in memory of Ustad Zia Mohiuddin Dagar at the Nehru Centre. Naseeruddin Shah co-directed 'Julius Caesar' in Bombay, and Muslims featured their own section in the Matrimonial Columns advertisements in *The Times of India.*

Moving on to February 1995, M. Rahman interviewed Shiv Sena's Bal Thackeray on the topic of problems in his party and his vision for the future. The Sena leader forthrightly expressed his attitude towards India's Muslim community.[66] *India Today* addressed election issues and the ways in which they could impact India's Muslims.

Chief Minister Laloo Prasad Yadav of Bihar promised the Muslims 10 per cent reservations, in Assam Saikia promised 24 per cent, and in Karnataka and Andhra Pradesh the Congress(I) offered 27 per cent. 'For Muslims, Laloo has succeeded in creating an era of Peace,' stated Mojahidul Islam Qasmi, Chief Qazi, Imarat Shariya, Patna.[67]

No paper on Muslims in India would be complete without reference to the world of film (Bollywood), for India can boast the largest film industry in the world. By 1994, the perceived Hindu–Muslim divide had for the first time penetrated the film industry, according to Madhu Jain. Screenwriter Javed Akhtar noted: 'When it comes to the "Hindu–Muslim problem", popular Indian cinema usually shuts its eyes and turns the page, unless [the film is] the kind of saccharine *bhai bhai* treatment [in which] the Muslim characters were unbelievably angelic.'[68] In the film industry, Partition was, at the time, a taboo subject and, if and when addressed, religious identities were deliberately left ambiguous. Art, in the world of film, appeared not to lend itself to discrimination:

The influx into the Hindi film industry of such distinguished poets and writers as Sardar Ali Jafri, Kaifi Azmi, Rahi Masoom Raza and lyricists like Naushad, Majrooh Sultanpuri, Indivar and scores of others brought in the cadences and eloquence of the Urdu language to screen dialogue and songs. The Urdu language became rooted in Hindi films, from where it rapidly found a mass audience, as did the *qawwali* and the *ghazal* ... In the film industry, Muslim writers, directors, producers, actors and technicians could move up the ladder as fast as the Hindus, quite unlike what was happening in the world outside.

However, according to Madhu Jain's article (post 1992–3 Bombay), polarization had occurred. Mani Ratnam's *Bombay* drew adverse reaction in many areas of India and, according to A. Chandra writing in *India Today*, Muslim leaders sought to ban the film.[69]

In researching this section of the paper, an attempt was made to trace the degree of reference to Muslim affairs demonstrated by India's English print media. From a secular and muted approach following Partition, over the decades a more outspoken reference (albeit minimal) becomes manifest, one of frankness but as yet not challenging. Was this because (a) the works of Indian Muslim writers still did not find publication opportunities in India's press; (b) Muslim writers were by now more inclined towards mainstream India; (c) they were confining their writings to the Urdu press; (d) they were not writing seriously in which case they did not invite publication opportunities; or (e) they were bowing to what they saw inevitably as their minority role?

INDIAN MUSLIMS, THE VERNACULAR PRESS, WRITING, AND MODERNITY

A distinctive Muslim press grew in pre-Partition India as a result of a national awareness and an increased political consciousness which were engendered in India's Muslims during the late 1930s. If the push for Pakistan was to succeed, Mohammed Ali Jinnah needed to organize Muslims in order to consolidate a Muslim press. By the mid-1940s, a Muslim press had become established in the subcontinent, albeit a press plagued by poor finances, low circulation numbers, sparse advertising, shortages of newsprint, and the high cost of printing.

In his article 'The Youthful Muslim Generation and Urdu', published in the *Weekly Hindustani* in the Devnagari script, Ather Farouqui suggests that the support Jinnah gained from Aligarh Muslim University, along with that of the Uttar Pradesh elites, contributed more than anything else to the creation of Pakistan. This *shariif* community, along with the Urdu speakers of Delhi, considered themselves to be masters of the Urdu language. However at the time of Partition, there was an exodus of UP intellectuals from the area and, as a result, the political strength of the remaining (generally middle-class) Muslims suffered depletion. Many among those who remained behind succumbed to depression, perhaps troubled by what they perceived as loss of Muslim identity and by relegation to a perceived second-class social status.[70] Here I raise the question of where the blame should lie? Did those more fortunate, who rushed to the newly created state to take advantage of commercial prospects, ever stop to consider the consequences for those left behind? (This of course does not deny the tragic plight of those who became caught up in fear and hysteria and suffered equally upon their arrival in 'Pakistan'.) Farouqui suggests that during the period 1947–89, the Muslims of India were unable to unite themselves linguistically. While some identified with the 'group', others opted for 'Indianness' (their lived reality and all they really knew). However, this was to change after the Babri Masjid incident in 1992.[71]

Farouqui's article, which questions the legal status of Urdu, suggests that the Urdu language was to a certain extent available to Muslims. For example, Urdu could be used for the written submission of government office applications, on railway stations, and on billboards, if requested. Urdu language courses were offered in the madrasas (religious schools) in UP because apart from the Koranic texts (written in Arabic), Indian Muslim religious texts are written in the Urdu script. It seemed impractical to enforce the UP Assembly Second National Language Bill because Urdu-speakers in UP were largely a minority group. Although some institutions in the area supported a department of Urdu and offered Urdu at BA and MA levels, students in general did not avail themselves of classes because they were unable to write Urdu's Persianized Arabic script. Rather, they tended to take notes in Devanagari.

In a second article published in the *Weekly Hindustani*, under the title of 'Urdu Journalism and Indian Muslims', Farouqui highlights the differences that exist between the Hindi press and India's Muslims. He suggests an uneasy relationship between the two, the reason being that the national press was perceived by some to take the wrong approach to Muslim issues and that press opinions lacked foundation. The situation appeared to be different in south India. According to Farouqui, language and culture were not in contestation with regional religious values in the south: the south Indian Muslims were generally more progressive, particularly in the field of education. Since 1947, newspapers had appeared regularly in south India, and journalism had thrived. Prior to 1980, there was no place for Urdu journalism in the area Farouqui refers to as 'West India', including the Delhi area where Muslims felt they had lost the language battle. 'A wall is growing higher between India's Muslims and all of the newspapers of India connected with the majority group.'[72]

The top-selling Urdu language weekly in the 1990s was the Delhi publication *Akhbar-e-Nau*. *Qaumi Awaz*, published in Lucknow and described by Farouqui as 'the Congress paper read by Urdu speakers', ceased publication. The top-selling Urdu daily in Bombay (Mumbai) was *Inqilaab* published by the Midday Press. 'The only serious daily was *Al Jamiat*, published by editor Maulana Usman Farqlid. This also closed after the Maulana's death.'[73] The Urdu *Blitz*, which catered for the interests of Muslims India-wide, was published in Bombay along with two other successful dailies, the *Urdu Times* and the

Hindustan. Three Urdu dailies were published in Hyderabad: *Siyasat,* *Rehnuma-e-Deccan* and *Munsif.* Apropos of the aforementioned Babri Masjid incident in 1992, Farouqui states: 'During the period of the Babri Masjid movement, two more papers, the daily *Faisal Jadeed* and the weekly *Hamara Qadam* were launched. After the demolition of the mosque, this resulted in the virtual collapse of the movement for its protection, both of these papers almost ceased publication.'[74] (In Australia, the *Muslim Times*, a Sydney publication, included a page in Urdu, one in Arabic, one in one of the languages of Indonesia, and in earlier times a page on Bosnia. However this too ceased publication.)

In the Delhi publication *Akhbar-e-Nau*, in February 1990, Mahommad Hasan threw light on the recommendations of the Gujral Committee, commenting that:

In various ways, efforts will be made to complicate the issue of Urdu. The first effort will be that *Hindi–Urdu should be one whole language and the question is only one of script. Urdu script should be changed to enable easy access by all* (emphasis added).

This was unconstitutional; that is to say, it was contrary to the Constitution of India in which Hindi and Urdu are designated as two separate languages. Nowhere in the Constitution is it written that apropos of the rights of Urdu the time would come when any one person or group should select the script. Every language has the right to constitutional facilities and the right to keep the language alive within a particular script. Urdu also has this right, and the Constitution gives this guarantee. In short, from the recommendations of the Gujral Committee, the struggle for Urdu was already a thing of the future. The government had expectations that with the passage of time the enthusiasm for Urdu would dissipate and that the heat would go out of the debate. Urdu-speakers could only hope that in the final analysis, justice would one day be done.[75]

Fitrat Ansari, writing in the Lahore publication *The Nation* on the topic of India's Muslims, observed as follows: 'The true picture of Muslim politics, their understanding and psychology, is best projected by Urdu papers only.'[76] Would this preclude a couple of generations of Indian Muslims' (who had either been denied the opportunity to learn Urdu in India's educational system or had chosen to use Hindi in order to go with mainstream India) access to 'the true understanding and psychology' of their fellow Muslims? However also in *The Nation*, O.P. Shah presented an opposing view, stating that 'the National Press, as a whole, has been playing a constructive and positive role as far as Muslims are concerned. This perhaps cannot be said with surety about the language press which more often plays the so-called popular tune.'[77] Again in *The Nation*, Maulana Waheed-ud-Din Khan commented:

My complaint is not against the national Press but against the Muslim Press. At present, all Muslim newspapers are trading in protests [and] complaints, and the community is suffering. It is a fact that the present Muslim journalism is protest journalism. What are the Muslim newspapers doing? They are indulging in convincing the Muslims that they are an oppressed and deprived minority, for whom all avenues of living and progress are closed.[78]

As an aside, during approximately four years of research in Pakistan and the Northern Areas, I had the privilege of observing at first hand the various communities of the country. For this reason, questions must be raised regarding the following sweeping and misleading piece of journalism, which appeared in *The Nation*, August 1992. It read: 'Pakistanis are much better off than the citizens of any other country in South Asia.'

To start with, in the interests of responsible journalism, one has to first clearly define the term 'Pakistani' (which includes Pathans, Baluchis, Punjabis, Sindhis, and Mohajirs, extended nowadays to the Gilgitis and Baltis of the perceived 'Northern Areas'). Undoubtedly Pakistan has an affluent—and by extension well-dressed middle-class and elite, visible mainly in the relatively affluent cities of Islamabad, Karachi, and Lahore. However, scrutiny of the Karachi publication *Newsline* December 1992 revealed articles entitled 'Enslaved by the System' and 'The Living Dead' by Hasan Mujtaba, articles which described the plight of the Hari community of rural Sindh. Mujtaba wrote at the time: 'Burdened by debt they can never repay, Sindh's haris are shackled to lives of virtual slavery.'[79] An article by Nusrat Rehman appeared in the *Herald*, September 1988, describing the plight of the Thar Desert-dwellers. Rehman wrote:

'Thar has captured public attention. Stories of starvation and water scarcity have been widely reported. But Thar's crisis is not simply a drought-induced problem; it is symptomatic of a deeper change that is taking place in many of Pakistan's rural areas.'[80] In *Newsline,* November 1995, journalists S. Daudi and M. Khan stated in an article titled 'The Poor get Poorer': 'As prices continue to rise, just staying alive has become a struggle for the country's impoverished millions.'[81] In light of my own experience working in a Free Eye Clinic for the poverty-stricken in Baluchistan, the term 'Pakistani', as used in that article, requires clearer definition in terms of privilege and class. In 2007, many of Pakistan's rural dwellers, the under-privileged Balti/Urdu-speaking Balti people of the Northern Areas, for example, might well ponder the notion that they are among those 'better-off than citizens of any other country in South Asia'.

Articles written by India's Hindu (and other) journalists in the English press of the 1990s revealed such catch phrases as 'venture capitalists', 'voice-recognition devices', 'interactive TV set-to boxes', 'net-working protocols', 'Himachal Futuristics', etc. The question may be raised yet again: where in all this grand verbosity were the Muslim writers? For what reasons did their work not appear in quantities to equal the output of the Hindu writers and others? Were they given fair access to the press? Ather Farouqui suggests:

The management of the prestigious fortnightly *India Today* and also some other newspaper houses on several occasions decided to start publication of Urdu versions. However, each time Urdu editors discouraged them by presenting to them distorted facts about the Urdu readership. They were told that the Muslims did not trust the National Press and by nature tend to be 'anti-establishment'. As a result, such proposals had to be shelved.[82]

Is it that India's Muslims at the time were caught in a dilemma of continuity versus change? Is it essential that *all* of India's Muslims have access to an Urdu press? My research suggests that there are groups of Muslims residing in communities in which all ethnic groups speak the regional language, the Muslim women wear saris, all community members are peace-loving, and as a group the Muslims are barely distinguishable from the 'others'. Does lack of differentiation result in lack of bias and discrimination? De Vos and Romanucci-Ross maintain:

Social theory could ... benefit from a better understanding of why certain people insist on maintaining symbolic forms of cultural differentiation for centuries, despite a lack of political autonomy or even a particular territory. An adequate answer to this question must involve a psycho-cultural approach.[83]

According to Sumanta Banerjee, in an article addressing discrimination written in 1973 and titled 'India's Monopoly Press: A Mirror of Distortion', the press felt that papers owned by businessmen or industrialists would welcome editorial policies advancing the interests of the business community. The Press Commission also held that the bulk of those who owned and published newspapers favoured continuation of the present order, discouraged opposing views, and 'blacked out' news from the other side. Banerjee wrote at the time: '... distortions took the form of "blacking out" ... discrimination in the allotment of space and position [for] contrary views, and a disproportionate display of news ... favouring "continuance of the present order".'[84] However, it may be that discrimination in this instance did not single out any specific community.

Several notable Muslim media-persons attended a meeting of the Indian Association of Muslim Social Scientists in Bangalore in 1994. Yoginder Sikand commented: 'It was the general view of the discussants in the mass media panel that there exists a fairly widespread bias, both unwittingly as well as deliberate, in a significant section of the mass media, not just in India but in the west as well.'[85] The sensationalism and counter-productivity of sections of the Urdu tabloid press came under sharp attack. (This prompts this writer to look back at the same sensationalism that marked the Urdu press, which emerged in Karachi concomitant with the settlement of the Mohajirs there immediately following Partition.)

January 2000 saw the emergence of the daily *Milli Gazette*, a 32-page publication considered to be the only Indian Muslim media source in the English language. The standard of journalistic writing is arguably inferior to that produced by contributors to what could be termed India's 'mainstream publications'. The Aligarh Muslim University (AMU) recently introduced a course in journalism aimed at improving Muslim writers' journalistic skills. Is this a tacit recognition of the fact that Muslim writers lack the necessary skills to either compete or succeed in India's journalism community? While teaching English language to hospital staff in Mehdiabad (a village in Kharmang valley, Baltistan) in 1999, I used examples of Pakistani journalists' incorrect use of the English language to demonstrate how not to use it. So the problem of Muslim writers is not confined to India. At the same time, however, Muslims living outside of these homelands produce a far better standard of writing. One only needs to explore *Islam Online*[86] to find quality first-class Muslim contributors. Could it simply be that after having taken domicile in the diaspora, away from his/her homeland and the need to be seen to conform to the often restrictive influences that may pervade society, the writer has the freedom to hone his/her skills to a degree which is acceptable to the media in general?

In Pakistan, there is arguably a tendency to perpetuate an English Raj (outdated) style of writing, in the same way that there is a curiously nostalgic perpetuation of the institutions of English-style clubs in India, with their 'gin rummy and tiffin at four'. It must not be overlooked, however, that shifts in language use occur constantly. The British departed the subcontinent some sixty years ago, taking with them a form of language use that has undergone considerable change in the interim. For example, cars no longer 'turn turtle', they roll! However, a school of thought is emerging which believes that 'Indian English' and 'Pakistani English' are as legitimate as 'Australian English', for example. But I would suggest that 'Australian Urdu' will never be acceptable in Pakistan!

As a former student of Urdu *shairi* (poetry) the writer of this paper felt some dismay upon reading Firoz Bakht Ahmed's reporting of an 'Indo-Pak international mushaira' (published in the 1–15 May 2004 edition of the *Milli Gazette*).[87] Apart from the fact that the standard of writing fell below expectations, as evident in 'Most hilarious moments came when poets took a dig at politicians', 'pulled their legs', and 'taking *shairi* connoisseurs for a ride', the standard of composition demanded by the 'disgruntled' audience falls far below the often exquisite traditional ghazal structure and content. Certainly there is a place in Urdu shairi for comedy and satire. Along with panegyric, love themes, eroticism and bacchic odes, satire and comedy have persisted in thematic form throughout successive generations of Urdu poetry. But one questions the quality of '... *phir bhi hum good feel karen*' and '*ehlu pehlu bollywood, buddhe neta feeling good*'. One can only cast one's mind back to the mastery of Faiz.

Is it simply that today's Indian Muslim Urdu poets no longer possess either the knowledge or skills required to work within this rich (perceived) Arabo–Persian literary heritage? Is there a latent antagonism in India's younger generations towards the highly respected Ahmad Faraz's 'old and oft-repeated couplets' and does this antagonism extend to Indian Muslim journalists/writers? Do memories of the agony and separation of Partition still persist? Is this why Indian Muslim writings lack representation in the free press and why the said writers have distanced themselves, retiring into the exclusivity of the *Milli Gazette* where they may continue to produce less than quality writings in the English language?

It seems that there may in fact be more Muslim representation in India's free press in recent times. A short perusal of the columnist section of *The Times of India* revealed the rather flamboyant literary style of Rashmee Z. Ahmad writing on the topics of corporal punishment and Tony Blair holidaying in Barbados.[88] Again, it is difficult to identify the authorship of 'By our Special Correspondent' and 'By our Staff Reporter'. In a 'Special Report', in *The Times of India,* Sakina Yusuf Khan writes: 'Yes Minister? No, just do what's right'. Khan appears to be interviewing Cabinet Secretary B.K. Chaturvedi, demonstrating her interviewing skills and journalistic style, which includes terms such as the 'Cabinet Secretary's earlier "clout"' and the Principal Secretary 'calling the shots'.[89] Can it be (or not be) that this writer is an avid reader of *Time* magazine?

In the interview section of *The Times of India,* in an article titled 'Gandhi's Khandaan', Humra Quraishi interviews Asfandyar Wali Khan about his grandfather Khan Abdul Ghaffar Khan, known in his time as the 'Frontier Gandhi'.[90] In the columnist section of *The Indian Express,* Husain Haqqani provides a well-written expose of US tolerance of Pakistan's 'misplaced priorities' and lack of 'long-term stability' among other perceived vagaries of successive Pakistani government institutions.[91] Again in the columnist section of *The Indian Express,* Saeed Naqvi's 'Through their eyes and ears' is a well-constructed informative article focused on the perceived imbalance evident in western multi-media.[92]

CONCLUSION

India in 2007 is a burgeoning economy, an influential decision-maker in world political and economic affairs, a voice to be reckoned with.

Within this rapidly-expanding socio-economic framework, has Indian Muslim journalism found *its* voice, and kept equitable pace with 'others' among India's writers/journalists?

One notes the emergence of female Muslim writers with an exceptionally good command of English. Nigar Ataulla, associate editor of the Bangalore-based English-language magazine *Islamic Voice*, writes in her well-structured comprehensive article titled 'Indian Muslims and the Media' that September 11 has given rise to negative stereotyping and misinformation about Islam and Muslims in mainstream media, further adding that the Indian Muslim media *could* (my emphasis) counteract such misinformation.

Ataulla adds:

Muslim representation in the Indian media is dismal, while Muslims' share in media ownership is even more pathetic. Muslims do not have any considerable hold over the media. In northern India, several Urdu newspapers owned by Muslims have gradually closed down or lost circulation ... Muslims are yet to have any major presence in TV channel ownership ... the two or three that exist today devote a large share of time to religious issues, rather than on other social-economic issues facing the community.[93]

Ataulla further writes that several Muslim-owned newspapers are published not primarily in Urdu but in languages including Tamil, Telugu, Urdu, Kannada, Malayalam, Bengali, Gujarati, and Hindi. Success stories appear in the main to be in areas where languages other than Urdu are used. On the other hand, she claims:

... the launch of an Urdu service of UNI, the Urdu channel of Doordarshan on August 15 2006, and completion of six years of the Urdu channel 'ETV Urdu' from Hyderabad are distinct milestones of success as regards the Indian Muslim media ... The quality of Urdu journalism [has] improved in Mumbai, Bangalore, Hyderabad and Aurangabad from the late 1980s and the survival of magazines like *Urdu Mein Science, Shayar, Gagan, Sanaat-o-Harafat* from Kolkata and *Khatoon-e-Mashriq* from Delhi [among others Ataulla lists] is worth mentioning.[94]

It is difficult to assess accurately (from distant Australia) the prevailing situation vis-à-vis Indian Muslims and the free press in India. I would suggest that Muslim reticence in the past to embrace modernity has left Muslim writers in 'a catch-up' mode. The mere fact that the AMU, the Jawaharlal Nehru University, and Jamia Millia Islamia in New Delhi, along with the Osmania University in Hyderabad are introducing journalistic courses to improve Muslim writers' English-language journalistic skills reinforces this assumption. One could suggest that retiring into the exclusivity of the *Milli Gazette* will only serve to both enhance and perpetuate Muslim journalists' English language literary shortcomings.

Part of the ongoing problem may lie in the fact that Indian Muslim journalists often tend not to be research-oriented, with few able to competently address and explore today's socio-economic issues. India today, as a diverse and complex society, invites journalistic coverage of what one could term a 'smorgasboard' of issues, that is, politics, economics, religion and religious/ethnic conflict, military and security-related issues (including India's nuclear programme), personalities, arts, entertainment, history, and culture. Ataulla states that in the madrasas in which the ulema or Muslims clerics are trained, students are often kept ignorant of the contemporary social reality. They graduate unable to write on anything more than strictly religious issues.[95]

According to Ataulla, Muslims often complain that the national media is biased in its coverage of issues and events pertaining to the [Muslim] community. Is it that bias and mis-reporting are still exercised by the mainstream media, by 'others' in India? I would suggest that in the aftermath of September 11, bias and misinformation pertaining to the Islamic world may be visible in many of the world's media. Do Muslim journalists function under some form of restraint in India? Has the obsession of some with the preservation of the Urdu language diminished their ability to acquire English-language skills that can match the skills of non-Muslim Indian journalists?

As regards Urdu-language publications, according to G.D. Chandan, the shortfall in Urdu newspapers publication is 'more visible in states like Bihar, Andhra Pradesh, Maharashtra and the Punjab, areas in which Urdu language media previously enjoyed considerable popularity.' Chandan adds that although all of the states 'have accepted the three language formula, none of them has seriously and honestly put it into practice'. Whereas in 2000 the publication figure for Urdu newspapers was 61,20,317, by 2001 it had declined to 516,182.[96] Chandan further states that: '... [A] fairly large percentage of Urdu newspaper readers consisted of refugees of West Punjab who are now leaving this place one after the other. [The] new generation is ignorant of Urdu.' He stresses the important role of the Urdu language vis-à-vis promoting mutual relations with the neighbouring country of Pakistan, in which Urdu is the country's lingua franca.

It would seem that the Urdu language that played such an important role in the Partition movement—particularly in the case of the Muslims in UP—and was transported to Pakistan by the Mohajirs may simply have had 'its place in time'. The preoccupation of some Urdu writers with a 'glorious past' may not have left room for adaptation to the English-language journalistic demands of the time, of modernity. All those employed in the mass media have a role to play in the shaping of the modernity of the age, even if this requires a shift, from (but not necessarily abandoning) the perceived rich traditions and values that marked their past, to the realism of a lifestyle in which religion may be relegated to a lesser role, a lifestyle dominated by rapidly-moving technologies, materialism, and consumerism. This paper suggests that achieving success in the world of India's mass media requires Indian Muslim writers to address these challenges and to strive to surpass the journalistic skills of the nation's 'others'.

As Marshall Berman maintains:

In order for people, whatever their class, to survive in modern society, their personalities must take on a fluid and open form of this society. Modern men and women must learn to yearn for change: not merely to be open to changes in their personal and social lives but positively to demand them, actively to seek them out and carry them through. They must learn not to long nostalgically for the 'fixed fast-frozen relationships' of the real or fantasized past, but to delight in mobility, to thrive on renewal, to look forward to future developments in their conditions of life and their relations with their fellow men.[97]

NOTES

1. Khalid Hasan, *The Union and the Dancing Girl* (New Delhi: Allied Publishers, 1988), p. 46.
2. Mohammed Peer, citing M. Mujeeb, 'Urdu Language and the Indian Muslims', *Guru Nanak Journal of Sociology*, 4(2), 1983, pp. 138–49.

The Urdu language takes a Persianized Arabic script. For details about the origins of the Urdu language, see E. Dryland, *Faiz Ahmad Faiz: Poet of Social Realism* (Lahore: Vanguard, 1993).

3. A. Rahman, 'Indian Muslims—A[n] Historical Perspective', in Ratna Sahai (ed.), *Muslims in India,* produced for the Ministry of External Affairs by FORMAT, New Delhi [n.d.], pp. 4–18.

4. Mohammed Peer, 'Urdu Language and the Indian Muslims', p. 138.

5. Yunus Ahmar, 'Sarshar Siddiqi: A Poet without a Name', *Morning News,* 17 May 1983.

6. M. Peer, 'Urdu Language and the Indian Muslims', p. 138, citing M. Brecher, *Nehru: A Political Biography* (London: Oxford University Press, 1959).

7. S.K. Zaidi, 'Urdu in India: Problems and Prospects', in IIAS (ed.), *Language and Society in India—Papers and Proceedings of a Seminar* (Simla: Indian Institute of Advanced Study, 1967), p. 236.

8. Jawaharlal Nehru, 'Jawaharlal Nehru's Speeches, September 1957–April 1963' (New Delhi: Government of India, Ministry of Information and Broadcasting), p. 63. I am uncertain from Peer's references whether the year was 1963 or 1965.

9. S. Irtiza Husain, 'The Enigma of Firaq', *Newsarticle* (Pakistan), 16 August 1983.

10. Specifically the *Bombay Chronicle, The Times of India, March of India, India Today, The Hindu, Indian Horizons, The Sunday Times of India, Weekly Hindustan,* and *Nation.*

11. Sharad Karkhanis, *Indian Politics and the Role of the Press* (New Delhi: Vikas, 1981), p. 87.

12. P.N. Malhan, 'Liberty of the Press in India', *March of India,* 5(6), 1953, pp. 52–6.

13. Editorial, *Bombay Chronicle,* 11 November 1948, p. 4.

14. 'Proceedings in Hindi', *The Times of India,* 30 September 1948.

15. *The Times of India,* October 1949.

16. 'National Language—Hindustani in Both Scripts', *Bombay Chronicle,* 11 November 1948, p. 8.

17. Ibid.

18. Ibid., p. 7. There is a suggestion, of course, that Sanskrit, having been introduced by the Aryans, could also be considered a 'foreign' language.

19. *Bombay Chronicle,* 15 November 1948, p. 3.

20. *Bombay Chronicle,* 10 November 1948, p. 10.

21. A *tazia* is a replica of the mausoleum dedicated to the two Shia martyrs Hasan and Husain. It is constructed out of bamboo sticks, coloured paper and fabric.

22. *Bombay Chronicle*, November 1948, p. 9.

23. *The Times of India*, 30 September 1950.

24. S.F. Hussain, 'Muslim Wedding', *March of India*, 6, July–August 1953, pp. 60–3.

25. C.J. Chacko, 'India: A Living Democracy', *March of India*, 5(6), July–August 1953, p. 5.

26. 'Hindi in the South', *The Times of India*, 22 November 1957, p. 6.

27. *The Times of India News Service*, 11 November 1957.

28. The Mustalian Ismailis are primarily found in North Yemen.

29. *The Times of India*, 29 November 1957, p. 9.

30. *The Times of India*, 27 November 1957.

31. Tara A. Chandravarkar, 'Strictly Purdah', *The Times of India*, 26 November 1957, p. 6.

32. 'Mr. S. Narayan's Appeal', *The Times of India*, 26 November 1957, p. 5.

33. '"English Complex Must Go", says leader', *The Times of India*, 24 November 1957, p. 7.

34. S. Chakravarti, *India Today*, 28 February 1995, p. 100.

35. 'Urdu Literature', *March of India*, 11(9), September 1959.

36. K. Nath, 'Masters of the Urdu Ghazal', *March of India*, 15(1), January 1963, p. 23.

37. Inder Jit Lal, 'Khwaja Mir Dard—Famous Sufi Poet of Urdu', *March of India*, 15(9), September 1963, p. 14.

38. Anonymous, 'Aligarh Muslim University', *March of India*, 15(7), July 1963, p. 19.

39. Anonymous, *March of India*, 11(6), June 1959, p. 19.

40. Maulana Maudoodi, a Sunni Muslim cleric, opposed the creation of what he saw as Mohammad Ali Jinnah's secular Pakistan, claiming that he planned to Islamize undivided India. Founder of the Jamiat-e-Islami, Maudoodi insisted that where Islam exists, there is no place for nationalism. However, the Muslim Ulema recognize a concept of 'Islamic Nationalism'. Following Partition, Maudoodi finally relocated from India to Pakistan, the creation of which he had opposed. The Ahrar Party was a semi-military political organization in pre-Partition India.

41. The Punjab-based Ahrar Party opted not to join the Muslim League, calling it a 'party of reactionaries'. The Punjab's strong Unionist Party was outside of the League's control. President Ayub Khan, born in

Hazara, India (1907), died in Islamabad (1974). President of Pakistan from 1958–69, he was educated at Aligarh Muslim University. The Jamiat-e-Ulema-e-Hind was formed in 1919 by leading Islamic ulema (scholars). Their involvement in the Khilafat movement drew members close to Gandhi and the Indian National Congress.

42. Hamid Dalwai, 'Muslims and India', *The Times of India*, 28 October 1968, p. 6.
43. M.A. Karandikar, 'Muslims in India', *The Times of India*, 4 November 1968, p. 9.
44. 'Action against newspapers in five states', *The Times of India*, 29 October 1968, p. 8.
45. 'Persecution Bogey', *The Times of India*, 29 October 1968, p. 8.
46. Ibid.
47. 'Muslims misled by League', *The Hindu*, 19 October 1969, p. 10.
48. 'Communalism in Politics', *The Hindu*, 6 November 1969, p. 8.
49. 'Gandhi Award for Hindi Propagation', *The Hindu*, 4 November 1969, p. 14.
50. L.M. Khubchandani, 'Language Situation in India', *Indian Horizons*, 22(2), 1973, pp. 64–74.
51. *Indian Horizons*, 23(2–3), 1974, pp. 67–80.
52. C. Bakshi, 'An Alien at Home', *The Times of India*, 3 September 1978, p. 11.
53. The Dawoods, Fancys, Adamjees, Memons, Ragoonwalas, and Jaffars, among others.
54. C. Bakshi, 'An Alien at Home'.
55. 'Imam warns Janata of Minorities Issue', *The Times of India*, 11 September 1978.
56. Asghar Ali Engineer, 'As much a Romantic as a Radical', *The Times of India*, 10 September 1978, p. 13.
57. 'Confiscation of Copies of Dailies Criticised', *The Times of India*, 10 October 1978, p. 9.
58. 'Hindi is opposed for political reasons', *The Times of India*, 15 October 1978, p. 5.
59. 'Simplify Sanskrit, suggests Jatti', *The Times of India*, 15 October 1978, p. 7.
60. 'Clashes of interest in promotion of Urdu in Bihar', *The Times of India*, 17 October 1978, p. 5.
61. 'Political Trends', *The Times of India*, 3 October 1988, p. 3.
62. 'Banning of a Book', *The Times of India*, 8 October 1988, p. 6.

63. 'Jamia's Ethos' and 'Jamia, a Lesson', *The Times of India*, 10 October 1988, p. 3.

64. P. Prasannarajan, 'Children of Another Gulag', *The Sunday Times of India*, 4 October 1992.

65. 'Pak bid to rewrite history', *The Times of India*, 5 October 1992, p. 12.

66. M. Rahman, 'Bal Thackeray: I won't be CM', *India Today*, 28 February 1995, pp. 24–5.

67. Raj Kamaljha and Farzand Ahmed, 'Laloo's Magic', *Indian Today*, 30 April 1995, p. 26.

68. M. Jain, 'Reeling from the Impact', *India Today,* 15 September 1994.

69. A. Chandra, 'Mani Ratnam's film incenses Muslim Leaders of the City', *India Today*, 10 April 1995, p. 18.

70. Ather Farouqui, 'The Youthful Muslim Generation and Urdu', *Weekly Hindustani*, p. 27.

71. The Babri Masjid is believed to have been constructed in 1528 at the behest of the Mughal Emperor Babar. It was demolished by Hindu militants on 6 December 1992, the reason given being that it was believed to have been built on top of an eleventh-century Hindu temple (*Sword of Truth*, December 1999).

72. Ather Farouqui, 'Urdu Journalism and the Indian Muslims', *Weekly Hindustani,* December 1990, p. 26.

73. Ibid. (Consultant: Mr Zafar Siddiqui, *Anjuman-e-Taraqqi-e-Urdu,* Sydney, Australia.)

74. Ather Farouqui, 'The Emerging Dilemma of the Urdu Press in India: A Viewpoint', *South Asia,* 18(2), 1995, pp. 91–103. p. 96.

75. Mohammed Hasan, 'Recommendations for the Gujral Committee', *Akhbar-e-Nau,* February 1990, p. 2.

76. F. Ansari, 'Indian Muslims and the Press', *Nation*, 8 October 1993, p. 7.

77. O.P. Shah, 'National Press and Indian Muslims', *Nation*, 4 September 1993.

78. 'Indian Press and the Muslim', *Nation,* 9 July 1993, p. 18.

79. Hasan Mujtaba, 'The Living Dead', *Newsline,* December 1992, p. 49.

80. Nusrat Rehman, 'Thar: Cycle of Despair', *Herald*, September 1998, p. 71.

81. S. Daudi and M. Khan, 'The Poor get Poorer', *Newsline,* November 1995, pp. 31–4. p. 31.

82. Ather Farouqui, 'The Emerging Dilemma'.

83. G. de Vos and L. Romanucci-Ross (eds), *Ethnic Identity* (Chicago: University of Chicago Press, 1975), p. 8.

84. Sumanta Banerjee, *India's Monopoly Press* (New Delhi: IFWJ Publications, 1973), p. 83.

85. Yoginder Sikand, 'Muslims and the Mass Media', *Economic and Political Weekly*, 29(3), 1994, 2134–5.

86. Nigar Ataulla, 'Indian Muslims and the Media', Available at: mhtml: file: //E: \Khabrein_info.mht

87. Firoz Bakht Ahmed, 'Indo-Pak international mushaira', *Milli Gazette*, 1–15 May 2004.

88. *The Times of India*, Columnist Section, 29 July 2004.

89. *The Times of India*, Special Report, 29 July 2004.

90. Humra Quraishi, 'Gandhi's Khandaan', *The Times of India*, 29 July 2004.

91. Husain Haqqani, *The Indian Express*, 19 July 2004.

92. Saeed Naqvi, 'Through their eyes and ears', *The Indian Express*, 29 July 2004.

93. Nigar Ataulla, 'Indian Muslims and the Media'.

94. Ibid.

95. Yoginder Sikand, 'India's Largest English Islamic Magazine's Woman Editor', *Indian Muslims: Indian Muslims News and Information*, p. 1, Available at: http: //www.indianmuslims.info/interviews/indias_largest_english_islamic_magazines.

96. 'Reasons for decline of Urdu journalism', *Milli Gazette Online*, citing G.D. Chandan, Available at http: //www.milligazette.com/Archives/2005/01–15July05-Print-Edition.

97. Marshall Berman, *All that is Solid Melts into Air* (London: Verso, 1983), p. 88.

13

Islam and the West
Ominous Misunderstandings

Susan B. Maitra

For some time now the Western press has been busy building up Islam and Muslims as the new public enemy number one. This a campaign that began, at least, with the revolution in Iran in 1979, and was carried forward during the early 1980s via periodic crises over Libya. It got a final big boost with the Western assault on Iraq in 1990. The propaganda campaign is taking roots in the fertile ground of the ignorance of Westerners about Islam and its history, and in the midst of a worldwide crisis of economic stagnation and moral and institutional breakdown, an environment in which scapegoats are eagerly sought by discredited and corrupted governments. In the meantime, the collapse of the Soviet Union and the Berlin Wall signalled the end of the post-Cold War era, and public perceptions of the so-called New World Order are increasingly coming to be associated with a confrontation between Islam and the West.

To allow this confrontation to proceed would be the greatest folly for Westerners and Muslims alike. As I shall try to show, it is not a real conflict—the problem is not a clash of religious views and beliefs. The problem is geopolitics, or the rule of international relations by the overt and covert activity of private elites who use religion (like money and other things) as a tool of manipulation of entire peoples in their game of maintaining world dominance, endlessly pitting one group or region against the other. Now, in the absence of the East–West (communists versus non-communists) conflict, these elites are trying to set up the 'Muslim World' (read, fundamentalist) as the chief adversary of the 'Christian West'.

The press is for the most part a handmaiden in this sinister business. Except for those cases of writing involving planting of false or inflammatory information and analysis, the press is generally compromised by its craving for sensationalism and its perceived need to be at the front of whatever bandwagon is currently going through town. The commercial situation of the press drives this in part. But the notion that the press should somehow reflect or speak for so-called 'public opinion'—as opposed to carrying out an educational mission guided by the search for truth—tends to eliminate the critical faculty. As a result, this terribly powerful medium, which admittedly shapes what most people think about the world, performs a kind of brainwashing function, including a worldview that has little to do with reality.

VILIFYING ISLAM: 1993

A review of some high points of the 1993 campaign to vilify Islam in the United States will make clear the concerted nature of this operation and the critical role of the press in it.

On 26 February, a powerful bomb ripped through the World Trade Center, killing five and injuring more than 1,000, and causing billions of dollars in damages and lost business for corporations and government agencies operation in the lower Manhattan financial district. The incident triggered a media barrage about 'Islamic fundamentalism' as the gravest threat to the United States. The first to claim that Islamic fundamentalists were behind the bombing was the News Network reporter Wolf Slitzer, a former reporter for *Jerusalem Post*.

Days after the blast the Federal Bureau of Investigation (FBI) arrested one Mohammed Salameh, a follower of Sheikh Omar Abdel Rahman, a blind Egyptian cleric living as a permanent resident in the United States after a series of missions back and forth to Afghanistan during the 1980s. Rahman, it was charged by US officials months later (in June), was the mastermind of the fundamentalist World Trade Center bombing, and, with the Sudanese mission to the United Nations (UN), was also plotting to bomb the UN headquarters and kill Egyptian President Hosni Mubarak. The charges propelled the blind cleric from obscurity to being dubbed the 'Khomeini of Egypt', and his expected deportation to Egypt, an action which will ensure that he acquires the status of an Islamic super-hero or a martyr. Significantly, in a meeting with newspaper editors on 26 May, the Egyptian President Hosni Mubarak charged that the Sheikh has been a Central Intelligence Agency (CIA) agent since his days in Afghanistan.

Heedless of such fine details, Western media coverage of the ongoing wave of 'Islamic terrorism' in Egypt, attributed to Rahman and Sudan, has been propagandistically preparing Europeans and Americans to expect President Mubarak's overthrow.

On 14 June the *Wall Street Journal* declared that the Mubarak regime's days were numbered. On 23 June the FBI announced it has 'crushed' the plot to blow up the UN and kill President Mubarak: of the eight persons arrested, several were associated with Rahman and six were Sudanese nationals. ABC 'Nightline' the following evening claimed that the bomb plot was aided by two Sudanese diplomats at the UN. On 1 July Sheikh Rahman was detained in the US, pending deportation to Egypt. Attention then shifted to Sudan, now established as a fundamentalist and terrorist country. After several months of propaganda about it being taken over by Iranian fundamentalists, and after the World Bank had frozen lending and the International Monetary Fund (IMF) suspended the country, Sudan was put on the US State Department's 'State Terror List' on 18 August. A few days later, *US News and World Report* claimed that Sudan was aiding Somalia's General Mohammed Aideed, another recent target of the Anglo-Americans.

In the midst of this, in April, a book called *Target America* appeared in the US. The book describes itself as 'the full story of who declared a holy war against America and Canada, and why.' The author, Yossef Bodansky, identified as an 'international terrorism expert', is director of the House Republican Task Force on Terrorism and Unconventional Warfare. Left unsaid anywhere in the book is the fact that Bodansky is the former editor of the Israeli Air Force magazine or that he was implicated in the Jonathan Pollard spy scandal. (Pollard was arrested when caught red-handed stealing secret US documents for Israel in 1985, and it is widely acknowledged that Bodansky may have been Pollard's controller.)

Here is how this 'terrorism expert' described the threat to the United States:

The explosion that shook the World Trade Center, and the rest of America, was only the beginning .... a prelude to an escalation in Islamist terrorism in the United States and Canada. The terrorist sponsoring states led by Iran, Syria and Sudan consider international terrorism an indispensable instrument of state policy. Moreover, the decline of the war in Afghanistan enabled scores of 'Afghans' to redirect their attention and zeal to Islamist causes, from Kashmir to Bosnia-Hercegovina, from Algeria to the United States and Canada.

Bodansky's book is a good summary of the message being delivered through the media to the American people. It is the 'politically correct' view of the day, an accurate reflection of what most people in America now believe.

In this vignette it is clear that in the interplay of propaganda and incident, the public is being led to believe that Islam equals Muslim fundamentalist equals terrorist equals threat to our way of life. Thank goodness the FBI and the State Department are determined to crush this menace and protect the American people! The equation is simple, no matter how false to reality.

A CONTRADICTORY REALITY

And false it is, for sure. Apart from the editing of his own bio-data, Bodansky's 'full story' on Islamic terrorism nowhere explains how it is that the fearsome terrorist mastermind, Sheikh Rahman, managed to get a series of entry visas into the US, and then a permanent residency permit or green card. Further, Bodansky nowhere mentions the peculiar behaviour of US officials in Egypt, for example, where Ambassador Robert Pollitreau made increasingly insistent demands on President Mubarak to liberalize the economy and ease up repression of the Islamic movement, and how the CIA station chief James Soriano's met with Islamic fundamentalist representatives, including those the State Department condemned as tied to 'Sudanese terrorism'.

Take the case of Sudan, now officially a 'terror-sponsoring' nation. Why is it that when announcing the decision to blacklist Sudan on 18 August, State Department officials could not explain why it was not placed on the list in April, when the annual list (which also includes Iran, Iraq, Libya, Cuba, and North Korea) was released? Why is it that State Department officials could not cite what new evidence had been gathered since April justifying the decision? Interestingly, Sudan was one of the small group of nations that refused to back the Anglo-American war on Iraq, and since that time has increasingly been targeted by the US and the British media and by the myriad of non-governmental organizations that makes it their business to destabilize sovereign nations.

That terrorism in the US and elsewhere may be making a comeback cannot be discounted. But who is running it, and why? An actual terror wave was signalled on 24 June, when Turkish embassies, missions, and businesses in 29 European cities were simultaneously attacked, with some offices briefly occupied and hostages taken. But the assailants, the so-called Kurdish Workers Party, like the fearsome Sheikh Rahman and other Middle East terrorist organizations, emphatically including some of the 'Islamic' ones, are infiltrated if not covertly steered by Anglo-American and Israeli agents. It is the same crowd that funnelled thousands of Arabs into Pakistan in the 1980s to be trained by US Special Forces and Mossad and then fed into the Afghan resistance—the bulwark against Soviet communist expansion. It is the same crowd that is now taking advantage of that pool of now-unemployed irregular warriors and mercenaries for use in orchestrating the projected war between the 'Christian West' and Islam.

THE SCOURGE OF GEOPOLITICS

The Anglo-American elite and their Israeli juniors play the game of world politics according to the doctrine of geopolitics, a doctrine spelled out by British imperial strategists in the late nineteenth and early twentieth centuries.

Essentially a rationalization for the maintenance of the British Empire, the doctrine's theoretical premise draws heavily on two apologists for British colonial rule, the Reverend Thomas Malthus and Charles Darwin. Malthus, it will be recalled, propagated the unscientific theory that population growth will necessarily outstrip increases in agricultural production—and that famines, wars, epidemics, etc., were not only natural but necessary for stability. Proceeding from an identical view of man, Darwin argued that life was a battle for survival that only the physically fittest would win. Geopolitics postulates that geographical, climatic, and demographic factors determine the course of history. Historically and in international relations, geopolitics consistently assigns priority to 'objective' factors of space and human masses over such 'subjective' factors as cultural and technical development. Wealth, in this view, like that of the eighteenth-century physiocrats, is defined exclusively as the organic and inorganic bounty of the soil. Thus it is the 'objective factor' of the scarcity of land and raw materials compared to the growing population that takes priority in determining policy over such 'subjective' factors as mankind's ability to improve his condition by extending available resources through scientific and technological advance. In this view there will always be battles among nations and peoples for land and raw materials.

Friedrich Ratzel (1844–1904), whose book *Political Geography* (1897) gave the overall theoretical foundation of geopolitics, described the 'necessary' struggle among peoples in the following words:

For man and his history the size of the land surface is un-changeable. The number of people grows, but the soil on which they must live and work remains always the same ... [The land is] the only material cohesiveness in each people ... In the progress of history this bond does not tend to become loose through the progressive liberation of intellectual forces, but rather it grows with the number of people. From this also comes historically the growth of the tendency of the people to become more tightly bonded with the soil, so to speak to take root in it. Ample space confers the protection of distance to the life forms which spread out over it. Therefore we see in the competition of stronger and weaker peoples, that the weaker ones are more quickly consigned to narrower spaces. We may seek a formula which shall express certain aspects, at any rate, of geographical caution in universal history ... The actual balance of political power at any given time is of course, the product, on the one hand, of geographical conditions, both an economic and strategic, and on the other hand, of the relative number, virility, equipment and organization of the competing peoples. And the geographical quantities in the calculation are more measurable and more nearly constant than the human.

The doctrine of geopolitics is reflected systematically in British foreign policy since the turn of the century, and continues to dominate its international policy making to date. At the end of the nineteenth century, the British leadership recognized that the economic, scientific-technical, and military basis of the power of the British Empire was fast dwindling in comparison with the United States on the one hand and the major nations of continental Europe (Germany, Russia, and France) on the other. A round table was convened at the top level of the British oligarchy, to which Cecil Rhodes, Lord Milner, Lord Grey, Lord Rothschild, and others belonged, and which formulated a policy of 'new imperialism' for the empire. Halford Mackinder, the geopolitical strategist, was a member of this group, sometimes called 'Milner's Kindergarten'.

The main goal of British diplomacy before World War I and indeed for the whole of the nineteenth century had been to prevent by any means a continental convergence of interests among France, Germany, and Russia. After 1871, in particular, when Germany took over the leading role on the continent from France, British strategists found themselves faced with a new kind of 'danger'. The sweeping industrial–technical progress taking place on the continent, especially in transportation technology, offered the prospect that mutual economic interests would increasingly subordinate rivalries among the three powers. And, in particular, the Trans-Siberian and Berlin–Baghdad railway called into question the British domination of international trade by sea.

Mackinder came up with suitable geopolitical categories for this: he divided the Eurasian space into the 'heartland' proper (Russia) and a west-central European 'Rimland', which stretched over the Mediterranean into the Middle East. In this way the Balkan peninsula emerged as the area of confrontation in which the most frequent and long-lasting tensions among Germany, Russia, and France were kindled in the decades before World War I. It is no accident that the conflicts in the Balkans became the trigger for World War I, in which the three great powers of the continent butchered one another mercilessly.

Two World Wars and Beyond

The defeat of Germany in 1918 achieved Great Britain's main geopolitical goal for a new balance of power on the continent, and led to its overall weakening. The Treaty of Versailles imposed new exactions on defeated Germany, and the onerous reparations— not unlike today's IMF 'condititionalities'—sowed the seeds for World War II.

What 'Milner's Kindergarten' also realized in the early years of the twentieth century was that it would be futile to challenge the United States militarily for a third time, having lost the wars of 1776–83 and 1812–14. Instead, British diplomacy set about turning the United States into a partner and close ally of the British empire. Taking off on the work of the American geopolitical strategist, Admiral Alfred T. Mahan, Halford Mackinder postulated a geopolitically based identity of interests between American naval power and the British empire. The so-called insular crescent and outer continents constituted a kind of natural opposition to the Eurasian heartland, according to Mackinder. If a nation or alliance of nations were to achieve hegemony over the Eurasian continent, this would be a mortal threat to the sea power of the 'World Island'.

After the fall of France in 1940, Winston Churchill asserted that, given the new situation of the alliance of the sea powers (Great Britain and the United States), the more immediate priority was to bring down Germany. By 1945 Nazi Germany was totally vanquished, but the victory had essentially been won by the United States and Stalinist Russia. Great Britain played only a secondary role by now, and its empire was getting harder and harder to hold together. Great Britain alone could no longer direct the 'concert of Europe' or enforce the balance-of-power policy on its own. However, Great Britain could induce the American leadership to carry forward the geopolitical premises of the Treaty of Versailles under the new post-war conditions in the form of the Yalta system.

The Eurasian landmass was radically partitioned by the Iron Curtain cutting straight through Germany and Europe. The heartland was surrendered to the Soviet Russian Empire, and the west-central European Rimland was placed under the direct control of the Anglo-American sea powers. Thus the British leadership, through its 'special relationship' with America, held on to a decisive influence over the fate of Europe. And the foreign policy establishment of the United States from George Kennan through Henry Kissinger and down to George Bush and Bill Clinton think in the categories of Halford Mackinder, the geopolitician.

The fall of the Berlin Wall in 1989 ripped the foundation out from under the Yalta system, an earth-shaking development which brought us to the situation we face today. Ending the division of Europe and Germany meant that Europe's economically drained East could not cope up with the economically strong central-western Europe. Out of the economic combination, not only could the reconstruction of the East be accomplished relatively quickly and practically, but at the same time, proposals going in that direction, such as the 'productive triangle' programme of American statesman, economist, and founder of *Economic Intelligence Review* (EIR), Lyndon LaRounche, would have had a 'locomotive effect' to put the world economy as a whole back on its feet. But in the world of geopolitics, such a developmental possibility was instinctively perceived as a nightmare, an acute threat to the Anglo-American powers.

According to the absurd premises of geopolitics, France, Germany, and the former satellite states of the Soviet empire had to be prevented from proceeding with the real economic and infrastructural reconstruction of the 'Eurasian economic zone'. Such a great zone of economic development would mean, supposedly, a shift of world economic weight to the disadvantage of the economically weakened US and Great Britain—as if the US and Great Britain could not constructively participate in the rebuilding of the Eurasian zone to their own real economic advantage! Instead, according to the foolish and dangerous doctrine of geopolitics, the reconstruction of Europe was to be rejected and obstructed. Instead of optimism and hard work in the former Eastern Europe, there was cynicism and anger and mounting political instability. Instead of optimism and regeneration in Western Europe, there was frustration and despair. And, hardly surprising, there was war.

The Gulf War—cleverly engineered by the Bush administration—drained Europe's coffers. And just four months after its end, the war in former Yugoslavia began. For more than a year, the nations of Europe sat by, at best, while the hideous spectacle of genocide in the name of 'ethnic cleansing' played nightly on the television news. Of course the Balkan war had origins in its own internal, centuries-old conflicts. But that is only part of the truth about this war. The decisive truth, the only thing which explained the Anglo-Americans' open support for the war's continuation, is that since the end of the nineteenth century Serbia has been 'reared' as a geopolitical counterweight by the British, French, and Russians to Germany and the Hapsburg monarchy. The ruthless domination of the Serbs over the other south Slavic peoples has been systematically promoted since 1919 in the interest of a Yugoslavia as the strongest possible geopolitical counterweight against Germany.

Precisely in this geopolitical continuity lay the attitude of the governments of London, Washington, Paris, and the Moscow elite in June 1991. Soviet Defence Minister Dmitri Yasov, US Secretary of State James Baker, and Major and Chirac's governments encouraged the Serbian leadership to frustrate Slovenian and Croatian independence. In the spring of 1992 the same thing occurred with Bosnia-Herzegovina. The additional geopolitical 'benefit' of the

Serbian communal holocaust against Bosnian Muslims in the name of 'ethnic cleansing' is a massive provocation of the Muslim *Ummah* and a powerful weapon in the hands of communalists within the Muslim fold who wish to grab the bait for their own purposes. For two years, the endless Carrington-Owen-Vance negotiations offered a diplomatic cloak to Serbian aggression to carry forward and widen its Greater Serbian scope of conquest. The result is a festering wound in the heart of Europe, and a situation which, along with the consequences of the obstruction of reconstruction efforts in Eastern Europe and the Soviet Union, could help trigger World War III.

GEOPOLITICS CLOSER TO HOME

At about the time that the British elite's 'Kindergarten' began the drive to harness American muscle to the British imperial brain, other major projects of geopolitical significance were underway at the Empire's newly established Arab Bureau and the Crown's India Office. At the time, the Arab Bureau's best-known operative, the famous T.E. Lawrence 'of Arabia', was at work in the Hijaz region of the Western Arabian Peninsula to encourage an Arab independence movement aimed at the disintegration of the Ottoman empire. In the words of T.E. Lawrence:

If the Sultan of Turkey were to disappear then the Caliphate by the common consent of Islam would fall to the family of the prophet, the present representative of which is Hussein, the Sharif of Mecca ... Hussein's activities seem beneficial to us, because it matches with our immediate aims, the breakup of the Islamic bloc and the disruption of the Ottoman Empire, and because the states he would set up to succeed the Turks would be as harmless to ourselves as Turkey was. If properly handled the Arab states would remain in a state of political mosaic, a tissue of jealous principalities incapable of cohesion, and yet always ready to combine against an outside force.

As it happened, Lawrence and his patrons in the British oligarchy did not figure in Kemal Ataturk in their plan to reduce the Ottoman empire to smithereens in the immediate post-World War I period, but other projects were afoot which would fructify in the smouldering ashes of World War II.

Earlier, in the mid-nineteenth century, in India, where the East India Company had taken the place of Muslim and Hindu kings to conquer and loot the region, a joint Hindu–Muslim uprising against

British colonial rule—the so-called 1857 Mutiny—had been put down through bribery and force. It was at this time that the effort to drive an unbridgeable wedge between these two communities on the Indian subcontinent was made top priority. The promotion of Muslim separatism—which later became the so-called two-nation theory—by the British India Office and its minions took up from the Arab Bureau's more extensive experience in manipulating the myriad Arab tribal, ethnic, and religious groups.

The Partition of India in 1947, institutionalized a rift between Hindus and Muslims which had not existed previously and which took more than fifty years to inculcate, was a signal success from the standpoint of Anglo-American geopoliticians. In the same period, the engineering of the sudden declaration of the state of Israel scored a geopolitical success in the Middle East. In both cases, ethnic and religious differences were exploited to serve the strategic agenda of a foreign imperial power, with long-lasting negative consequences for the peoples involved. In both cases, institutions, no less than states, were set up, arbitrarily, to perpetuate the consequent strife and to act as avenues of intervention for the imperial powers in the area. The Partition of India, like the Balfour Declaration and all that led up to it, had the effect of establishing a permanent open wound in the body politic of an important region of the globe. These permanently festering wounds would consume the energies and attentions of the population as well as the political and spiritual leaderships of these regions for the next fifty years or so, frustrating all healing efforts, and creating a perpetual drain of funds and energy from the urgent post-war tasks of cooperative nation building.

The Kashmir conflict, now pompously decried as an example of 'ethnic and religious conflict' by no less than the American President from a podium at the United Nations, is a case in point. The origins and perpetuation of this dispute betray its classification as an 'ethnic and religious conflict'. The Partition was a classic 'divide-and-conquest' geopolitical manoeuvre by the British, which an egotistical Jinnah embraced for his own reasons and which a tired and gullible Congress leadership accepted. It was intended to permanently set Muslims and Hindus against each other in the region and to make sure that the smaller of the new states remain dependent on Western protection. By an outrageous perversion of reason, the arbitrary establishment of two nations where one had existed for centuries was intended to establish the 'one country, two nations' slogan as truth.

One look at the map shows that Jammu & Kashmir is in a most strategic location—almost like a cockpit from which three large nations, China, India, and Pakistan, could be watched and interfered with. Today, in the post-Cold War days, Kashmir provides a close lookout on Afghanistan and the nations of Central Asia, which are now in a highly unstable state. There is no question that whoever controls Central Asia—and to some geopoliticians it is an easier prospect than controlling China or India—controls not only vast amounts of raw materials but also a highly valuable piece of real estate, strategically speaking.

Indeed, before the gunfire from the 1947 raiding party from Pakistan had subsided, a proposal to make Kashmir an independent nation was circulating over tables in New York and London, and was being advocated in Srinagar, not to mention the fact that the Indian governor of the northern Kashmir province of Gilgit was taken prisoner as the raid began by the British Commander of the Gilgit Scouts, Major Brown, who had suddenly switched loyalty to Pakistan! The long-standing British interest in Gilgit is a matter of historical record. According to Karan Singh, scion of the erstwhile royal family of Kashmir, the British had 'pressurized' has father into leasing the Gilgit Agency to them for 60 years in 1935.

Note that the uprising in Kashmir is undeniably fuelled to a certain extent both by intervention from across the border in Pakistan and by arbitrary governance on the part of India, but not being waged for the glory of Islam or on behalf of the Kashmiri Muslim community as a whole. The fact is that a section of Kashmiris, who happen to be Muslims, are trying to carve out a separate state for themselves. They have been aided and abetted by interested parties thousands of miles away, whose commitment is neither to Islam nor to the Kashmiris. There is little doubt that once Kashmir is taken out of Indian bands, the militants will train their guns on the authorities and institutions of Pakistan Occupied Kashmir. There is ample evidence of this in the form of Sunni–Shia conflicts and the resentment among Pakistani Kashmiris against the proposition of merging Azad Kashmir into Pakistan.

An independent Kashmir has several other attractions for the geopoliticians of Washington and London. A nominally Muslim, independent nation having broken away from India would give new authority to the old two-nation theory, which suffered a serious loss of credibility when Muslim Bangladesh was forced to separate from Muslim Pakistan, it will be recalled. Even more important, an independent Kashmir will provide an opportunity to meddle in the otherwise impregnable defence of China. Attempts have been made to tamper with the Uighur Muslims of Xinjiang, but with little success so far. An independent Kashmir, emerging after a fierce struggle with, first, India, and later Pakistan may provide the necessary inspiration to the Uighurs in China.

An Alternative to Geopolitics

One must conclude that exposure and overturning of the geopolitical worldview is not only long overdue but quite urgent, and that a more appropriate strategic doctrine needs to be adopted to govern relations among nations and the making of policies—no less than a grand strategic design which counters the method employed by the Anglo-Americans throughout this century is required.

The need for a broad ecumenical dialogue and movement on the part of the world's great religions to accomplish this is defined not only by the immediate need to head off the planned bloody confrontation between Islam and the 'Christian West' but also because the doctrine of geopolitics that is pushing mankind toward the abyss is based on a concept of man that is totally immoral and unacceptable to any genuine human being.

Geopolitics is based on the premise that man is essentially a talking beast, a mean creature of instinct, who is born, fights to consume as much as he can of limited resources, and then dies. For the geopoliticians' man, knowledge is sense-certainty—such things as reason, truth, charity, and the meaning of life do not exist. The British philosopher Thomas Hobbes described the 'natural' relations among such individuals as well as the states they form as a 'war of all against all'. In the world of geopolitics, might makes right.

The point of departure, then, for defining an alternative to geopolitics must be the concept of man. What distinguishes man absolutely from all other species of creation is his high capacity for reason, that he was made in the image of 'God', a concept of perfection, with the capacity to generate ever more adequate hypotheses, which when applied in the material realm lead to a more effective domination of the physical universe and result in the physical bases for mankind to grow and flourish. The survival and advance of mankind is proof of the coherence between the laws of human reason and nature.

For example, contrary to the propaganda of pagan interest groups, the problem in the developing countries is not one of overpopulation, since their population density is mostly only a tiny percentage of that of the most highly developed industrial nations. The problem is that the existing technologies are being denied to the larger part of humanity—this is what is openly called technological apartheid. There are not too many human beings, but as a result of neo-Malthusian policies, agricultural and industrial capacities have dropped below the level required to sustain the actually living individuals on an adequate level. A continuation of these monetarist economic policies is threatening to lead to the depopulation of entire continents, and could eventually lead to the collapse of human civilization. Mankind is the only species in creation, which has the capacity to wilfully increase its potential population density, but at the same time it is the species which must do this as the precondition for continued existence. Because at each level of development, the so-called natural resources are relatively finite; their development becomes relatively too expensive, so that a continuation of production on the same technological level indeed reaches relative 'limits' to growth.

The population potential on the Earth at the level of the 'hunting-and-gathering' society was only 5–10 million individuals because a specific number of square kilometres are necessary to maintain every individual. It was only the unique, continued ability of man to again and again generate scientific and technological progress on the basis of his creative reason that, applied in the productive process, always led to renewed definitions of what represented natural resources and to a related increase in the potential population density of the society.

The survival of a society depends on the condition that the physical standard of living with respect to nourishment, healthcare, education, etc., increases per capita, and that life expectancy also increases, which is reflected in per capita and per square kilometre energy use in production and consumption. Technological progress and the increase in the potential population density are existentially necessary—because of the increasing division of labour. They are not a choice, but part of evolution as a law. When mankind follows this law, there is progress; when he violates it, society collapses as it is doing now.

Thus, contrary to the geopolitician's claim that a society's wealth lies in its raw materials and its right to extract usury, the only source of wealth in a society is the creative capacities of its population. Therefore it is in the highest self-interest of the state to develop all the creative potentials of its citizens to the maximum. A true definition of human rights therefore is not only the inalienable right of each individual to life, food, housing, employment, etc.—to 'development' as the Non-Aligned Movement (NAM) had championed it—but also the inalienable right of each individual to develop all the creative potentials embedded within him or her, not as limited self-interest but because individuals contribute optimally to the benefit of society and the improvement of life for coming generations.

The nation which is committed to this principle, and which pushes the material and intellectual development of its own citizens to the maximum, will readily recognize that similarly maximal development of all other nations is in its own national interest. On this basis there is a community of principle—namely, maximal self and mutual development—among nations.

The sovereignty of the nation state so committed must be upheld absolutely. Fuzzy notions of 'world government' and other slogans whose effect is to render people vulnerable to arbitrary foreign intervention and manipulation will not suffice. Though the modern nation-state, which is based on a common language or languages, a common culture, and common duty to participate in self-government is a relatively new institution, it has proven the most efficient means by which the reason of the individual participates in the affairs of mankind and through which a rational deliberation of a people together over their own affairs can take place. Working practically to achieve such a reordering of world affairs would seem to be the most appropriate way for people from different cultures and religions to strive together, as in a race, toward all that is good.

REFERENCES

Breda, Joseph. 'Sudan is Next Target for Assault by New World Order', *Economic Intelligence Review*, 3 September 1993, p. 12.

Brewda, Joseph. 'Mossad Script Sets US Against Islam' [Book Review], *Economic Intelligence Review*, 23 July 1993, p. 58.

H. LaRouche, Jr, Lyndon . *The Science of Christian Economy and Other Prison Writings* (Washington DC: Schiller Institute, 1991).

_____. 'The Planet Cannot Survive Without a New Golden Renaissance', *The New Federalist*, 20 September 1993.

Liebig, Michael. 'Geopolitics: the Root of Bush's Tantrum in November 1989', *Economic Intelligence Review*, 16 April 1993, p. 18.

Mirak-Weissbach, Muriel. 'Islam: Friend or Foe?', *Economic Intelligence Review*, 5 March 1993 (Part I), p. 49; *Economic Intelligence Review* 19 March 1997 (Part II), p. 12.

_____. 'Why the Israel–Palestine Accord Must Succeed', *Economic Intelligence Review*, 17 September, p. 18.

Schlanger, Harley. 'Why British Geopolitics Will Lead Inevitably to World War III', [Book Review], *The New Federalist*, 30 August 1993, p. 6.

Steinberg, Jeffrey. 'Trade Center Bombing: Strategy of Tension?', *Economic Intelligence Review*, 12 March 1993, p. 70.

Zakaria, Rafiq. *The Struggle Within Islam* (New Delhi: Viking [India], 1988).

Zepp, Helga. 'For an Ecumenical Dialogue Based on an Economic Science in Cohesion with the Laws of God's Creation', A speech delivered to the International Conference on Religions in Khartoum, Sudan, 26 April 1993. Reprinted in *Economic Intelligence Review*, 14 May 1993, p. 41.

'Why U.N. Plans for World Government Must be Stopped', *Economic Intelligence Review* Special Report, 1993.

PART III
MUSLIM JOURNALISM
A PHENOMENAL DICHOTOMY

14

Urdu Newspapers in India
Waiting for Citizen Kane?

Robin Jeffrey

Spreading across India after the end of the Emergency in 1977, technological change in the form of the personal computer and offset press revolutionized the newspaper industry. The circulation of daily newspapers in all languages trebled between 1976 and 1992, from 9.3 million to 28.1 million; and the dailies-per-thousand people ratio doubled, from 15 daily newspapers per 1,000 people to 32 per 1,000.

Regular reading of something called 'news' both indicates and causes change. Expansion of competing newspapers clearly signals the vitality and growth of capitalism: newspapers have owners and owners must have advertisers. The changes of the past 20 years are obvious yet largely unstudied. This essay is part of a larger project to map, analyse, and try to understand the transformation of the Indian-language newspaper industry.

Of all the Indian-language newspaper industries, Urdu poses the most intriguing questions, and, ultimately, best highlights the

Table 14.1: Population Change among Urdu-Speakers and
Newspaper Change in Urdu, 1961–91

	1961	1971	1981	1991
Urdu speakers (millions)	22.0 (estimated)	28.6	35.3	43.0 (estimated)
Urdu papers daily circulation (thousands)	303	376	734	1,440
Urdu dailies per thousand	14	11	21	33

Sources: Statistical Outline of India, 1989–90 (Bombay: Tata Services, 1989), p. 44 and SOI, 1984, p. 42. *Press in India* for relevant years.

way in which capitalism—and its companion, the modern state—affect the way people speak, read, and write. From one perspective, the place of Urdu in India can be seen as a distorted reflection of the place of English. Both are used all over India. Both are sometimes portrayed as the languages of conquerors or traitors. But where English is considered to be the language of the wealthy, Urdu is now regarded as primarily a language of the poor, particularly of poor Muslims.

As a foreigner, I wrestle with the questions 'What is Urdu?' and 'What is Hindi?' What I know is that when fellow travellers on a train or bus in north India want to be kind to me, they will generously but falsely say: 'You speak very good _____', and they will fill in the blank with the name of the language they esteem—either 'Hindi' or 'Urdu'. My halting remarks about the price of papayas or the punctuality of trains will have been scraped from the pigeonholes of my mind where they were deposited thirty years ago through study of a grammar book called *Conversational Hindi–Urdu*. Obviously I speak both languages. (Some might say I am torturing both.) Mahatma Gandhi made the distinction in a way that I can understand: 'Hindi, Hindustani and Urdu are different names for the same speech just as dialects of Cornwall, Lancashire, and Middlesex are different names for the same language.'[1] Speakers and writers of 'High Urdu' and 'High Hindi' can no doubt make themselves as unintelligible to each other as a Scot from Glasgow to a Black American from Harlem; but they can, if they choose, also make themselves readily understood. As I understand it, 'Hindi' and 'Urdu' have the same grammar and a common basic vocabulary; differences in pronunciation of some sounds begin to mark one from the other ('j' and 'z', for example); and for more sophisticated vocabulary, those who would speak 'Hindi' reach into Sanskrit and those who would speak 'Urdu' into Persian and Arabic. The most contentious difference—over script—has been made acute by the printing press and bureaucratic government. Akbar and Ranjit Singh were, we are told, illiterate. At the beginning of the nineteenth century, a number of writing systems were available in which the language of north India could have been recorded, but by the early twentieth century only two were realistic candidates: Devanagari and Perso-Arabic.[2]

The story of Urdu in India after Independence illustrates the role of governments and capitalists in language evolution. National and state governments have been cruelly kind to the Perso-Arabic script. At one level, they have patronized it: Urdu newspapers readily get government recognition and the perks that go with it because this has seemed a painless way to please Muslim voters. But no government has done what is crucial to make a script flourish under capitalism: use it as the chief script of schools and administration. At the same time, the association of Perso-Arabic with Muslims has led capitalist advertisers to associate it with people who are mostly poor. Thus commercial advertising for Urdu newspapers does not come easily. Part of the outcome is the intriguing paradox examined below: according to government figures, the circulation of Urdu dailies has risen steadily over the past twenty years;[3] according to commercial figures, circulation of Urdu dailies has declined noticeably. Strangely, both may be correct.

Virtually everyone who writes about Urdu and Urdu newspapers contends that the language and the industry are failing fast. Yet according to the Government of India's figures, the circulation of Urdu dailies grew from about 400,000 copies a day in 1974 to 1.5 million a day in 1994, an increase of 275 per cent, higher than the total rise for Indian dailies in all languages.[4] In 1991, the ratio of Urdu dailies to Urdu speakers was about 30 daily newspapers to every thousand speakers (30:1000)—about the same as the national average and better than the ratio for, say, Bengali or Tamil (both roughly 20:1000).

However, the figures of the Audit Bureau of Circulations (ABC)—the figures of commerce—tell a different story. The total circulation of Urdu dailies affiliated to the ABC fell in the 1977–94 period, from 128,000 to 113,000 copies.[5] The number of Urdu dailies belonging to the ABC also fell, from five in 1976 to four in 1994.[6]

What was happening? Observers of the Urdu press have long proclaimed that it was going through 'the process of a slow, painful death'.[7] Equipment was ancient, journalists poorly paid, and owners unscrupulous.[8] Urdu newspapers, according to a Muslim critic, were 'prone to reinforce a sectarian and emotional outlook among readers'.[9] The main task of the tiny, threadbare staff of most Urdu newspapers was 'to select ... stories from various newspapers and mould them ... so that they appear provocative and anti-Muslim'.[10] And the numbers of people who could read the Perso-Arabic script were said to be falling fast, since it was neither a language of business nor a first language of education in any state.

Could the rising circulation trend reported by the Registrar of Newspapers therefore be genuine? Is the Urdu-reading public in India being renewed? The answer to both questions, I think, is yes. Even though Urdu in the Perso-Arabic script is not a first language of instruction in government schools in Indian states, tens of thousands of Muslim children still learn the script in an elementary way in religious schools.[11] These students become the readers of Urdu dailies and weeklies—'the lowly educated and politically ill-informed poor Muslims', as a Muslim analyst characterizes them.[12] Such a socio-economic category may not make an advertising manager's heart beat faster, but it may well result in the sale of hundreds of thousands of small, cheaply produced newspapers.

To be sure, the Registrar of Newspapers for India (RNI) circulation figures probably exaggerate the number of Urdu dailies and their circulations, because people keenly seek such recognition—it brings rewards. Even in the 1990s, up to a third of Indian newsprint was imported, and since 1962 government has controlled its allotment through the RNI.[13] A robust black market quickly grew. A newspaper with more newsprint than it needed has often been able to sell the excess at a premium. If a newspaper is a virtual phantom, printing only a few hundred copies but drawing a newsprint quota for thousands, money can be made by selling newsprint. Similarly, a newspaper recognized by the state or Union government draws regular government advertising. Circulation claims are rarely checked, particularly for small newspapers, and a proprietor need print only a few score copies to satisfy government authorities that the advertisment has appeared. A reliable income results from this fraud. Journalists and proprietors also enjoy travel privileges, admission to buildings and events, and sometimes the opportunity to acquire land or accommodation at bargain rates.[14] Finally, a small newspaper can be used for blackmail: officials or politicians or political parties may be told that unless particular actions are taken, certain stories will appear.[15]

These practices are found in newspapers in all languages,[16] but they are more significant for the Perso-Arabic script because Urdu is seen to be the language of Indian Muslims. Politicians of all parties have seen virtue in keeping 11 per cent of the electorate quiescent and sympathetic. If newspaper proprietors, claiming to represent 'the Muslim community', could be kept happy with advertisements and newsprint, this was a price many politicians would gladly pay. What was written could not be read by the vast majority of non-Muslim voters, and this was therefore a far less provocative way of 'supporting' Urdu than using it widely for administration or in schools. Thus we may guess that the RNI and state governments generally, have been under steady pressure for many years to be lenient when examining the existence and circulation of Urdu newspapers. We should perhaps add to this a further ingredient. Because Perso-Arabic has little commercial value in India today, there is an incentive for those who know it to cash in on it in one of the few ways they can: through the advantages available to newspapers.

To analyse the Urdu press—and tease out wider hypotheses from the Urdu experience—let me look at four newspapers, each with particular characteristics. Two examples illustrate Urdu newspapers that will, I believe, eventually close, or, if they survive, transform themselves radically; but the other two provide evidence of why Perso-Arabic is *not* in imminent danger of disappearing from India, in spite of its lack of commercial value or meaningful—as opposed to condescending—state support. Overall, the evidence suggests that Perso-Arabic newspapers—though perhaps not dailies—have a future and, indeed, that there is a market waiting to be catered for.

The most widely circulated and financially successful Urdu daily in India is Hindu-owned and published in Punjab. *Hind Samachar* (ABC, January–June 1996: 44,348), founded in 1948, was the first newspaper in Lala Jagat Narain's empire. As late as the Partition, Perso-Arabic was the script for educated, employable males in north India, which is why Jagat Narain's first newspaper was in Perso-Arabic—he knew who his readers were. It was also his only paper until 1965, and it still gives its name to the Hind Samachar Group. Today, the group produces *Punjab Kesari*, the country's largest selling Hindi daily, and the Gurmukhi daily, *Jag Bani*. In 1996, the circulation of the Urdu daily *Hind Samachar* was 15 per cent lower than it had been twenty years earlier (ABC January–June 1976: 51,000), and its advertising rate was a quarter that of *Punjab Kesari's*.[17] Lala Jagat Narain (1899–1981) started *Hind Samachar* to cater to the Hindu and Sikh elite of old Punjab—men (seldom women) who had learned Urdu particularly because it was the language of government.[18] In the 1990s, that audience is fast disappearing: Hindu and Sikh children have generally not learned the Perso-Arabic script in north

Indian schools for more than 40 years. *Hind Samachar*'s circulation has been partly sustained by sales in Jammu and Kashmir, where the script is taught in schools and used in offices. In 1992, 17 per cent of circulation went to Jammu and Kashmir; the rest was dispersed over Punjab, Haryana, Himachal Pradesh, Delhi, Chandigarh, and western Uttar Pradesh.[19]

The Hind Samachar Group perhaps maintains its Urdu newspaper partly out of sentiment—in memory of the founder whose bust sits in the office of the present editor-in-chief. But it is also a commercial decision. *Hind Samachar* still makes money because it is cheap and easy to produce. The same newsroom in Jalandhar prepares all three newspapers—in Urdu, Hindi, and Gurmukhi. In 1993, the news editor sat on a raised platform, the horseshoe-shaped desk of the *Punjab Kesari* (Hindi) staff immediately around him, and with the sub-editors for *Hind Samachar* on his left and those for the Gurmukhi paper (*Jag Bani*) on his right. Stories were translated and passed back and forth among the three desks; one newsgathering system served all. Similarly, the technology, production and advertising staff that served one newspaper could with only a little more effort produce another one, particularly if, as is the case of Urdu, the deadlines were less tight and the business less competitive.[20]

Thus in the 1990s, India's largest-circulating Urdu daily considered Muslims to be a minor segment of its readers.[21] Yet its advertising rate was 50 per cent greater than that of the second largest Urdu daily in the ABC—*Siasat* of Hyderabad. It cost Rs 55 to buy a column centimetre in *Hind Samachar* in 1995, and only Rs 36 in *Siasat*.[22] The contrast highlighted the different styles of the two newspapers, and the way in which the Indian state and Indian capitalism profoundly affect—often unwittingly—the languages and scripts that people use. *Hind Samachar* survives as part of a burgeoning commercial enterprise, characterized by a market-consciousness that has led the group to start new newspapers when state sponsorship of particular languages makes it profitable (that is, when there is a substantial readership in those languages). Given the group's close attention to commercial considerations; it seems likely that *Hind Samachar* will be closed when its circulation and advertising revenues fall below an acceptable level. This appears inevitable as the older generation of Urdu-reading Sikhs and Hindus dies off.

While the Hind Samachar Group's headquarters in Jalandhar conveys a sense of brash bustle, *Siasat* in Hyderabad has an air of gentility. It also has a rising circulation. Where the circulation of *Hind Samachar* has fallen by 17 per cent between 1976 and 1996, that of *Siasat* has risen by 330 per cent—from 10,000 to 44,000 copies a day. The difference lies in the fact that Hyderabad and Andhra Pradesh have a large Muslim population and a relatively large network of government-run Urdu primary schools. Large numbers of Muslim children are also taught the Perso-Arabic script in madrasas and maktabs.[23]

The contrast between the two newspapers is instructive. Both were founded immediately after Independence in places that had experienced upheaval. Jagat Narain was a refugee of the Partition. When Abid Ali Khan (1920–1992) founded *Siasat* in 1949, Hyderabad state had just been absorbed into India through the Indian army's 'police action'. Both newspapers were family companies, and both offered distinctive views of the world based on the experience and interests of their founders. *Hind Samachar* presented that of male, upper-caste, commercial, and official Sikhs and Hindus of Punjab. Abid Ali Khan, on the other hand, came from the Progressive Writers Association, of which he had been secretary from 1943–7. He belonged to a strand of Urdu writing and writers associated with leftist causes and Soviet sympathies. 'After the advent of *Siasat*', a company brochure declared, 'he kept himself aloof from active politics, but infused the progressive spirit, secular thinking and nationalism through his paper ... He always looks on the profession of the Press as a mission.'[24]

This sense of a civilizing mission lingered at *Siasat* in the 1990s. Advertising was not pursued with the relentless enthusiasm that it was elsewhere. Rather than 'run promotions'—campaigns aiming to do public good and boost circulation—*Siasat* supported demure literary trusts; and, unlike the Hind Samachar Group, the *Siasat* family company had not started newspapers in other, more profitable languages. 'We are clapped', Zahid Ali Khan, the editor-owner said in 1993, 'in only one shell. This is a self-sufficient, independent Urdu paper coming out from India. We don't have anybody to go out of our office to beg for the advertisements.'[25] A new reporter at *Siasat* in 1993, a young Hindu woman, hired to cover commercial and financial stories though unable to write Urdu (her copy was translated at the news desk), spoke of the friendly, family-like atmosphere of the *Siasat* newsroom.[26] This contrasted with the large size and Dickensian discipline of the newsroom at the Hind Samachar Group in Jalandhar.

In one respect, *Siasat* represents something that is not uniquely Urdu: a disappearing type of Indian newspaper, which has not yet been swamped by commercial requirements. *Siasat* has been able to afford such gentility because of painstaking management—'I've been trained [since 1964] for keeping [an] eye on the complete administration'[27]—and the singular position of Urdu in Hyderabad. The city still has the remnants of a cosmopolitan population able to read the Perso-Arabic script; and at the same time a large Muslim population means that writers of the script and speakers of the language are being renewed through government and religious schools. Because it is efficient, well-produced and has thorough news and picture services, *Siasat* has also acquired a wide reputation and points proudly to subscribers all over India and in more than thirty countries from Japan and Russia to the United States.[28]

Astute management and the special circumstances of Urdu in their regions help explain why *Siasat* and *Hind Samachar* are the two most successful commercial Urdu dailies in India. But what of the scores of small Urdu newspapers that rise, fall, and scrape along? And what are the grounds for arguing that Urdu and the Perso-Arabic script have a vigorous long-term future?

Siasat Jadid (new politics) of Kanpur represented in 1993 an example of a newspaper in decline, suffering both from the absence of a supporting state, which affects all Urdu newspapers, and the inability to adjust to the commercial conditions imposed by the spread of capitalism. Founded in 1953 by K.G. Zaidi (1916–1992), a strident advocate of Muslim concerns, *Siasat Jadid* was sufficiently commercial to join the Audit Bureau of Circulations between 1971 (when it had a circulation of 9,000) and 1983. For a time Zaidi also ran a newspaper in Devanagari script in order to cater to the young Muslims who could not read Perso-Arabic; it lost money and he closed it in 1992. By the time of his death in October 1992, circulation of *Siasat Jadid* had fallen to 7,500, and the paper's office gave the appearance of a small cottage industry, but instead of pickles or *papad*s, it produced a newspaper.

Zaidi's son, Irshad Ilmi, who became editor after his father's death, recognized that the paper was poorly distributed: 'We are partly responsible ... for the falling readership, because we don't supply [people] with the newspaper.' Where *Siasat* of Hyderabad and *Hind Samachar* had used computers to create Perso-Arabic script in camera-ready form since the late 1980s, *Siasat Jadid* still had only 'three calligraphers, just three. And each writes two full pages.' This had advantages because the 'the calligrapher who writes the paper is an editor by himself; he knows what he has to give.' In that sense, the slow-moving, hand-written *Siasat Jadid* maintained a link with an earlier time when the reporter may have—literally—written the story for the lithographic stone that would print the newspaper. The small staff had known what Zaidi wanted: passionate stories of pointed concern to Muslims. 'The [Gulf] war [of 1991] was a big hit', with readers, Ilmi recalled. Similarly, Zaidi's ardent campaign to preserve the Babri Masjid in Ayodhya had been good for circulation; but after the building was destroyed on 6 December 1992, the paper looked as if it had lacked foresight, and it was left bereft of purpose.[29]

In spite of rudimentary technology and apparent disorganization, *Siasat Jadid* in 1993 seemed to make a small profit on its selling price of Rs 1.50 for a four-page broadsheet. Given the low salaries of the half-dozen employees, and allowing for the cost of newsprint, ink, and commission to hawkers, I calculate that there was a possible surplus of up to Rs 10,000 a week. Such circumstances, however, left the paper vulnerable not only to the decline in the number of Urdu-reading people but also to the possibility of a more efficient and attractive publication supplanting it.

Such prospects exist: the New Delhi weekly *Nai Duniya* (new world) exemplifies a fourth category of publication, one which suggests the strengths of Urdu in India and the potential for developing Perso-Arabic publications. There is nothing unique to Urdu about two aspects of *Nai Duniya*. First, the family that produces it has made what appears to be a successful transition from one generation to the next. Second, in doing so, they have introduced new technology and experimented with different genres of publication. In short, unlike *Siasat Jadid*, they appear to be adapting to the peculiar circumstances of Urdu in India. The 'lessons' of *Nai Duniya* help to clarify those circumstances.

The first *Nai Duniya* was founded as a daily in 1950 by Abdul Waheed Siddiqui (c. 1895–1981), a journalist and political activist whom his youngest son describes as 'a nationalist Muslim who fought the Muslim League'. Intended to promote Muslim interests, the paper often ran afoul of authorities in the 1950s. Though it closed in 1964, the family had meanwhile developed popular and profitable magazines or 'digests' in Urdu. These were printed on an offset press—much faster than lithography—more than twenty years before offset became widely used in India. Shahid Siddiqui (b. 1951) started his first Urdu magazine in 1970 when he was a college student and a member of the CPI(M). The paper failed, largely, he believed, because of its treatment of the Bangladesh struggle of 1971:

I went to Bangladesh at that time ... I wrote the truth which was not acceptable to Muslims, because for them the creation of Bangladesh was a turning point, because [it was] the destruction of the idea of Pakistan, the two-nation theory.[30]

Circulation fell and the paper closed in 1972. The perceived effect of the Bangladesh war on circulation confirms the view of other Muslim editors that Muslim affairs at an international level fascinate readers and rapidly affect circulations. In the following year, Siddiqui and family started *Nai Duniya* weekly, and it benefited from a similar chance: the Arab-Israeli war of 1973. Circulation reached around 30,000 within a few months.

Over the next 20 years, circulation fluctuated widely: down during the 'Emergency', up to 200,000 during the overthrow and trial of Zulfiqar Ali Bhutto in Pakistan, down thereafter to 50–60,000, and up to 350,000 during the Gulf war of 1991. By 1993, it had settled at about 120,000. (*Nai Duniya* is not a member of the ABC. In 1992, it claimed a circulation of 45,000).[31] Unlike most major newspapers in India, Urdu publications usually make a profit on their selling price. Priced in 1993 at Rs 5 for 20 tabloid pages (the equivalent of 10 broadsheet pages), *Nai Duniya* garnered a considerable profit, even after salaries, commissions, and other expenses were accounted for. During the Gulf war, *Nai Duniya* introduced full colour for its front and back pages, and 'once we started we couldn't go back.' Photocomposing came later in 1991, and calligraphers who had previously written the paper were retrained as computer operators. In 1992, to attract Muslims who had studied Hindi in Devanagari at school and did not know the Perso-Arabic script, Shahid Siddiqui began *Nai Zameen*, a weekly that was heavily, though not exclusively, a Devanagari version of *Nai Duniya*. The ability to experiment helped to explain *Nai Duniya's* apparent vitality. And unlike *Siasat Jadid's* experiment with a Devanagari version, *Nai Zameen* was a weekly—able to circulate at a leisurely pace around the whole country.

Siddiqui contended that Urdu weeklies like *Nai Duniya* prospered because they were suited to the fact that Urdu speakers were dispersed throughout India. In that sense, Urdu, even more than Hindi, is a countrywide language because it elicits little opposition in the towns of the south where it is read and studied—provided it is an option, not a compulsion.[32] These dispersed populations are rarely so concentrated as to sustain a daily newspaper, but they can be reached by a weekly. And a weekly can make a profit on its selling price alone: it does not have to depend on advertising, of which Urdu newspapers get little.

We don't get ads. The reason is that in the ad agencies, the Muslims belonging to the upper strata ... are there. Or those who are there ... have got friends among the Muslims who belong to the upper strata ... They tell me, Can your paper have any influence? Because I know so many Muslims and they tell me they don't read Urdu at all.

Even if advertisers believed that large numbers of Urdu readers existed, they would discount their purchasing power. 'My paper', Siddiqui of *Nai Duniya* continues, 'is mainly popular among Ansaris, weavers, lock-makers, all kinds of artisans all over the country.' These are not the people that most big-spending national advertisers are trying to reach.

The fate of Urdu in the Perso-Arabic script highlights important propositions about languages. Urdu readers in India are dispersed across the country, and Urdu is a language without a state apparatus to support it. Languages and scripts need *state* support—first-language status in administration and education—if they are to become embedded in a capitalist world. The sheer number of small Urdu dailies and weeklies—close to 250 recorded by the Registrar of Newspapers for 1994[33]—suggests that Urdu experiences a certain moth-eaten patronage: concessions to small newspapers encouraged by politicians with the goal of keeping Muslims happy for the next election. Such patronage helps to sustain haphazard publications, but it is not the kind of state support that embeds languages under capitalism.

Government inducement alone, however, is not enough to propagate a language successfully or undermine it completely. As David Laitin writes in a book about Africa, 'the sum of incentives to develop individually rational language repertoires can override the best-laid plans of ideologues and planners.'[34] Those 'incentives' may well be religious. It may be 'rational' to teach one's children a script and a language that brings them closer to God, not the secretariat (though proximity to both is desirable and may require learning another language).

The RNI's figures for Urdu circulations, though probably inflated, suggest that the pool of Urdu readers in India is being renewed. Such renewal assures the future of the script. In thousands of schools throughout India, students of all religions may study Urdu as an optional language. Because in north India it is sometimes seen as an easy option—one has only to learn the script, not the vocabulary or grammar—non-Muslim students choose to study it. They may not learn well; they may not become readers of Urdu publications; but some will have the ability to do so. And Muslim students in such schools study Urdu as a desirable choice. Moreover, there are thousands of madrasas all over India where a child is sent. In the villages a child goes to the government school in the daytime and in the evening he goes to the madrasa for two hours. Everywhere you have this network of madrasas and there children learn Urdu. But the children of the middle-classes and upper-classes don't. If you talk to most of these people they will tell you that nobody is learning Urdu.[35]

The students who come from the madrasa, or who have studied Urdu as a second language in government schools, are the audience for Urdu periodicals like *Nai Duniya*. Numbering in millions, such people provide the new generations of Urdu readers and exemplify the *social* support that secures the survival of the Perso-Arabic script.[36]

Popular desire—in the case of Urdu, of Muslims to have their children study a script associated with the Koran—can maintain a language even without much government support. Urdu in Perso-Arabic, however, has a predicament: the social factors that ensure its survival—primarily madrasa education available to Muslim children—have so far limited its potential as a vehicle for capitalism.

Depending heavily on madrasa education makes Urdu the language of Muslims, which means that publishers in Urdu produce magazines and newspapers geared overwhelmingly to Muslim interests. And since major advertisers regard Muslims as among India's poorest people, they decline to commit the large sums of advertising money that would encourage more widely focused news-gathering publications capable of eliciting the interest of non-Muslims.[37]

The modern history of the Irish language—surviving under British imperialism yet far from flourishing under a free government dedicated to propagating it—highlights contrasts between government support and social support for a language. Contrast the experience of Irish with that of Hebrew in Israel or Punjabi in the Gurmukhi script, both of which have taken firm hold in popular, commercial, capitalist ways in the past two or three generations. They have had *both* social and government support, and that social support came initially from religious association. The Perso-Arabic script and Urdu in India since 1947 have had powerful social—but only token government—support. As in Punjab and Israel, the social support has stemmed primarily from a religious base. (Would the Irish language have gone deeper into modern Ireland if Catholic scripture had a tradition of being written in a distinctive Irish script?) The paradox, as I see it, is that the combination of government and social backing that embeds a language may ultimately reduce the religious emphasis—that is, it may ultimately secularize the language—as it becomes a vehicle for capitalism.

Today, the structure of Urdu newspaper publishing—scores of small operations scattered all over India and surviving chiefly on their selling price—insulates it from such capitalism and accompanying non-religious tendencies. But as capitalists awaken to the fact that the Urdu-reading public *is* being renewed and that 'Ansaris, weavers, lock-makers, [and] all kinds of artisans' are now part of a lower middle-class keen on consumption,[38] Urdu in India is, I suspect, a language awaiting its Northcliffe, Murdoch, or Citizen Kane.

NOTES

1. *Collected Works of Mahatma Gandhi*, vol. 62, pp. 408–9, quoted in Peter Brock, *The Mahatma and Mother India. Essays on Gandhi's Non-Violence and Nationalism* (Ahmedabad: Navajivan, 1983), p. 200.

2. Christopher R. King, *One Language, Two Scripts: The Hindi Movement in Nineteenth Century North India* (Bombay: Oxford University Press, 1994), pp. 8, 178.

3. Robin Jeffrey, 'The Mystery of the Urdu Dailies', *Vidura*, January–February 1988, pp. 38–40.

4. *Press in India, 1995* [hereafter *PII* + year] (New Delhi: Ministry of Information and Broadcasting, n.d. [1996]), p. 42; *PII, 1975*, p. 35. Total circulation of dailies in all languages increased by only 240 per cent in this period—from 9.3 million to 31.6 million.

5. *PII* and *Preliminary List of Circulations Certified for the Six-Monthly Audit Period* (Bombay: ABC) for appropriate years. In the case of the ABC, of the two six-monthly figures available for each year, I have chosen the higher one.

6. In 1976, the five were *Hind Samachar* (Jalandhar), *Inquilab* (Bombay), *Siasat* (Hyderabad), *Siasat Jadid* (Kanpur), and *Milap* (Delhi). *Siasat Jadid* and *Milap* left the ABC in 1983–4; *Urdu Times* (Bombay), joined in 1990. The number of dailies registered with the RNI also fell from 94 in 1976 to 82 in 1994, though circulation rose. *PII, 1977*, p. 11; *PII, 1995*, p. 48.

7. *Vidura*, February 1982, p. 41; October 1982, p. 284.

8. Yoginder Sikand, 'Muslims and Mass Media', *Economic and Political Weekly*, 13 August 1994, pp. 2134–5.

9. Ather Farouqui, 'The Emerging Dilemma of the Urdu Press in India: a Viewpoint', *South Asia*, 18 (2), December 1995, p. 91.

10. Ibid., pp. 102–3.

11. R.S. Newman, *Grassroots Education in India* (New Delhi: Sterling for the Asian Studies Association of Australia, 1989), pp. 74–108, has written feelingly of the maktabs of Uttar Pradesh and the support they commanded in the 1970s and 1980s.

12. Farouqui, 'Emerging Dilemma', p. 97.

13. *PII, 1992*, p. 330. From 1962–76, the Ministry of Commerce was also involved. Since 1976, the Ministry of Information and Broadcasting has been in charge of the allocation procedures.

14. See Press Trust of India, 5 February 1997, on the Press Council's intention to investigate such privileges, especially 'land and houses at nominal prices'. From *India News Network Digest*, 7 February 1997, INDIA-L@INDNET.org.

15. Farouqui, 'Emerging Dilemma', p. 92, discusses all these in relation to Urdu newspapers.

16. T.J.S. George, *The Provincial Press in India* (New Delhi: Press Institute of India, 1967), pp. 6–7. *In Defence of Press Freedom: Minute of Dissent to the Report of the Second Press Commission 1982* (Calcutta: The Statesman, 1982), p. 59. *Press Council of India Review*, 13 (3), July 1992, pp. 122–4.

17. *Press and Advertisers Year Book, 1994–5* [hereafter *PAYB* + year], pp. 104c–8c. Rs 55 against Rs 275 a column centimetre.

18. Prakash Tandon, *Punjabi Century* (Delhi: Orient Paperbacks, n.d.; first published 1961), pp. 67–8.

19. *A.B.C. Certificates. Audit Period: 1st January to 30th June 1992*, Serial No. 87 (Bombay, Audit Bureau of Circulations, 1993), no. 87/510. Interview, Vijay Kumar Chopra, Chief Editor, Hind Samachar Group, Jalandhar, 20 May 1993.

20. Interviews and observation, Hind Samachar Group, Jalandhar, 20 May 1993.

21. Interview, Vijay Kumar Chopra, 20 May 1993.

22. *PAYB, 1994–5*, pp. 104c–5c, 128c–9c.

23. More than 1,100 such schools, according to *Muslim India*, no. 113, May 1992, p. 225, quoting the Ali Sardar Jafri Committee Report, October 1991, to the Government of India. Ather Farouqui, 'Urdu Education in India: Four Representative States', *Economic and Political Weekly*, 2 April 1994, p. 784.

24. *Four Decades of the 'Siasat' Hyderabad, 1949–1991* (Hyderabad: Siasat, 1991), inside front cover.

25. Interview, Zahid Ali Khan, Editor, *Siasat*, Hyderabad, 3 March 1993.

26. Interview, Ratna Chotrani, Reporter, *Siasat*, Hyderabad, 3 March 1993.

27. Interview, Zahid Ali Khan, 3 March 1993.

28. *Four Decades of Siasat*, p. 5 and back cover.

29. Interview, Irshad Ilmi, Editor and Owner-Partner, *Siasat Jadid*, Kanpur, 13 May 1993.

30. Interview, Shahid Siddiqui, Editor and Managing Director, *Nai Duniya*, New Delhi, 10 May 1993.

31. *The Indian Newspaper Society Press Handbook, 1992* (New Delhi: INS, n.d. [1992]), p. 473.

32. The outbursts in Bangalore over an Urdu television news bulletin illustrate the way in which enforced, ill-considered government policy can provoke rapid opposition. *The Indian Express* (New Delhi), 9 October 1994.

33. *PII*, 1995, p. 48.

34. David D. Laitin, *Language Repertoires and State Construction in Africa* (Cambridge: Cambridge University Press, 1992), p. 153. Laitin's book is puzzling in that he entirely overlooks the role of newspaper and advertising industries in the propagation of languages.

35. Interview, Shahid Siddiqui, 10 May 1993.

36. It must of course be pointed out that the new owners closed *Urdu Blitz* in 1996. Was that decision more ideological than commercial?

37. Farouqui, 'Emerging Dilemma', p. 103, reports that *India Today* considered starting an Urdu edition but dropped the idea because 'Urdu editors' told them 'that Muslims do not trust the national press and ... [are] "anti-establishment".'

38. S.L. Rao and I. Natarajan, *Indian Market Demographics. The Consumer Class* (New Delhi: Global Business Press, 1996), pp. 214–32.

15

Urdu Press in India

Ather Farouqui

This article is concerned with the state of Urdu journalism in contemporary India. In attempting this analysis my purpose is to address the question of whether or not Urdu journalism has played a constructive role in shaping Muslim sensibilities in post-Independence India, in the sense of enabling the community to face up to the challenge of adjustment as a large minority group in secular India. I shall argue that Urdu journalism during the post-Independence period has very largely failed to perform this expected role. For reasons which are partly inherent in the nature and character of the Urdu readership, and which partly arise from the political and economic proclivities of individual Urdu journalists as well as from their linkages to political parties, Urdu journalism has more often than not been prone to reinforce a sectarian and emotional outlook among readers. At any rate, Urdu journalism has often disturbed Muslim positions on substantial issues of concern to the community and the country at large, ignoring the emerging social realities within the community. Accordingly, this discussion of Urdu journalism in India is set against the changing position of Urdu and the socio-economic changes Muslims in India have experienced during the past sixty years.

It is significant to note that a glance over the journey of Urdu journalism reveals that except for a few minor changes in north Indian Urdu journalism (like a few new newspapers appearing on the scene and the emergence of electronic media), mainstream Urdu journalism has by and large remained static. The ethos and subject matter has hardly changed. With the settling of the dust of the destruction of the Babri Masjid, the Urdu print media has come back to square one, and there is no sign of change in its mentality.

The electronic media has slightly changed its attitude in respect of the Urdu linguistic minority, but that is a different field of study. However an important fact in this respect is that if the problems associated with Urdu are political, and if Urdu means a language that is identified by script rather than speech, then the language used by the electronic media, irrespective of its Perso-Arabic lexical terms and words has to be seen differently. Urdu in its spoken form is called either Hindustani or Hindi (the classic examples are *Mughal-e Azam* and *Razia Sultan,* which are branded and even certified as Hindi films). Constitutionally speaking, even Hindustani is a form of Hindi, along with many other major languages of the north like Braj, Avadhi, Haryanavi, Rajasthani, Magahi, Bhojpuri, etc. Earlier Maithili was also included in the canon of Hindi but now has its independent existence. Hence, in its spoken form Urdu also becomes Hindi, and thus even the newly sprouting Urdu TV channels automatically become Hindi channels.

This unfair treatment meted out to major and rich languages of north India by illiberal forces has penetrated even the Constitution. In a true democratic state, this needs to be immediately rectified. Under Article 351 of the Constitution, Hindustani is stated to be a form or Hindi. But one must not forget that Hindustani was to be declared (in two scripts, Urdu and Devanagari) as the national language of free India. But before that could happen our country was partitioned into two, and Gandhi was assassinated by reactionaries.

As far as the Urdu print media is concerned, a small visible change has occurred in north India because caste politics has fragmented society. As a by-product, an Urdu newspaper, *Rashtriya Sahara,* has sprouted (morphing from monthly to weekly to daily) in many cities of India. The claims of circulation made by the management need to be verified and the phenomenon of growth too needs proper study. This newspaper, with obvious political leanings, has been pandering to the needs of a casteist-cum-Muslim populist like Mulayam Singh Yadav, in the same way as Urdu weeklies of the north had been fanning fundamentalist tendencies for their petty gains. This is a contemporary example of sectarian political clout. On the other hand, despite tall claims, the Congress has failed to address the problems of Muslims or to start the process of their social cohesion and economic development. In a worsening situation, it also lost its only link to Urdu-speaking Muslim society (which is mainly based on women and madrasa graduates) with the degeneration of the daily *Qaumi Awaz* and ultimately the closure of its Lucknow edition. Although people who know Urdu (that is, know the script) in UP are very few, but post-6 December 1992, their assertion of their Urdu-based identity has been fortified.

After Partition, Urdu was seen by average Muslims in India as the language of their cultural identity and the medium of religious instruction. It has become the sole medium of dini madari education and for this reason evokes a deep attachment. But Muslim identity was not always bound up with the language. Historically, Urdu was the language of the ruling Muslim elite and the elite Hindus who came in touch with Muslim rulers. The common masses communicated in regional languages without feeling tension over whether it was Urdu, Hindi, or some other language.

Urdu suffered a decline after India was partitioned. It was threatened by the official support extended to Hindi by the government in free India. The Muslim leadership of post-Partition India campaigned for Muslims to declare Urdu as their mother tongue and to consider it as a symbol of their cultural identity. Also, the political compulsions of the north Indian Muslim elite, who needed to consolidate the Muslim community, which is otherwise internally differentiated, strengthened this campaign. One of the consequences of this development—namely, the subsidy given to Urdu publications by the government—was that it made sure that Urdu journalism would die, particularly in north India.

In India the Urdu press is by and large a Muslim press, although in some southern states a few good Muslim newspapers are being published in regional languages. A large number of representative Muslim weeklies are published from Delhi. But in this assessment I have included only those Urdu newspapers, mainly weeklies and dailies, which have played a role, even if negative, in the lives of India's Muslims in general.

The concessions granted to Urdu newspapers by the government to appease Muslims are readily exploited by some people, although most of them have no relation with journalism. These people get a registration number for an Urdu paper and publish fifty or a hundred copies. However, in order to obtain government advertisements and the quota of newsprint, they falsely claim that they publish greater numbers. Surprisingly, the office of the Registrar of Newspapers plays a passive role and does not try to find out if the figures submitted to it by the respective newspapers are authentic. Most of the owners of these newspapers (who also happen to be their editors) indulge in blackmailing one or other political party in the name of their newspaper.

Out of the 347 registered publications, there may be hardly forty to fifty which in fact reach public hands. Most of these publish file copies only for the government's records.[1] In this assessment I have included only those newspapers which really reach the public, and are published regularly. These papers possess the capability of motivating public opinion.

Without doubt, the Muslims of south India, particularly Karnataka, are today recognizing Urdu as their language and a symbol of their religious identity in the changed political milieu, even if Urdu was never their language in the past when they were greatly distanced from the Muslims of north India. Culturally, north Indian Muslims always considered themselves different from Muslims in the rest of the country. They were also victims of a pronounced sense of superiority. This cultural distance and the strong sense of superiority on the part of north Indian Muslims became a great hurdle in linking them with south Indian Muslims.

This factor also prevented the movement for Pakistan from reaching south India. Except for a few big cities, migration to Pakistan from the south was limited. (Precisely because of the hold of north Indian Muslims, particularly the ashraf (gentry) and the middle-class, over the Muslim League, linguistic and cultural conflicts have arisen there even after the formation of Pakistan.) The subsequent establishment of Bangladesh and the remarkable rise of the MQM in the refugee-dominated urban areas of Sindh province are ample proof of this.

Muslim politics in contemporary India are not particularly different from what they were in the past. The hold of north Indian Muslims on Muslim political campaigns has been strong even after Independence. This prompted the presumption that the north Indian Muslim leadership would also be successful in the south. However, the defeat of Syed Shahabuddin in Bangalore during the 1989 general elections made the north Indian Muslim leadership acutely aware of its real standing in the south.

Over the recent past, Muslims in India have been at the centre of two public controversies. The first controversy centred on whether a divorced Muslim woman, Shah Bano, was entitled to maintenance from her husband under certain provisions of the Criminal Procedure Act, entitling women to claim such maintenance to avert their taking to vagrancy or prostitution. Under Muslim Personal Law, a husband's responsibility towards his wife ceased after divorce. The second controversy concerned the claim of a section of chauvinist Hindus to build a Ram temple on the site of the Babri Masjid, allegedly built by Mughal emperor Babar after bringing down a temple in the sixteenth century. Muslims waged fierce struggles for the enactment of a law to annul the Supreme Court judgement[2] in the Shah Bano case, and for the protection of the Babri Masjid (which was, eventually, forcefully demolished by fanatical Hindus on 6 December 1992, plunging India into serious Hindu Muslim strife).

The Muslim leadership's short-sighted campaign to annul the Supreme Court judgement upholding a Muslim divorcee's right to maintenance through a legislative enactment[3] enabled the chauvinist Hindu leadership to convince common Hindus that in matters of faith the judgement of the court had no place. Accordingly, when the Supreme Court directed that the structure of the Babri Masjid should not be disturbed, as no available evidence indicated that a temple originally existed on its site, the Hindu leadership started arguing that the ruling of the court had little validity when the people believed that a temple actually existed there. This stand has not changed and has been emphasized by the VHP.

The style and objectives of the Muslim leadership in the Shah Bano and the Babri Masjid campaigns were ill-conceived, as, arguably, was Muhammad Ali Jinnah's Muslim League campaign to have a separate homeland for Muslims carved out of the Muslim-majority areas of undivided India. It was sheer luck for Indian Muslims that those running the Shah Bano and the Babri Masjid campaigns lacked Jinnah's mobilizing skills.

To be able to appreciate the role of the Urdu press in the lives of Indian Muslims, we need to divide Urdu publications between Urdu weeklies, fortnightlies, and monthlies on the one hand and Urdu dailies on the other. Urdu weeklies, fortnightlies, and monthlies published on a regular basis enjoy the patronage of the Muslim leadership of

Delhi in particular and north India in general, and it is widely known that they receive their funding from the same sources which finance the activities of fundamentalist Muslim leaders. These publications can, therefore, be regarded as truly reflecting the mentality of north Indian Muslims. Nonetheless, among the publications belonging to this category, the number of those published on a regular basis is limited to one or two. Most of them are open advocates or official organs of political parties or ideological organizations. Therefore, their circulation and area of influence are greatly restricted.

The weeklies published from Delhi command a comparatively larger readership among Muslims. Their role in the formation of Urdu journalistic thinking is substantial and a true reflection of the sentiments of north Indian Muslims and their social situation. Muslim readers in the north are educationally backward. Muslim readers from many organizations (which are in fact are unconcerned with the real problems facing Muslims, particularly those relating to their educational backwardness and under-representation in public employment or even their general poverty) find the north Indian soil extremely fertile for their campaigns. Therefore, most Delhi-based Urdu weeklies keep giving currency to self-created stereotypes and misconceptions which place severe limits upon their potential for growth.

The sources of such stereotypes and misconceptions are varied. There are some stereotypes and misconceptions which anti-Muslim forces have deliberately given currency to in an organized fashion. Even so, a good many of the stereotypes and misconceptions have been popularized by Delhi-based Urdu weeklies too. For instance, Urdu publications have all along harped on the discriminatory treatment meted out to Muslims in India, often explaining the social and economic backwardness which characterizes this community as entirely and exclusively the result of the failure of the government to protect Muslim interests or to secure economic advantages for them. One is not suggesting that there is no discrimination against Muslims in contemporary India. What one is suggesting is that discrimination is only a part of the story. A number of internal factors as well as their post-Partition psychological orientations can equally be a factor in the continued backwardness of the community. However, the Urdu press has never even raised the question that there might be other factors which have contributed to their continued backwardness. Even if proved wrong on subsequent scrutiny, such searching analyses would have broadened Muslim viewpoints to understand their predicament in post-Independence India, and thus enabled Muslims to come to terms with their existential realities. Unfortunately, Urdu journalism has been content with reiterating the common clichés.

For a while in the 1980s a slight change in Urdu journalism was discernible. At that time some new newspapers started appearing and several of the old publications reoriented their outlook in order to reflect emerging realities. The *National Herald*, an organ of the Congress, started its sister publication in Urdu, known as *Quami Awaz*, from Delhi. *Quami Awaz* set a new trend of healthy journalism in comparison with other Urdu dailies of north India, and, despite being an organ of the Congress, it became necessary reading for enlightened and sober Muslims in some parts of northern India, particularly in western Uttar Pradesh in the 1980s. *Nai Duniya*, which had resumed publication in 1973 as a weekly newspaper, assumed extraordinary popularity in 1980, when communalism and extremism were at a peak. Another weekly newspaper, *Akhbar-e Nau*, appeared on the scene in the mid-1980s. *Akhbar-e Nau* indulged in blindly backing Imam Bukhari. During the Muslim Personal Law movement and later on during the Babri Masjid movement, it assumed great importance, and by 1990 it was among the leading Urdu weeklies of the country. When the Janata Dal came to power, the then prime minister V.P. Singh, on the recommendation of the Imam of Jama Masjid of Delhi, Abdullah Bukhari, granted a Rajya Sabha seat to its editor Muhammad Afzal, who was consequently elected as a Rajya Sabha MP on a Janata Dal ticket. After stepping into the political arena, Muhammad Afzal's interest in the newspaper, and simultaneously the influence of the paper on the common Muslim, started fading. During the period of the Babri Masjid movement two more papers, the daily *Faisal Jadeed* and weekly *Hamara Qadam*, were launched. The daily *Faisal Jadeed* was a newspaper without news.[4] It was more a 'views-paper' of people who were extremely narrow-minded. Instead of bringing about an awareness among the Muslim masses of the issues involved, it worked towards inciting Muslims to fever pitch. It remained very popular during the heyday of the Babri Masjid movement.

After the demolition of the Babri Masjid, which resulted in the virtual collapse of the movement for its protection, *Hamara Qadam* and *Faisal Jadeed* almost ceased publication. *Nai Duniya*, a publication brought out by another member of the Urdu press magnate family which has dominated the Urdu journalistic scene, played a vital role in orienting Muslims towards political aggressiveness in north India. *Akhbar-e Nau*'s editorial comment on the eve of the launching of *Hamara Qadam* gives an idea of the opportunist attitude of this as well as other newspapers, including *Nai Duniya*. It reads:

In the journalistic brotherhood of Delhi, the name of Siddiqui brothers is worth mentioning. Maulana Abdul Waheed Siddiqui, the founding father of *Nai Duniya* (weekly), *Huma* and *Huda* (monthly digests) had four sons who were publishing separate newspapers and magazines. *Nai Duniya* is edited by his youngest son Shahid Siddiqui whereas his eldest son Ahmad Mustafa Siddiqui Rahi brings out the magazine *Huda*. As compared to *Nai Duniya*, Rahi had brought out a more bulky weekly *Humara Qadam* ...

What is interesting is that the political experience and outlook of Shahid Siddiqui and Ahmad Mustafa Siddiqui are sharply contrasting. Shahid Siddiqui, a staunch communist from his very early stages, was an atheist, whereas Ahmad Mustafa Siddiqui was pro-religion, anti-Communist, and a staunch Congressman from the political point of view. However, after the starting of their respective newspapers, the outlook and ideology of both of them has entirely changed.[5]

Elsewhere the editor of *Akhbar-e Nau* openly conceded the sub-standard level of Urdu journalism. His contention is that Urdu journalism acts as a mouthpiece of the communal Muslim leadership. But he holds the government responsible for these problems. He feels that if communal riots did not occur and if the government took an interest in solving Muslims' problems, then Urdu newspapers would not be able to misguide and exploit innocent Muslims.[6]

Similar sentiments had been echoed by Masoom Moradabadi when he launched *Khabardar Jadid* in 1991. Indeed, *Khabardar Jadid* was launched with the explicit objective of rooting out the destructive orientation of Urdu journalism. However, after some time he himself drifted towards the same kind of provocative and destructive journalism. His views on Urdu journalism, based on his association with the profession over several years, are nonetheless pertinent:

The majority of Urdu newspapers wishes to keep their readers buried under grief and pessimism and also wants to keep them mentally retarded so that they may be rendered inactive in practical life. Since independence the majority of Urdu newspapers have done nothing except lamentation. They deliberately search and compile such material which would push Muslims into pessimism and hopelessness. These newspapers have published stories of this tyranny on the community with renewed vigour, but they never care to educate them and tell them that there are ways and means to come out from these circumstances and live a respectable life. These newspapers are scared that they will educate and adequately guide the readers, that no one will buy their blood-drenched newspapers.[7]

Another tragedy of the Delhi-based Urdu publications is that despite a sea change having taken place in the political situation of Muslims in India, their orientation remains what it was around the 1970s. They openly aroused Muslims to a high pitch, almost trying to build mass Muslim hysteria over the Babri Masjid issue, and prompting Muslims to take to militancy during the movement. This orientation was reflected by several newspapers between September and December 1990.[8]

Today their circle of readers comprises the less educated and politically ill-informed poor Muslims. Among the stable readership of Urdu journalism and particularly Delhi-based weeklies, one section comprises those persons whose political temperament has been shaped by those papers which have, by creating misconceptions about Muslims and about Urdu journalism, rendered the situation extremely complex and perhaps beyond redemption. They carry an image of themselves as a backward, discriminated against, and culturally threatened community.

The trouble is that the Delhi-based weeklies and other Urdu papers and magazines have not familiarized themselves with the changing situation of Muslims. Nor have they thought of giving space to the problems of the newly educated and emerging middle-class (whose size is nevertheless quite small) among north Indian Muslims. Precisely because of this, journalism continually harps back to the image of Muslims as backward and discriminated against, a perception that is not universal to Indian Muslims in view of distinctive regional variations in the standing of Muslims in different parts of the country. Because it does not reflect issues of concern to the emerging Muslim middle-class, it has failed to establish all-India credentials for itself at any time. It is only in situations of extreme emergency, when an issue that seems to threaten Muslim cultural identity comes to the fore, that the reach of such papers extends beyond north India.

Since the 1970s a new generation of Urdu journalists has come up in north India. Even so, neither the tenor and temperament of Urdu journalists nor their attitude, which compels them to analyse things from the perspective of the 1970s, has changed. Urdu journalism is entirely indifferent to the importance of the mass media in the changed circumstances and the advent of new printing technologies. Among the over-simplified explanations offered by Urdu journalists for the sad state of their affair are the reluctance of average Muslims to buy newspapers and the inability of Urdu newspapers to secure advertisements as readily as English, Hindi, and some other regional newspapers.

Around the early 1970s the educated stratum among north Indian Muslims was almost non-existent, and the Muslim middle-class had become greatly diminished through migration to Pakistan. Yet at that time a good many Urdu magazines and newspapers were published in large numbers. But today, when the Muslim middle-class has expanded, education among south Indian Muslims has become common, and the economic situation of even north Indian Muslims has improved, it is surprising that the print orders of Urdu newspapers and magazines have declined substantially, and several such papers and magazines have ceased, or are about to cease, publication. This exactly illustrates the predicament which confronts Urdu journalism today.

Leading Urdu weeklies which focus on north Indian Muslim problems and politics are no longer relevant outside north India. The pattern of Muslim politics in south India is quite different from that of north India. North Indian Muslim politicians have never thought of undertaking measures to truly improve the lot of their constituents and their empty and meaningless political rhetoric does not echo a sympathetic chord in south India.

After the collapse of the highly emotionally charged Muslim Personal Law and Babri Masjid issues, the scope for Urdu newspapers to carry on those polemics has virtually ended. The Muslim youth is also gradually realizing that the solution to the frequent outbreak of communal riots does not really lie in reinforcing a ghetto mentality or promoting the idea that all Muslims constitute a well-knit and unified community, as north Indian Muslim politics has traditionally recommended. It is also beginning to see that Urdu newspapers have been using Muslim youth as fuel to feed the fire of Muslim fears, to see themselves as a well-knit community threatened by conscious efforts to erode their distinctive identity under the patronage of the state, through presentation of extremely emotional analyses of the communal scenario.

Another factor responsible for the decline of influential Urdu newspapers published from Delhi is the eclipse of Urdu in this region. The new generation of Muslims, in some north Indian states, particularly Uttar Pradesh, is hardly conversant with Urdu, as Urdu ceased to be taught as a language in schools except those run by Muslims. Historically, Urdu was culturally refined in Uttar Pradesh and became a popular lingua franca in this region under the patronage of the Awadh rulers during the eighteenth and nineteenth centuries. Thus, Urdu was learned by Muslims as well as by non-Muslims as a matter of course, and facilities for teaching Urdu existed in all schools. During the Congress raj in 1937–9 and after Independence, the state policy in respect of teaching Urdu was dramatically changed with the Urdu script being replaced by Devanagari. Today the result is those young Muslims who are unable to go beyond primary education are modestly conversant with Hindi but know no Urdu.

It is the educationally backward Muslims who stayed on after Partition in north Indian provinces and who had at least a smattering of Urdu that constitute the regular readership of Urdu newspapers. Indeed, Urdu newspapers and Muslim politicians evolved their political strategy of reinforcing a ghetto mentality by playing on the sensibilities of this very section of north Indian Muslims. But the reality is that poor and ill-educated Muslims have little choice other than to read regional Hindi newspapers, despite the anti-Muslim communal biases of these newspapers.

After Partition, such Muslims demonstrated a very emotional attitude towards Urdu. They also lent a degree of support to campaigns for Urdu and whenever necessary they made sacrifices for it. However, because of the short-sighted and self-serving politics of the Muslim leadership, Urdu has become merely a part of their past cultural heritage. Urdu's decline has rendered the existence of a prestigious Urdu newspaper virtually impossible. Urdu magazines get a larger quota of government-sponsored advertisements than some of the regional language magazines, the size and standard of which far exceeds that of Urdu magazines. As the figures in Table 15.1 show,

Urdu newspapers are the fifth largest recipients of state-sponsored advertisements.

As far as advertisements of corporate and private firms are concerned, it stands to reason that they would be reluctant to put advertisements in Urdu magazines whose readers represents the most backward section of Muslims. One is not talking here of Hindu–Muslim differentiation. Even Muslim business firms give very few advertisements to Urdu publications compared with English and Hindi periodicals. It is the middle-class that by and large constitutes the consumer class in India and the purpose of advertising is to influence it. If Urdu periodicals do not reach the consumer class, why should any firm give them advertisements?

The state of Urdu journalism is far more favourable in those linguistic regions of India where Muslims are proud of their religious identity and are actively sharing the region's cultural ethos. In all such regions the percentage of the population that knows Urdu is

Table 15.1: Government-sponsored advertisements in periodicals
(language-wise)

S.No.	Language	Total Amount (in Rs) of government-sponsored advertisements
1	English	8,82,84,356
2	Hindi	6,65,08,844
3	Urdu	97,78,363
4	Punjabi	60,73,918
5	Marathi	1,33,88,180
6	Gujarati	80,76,155
7	Sindhi	5,18,244
8	Assamese	17,68,736
9	Bengali	1,16,72,781
10	Oriya	34,59,288
11	Tamil	66,73,358
12	Telugu	28,40,188
13	Malayalam	87,49,789
14	Kannada	32,46,885
15	Sanskrit	27,373
16	Nepali	2,88,020
17	Mizo	82,570.0
18	Khasi	36,248
19	Konkani	34,528

Source: Annexure referred to in reply in Rajya Sabha to unstarred question no. 4305 on 22 December 1992.

much smaller than in north India. Even in those regions where Urdu is not the mother tongue of Muslims, the situation of Urdu is much better than in north India, and the attitude of Muslims towards Urdu is pragmatic, not emotional. From the organization of education to other spheres of practical life, the position occupied by Urdu has neither become a hurdle to development nor come in conflict with their regional identity.

Let us undertake a brief evaluation of Urdu journalism in the Urdu-speaking and non-Urdu-speaking linguistic regions. The Congress party's Urdu daily, *Qaumi Awaz*, published from Delhi, whose circle of readers until 1995 was extremely wide, includes Muslims of Uttar Pradesh and Delhi. Even the hostile Muslim reaction against the Congress after the demolition of the Babri Masjid could not erode the popularity of this daily. The print order of Urdu dailies published from other cities and towns of Uttar Pradesh and Delhi would number not more than a few hundred. (As stated earlier, most of these dailies publish only file copies for securing newsprint quotas and other facilities.) This number also includes Urdu dailies like *Pratap* which is owned by a refugee Punjabi establishment, and whose readership by and large comprises that section of Punjabi and Sindhi Hindus and Sikhs who had learnt Urdu as a second language in pre-Partition days. They represent the last generation of Urdu-knowing Hindus and Sikhs. The succeeding generation of Punjabi Hindus and Sikhs is unfamiliar with Urdu, and some Hindus form the hardcore of fanatics. Therefore, the attitude of this group, as well as *Hind Samachar* (51,264), which was the largest circulation in this part of the country, is openly hostile towards Islam and Muslims.[9]

In Bangalore, one popular Urdu daily, *Salar* (11,871), is doing well even though the size of the Urdu-speaking population of Bangalore is substantially lower than in the main cities of Uttar Pradesh and Delhi. The picture is not vastly different in Calcutta. The attachment of Bengali Muslims for their language is proverbial. Throughout the struggle of the Bengali Muslims to carve East Pakistan out as a distinct country the issue of Urdu verses Bengali remained at the core. The protagonists of Pakistan, an eminent Muslim scholar Maulana Syed Sulaiman Nadvi and Maulvi Abdul Haq, who earned the title of the grand old man of Urdu, argued that Bengali Muslims should not express hostility towards Urdu as the national language of unified Pakistan. They asserted that Urdu contained many Arabic words and is written in the Arabic script, the language of the Koran. The East Bengali Muslims rejected this logic and established Bangladesh with Bengali as the national language. By contrast, two popular Urdu dailies, *Azad Hind* (15,351) and *Akhbar-e Mashriq* (12,882), are published in Calcutta.[10]

Urdu is not widely spoken in Maharashtra or Andhra Pradesh. Muslims constitute a relatively small section in both these states. Moreover, education in both states is conducted predominantly in the regional language. Over the years, in a bid to support the campaign of north Indian Muslims to have Urdu declared as the second official language, Muslims of both states have started Urdu schools and claimed Urdu to be their mother tongue. However, Marathi in Maharashtra and Telugu in Andhra Pradesh remain the languages of everyday communication. Even so, three prominent dailies—*Inquilab* (23,531), *Urdu Times* (19,746), and *Hindustan* (8,612)—are published in Bombay. Three Urdu dailies—*Siyasat* (39,949), *Rehnuma-e Deccan* (20,982), and *Munsif* (9390)—are published from Hyderabad.[11]

In Bihar, where a substantial number of Muslims are concentrated and Urdu is the recognized second official language, the state of Urdu journalism is discouraging. In Patna alone, nearly fifty dailies or weeklies are published, but the real print order in a majority of cases is limited to fewer than a hundred copies.

It is being recognized belatedly that Urdu journalistic establishments in Delhi and other north Indian states will have to change their linguistic policy, in view of the emerging reality that the new generation of north Indian Muslims is unfamiliar with Urdu. It will also be necessary that rather than exclusively focusing on the issues of north Indian Muslims, they will have to give greater space to Muslims in the rest of India, particularly south Indian Muslims. The Hindi weekly *Nai Zameen* (47,901) is largely a response to this emerging reality. It will provide an alternative to the highly communal anti-Muslim local dailies to which the Hindi-knowing Muslim youth are willy-nilly exposed. Other newspapers that wish to restrict themselves to north India will also have to increasingly publish Hindi editions like *Nai Duniya*. As they do so, they will have to shift from emotional and provocative issues that have traditionally appealed to Muslims in north India, and accord greater space to serious socio-economic and employment-related issues which educated Muslim youth are increasingly facing in contemporary India.

CONCLUSION

The system of most of the Urdu newspapers is at least one century old. In today's modern world one is at a loss to understand how these newspapers, which are printed so carelessly and frivolously, survive and serve as vehicles of Muslim journalism in India. The office of most of the newspapers consists of one room. In the name of the working staff, there are one or two Urdu DTP operators or calligraphers and one or two sub-editors. The job of the sub-editors is to select the already published stories from various newspapers and mould them according to their own policy and ideology so that they appear provocative and anti-Muslim. Proof-readers and copy-editors have no role in Urdu newspapers in India. Sub-editors are generally not very well educated. The only quality they have is that they have a working knowledge of Urdu and Hindi. Normally they do not know English, the reason being that they are products of orthodox dini madaris (religious educational institutions). The salary of a sub-editor in most of the cases is a third of an orderly in a national daily. They are usually paid as little as Rs 2,000.

These Urdu newspapers generally have no column for intellectuals or for commissioned articles. Therefore, there is no question of paying an honorarium to writers. Thus, it is the owners of the papers who generally occupy the posts of editors and become wealthy, as their publications, despite being sub-standard, are quite popular among the Muslim masses.

This picture is gradually changing with the slow increase in the size of the Muslim middle-class. Educated Muslims who have some familiarity with the English language, and are interested in national problems, are turning to Hindi and English newspapers. English newspapers, unlike Urdu ones, are more beneficial to them because they provide information about jobs and admissions to universities. The management of the weekly *India Today* and also some other newspaper houses have on several occasions decided to start publication of Urdu versions. However, each time Urdu editors discouraged them by presenting to them distorted facts about Urdu readership. They were told that Muslims do not trust the national press and by nature they tend to be 'anti-establishment'. As a result such proposals have been shelved. However, it is almost certain that if some prominent newspapers or magazines were to publish an Urdu version, it would be a sure success because Urdu is a symbol of the culture and identity of the Muslims throughout the country. Until this happens, the prospects remain that Urdu journalism will continue the traditional game of arousing Muslim sentiments through provocative writing, and render them susceptible to the influence of the communal leadership, with which a good many Urdu journalists are themselves aligned due to their own ambitions for political prominence and professional clout.

NOTES

1. Rajya Sabha (Upper House of Indian Parliament) Proceedings— Annexure referred to in a reply to parts (a), (b), and (c) of the Rajya Sabha Unstarred Question no. 3294 for 15 December 1992.
2. The Judgement of the Supreme Court of India, Criminal Appeal Number 103 of 1981, D/-23.4.1985, *Mohd. Ahman Khan* (Appellant) vs *Shah Bano Begum* and others (Respondents).
3. Ibid.
4. Its circulation was not recorded. But a reliable source holds that its circulation was between 75,000 and 1,000,000, which is a record in Urdu journalism in India.
5. *Akhbar-e-Nau* (Urdu Weekly, New Delhi), 19 March 1991.
6. This assessment of Mohammad Afzal is based on a number of interviews conducted with him in 1991–3. One of them was published in *Saptahik Hindustan* on 24 March 1991.
7. *Saptahik Hindustan*, 28 April 1991.
8. *Nai Duniya* declared that after 30 October 1990 India will become a Hindu theocratic state. 30 October 1990 was chosen by the fundamentalist Hindu organizations to start the construction of a Ram Mandir at the site of Babri Masjid. But their attempts were foiled by Mulayam Singh Yadav, the chief minister of Uttar Pradesh. Again, these 'fascist' Hindu organizations chose 6 December 1992 for the same purpose and subsequently succeeded in demolishing the Babri Masjid. See *Saptahik Hindustan*, 9 December 1990. *Faisal Jadeed*, in its issue of 10 November 1990, demanded that the government provide arms to the Muslims for self-defence.
9. Rajya Sabha Proceedings in reply to question number 3294, 15 December 1992.
10. Ibid.
11. Ibid.

16

Muslims and the Press
Wahiduddin Khan

The power of the press can be gauged by the use of the term 'Fourth Estate'. Although its origins go far back in time, it did not acquire the definite and effective form of an organized means of mass communication until a course in journalism was given at the University of Missouri, Columbia, from 1879 to 1884. Throughout the twentieth century it has gradually gone from strength to strength. By the end of the nineteenth century, the Muslims as a community had entered the field of journalism in earnest. Probably the first notable Muslim paper was *Al-Urwatul Usqa* (1883), brought out by Sayyed Jamaluddin and Mufti Mohd. Abduhu. Anti-British in sentiment, its objective was to unite Muslims all over the world as a means of putting an end to British colonialism. Since that time tens of thousands of magazines and periodicals have been brought out in a variety of Muslim languages. I myself have been reading Muslim periodicals in the original in three languages—Arabic, English, and Urdu—and have to some extent read periodicals in other languages in translation. In this paper, I propose to make an evaluation of the Muslim press in the light of the considerable information which I have at my disposal. But first of all, a set of criteria shall have to be adopted by which we may judge the two basic aspects of journalism: namely, presentation and content. I would suggest that our yardstick for presentation should be the Western press, and our criterion for content should be the Koran.

Setting up the Western press as a model of presentation is perfectly justifiable, since no other press in the world can match its level of excellence. Judged by this standard, the Muslim press is so far behind in every respect that assigning a place to it in the hierarchy of standards is simply not possible. In terms of circulation, the Western press, with its direct access to global news, has already achieved an international status, whereas the Muslim press, with its dependence on indirect sources of information, suffers from such limitations as to make it barely of regional interest. Today the whole world looks to the Western press for international news, while the Muslim press is not, so far, an accepted source even of Muslim news. This difference of standards between the two is underscored by the fact that, to date, all over the world, important Muslim news is sought after in the Western press, not only by non-Muslims but also by Muslims themselves. An instance of this reliance on the Western media was demonstrated during the period leading up to the signing of the agreement between Israel and the PLO on the subject of mutual recognition, surely one of the most important events of the Muslim world. Right from the beginning of the negotiations till the actual signing of the agreement in Washington on 13 September 1993, the Western media, and not the Muslim press, remained the principal source of all information on this topic for both Muslims and non-Muslims.

One very important asset of the Western press is the high intellectual calibre of its staff, which is the main reason for the excellence of its academic and journalistic standards. Muslim journalism, on the contrary, has suffered from the general lack of awareness among the community, which has in turn discouraged men of superior intellect from engaging themselves in the field. In its failure to measure up to the high standards of the present day, the Muslim press has had little or no impact upon public opinion. It would be quite correct to say that it exists in name only.

Now let us examine the content of Muslim journalism from the standpoint of Koranic standards. The writing of the Koran took place—without ascription—in the manner of modern journalism. That is, the contents of the Koran were not revealed all together in the form of a book, but came in instalments, or as men of religion would say, in separate revelations over a period of 23 years. So, the Koran was like a periodical which was started in 610 AD, reaching its completion only in 632 AD. As well as providing the archetypal form for modern journalism, the Koran had the same objectives as those of our modern press, namely, to guide people at critical moments, to help solve their problems, and then set the course for their thinking and action. Now let us see what method was adopted in the Koran over this period of 23 years.

The revelation of the Koran started in ancient Mecca. At that time, a number of pressing issues presented themselves not only in Mecca but throughout Arabia. For instance, the holy Kabah housed 360 idols. The Roman and the Iranian empires had made political inroads into Arabia. There were many evils, and crime was widespread among the tribes. Yet the first commandment revealed in the Koran made no reference to any of these problems. On the contrary, the first commandment of the Koran was *Iqra* (read). Given Arabia's condition at that time, it might have been expected that the first verse of the Koran would be either a protest, or a command to wage war. But it was not. Instead, the Koran gave the very positive injunction to read! In other words, to think positively in the face of adversity. Let others follow the path of destruction: one's own course should be that of construction. It was strong in its advocacy of the power of peace as opposed to that of violence. It guided the oppressed to shun the path of violence in favour of adherence to the principle of non-violent activism.

This means that the first part of the Koran counsels against head-on confrontations in the attempt to deal with life's problems. It advises one to get at the root of the cause of the trouble. The most obvious root cause of many problems is the lack of perception and judgement, which stems from poor education or no education at all. With the spread of education, this ignorance, which underlies so much of the evil in the world today, could be banished. This in turn would facilitate the solution of many different kinds of problems.

A similar revelation was made on the occasion of the Hudaybiyya controversy, when Meccan leaders refused to let Muslims enter Mecca for the performance of Umrah (a minor pilgrimage, which can be performed at any time of the year). This revelation in no way incited the Muslims at that point in time to wage war against the enemy. Instead, it enjoined the Muslim to adopt the path of avoidance in order to counter the display of arrogance and prejudice on the part of the Meccans, and to go back after entering into a peace treaty with them. Thus, on such a delicate and sensitive occasion, Muslims were advised that the power of peace was greater than the power of war. They were advised, therefore, to forsake the path of war and taste the fruits of peace.

Judged by Koranic standards, Muslim journalism falls far below that of the others. While the Koranic periodical was run on positive lines, the entire Muslim press of the present day is plunged in negativism. Where the Koran stressed the importance of action and the avoidance of reaction, present-day Muslim journalism as a whole is oriented towards and motivated by reaction. During the last day of the Muslims in Mecca (shortly before the emigration), when they had been cruelly persecuted by the Meccan non-Muslims, this verse of the Koran was revealed: 'Every hardship is followed by ease' (94: 6–7). That is to say that for this world God has decreed this facility, or ease, which should exist side by side with difficulty and hardship. One should, therefore, ignore difficulty, seek opportunities and avail of them. But today Muslim journalism has devoted itself entirely to the ferreting out difficulties, mainly plots and conspiracies of others against them.

If we were to place the revelations of the Koran on parallel with investigative, informative, and advisory functions of the modern press, the most appropriate, although anachronistic, term for them would be constructive journalism. Where the parallel ends is in the failure of modern Muslim journalism—unlike the Koran—to be constructive. I would say that, on the contrary, it is run on the very opposite principle.

Hundreds and thousands of newspapers and periodicals are brought out by Muslims but although they all appear under different titles, they might well be lumped together under the single title of 'protest'. If we substituted 'Protest Daily', 'Protest Weekly', or 'Protest Monthly', for their original titles, this would in no way be inappropriate to their contents. In the light of Koranic wisdom, nothing but negative reaction with constant repetition builds up a paranoid mentality. It encourages peevishness and irritability, which are hardly the mental states we need for a positive, practical struggle. Of course, we need our press to have a powerful reach, but it must cultivate the kind of constructive thinking which will lead to a regeneration of the Muslim community. Regeneration can come about only through self-construction. It can never result from the mere lodging of protests against others.

Now, the question arises as to how the Muslim press developed into a medium of protest. In the nineteenth century, when the power of the press was building up, the Muslims were divested of political power. It was this concatenation of events which produced the mindset due to which the entire Muslim press has taken the shape of an organ of protest in modern times. This is the reality, but Muslim leaders, then and now, have projected the loss of power as a matter of usurpation, brought to fruition by plots and conspiracies. It is surely a law of nature that those who progress are entitled to a position of dominance. The reverse is also necessarily true. So why should the Muslims consider themselves an exception to that rule? If they remained backward, they deserved to fall from power. Muslim leaders, however, unwilling or unable to face the facts, traced the decline of their community to the machinations of the West. It was this rigidity of thinking which turned past and present Muslim journalism into a platform of protest. Immersed in such ideas, they became engaged in vociferous outbursts against all Christian, Jewish, and European powers. The real task to be performed, according to them, was the continual registering of complaints.

Had the Muslim leaders been of a different mentality, they might have made a more profound study of the situation: Muslims were, in fact, unable to move with the times due to their own inabilities. This would have resulted in their urging the press to devote itself to Muslim reconstruction. Journalists would then have worked towards bringing about an awareness among Muslims for the need for modern education. Only in that way would their feet have been set on the path of progress. Only then would they have realized that it was the time for self-preparation rather than the time for *jihad*. Had Muslim leaders and journalists subscribed to this way of thinking, they would have impressed upon their public how imperative it was for them to remain patient in the face of Western dominance, and to devote all their time and energy to the field of construction. Modern circumstances demanded patience, but Muslims could think of nothing but protest.

Today, Muslims—Indian Muslims in particular—place continuing emphasis on having their own press in English. Its aim, according to them, is the proper presentation of their case before other nations. It is probably due to this mentality that we see the unique phenomenon, unparalleled in any other community, of a number of papers being brought out with purely communal titles, such as *Voice of Ummah, Muslim Outlook, Call of the Ummah,* etc. The reason for such papers to have purely communal titles is traceable to the image the Muslims cherish of themselves as being faultless and above reproach. In their periodicals, they have felt—consciously or unconsciously—that the world was not being given a true picture of them, and as a matter of self-vindication wanted to publish papers which would correct what they felt were erroneous impressions—by projecting Muslims as absolutely perfect, but ill-treated human beings. It is significant that papers of this sort published in English over the last fifty years have either failed or ceased publication, or, if they are still in existence, take the form of highly abridged Muslim bulletins rather than full-fledged Muslim newspapers.

The reason for this failure is quite simple. Where the totality of issues is expected, the Muslim press gives only half the picture. For instance, take the case of the Bhagalpur riots in October 1989. Bombs were initially set off by Muslims. It was only after this that Hindus set fire to Muslim properties. The non-Muslim press described the acts of both the communities, including the fact that the Hindu destruction of Muslim property had been on a much larger scale than the damage caused by the Muslim bombs; yet, plying in the face of the facts, the Muslims wanted no mention of bomb-throwing. They wanted only the burning of their property by the Hindus to be highlighted. Similarly, when the Babri Masjid was demolished on 6 December 1992, the Muslims of Bombay wanted no mention of their subsequent rioting and destruction, which sparked off Hindu acts of revenge, again on a much larger scale. They wanted facts damaging to themselves to be suppressed, so that they might appear to be the innocent, injured party.

This attitude extends to every important sphere of Muslim existence. For example, the number of Muslims in government service is very small, mostly because very few Muslims attain the necessary level of education. When this subject is covered by the non-Muslim press, the paucity of Muslims in government office is underlined, but at the same time, the reason for this—namely, their lack of education—is also stressed. The Muslims, on the contrary, want everyone to know that they are under-represented in government service, but they want all mention of their backwardness to be omitted. Again, during the Afghanistan war, the non-Muslim press gave equal credit to the valour of the Afghani Mujahiddin and the assistance given by the Americans. The Muslim press, on the contrary, kept the Americans out of the picture—although the help they gave was quite extraordinary—and gave full credit to the Afghani Mujahiddin. They act in this way because they want to prove that Muslims are entirely virtuous and innocent of all wrongdoing. And that if they appear to have shortcomings, it is because of the harsh treatment meted out to them by others.

It is on the basis of this kind of one-sided and partial news reporting that Muslims want to create their own press. What they do not realize is that the world for which they want to create such a press has neither any need nor any interest in it. Such papers issued by Muslims are destined to be read by Muslims alone. In this world of cause and effect, such efforts cannot have any other result.

Another issue, which, despite massive coverage, the Muslim press has failed to influence, is that of Zionism vis-à-vis the Arab world. Over the last fifty years, Muslim journalists have devoted all their energies to writing against Zionism and the existence of Israel as a sovereign state, but to no avail. As a journalistic campaign, this was a complete failure. The Egyptian president Anwar Sadat recognized Israel in the Camp David agreement in 1979, and although the PLO continued to reject Israel, it finally surrendered after a period of 14 years, giving its formal recognition to Israel at a function held in Washington on 13 September 1993. This event, the culmination of so many years of struggle for the very opposite outcome, is to the discredit of all sections of the Muslim press. It could neither avert the tragedy of Israel being set up as a sovereign state nor could it lessen the pain of its consequences for the Arab world. The PLO's recognition of Israel ought to be an eye-opener for Muslim journalists everywhere. Now it is high time the basic weaknesses and shortcomings of the Muslim press are acknowledged so that it may be reshaped anew.

To me, the Muslim press has been suffering from what I can only call as unjustified self-righteousness on the part of the Muslim intellectuals. It is this innate weakness which has prevented them from seeing their own shortcomings. All they can see is the plots of others behind every problem their community faces. Consequently, instead of engaging themselves in constructive activities, they spend their time inciting members of their community to protest against others.

Journalism of this kind will only lull the community to sleep by providing it with doses of opium: it cannot become the means of its regeneration. This is the modern reality of the Muslim press. It must also be conceded that neither at present nor in the near future can Muslims bring their journalism up to the standard of the day. One basic reason is that modern journalism is fed by industry, and that is a field in which Muslims have yet to find a noteworthy place. For this reason, it is my firm opinion that, at the moment, Muslims are in no position to achieve an international status for their press.

That being so, what are we to do? I think in this matter our first step should be to heed the wisdom of the old saying: 'Begin at the beginning.' If we can adopt this realistic approach, we shall soon discover that, despite all deterrents, we are in a position to make an effective start by substantially improving the quality of Muslim journalism. By first setting aside the impossible, we must explore actual opportunities and from that point make our beginning, for the right beginning guarantees the right end.

1. One vital step is to provide good training to Muslim youths, and help them to enter various newspapers and news agencies. Over the last few years, a certain number of young Muslims have entered these fields. But this has only happened sporadically, as the result of their personal motivation. There is no such general awareness of journalistic imperatives and opportunities in the Muslim community.

2. Another important point is that any community paper which is brought out should be of a very high standard. Moreover, Muslim periodicals should be published in the mother tongue of their readers, so that language may not prove an obstacle in bringing about an awareness of the times and a sense of commitment at the community level. They should also stop encouraging their readers to achieve their objectives by the continual lodging of protests and instead point the way to modern opportunities, with exhortations to make the best possible use of them.

3. It is essential to cultivate journalistic consciousness among the educated class of Muslims. This paper constitutes an important step towards that. Efforts of this nature must continue and expand in their scope.

4. Muslim journalism's greatest shortcoming is that it presents no model of excellence to the young people of our community. Today, Muslim journalism is almost entirely filled with amateur journalists who resort to yellow journalism. The reason for its being of this hue is that, in the absence of any support from industry, it must resort to unscrupulous sensationalism in order to survive. There is really no alternative. That is the price that journalism pays for the Muslims industrial backwardness.

Exemplary journalism can only be brought into existence by making sacrifices. If a team of educated Muslims could muster enough courage to bring out a model paper, irrespective of recurring losses, and continue to maintain its high standard, this would indeed be a welcome breakthrough as well as a great feat. In the present circumstances, there is no other way to bring out a paper of quality.

5.   To ensure that Muslims make an effective entry into the field of journalism, one positive and result-yielding step would be to open a Muslim school of journalism, which should conform to the highest standards of the present day. One very necessary feature would be to have arrangements for journalistic training in all the Muslim languages. Once such a school were to be established, journalistic progress could be achieved by leaps and bounds, because it would attract the very best of our young aspiring writers. With proper direction, effort, and orientation, it could soon assume the position of an international institute.

17

Is Urdu Journalism in India a Lost Battle?

Arshad Amanullah

Sher Singh, a resident of a predominantly Hindu locality of New Delhi and the owner of the Sandeep Tea Stall where I usually have my breakfast, sometimes reads the Urdu daily *Rashtriya Sahara* (RS) and at times one of the Hindi dailies, usually *Dainik Jagran*. He belongs to the generation which had lived the experiences of the Partition of the Indian subcontinent. He vaguely recollects those days when it was not rare to see a person devouring an Urdu newspaper in the public domain. Now things have changed. Hindi newspapers have replaced their Urdu counterparts.

The feelings of 70-year-old Sher Singh are not isolated ones. Most of the writings about Urdu journalism in India are nothing but a requiem to a non-existent entity. Academic papers on the theme are replete with reasons and figures substantiating this narrative of decline. In contrast, the last decade, under the influence of the forces of liberalization, privatization, and globalization, has been witness to some visible changes in this atmosphere clouded with despair and dismay. The emergence of Urdu publications from Sahara India Mass Communications (SIMC) on the Urdu mediascape, launch of a number of dailies both in the southern and northern spheres of the country, and the boom in their readership in recent years defies the stereotypes of Urdu journalism and calls for a fresh look at the current scenario. This paper seeks to study this emergent interesting phenomenon.

THE NARRATIVE OF DECLINE

'Urdu journalism', says Mohan Chiraghi, the editor of the daily *Qaumi Awaz*, Delhi, 'is a lost battle. I am regretting after 25 years why I decided to switch to it from English journalism'.[1] This realization of loss on his part stems from two factors that plague Urdu journalism:

it pays its journalists very meagre amounts of money, insufficient for two meals with dignity; and they do not get any job satisfaction as there is no channel through which a journalist can get feedback of readers regarding his writings. Farhat Ehsas, a former colleague of Chiraghi, agrees with him. He says: 'Like Urdu, the journalism in the language also is a non-living entity.'[2] Elaborating his argument he further says that though there are Urdu newspapers, journalism is perhaps not the appropriate word to refer to the process of bringing them out. A symbiotic interaction among readers, market forces, and the intellectual capital of journalists, according to him, is very crucial for the existence of a lively and healthy journalism. 'This is simply absent in the Urdu Press,'[3] believes Farhat.

An honest investigation into what ails Urdu journalism presently cannot be imagined without studying trends prevalent during the Partition decades. Unfortunately, those from the politicians, including Muslim community, worked very hard to project Urdu as the language of the Muslims, and they succeeded in achieving this. Consequently, the lens through which one looked at news-making, editorial writing, and news analysis became myopic. It reduced the all-embracing status of the Urdu press to the representative of the concerns of only one community. This deprived Urdu newspapers of a section of readers who had migrated to India from Pakistan and were in search of newspapers they could identify with.

Urdu journalists belonging to the majority community who had migrated to India from Pakistan established their papers in Delhi. *Hind Samachar*,[4] *Milap*, *Pratap*, *Vir Arjun*, and many others very soon became apple of the eyes of the non-Muslim Urdu readers as they filled the gap. Though the reading material presented in them used to be in Persian script, their 'Urdu' was heavily laden with Sanskrit words. Their approach was communal and destructive. No one could blame them. They were driven out of their homes in Pakistan only because they were non-Muslims. *Pratap*, an Urdu daily uprooted from Lahore, was the most vociferous in spewing communal venom. The Jana Sangh, the political wing of the RSS, was now the champion of the Hindu cause. The main issues which were making headlines in the Muslim-owned Urdu newspapers as well were Urdu, whether Aligarh Muslim University was to be or not to be a minority institution, Common Civil Code, Article 370 on Kashmir, the Babri Masjid, and communal riots. Consequently, Urdu newspapers, unlike other vernacular print media, got divided into two camps: Hindu-owned newspapers and Muslim-owned newspapers. Both of them have locked horns in a battle of publishing sensational and sub-standard reading material about each other in their respective publications. Thus, according to G.D. Chandan, an authority on the statistics of the Urdu press, 'Urdu journalism is yet to recover from the shadow of two-nation theory.'[5]

With the departure of the Urdu-knowing generation of the refugees, the Hindu-owned Urdu newspapers are rapidly shutting down. Moreover, Muslim Urdu users who were products of secular education available in Urdu in the country before 1947 had almost come to an end in the 1980s. The hostility of the political class and societal apathy towards Urdu since Independence have, among other factors, been responsible for not allowing the emergence of a new generation of Urdu users among Muslims with a secular outlook. The void thus created in the domain of Urdu journalism was filled by madrasa graduates. This has culminated the process of transformation of Urdu journalism into Islamist journalism.[6]

Muslim-owned newspapers have in most cases not been honest even to the real problems of the Muslims. Turning a blind eye to the basic predicaments of the community—their continuously decreasing representation in different walks of national life, as is suggested in the recently compiled Sachar Committee Report—the Muslim-owned Urdu media made its readers believe that all they needed to do was to fight for the minority character of the Aligarh Muslim University, for the Babri Mosque, and against the Hindu fascist forces. Instead of acting as the debating platform for meaningful discussions and introspection on their social and educational backwardness, it compromised with journalistic ethics to supply them the reading material they were demanding as a result of their fear psychosis. The emerging middle-class among Muslims do not read Urdu newspapers as these papers do not address their needs and tastes.

The current scenario of the Urdu press has not been inviting enough to attract any big media house or corporate to launch any venture in the language. It is known that *India Today* and *Tehelka*, two of the top weeklies of India, were once flirting with the idea of launching Urdu publications. After getting negative opinions from economists regarding the revenue pattern of Urdu press, they threw their dummies into the dustbin.[7]

An overview of the circulation pattern of the Urdu press illuminates other dimensions of the decline debate. In its very first report (published in 1958), the Registrar of Newspapers for India declared that the total number of Urdu newspapers and periodicals in India stood at 513 in 1957. The Urdu press has since then been making good progress almost every decade, till 1997, as is evident from the following table:[8]

Table 17.1: Decadal growth in the number of Urdu newspapers and their circulation

Year	Number of newspapers	Comparative gain over previous decade	Circulation	Comparative gain over previous decade
1957	513	98	7,84,000	NA
1967	864	351	13,58,000	5,74,00
1977	1047	183	15,81,000	2,23,000
1987	1676	629	28,06,000	12,25,000
1997	2970	994	61,66,212	30,60,212

It is clear that the growth rate was remarkable between 1987 and 1997. It was 1.59 times in terms of number of papers and 2.19 times in terms of circulation. Further, a comparison between 1957, the base year, and 1997 shows that the number of Urdu newspapers had risen by 2,157 or 4.2 times, and the circulation by 53,82,212 or nearly seven times.[9] Also, they generally gained in most states, excluding the Punjab region, both in number and circulation.

With an eye on the astronomical number of dailies/periodicals and shortage of human resources in the office of the RNI, one can easily understand that it is almost impossible to verify data provided

Table 17.2: Statewise growth in number and circulation of Urdu newspapers (1957–97)[10]

States	Comparative growth between 1957 and 1997	
	Number (times)	Circulation (times)
Andhra Pradesh	18	26
Bihar	13	45
Karnataka	11	6
Uttar Pradesh	6	23
Maharashtra	5	5
West Bengal	5	2
Delhi	3.5	3.5

in the annual statements by the publishers under the provisions of Section 19 D of the Press and Registration of Books Act, 1867. Moreover, the RNI's 1998 report points out that a significant section of the newspaper establishments, particularly the Small Categories (to which the bulk of the Urdu Press belongs) do not submit their annual statements to the RNI office. RNI's report, *Press in India 2004–5*, acknowledges that out of 60,413 registered publications as on 31 March 2005, only 7,225 publications submitted statements for the year. 'Any information reflected in this Report, therefore, can not be construed as verified or accepted by the RNI.'[11]

According to the report, only 275 of the grand total of 2,906 Urdu newspapers submitted their circulation figures in 2001. The total circulation of the Urdu Press decreased to 51,16,182 copies in 2001 from 61,20,317 copies in 2000 (that is, by 16.41 per cent). The comparative picture in the hitherto leading states is given in the table below.[12]

Table 17.3: Decrease in circulation between 2000 and 2001

State	Total circulation (2001)	Total circulation (2000)	Decrease
Andhra Pradesh	3,27,116	5,06,731	1,79,615
Bihar	6,82,805	8,17,212	1,34,407
Delhi	11,43,454	12,87,496	1,44,04
Punjab	66,556	74,356	7,800

Though this is a highly depressing situation, the circulation of Urdu newspapers has seen an upbeat mood in the following two to three years. The total circulation of the Urdu Press in 2001 stood at 51,16,182 copies, which increased to 67, 90,697 copies in 2003 and further to 81,09,935 copies in 2004. The total number of registered newspapers was 3,078 but only 403 submitted their Annual Statements. This indicates an increase in the number of newspapers which made submissions, as this number was not more than 275 in 2001. It would not be out of context to point out that 31 newspapers were taken on RNI's record in 2004–5. A comparison between the statewise circulation patterns in 2001 and 2004 will render a clearer picture of recent trends.

Table 17.4: Number of newspapers and their circulation in different states

State/UT	2001		2004		
	Total number of newspapers	Total circulation	Total number of newspapers	Number of newspapers which submitted annual statements	Total circulation
Andhra Pradesh	495	3,27,116	510	59	8,25,050
Bihar	159	6,82,805	162	17	7,31,491
Chhattisgarh	NA	NA	1	NA	NA
Delhi	488	11,43,454	535	85	16,72,108
Gujarat	NA	NA	2	NA	NA
Haryana	17	2250	17	02	28,119
Himachal Pradesh	NA	NA	6	NA	NA
Jammu & Kashmir	251	99,489	271	16	4,06,345
Jharkhand	12	Not Supplied	15	03	1,17,762
Karnataka	133	1,75,537	141	06	2,19,705
Madhya Pradesh	30	77,397	33	05	83,388
Maharashtra	218	2,16,094	230	21	2,75,059
Orissa	05	1000	7	01	1000
Punjab	108	66,556	108	04	41,542
Rajasthan	22	Not Supplied	22	02	13,000
Tamil Nadu	17	43,541	17	02	43,752
Uttaranchal	14	3510	18	04	61,335
Uttar Pradesh	858	20,24,675	910	168	33,50,018
West Bengal	70	2,00,008	73	08	2,40,261
Grand Total	2906	51,16,182	3078	403	81,09,935

It would not be wise to take the official circulation figures of Urdu newspapers at face value, as government officials are assigned the role of issuing misleading statements highlighting the progress made in the promotion of Urdu. In the government files, of course, Urdu journalism is making steady progress. The growth of Urdu journalism is directly linked to Urdu education in common schools with secular curricula. Until there is no arrangement for teaching of Urdu in such schools, the Urdu-knowing population would remain confined to the madrasas and therefore Urdu newspapers, though unwillingly, would continue to publish only what madrasa graduates would like to read.

Unfortunately, after Partition, Urdu has not been included by the Congress leadership in the secular curriculum, especially in the cow-belt states. Consequently, Urdu education got relegated to madrasas. Moreover, due to economic backwardness, the *dini talim* gradually replaced secular education among poor Muslims. This proved detrimental to the overall progress of the Muslim community. It also symbolized the failure of the national education policy and the constitutional obligation to treat Muslims at par with non-Muslims in the education sector too. Obviously, an economically backward section of society, such as Muslims, cannot develop an educational system parallel to the state-sponsored education network. Sooner or later, civil society will have to provide Muslims with secular education at par with other religious groups.[13]

THE SOUTH IS DIFFERENT

The situation in the southern states of Andhra Pradesh, Maharashtra, and Karnataka is diametrically different from what we have discussed till now in the context of the northern part of the country. Though Chiraghi does not see the difference, his colleague Sohail Anjum thinks otherwise. With a few exceptions like *Nasheman*, Bangalore, the *jazbatiyat* (sensationalism) that marks the editorial policy of the northern newspapers is not that prevalent in the south. Anjum avers that they first go into the depth of news reports, verify them, and then prepare the news.[14] A survey of the content of these newspapers supports his views. *Azad Hind*, Kolkata, is the only daily newspaper which religiously adheres to the same journalistic ethics though it is not from the south.

Adding a different perspective to this, Parwana Rudolvi,[15] a veteran journalist from Delhi, informs that as the newspapers of the south are well off, they do not need to take recourse to cheap jazbatiyat. Citing the example of *Rahnuma-e-Dakkan*, Hyderabad, he says that it has a tendency to inject a staple dose of sensational and emotional content into the minds and hearts of its readers, as it was financially weak due to the insufficient number of advertisements it used to attract.[16]

Unlike the Urdu Press of north India and Hyderabad, the newspapers of Maharashtra try to cover the whole length and breadth of the country in the news they carry. They attach due importance to the news related to the Muslims of the north too. The reason is that migrants from the Gangetic regions to Mumbai, the business capital of India, constitute a sizeable section of their readers.

Though it is the *Urdu Times*, a daily from Mumbai, whose tagline reads: '*Urdu Awam Ka Bebak Tarjuman*' (a fearless spokesperson of the Urdu-knowing masses), Anjum acknowledges that 'the sobriety and the quality that mark the daily *Inquilab*, Mumbai, is simply unmatched in Urdu journalism in India today.'[17] Instead of being no less sober than *Inquilab*, lack of human resources prevents the *Qaumi Awaz* of Delhi from offering content that can address the needs and taste of the youth and the slowly emerging Muslim middle-class.[18] South Indian Urdu newspapers can afford to offer several special supplements because they have readership cutting across different age and social groups.[19] Parwana Rudolvi attributes the presence of this universe of readers in the south to two factors: unlike the north, there is a provision for secular education in Urdu in the academic institutions of the region, and the Urdu users of the south have the purchasing power.[20]

In the Age of Urdu E-Papers

It should be acknowledged that it is the south which has introduced the concept of the e-paper in Urdu journalism. The daily *Siasat*, Hyderabad, with the launch of its e-paper on 30 October 2004, was the world's first Urdu newspaper to enter the age of internet editions.[21] While a number of newspapers from the south now have well-maintained internet editions, only a few north Indian Urdu newspapers ventured into this new media domain. The daily *Rashtriya Sahara* is available on the internet from 6 February 2007. It is almost at the same time that the newly born *Hindustan Express* (*HE*), Delhi, has also made its presence felt in cyberspace.[22]

Internet editions have opened new vistas, both economic and journalistic in nature, to the Urdu media. With this, Urdu journalism is experiencing vertical expansion for the first time in its history of 184 years. E-papers are meant to tap the unexplored market of the Indian Muslim diaspora of the Gulf region as well as of the West. 'Curiosity about recent developments in their native places', says Khalid Anwar, editor of the daily *HE*, 'motivates the Indian migrants to log on to the internet editions of Urdu newspapers'.[23]

According to a media monitoring portal managed by Adarsh Mumbai News and Feature Agency, Mumbai, the daily *Inquilab* is the most widely read Urdu e-paper. Its total hits are 153,592. *Siasat* from Hyderabad attracts the second largest number of e-readers, as its website has been visited 136,048 times. *Munsif,* from the same city, and *Urdu Times*, Mumbai, stand third and fourth, as their web editions scored 128,857 and 117,812 hits respectively. India's Urdu e-papers have a total of 536,282 hits.[24] This is excluding 7,436 hits which denote the viewership of the just launched e-paper of the *RS*.[25] This new addition to the circulation profile of Urdu press has contributed in a significant way towards raising the stature of Urdu newspapers in the advertisement market. One can easily notice the blessings of this welcome change in the pages of the newspapers from the south.

Pointing out the limitations of the e-papers, Parwana Rudolvi draws attention to the sad reality that most Indian Muslims are keyboard-illiterate, and those who have acquired the skill cannot afford to buy a PC. Netizens are still a rare species among Urdu readers in India.[26] Web editions are no less a boon to the internet-proficient new breed of Urdu journalists as oceans of information are just a click away. However, blog journalism sounds a bit unfamiliar to even these Urdu media professionals. Asad Mirza, editor of the bi-monthly *British Jaiza* (BJ), informs that INPAGE, the only Urdu software which allows one to type in the prevalent Urdu script, is not compatible with machine language. So, to upload digitized Urdu information to any website is next to impossible. In this backdrop, blog journalism seems not likely to dawn on the horizon of the Urdu mediascape in the near future. Microsoft has recently, on a very limited scale, released in Pakistan a new Urdu software called *Urdu Pad*, which is said to go a long way in making digitized Urdu documents attuned to machine language.[27]

Connected with the revolution of information technology is the launch of the United News of India (UNI) news service in Urdu in 1992. With the help of 40 staff members including five women, UNI Urdu (UNIU) processes 150–200 news items during its business period extending to 18 hours everyday. It boasts of subscription from 70 newspapers which comprise around 80–90 per cent of the 'living' Urdu press. Sheikh Manzur Ahmed, who has been with UNI for 27 years and now heads its Urdu unit, has proudly stated that UNIU for the first time placed the Urdu newspapers 'at par with their English counterparts with respect to the availability of news stories'.[28] Moreover, the subscription fee for the Urdu dailies is subsidized to Rs 3,000 monthly, while English and Hindi subscribers have to pay Rs 15,000 for the same period. After the advent of UNIU, the number of suits filed against Urdu newspapers has significantly come down, while earlier this used to be a perennial problem due to the lack of any Urdu news agency.

It is interesting that though the advent of the UNIU has no doubt accelerated the process of establishment of new Urdu dailies, it has deepened the crisis of journalism in the language. 'The purpose of establishing UNIU is defeated,'[29] opines Mohan Chiraghi. He criticizes it on the ground that it has been reduced to a 'translation agency' where Hindi news stories (already translated from English news items) are rendered into Urdu. If an UNIU employee commits a mistake in translating news from Hindi to Urdu, it will be reproduced as it is in all except a few newspapers. Sohail Anjum relates that once 'ISI', the acronym for the international trade mark was typed as '151' in digits in a UNIU news-item. While copy-editing, he corrected the mistake. The next morning he found, to his wonder, that all newspapers published the same mistake, without fixing it.[30] This reveals the fact that Urdu newspapers, in general, are free from the obligations of copy-editing and proof-reading. It also suggests that instead of considering it a supporting agency, Urdu dailies, unlike other language newspapers, rely blindly on its stories. The UNIU is, in a sense, trying to standardize the variety of journalistic praxis (like translation) earlier in vogue in the Urdu press.

The Sahara Story

The Indian newspaper market witnessed a price war between *The Times of India* and *Hindustan Times* in Delhi,[31] in the last one decade in the history of the journalism in India, also known as the 'Samir Jain Years'.[32] The reach of the press (dailies and magazines combined) has increased from 216 million to 222 million over the last one year. According to National Readers Survey 2006, dailies continue to grow, adding 12.6 million readers from last year to reach 203.6 million. The Hindi belt has been witness to intense activity from large dailies and is an indicator of the general growth in the vernacular dailies segment. There are now two dailies that have captured more than 2 crore readers: *Dainik Jagran* (2.12 crores) and *Dainik Bhaskar* (2.10 crores).[33] Table 17.5 reflects the current circulation pattern of the vernacular press.

Robin Jeffrey, writing in the 1990s, foresaw this boom in the market of the vernacular press. He puts it down to three factors: the growth of literacy, the rise of capitalism, and the spread of technology. The last refers to offset printing technology coupled with communications technology that allowed the use of facsimile or satellite editions.[34] The Urdu press is not an exception to these new

Table 17.5: Shift in the circulation pattern in the vernacular press[35]

National Readers Survey 2006			National Readers Survey 2005		
Newspaper	Circulation (thousands)	Rank	Newspaper	Circulation (thousands)	Rank
Dainik Jagran	21,165	1	*Dainik Jagran*	21,244	1
Dainik Bhaskar	20,958	2	*Dainik Bhaskar*	17,379	2
Eenadu	13,805	3	*Eenadu*	11,350	3
Lokmat	10,856	4	*Hindustan*	10,557	4
Amar Ujala	10,847	5	*Amar Ujala*	10,469	5
Hindustan	10,437	6	*Daily Thanthi*	9,445	6
Daily Thanthi	10,389	7	*Lokmat*	8,820	7
Dinakaran	9,639	8	*Rajasthan Patrika*	8,651	8
Rajasthan Patrika	9,391	9	*Dinakaran*	1,485	39
Malayala Manorama	8,409	10	*Malayala Manorama*	7,985	10

trends. As the Hindi press is shocked at the success rate of the horizontal expansion of the daily *Dainik Bhaskar*,[36] media analysts still do not know how to react to the way the SIMC's intervention has changed the world of the Urdu newspaper market.

Before India opened its economy for foreign investment in 1991, the Urdu media had not attracted the attention of any corporate or big media house. So, the launch of the monthly *Sahara Urdu* in October 1991 added a new chapter to the history of the Urdu journalism. In 1994 it became a weekly, which was further transformed into a daily newspaper under the title of the *RS* based in Delhi in 1999. With its editions simultaneously coming out from nine cities,[37] presently the *RS* is no doubt the largest multi-edition Urdu newspaper of the country. *Aalami Sahara* (AS), the weekly Urdu publication, has been in publication since 2002. *Bazm-e-Sahara*, a monthly magazine for the upper-class Urdu users from the SIMC, has recently entered the market.

The driving force behind the print media intervention of the SIMC into Urdu is Aziz Burney. A parallel can easily be drawn between Burney, the editor of all the Urdu publications of SIMC, and Samir Jain,[38] the present boss of Bennett, Coleman & Company Limited (BCCL), as both of them have, through their newspapers, redefined the grammar of journalism in their respective languages. Like Jain, Burney did everything to keep pushing up circulation and offer a trendier newspaper for his predominantly anti-America Muslim readership—from colour supplements, different pricing and different number of pages in different city-editions, to cross-brand advertising packages. However, the newspaper comes nowhere near *The Times of India*.

The SIMC's staff is the highest paid lot in the Urdu world. Moreover, the daily *RS* pays a token honorarium for the contributions on the edit page, simply unprecedented in the history of Urdu journalism. It is in this backdrop that Ather Afzal, who was formerly with the *AS*, says, 'The situation of the Urdu journalism is not as bleak as it used to be around 10–15 years ago.'[39]

What further distinguishes the *RS* from contemporary Urdu publications is the vast network of reporters and stringers the SIMC has managed to spread across the length and breadth of the country. As the Sahara News Bureau (SNB)[40] has its presence in every strategically important city, the *RS* is in a position to not only report what others cannot but is also able to present a counter-perspective to recognized newswire agencies. Due to these two factors, it offers original reporting and attracts a number of quality writings on a range of issues. This is directly converting the readers of other newspapers into the Sahara fold.

Burney was quick to realize the fact that the Urdu journalism, in its essence, is 'views-oriented',[41] as its role in moulding Muslim public opinion is simply incomparable to the other vernacular press. The *RS* maintains a research wing which looks after bringing out its Sunday supplement called *Dastawez*. Started in June 1999, this four-page supplement provides a range of opinions on contemporary issues confronting Indian Muslims. Afzal Misbahi, who edited *Dastawez* from 2003 to 2005, informs that all its pieces are penned down on request by well-known scholars and experts on the concerned theme.[42] He further says that most of its issues deal with political developments. In only 5 per cent cases did it choose to discuss educational backwardness of the Muslim community, while only in 10 per cent cases has it devoted its pages to economic and social problems. During 2000–3, the issues related to the Babri Mosque demolition and the Gujarat carnage of 2002 outnumbered other issues discussed in the pages of *Dastawez*.[43]

Applying the technique of content analysis of mass communication research methodology a couple of years ago, this writer had studied the coverage of Muslim issues (2000–3) in the *RS*.[44] In this regard, some of the findings are as follows:

Table 17.6: Type of news about muslims

Types of news	RS (%)
Sports	6.36
Political	61.90
Economic	2.72
Accidents/disasters	1.36
Films/entertainment/personality	4.54
Development	10.90
Crime	2.72
Religion	9.09
Others	1.36

Table 17.7: Geopolitical categories of
news about muslims

Contries/continents	RS
India	57.27
Pakistan	9.09
Bangladesh	0.91
Afghanistan	5.00
Middle East	15.91
Europe	0.91
Americas	7.27
Others	1.36

Table 17.8: Sources of news

Source	RS
Home Agencies	48.18
Special correspondents	3.63
Reuters	15.91
AFP	1.37
AP	1.36
DPA	1.82
Agencies	11.36
Syndicated reports	12.27
Not mentioned	3.18

There is an accusation of 'sentimentality' against the RS. An overview of its coverage with reference to the death penalty awarded to Saddam Hussein, the former president of Iraq, confirms the accusation. For more than twenty days, the RS kept on devoting one complete page to news related to him and the developments in Iraq. After a small gap of some days, as the date of his punishment, 30 December 2006, approached, the *RS* resumed its allocation of the total space on page 5 to the reactions and writings regarding the controversy surrounding the execution of the death penalty. The caption this page used to carry read: *Saddam Ka Akhiri Salam* (The Last Salute of Saddam).[45] Here the newspaper applied a different technique. It provided its readers Urdu renditions of pieces that appeared in foreign newspapers like the *Independent*, the *New York Times*, the *Guardian*, the *Arab News*, etc. Moreover, it also kept on reproducing articles on the same theme from Urdu newspapers and websites from Pakistan and the Gulf region. It would be interesting to note that instead of acknowledging the source at the end of the piece, the *RS* had a tendency to superimpose the logo of the source newspaper somewhere in the upper third of the text of the piece.

With the use of some big names of world journalism, the *RS* sought to give the impression that it was not only this newspaper but the whole universe of the print media that was doing the same. However, this failed to hide the fact that no newspaper other than the *RS* was devoting that many column inches to just one issue. The sensationalization of the Saddam episode acquired a different dimension when, on the occasion of Muharram, Aziz Burney penned down his *Karbala Ka Paigham* (A Message from Karbala) which appeared in three parts as an exclusive editorial with his signature.[46] A special editorial which bears name of Burney is generally published in a column with green background. However, its background colour and placement varies in different editions. For example, the Delhi edition carried the above-mentioned Muharram message as a front-page editorial in a green background column, while it appeared on page 5 in a normal column in the Mumbai edition.

Burney has a tendency to write special editorials on emotive issues. On the 14th anniversary of the demolition of the Babri Mosque, he had written a front-page editorial titled '6 December', but the column in which it appeared in the Delhi edition had an off-green background. Moreover, before the above-mentioned three-part message, he had other editorials on the issue of Saddam death penalty to his credit. His special editorial *'Islam Dushman To Bush Hai, Saddam Nahi'* ('It is Bush who is the enemy of Islam, not Saddam') had already appeared on page 2 of the Delhi edition on 4 January 2007. It was followed by 'Saddam, Saddam, Saddam, Saddam', a front-page editorial, on 21 January 2007, in the Delhi edition.

A person tuned into the politics of colours may read into this practice of using green background an effort on the part of Burney to project himself as the spokesperson of Islam and Muslims. Also, while portraying the West as a self-conscious collective monolithic entity which is totally anti-Islam in its innate nature, he reduces the multiple identities of its people to a single identity, namely, the religious one. The line between fact and fiction is completely blurred in the narrative world present in these editorials by Burney. Mythologies, collective memories, and allusions towards different cultural markers and religious figures come together to construct an imaginary world where it does not take long to equate Saddam with Islam, the religion of the readers of the *RS*, and his execution with the subjugation of their religion. Arguing in this idiom, Burney easily morphs Saddam into Hussein, the nephew of the Prophet; and Bush into the twenty-first-century avatar of Yazid, a symbol of oppression in Muslim mythology. Now Iraq becomes Karbala, the battlefield where Hussein had attained martyrdom to become a stuff of legend. Against this backdrop, the whole of Iraq transforms into Karbala and acquires the sanctity of the soil of the latter. In this romanticized world, notwithstanding diversified social realities of lived Islam, all differences are sunk in the construction of a meta-narrative which is articulated in the binary opposition of Islam and *Kufr*, locked in a war for eternity.

I would like to reproduce here translations of a few excerpts from the writings of Burney.

EXCERPT 1
Saddam, Saddam, Saddam, Saddam

A sea of million heads chanting only one name, Saddam Hussein ...

The earth has swollen God knows how many skies

I had been hearing it for long but started believing in it after the departure of Saddam from this world.

Who says that Saddam is no more? Victims of big misconceptions are Bush and his followers who think that Saddam is no more in this world. One Saddam has definitely been eliminated from the earth but millions of Saddams were born. The lives of father and son have been ruined in settling score with one Saddam, it would be simply impossible till Doomsday to deal with millions of Saddams. Yes, I accept that I am Saddam Hussein from today onwards; every word that I utter will be a reply to the call which he gave at the last moments of his life ... My battle is that of Saddam, today I express my determination to fight against those anti-Islam forces Saddam was embattled with and I am not alone in this war.[47]

EXCERPT 2

... Whatever has been his past but there is no doubt that his (Saddam's) last war was against the anti-Islam forces and was not for his personal power. His war was for the cause of the unification of the Muslim world and also an articulation of *jihad* against forces inimical to Islam. Through this writing I make a humble request to my Shiite brethren to not to link with personal affairs the execution of Saddam Hussein by George W. Bush, the Yazid of the modern times. The reason is that the danger of invasion on Iran now looms large ...[48]

EXCERPT 3

... Whenever Islam will be in danger, Allah will find some way to protect it. And who knows better than Him whom He will select for what purpose? Is it possible to refute the fact that whether it was a matter of destroying Iraq or of devastating Afghanistan, it is Islam which has always been the target of the US President George Bush? ...[49]

Such tremendous coverage has never been given to the socio-economic problems of the Indian Muslims, as is the need of the hour, especially in light of the findings of the Justice Sachar Committee Report. While exploring the reason for this widespread sentimentality in the Urdu press, I have argued elsewhere that the majority of Urdu journalists are madrasa graduates who have neither training in the social sciences nor the interrogative spirit that is an essential quality in journalism. The main criteria of being a journalist in an Urdu newspaper is that one should be competent to write flowery language.[50] Though the same stands true in the case of the *RS* too, Burney defends the policy of the *RS*, saying, 'We offer what the readers demand.'[51] In this context, what Asad Mirza, editor of *British Jaiza* (*BJ*), has said about the *RS* assumes significance. According to him, 'The *RS* in its present form suggests just a tip of the iceberg of the possibilities in Urdu journalism but it does not offer the reading material it can.'[52]

Burney has almost redefined the concept of bringing out supplements on different themes as an aggressive marketing strategy.

Earlier there used to be four to eight pages in a supplement. Now an *RS* supplement may contain more than 100 pages. 'Sometimes people help us in choosing a theme for a supplement while on other occasions we draw the attention of a particular group/sub-community to a theme the *RS* will be interested in compiling a supplement on,'[53] says Burney, whose association with the SIMC dates back to April 1991. Any topic under the sky, ranging from the Holy Koran to a cult figure of a region or sub-community to a festival/Sufi celebration, can be the central theme of an *RS* supplement. As the supplement draws on the identity crisis or emotional attachment of a certain community to a particular theme, members of the community are keen to buy advertising space in it. It not only translates directly into revenue generation but sometimes ends up upsetting the balance between the advertisement space and the core content space. In this regard, I would like to reproduce for Burney what Sukumar Muralidharan has written for Samir Jain: 'Jain's achievement was to use simple marketing principles and good business sense to transform a down-in-the-dumps publishing company [read Urdu journalism here] into a profit machine.'[54]

It is interesting to note that the *RS* publishes two kinds of supplements: weekly supplements and *Khususi Zamime* (special supplements). There are only two weekly supplements which it offers on Sunday: *Umang* (passion) and *Dastawez* (Documents). As far as the special supplements are concerned, they are, unlike weekly supplements, sold separately and are not offered bundled with the core newspaper. It really takes around 60 to 70 days to bring out a special supplement. Though the *RS* invites contributions from the scribes for these supplements, and advertisements consume more than two-thirds of the space, staff of the SIMC's Urdu publications have to burn the midnight oil to fill the pages of theses supplements. The extra effort, in the form of overtime, that these faceless soldiers put into consolidating the SIMC empire generally goes unnoticed, as they neither get credit for their contributions nor any remuneration.

To bring out more than one edition of a daily newspaper was not new in Urdu journalism.[55] But the publication of the *RS*, an Urdu daily, simultaneously from nine cities is really remarkable. Its product differs in terms of number of pages as well as of price from edition to edition. Consequently, the content it offers to the readers varies and so does the quality.

Table 17.9: Pages and prices of different editions of the *RS*

No.	Place	Days	Pages	Price (INR)
1	Mumbai	Sunday	24 (16 + 4 + 4)	5.00
		Weekdays	16	3.00
2	Hyderabad	Sunday	28 (12 + 8 + 4 + 4)	3.00
		Weekdays	20 (12 + 8)	3.00
3	Kolkata	Sunday	16	3.00
		Weekdays	8	2.50
4	Lucknow	Sunday	20 (12 + 4 + 4)	3.00
		Weekdays	12	2.50
5	Delhi	Sunday	20 (12 + 4 + 4)	3.00
		Weekdays	12	3.00
6	Gorakhpur	Sunday	16(8 + 4 + 2)	3.00
		Weekdays	12	3.00
7	Patna	Sunday	16(8 + 4 + 2)	3.00
		Weekdays	12	2.00

It would not be out of context here to have a look at the pagewise break-up of the content-design the *RS* adheres to in its different editions. It is evident from Table 17.10 that except for the Mumbai and Hyderabad editions, there is not much difference among different editions of the *RS* when it comes to the content. However, its front pages as well as local pages vary from edition to edition. In this regard, the *RS* has a picture-perfect resemblance with *Dainik Bhaskar* (established 1948), which was a small Hindi newspaper till a couple of years ago but is now sweeping the market with its multiple editions.

According to Burney, his newspaper's distinction lies in its being significantly ahead of the curve when it comes to the lion's share of the Urdu readership. The *RS* is the choice of 80 per cent of readers in Delhi and of 65–70 per cent in Lucknow and Bihar. He acknowledges that in Mumbai it is a neck-to-neck competition with the daily *Inqilab* and *Urdu Times*. The Hyderabad edition, along with 12 pages of the main newspaper, carries an eight-page supplement titled '*Shahr-e-Char Minar*' (The City of Char Minar), which is devoted to news and activities of the city. Burney terms it a 'new experiment'. Kolkata's old newspapers are not in a position to offer a tough resistance.[56]

As the SIMC is not ready to release any data regarding the circulation of its publications, we are left with no choice but to listen to the opinions of contemporaries to measure the veracity of the claims made by Burney. Parwana Rudolvi and Farhat Ehsas are of

Table 17.10: Heads of content the *RS* provides in its different editions

Edition	Delhi	Lucknow	Gorakhpur	Kolkata	Patna	Mumbai	Hyderabad
Heads of Content	*Apna Des* (Our Nation)	*Apna Shahar* (Our City)	*Aas Pas* (Around the City)	*Apna Des* (Our Nation)	*Apna Shahar* (Our City)	*Mumbai wa Atraf* (Mumbai and around)	*Apna Des* (Our Nation)
	West UP	UP	*Apna Shahar* (Our City)	*Jharkhand wa Bihar*	*Aas Pas* (Around the City)	*Aina-e-Alam* (Mirror of the world)	Maharashtra
	Motafarriqat (Miscellaneous)	*Aas Pas* (Around the City)	UP	*Aina-e-Alam* (Mirror of the world)	*Jharkhand* (Miscellaneous)	*Motafarriqat* (Miscellaneous)	UP
	Bihar	*Motafarriqat* (Miscellaneous)	*Apna Des* (Our Nation)	*Kolkata Aas Pas* (Kolkata & Around)	*Aina-e-Alam* (Mirror of the World)	*Apna Des* (Our Nation)	Bihar
	Jharkhand/WB	*Khel Khilari* (Games & Sportsmen)	*Khel Khilari* (Games & Sportsmen)	*Apna Shahar* (Our City)	*Apna Des* (Our Nation)	UP	Jharkhand/WB
	Dehli wa Atraf (Delhi & Around)	*Apna Des* (Our Nation)	*Aina-e-Alam* (Mirror of the World)	*Khel Khilari* (Games & Sportsmen)	*Khel Khilari* (Games & Sportsmen)	Bihar/Jharkhand	*Dehli wa Atraf* (Delhi & Around)
	Ghaziabad/Noida	*Aina-e-Alam* (Mirror of the World)				*Apka Safha* (Your Page)	Business News
	Apna Shahar (Our City)					Maharashtra	*Khel Khilari* (Games & Sportsmen)

(contd...)

(Table 17.10 contd...)

Edition	Delhi	Lucknow	Gorakhpur	Kolkata	Patna	Mumbai	Hyderabad
	Khel Khilari (Games & Sports-men)					*Mehfil-e-Sahara* (In the company of Sahara)	*Aina-e-Alam* (Mirror of the World)
	Aina-e-Alam (Mirror of the World)					*Dehli wa Atraf* (Delhi & Around)	*Shahr-e-Char Minar* (The Char Minar City)
						Khel Khilari (Games & Sports-men)	*Hyderabad wa Atraf* (Hydera-bad & Around)
						Apna Shahar Mumbai (Mumbai: Our City)	*Bazm-e-Sahara* (In the Company of Sahara)
							Qariyeen Ka Safha (Readers' Page)
							Junubi Hind (South India)
							Andhra Pradesh

the opinion that except its Delhi edition, the *RS*'s other editions do not enjoy much circulation. Rudolvi thinks that it is commercially viable due to its multi-edition character while Ehsas thinks that the *RS* is doing so just to woo the advertising agencies. Asad Mirza believes that it is next to impossible for the *RS* to make a dent in the Urdu readership loyal to the old and local newspapers in Mumbai and Hyderabad. His argument gains strength from the fact that it is in these two cities that the *RS* is at its best. In Mumbai it offers 16 pages in weekdays for Rs 3 and 24 pages on Sunday for Rs 5. As

Inquilab offers three coloured supplements per week, the *RS* is also trying its best to make its product as attractive and engaging as it can. To woo readers, it is applying different mechanisms, ranging from different special reports on Muslim issues like Malegaon riots to introducing pages like *Apka Safha* (Your Own Page). For the latter the *RS* suggests some current issue, and requests readers to express their views so that they can be published in the newspaper. Though *Hindustan* does not stand anywhere in comparison to the *RS*, *Urdu Times* is one of its arch-rivals as it has deep roots in suburbia as well as nearby cities like Aurangabad, Nasik, etc.

Table 17.11: Pages and prices of some Urdu newspapers from Mumbai

Newspaper	Pages	Coloured Pages	Price (INR)
Inquilab	12	6	3.50
Urdu Times	12	2	4.00
Hindustan	6	2	2.00
RS	16	2	3.00

As far as Hyderabad is concerned, the largest number of Urdu newspapers come from this city. *Siasat* and *Munsif,* and *Rahnuma-e-Dakkan* also to a certain extent, have, by and large, been ruling the Urdu newspaper market for long. For the last four years, a new but very strong shareholder in this market has emerged in the shape of the daily *Etemaad*. What distinguishes it from the rest of the pack is that almost everyday a coloured supplement accompanies its main newspaper. It is these formidable rivals which render a sort of invincibility to the Urdu market of the city, especially for outsiders like the *RS*.

The same is the case, according to Asad Mirza, when it comes to the competition of the *RS* with the daily *Azad Hind* from Kolkata, which has deep roots in the history and people of the city. Excluding

Table 17.12: Pages and prices of some Urdu newspapers from Hyderabad

Newspaper	Pages	Coloured Pages	Price (INR)
Siasat	14	6	2.50
Munsif	14	4	2.50
Rahnuma-e-Dakkan	12	None	3.00
Etemad	16	6	2.00
RS	20	4	3.00

Akkas and *Aabshar,* two other dailies from the city, the daily *Akhbar-e-Mashriq* also has a strong grip on the market for the last twenty-four years. Only time will tell whether the *RS* will succeed in carving out its own niche readership. In Bihar and Jharkhand it is sweeping the market at the cost of other small newspapers like the daily *Qaumi Tanzeem,* bringing the diversity of Urdu journalism to an end.

When the *RS* had launched its Lucknow edition at the turn of the century, it was not difficult to secure its place as the market was almost devoid of serious, quality newspapers, after the closure of the city edition of the daily *Qaumi Awaz.* The situation at present is no longer as simple as it used to be. For a year or so the daily *Aag* (Fire), a newcomer, has appeared as a formidable competitor to the *RS* in the local Urdu media market. I will go into some details about it in the next section.

NEW TRENDS APART FROM *RASHTRIYA SAHARA*

The *RS* will complete a decade in the market in 2009. During this period, a number of its employees developed differences with the SIMC management and with the *RS* policies in particular. Khalid Anwar is one of the disgruntled journalists who left the *RS* to launch the daily *Hindustan Express* (*HE*), Delhi on 10 May 2006. Imbisat Ahmed Alavi,[57] Asfar Faridi, and Amir Salim Khan are prominent names among those who resigned from the *RS* to join this new daily. According to Anwar, it is the 'total journalism' which is missing in the *RS*. Being a corporate-owned newspaper which has explicit close connections with the Samajwadi Party, his efforts at doing 'candid reporting' invited wrath from the bosses on several occasions.[58]

Stating the purpose behind establishing this newspaper, the launching editorial reads:

As true servants of Urdu, we strive for the promotion of those higher journalistic values in the presence of which it will be impossible for sycophants and opportunists to survive in this walk of life, and, thus, Urdu journalism will be immune to the ominous influences of the embassy of Israel in India which it has been enjoying silently for many years.[59]

This shows that the *HE* wants to capitalize on anti-Israel sentiments among the Muslim community and does not accept journalism as a profession and a financial activity. Thus, the foundation of its edifice rests on very shaky grounds.

Anwar laments that there is no tradition of breaking-news in Urdu journalism. He claims that his newspaper is endeavouring to make it a regular practice in Urdu newspapers. In this regard, he mentions that it is the *HE* which broke the news of the decision on the part of the Jama'at-e-Islami Hind for limited participation in the general and assembly elections. Though this effort on the part of the *HE* should be appreciated, one needs to be careful of the dangers of the breaking-news culture, as is evident in the news reporting of the TV channels.

Urdu journalism has been very cruel to those who devote their entire lives to it. Their contribution generally goes unsung. Sohail Anjum has protested against the 'no byline culture', prevalent in the Urdu media. He accuses the editors of 'not promoting their subordinate colleague journalists'.[60] Likewise, Rizwanullah in his autobiography '*Kalkutta Ki Urdu Sahafat Aur Main*'[61] (Urdu Journalism in Calcutta and Me) has very poignantly elucidated how he had joined the daily '*Asr-e-Jadid*', now defunct, as a translator in June 1951, and was not promoted to the post of a journalist till he left it on 30 November 1975, despite the fact that he had, as a ghost writer, been writing editorials for the newspaper during crucial times like the Bangladesh war. Though the owners of Urdu newspapers have always been flourishing, their employees and journalists continue to languish in anonymity, negligence, penury, and poverty. Rizwanullah's book unravels illuminating accounts of the clash of interests between the workers and the owner classes in the domain of Urdu media. It also shows how a series of communal riots in country has time and again been forcing working journalists to withdraw their agitation against the owners or entrepreneur-editors of the Urdu newspapers for a handsome salary and amiable work culture.

It is against this backdrop one needs to see the *HE*'s practice of publishing photographs of the scribes along with their opinion pieces on the edit page. With this, it has become the second Indian Urdu newspaper, after the daily *Inquilab*, Mumbai, to accord such importance to its contributors.

There is no denying the fact that the trend of monitoring the predominantly Muslim Urdu media on a regular basis is on the increase in the post-9/11 India. Moreover, embassies and high commissions are working hard to engage the Muslim populace of the country in a very positive and intelligent manner. Their efforts culminated in the birth of two very trendy and quality bi-monthly magazines: *British Jaiza* (started in January 2005) and *Span* (started in April 2002), published by the British High Commission and the American Centre, New Delhi, respectively.[62] As far as the increasing influence of Israel on the Urdu press is concerned, a few articles recently appeared in Urdu dailies, but they did not produce any logical argument in support of their thesis.[63]

Burhanuddin Owaisi's *Etemad*, a daily from Hyderabad, is now four years old. It is said to have the backing of Sultan Salahuddin Owaisi of the All India Majlis-e-Ittehadul Muslimeen, a six-time MP from Hyderabad. Though it is at its nascent stage in comparison to old-timers like *Siasat* and *Munsif* from the same city, it does not lag behind in any respect. It provides a whole spectrum of content to attract all sorts of readers. Also, it has a well-maintained, colourful, and eye-catching website.

The daily *Aag* from Lucknow is one of the latest ventures into the Urdu press. In its old avatar, *Aag* used to be a fortnightly owned by Ahmed Ibrahim Alavi, a senior Urdu journalist. Maulana Kalbe Sadiq, the veteran Shia cleric, is supposed to be a shareholder of the True Media Indian Communication Ltd, which bought the newspaper from Alavi but retained him as the editor. The reading material it offers in its 12 pages for just one rupee is amazing. Also, in terms of variety of content and presentation, it has no parallel in north India. Unlike the *RS*, it devotes one page for literary writings, and the last page to comment upon and reproduce photographs of the epitomes of Indo-Islamic architecture. Everyday it keeps its readers aware of the developments in the field of economics as well as science. One should bear in mind that the Hyderabad edition of the *RS* carries a page titled 'Business News' but the Lucknow edition does not.

What adds further to the strength of *Aag* is its unique practice of reproducing editorials and opinion pieces from different Indian and Pakistani Urdu newspapers. It does so under the regular heading *'Moaqqar Akhbarat Ke Idariye'* (Editorials of Prestigious Newspapers) and devotes a whole page for this. The page carries an announcement on the part of the editorial collective which reads:

We have decided to publish, on this page, editorials from the prestigious newspapers of Urdu to furnish to our readers as much information as we

can, on all possible issues. For this we will be thankful to all Urdu
newspapers. Also, we request them to reciprocate without any hesitation,
to keep their readers aware of our views. We deem it useful and necessary
to maximize the scope of co-operation among ourselves.[64]

Though this practice by *Aag* per se bears a close resemblance
with what the *RS* did for more than a month to capitalize on the
pro-Saddam emotions of its readers, *Aag*'s reproduction differs from
the *RS*'s as it is not restricted to only Saddam/Iraq-centric writings.
This approach to collaboration of content lends to *Aag* a trans-
regional character without diluting its local Awadhi nature.

Another reason for being a tough competitor to the *RS* is the
strategy of *Aag* to straddle the worlds of the Urdu and Hindi print
media. Every issue has '*Nazar*', a free four-page supplement in Hindi.
Nazar contains only hardcore news. During the course of time, thanks
to the lack of Urdu education in government educational institutions,
a generation of Muslims has already come up who cannot decipher
Nastaliq, the dominant Urdu script. My sense is that with an eye on
this section of Hindi users in Muslim society, the *Aag* publishes this
Hindi supplement. Thus, offering 16 pages for just a rupee, it qualifies
as an ideal newspaper for a Muslim family of UP.

In complete contrast to the *RS* which refrains from publishing
stuff related to cinema as it has to go into mosques and madrasas to
reach a vast section of its readers, the *Aag* announces that it 'does
not carry religious articles' and hence it requests the contributors 'not
to send such pieces'.[65] However, it is interesting to note that when the
central government was organizing camps for Polio vaccination, *Aag*
published a fatwa in opposition of the Polio campaign. Categorizing
it anti-religious, the fatwa regarded the campaign as a conspiracy
against Islam. To the utter embarrassment of the newspaper, a few
days later the Ministry of Haj of the Kingdom of Saudi Arabia in a
communication to the Haj Committee of India asked to make sure
that every prospective pilgrim was vaccinated for Polio.

Notwithstanding events like this, *Aag* is very rapidly gaining
currency in the region of Awadh. It would be wise to listen what
readers have to say regarding the newspaper. A letter to the editor
reads: '... Its language is what can exactly be referred to as *Durust
Urdu* (correct Urdu) ... This sobriety and logical way of writing is
generally absent in Urdu newspapers ... You should charge at least

Rs 2 for an issue ...'[66] Thus, with so many feathers in its cap, *Aag* poses strong challenge to the *RS* in Lucknow.

CONCLUSION

Old and experienced media professionals are very pessimistic about the future of the Urdu press in India. However, this does not prevent others from venturing into it. In the midst of this shut-start cycle, the *RS* experiment, despite its limitations, stands very apart from the rest. Though one has to wait to see how sustainable the rapid horizontal expansion the *RS* is undergoing will be, it has no doubt kindled the lamp of hope in hearts of the otherwise disheartened Urduwallahs. Burney, editor of the *RS*, says, 'In the coming five years, the Urdu media market will attract the attention of all the big media houses.'[67]

NOTES

1. Interview with Mohan Chiraghi on 14 November 2006 in Delhi.
2. Interview with Farhat Ehsas, on 8 November 2006 in New Delhi. He is the assistant editor of *Islam And Modern Age*, a quarterly journal brought out by Zakir Husain Institute of Islamic Studies, Jamia Millia Islamia, New Delhi.
3. Ibid.
5. It has been enjoying the largest circulation among Urdu newspapers till 1991. In 1993, *Ludhiana Post* surpassed *Hind Samachar* in circulation, claiming its circulation stood at 55,853 copies per day.
5. Interview with Gurbachan Das Chandan on 20 November 2006 in Delhi.
6. For a candid discussion on this theme, see Ather Farouqui, 'The Emerging Dilemma of the Urdu Press in India: A Viewpoint', *South Asia Journal*, XVIII (2), pp. 91–103.
7. On 18 June 2007, Planman Media Pvt Ltd has launched the Urdu avatar of its *Sunday Indian Magazine*. The weekly, which comes out in 12 more languages, has been in the market since October 2006. It is a hard-core 'translation-based' magazine which is originally compiled in English. Though Malik Rashid Faisal, who looks after the Urdu edition, puts its circulation figure at somewhere near 15,000, it is no different from other language editions of the weekly. The variety manifested in the reading materials offered by the magazine is simply unprecedented in the contemporary Urdu press. It has attracted rave

reviews in prestigious journals like the *Urdu Book Review* (July–September 2007, pp. 71–2) of Mohammad Arif Iqbal though it is the readers who have the final say in deciding the fate of any new venture in the domain of Urdu journalism.

8. G.D. Chandan, 'Urdu Press In India' in *Mass Media In India 2004* (New Delhi: Publication Division, Ministry of Information & Broadcasting, Government of India, 2004), p. 5.

9. Ibid.

10. Ibid., p. 6.

11. Vide opening page of *Press In India, 2004–05*, 49th Annual Report of the Registrar of Newspapers for India (New Delhi: Ministry of Information & Broadcasting, Government of India).

12. Chandan, 'Urdu Press in India', pp. 9–10.

13. I am thankful to Ather Farouqui for drawing my attention to this dynamics of Urdu education which is, among other factors, shaping the contours of contemporary Urdu journalism in a major way. He has shed light on this in his edited volume, *Redefining Urdu Politics in India* (Delhi: Oxford University Press, 2006), pp. 1–10, 177–92.

14. Interview with Sohail Anjum, sub-editor of the daily *Qaumi Awaz*, Delhi, on 5 November 2006. He has devoted a whole chapter entitled 'Urdu Press Aur Jazbatiyat' to discuss the sensationalism prevalent in the Urdu Press. See his book *Media Roop Aur Bahroop* (Faces of the Media) (Delhi: Educational Publishing House, 2006), pp. 197–202. Zoe Ansari, in his illuminating essay 'Urdu Sahafat Ka Mizaj' (Nature of Urdu Journalism), has engaged the theme in a more philosophical and analytical way. See Mahboobur Rehman Farooqui and Mohammad Kazim (eds), *Ajkal Aur Sahafat* (New Delhi: Publication Division, Ministry of Information & Broadcasting, Government of India, 2000), pp. 1–10.

15. Born on 11 November 1933 in Barabanki of Uttar Pradesh, Parwana Rudolvi started his journalistic career in 1952 when he joined the daily *Nai Duniya*, Delhi. Later, he worked with several newspapers, ranging from *Siasat* (Kanpur), *Hindustan* (Bombay), and *Dawat* (Delhi), to *Qaid* (Lucknow). The daily *Pratap* (Delhi), proved to be his last employer. He joined the newspaper in 1968 and retired in 1990. An entire generation knows Parwana for his stories he often used to write for *Khilauna*, a children's magazine. Several books including two novels— *Aazmaish* and *Weerani Jati Nahi*—are to his credit.

16. Interview with Parwana Rudolvi on 8 November 2006 in Delhi.

17. Interview with Sohail Anjum.
18. Unfortunately, *Qaumi Awaz*, Delhi ceased publication from 2 April 2008. It signifies the fall of the last citadel of sober Urdu journalism in north India.
19. For example *Inquilab*, Mumbai offers three coloured supplements every week: *Juma Inquilab* on Fridays, *Family Inquilab* on Wednesdays, and *Sunday Inquilab*. Likewise, the daily *Etemaad* from Hyderabad provides a supplement every day: *Jahan-e-Nau* (New World) on Saturdays, *Jaiza* (Survey) on Sundays, *Awraaq-e-Adab* (Pages from Literature) on Mondays, *Aanchal* on Tuesdays, *Science and Technology* on Wednesdays, *Phulwari* (Garden) on Thursdays, and *Sirat-e-Mustaqim* (The Straight Path, on religion) on Fridays.
20. Interview with Parwana Rudolvi.
21. See http://www.siasat.com/english/index.php?option = content&task = view&id = 63&Itemid = 75&cattitle = Useful % 20Links
22. The daily *Rashtriya Sahara* may be accessed at http://saharaurdu.in/, while the website of the Hindustan Express is at http://www.hindustanexpressdaily.com/.
23. Interview with Khalid Anwar on 21 November 2007 in Delhi.
24. As per the data available on 10 January 2007 at: http://www.indiapress.org/index.php/Urdu/400x60
25. As per the data available on 10 January 2007 at http://saharaurdu.in/.
26. Interview with Parwana Rudolvi.
27. Interview with Asad Mirza, editor of the bi-monthly *British Jaiza*, on 23 November 2006 in New Delhi.
28. Interview with Sheikh Manżur Ahmed, editor-in-charge of UNI Urdu, on 16 November 2006 in New Delhi.
29. Interview with Mohan Chiraghi.
30. Interview with Sohail Anjum.
31. For an illuminating discussion on the issue see Sukumar Muralidharan's piece entitled 'The Times of India's Final Frontier', *Himal*, August 2006 at http://www.himalmag.com/2006/august/essay.htm.
32. See Vanita Kohli-Khandekar, *The Indian Media Business* (New Delhi: Response Books, 2006), p. 33.
33. http://thehoot.org/story.asp?storyid = Web591766177Hoot125650 % 20AM2286&pn = 1
34. See Robin Jeffrey, *India's Newspapers Revolution*' (Delhi: Oxford University Press, 2000).

35. Ibid.
36. For example, Chandigarh had no culture of any Hindi daily. *Dainik Bhaskar's* city edition is now selling more than other old English and Punjabi dailies. For the amazing success of the Bhaskar Group venture into the vernacular press, especially Hindi, visit http://www.bhaskar.com/defaults/aboutus.php.
37. Apart from Delhi, the capital city, its other editions come out from Lucknow, Gorakhpur, Mumbai, Kolkata, Patna, Hyderabad, Bangalore, and Srinagar. It constantly announces that its editions from cities of Punjab will enter the market very soon.
38. For Samir Jain's contribution to the Indian newspapers market see Kohli-Khandekar, *The Indian Media Business*, pp. 33–6.
39. Interview with Ather Afzal on 3 December 2006 in New Delhi.
40. The SIMC runs *Sahara News* (a 24x7 Hindi news channel), *Rashtriya Sahara* (a daily newspaper in Hindi), and *Sahara Times* (an English weekly tabloid).
41. Interview with Aziz Burney, editor of the Urdu publications of the Sahara India Mass Communication, on 25 November 2006 in Noida, UP.
    This can also be understood in the backdrop that the editorial of a Urdu newspaper is its most read item. Sohail Anjum has shed light on this unique feature of Urdu journalism and readership in his interesting article titled 'Idariya Nawesi'. See Humayun Ashraf (ed.), *Urdu Sahafat: Masail Aur Imkanat* (Delhi: Educational Publishing House, 2006), pp. 126–31.
42. Interview with Afzal Misbahi on 29 November 2006 in Delhi.
43. Afzal Misbahi, (2005), '*21 win Sadi Ke Siyasi,Samaji Aur Tahzibi Masail:Roznama Rashtriya Sahara Ke Hawaley Se*' (Politico-Social and Cultural Problems of 21st-Century India: With Reference to the Urdu Daily *Rashtriya Sahara*). In this unpublished M.Phil. dissertation for the University of Delhi, Afzal has studied issues of *Dastawez* from January 2000 to December 2003.
44. See Arshad Amanullah, 'Islam as News in Indian Newspapers', *Islam and the Modern Age*, vol. XXXV, no.4, November 2004, pp. 75–92.
45. The Delhi edition carried this (*Saddam Ka Akhiri Salam*) on page 5. It appeared on different pages in different editions but the amount of space allocated for it remained constant.
46. See: http://saharaurdu.in/index.php?id = 594

47. Front page editorial by Aziz Burney, '*Saddam, Saddam, Saddam, Saddam*', *Rashtriya Sahara*, Delhi, 7 January 2007.

48. Special editorial by Aziz Burney, 'Karbala Ka Paigham, Part 2' (A Message From Karbala), *Rashtriya Sahara*, Delhi, 27 January 2007.

49. Special editorial by Aziz Burney, 'Karbala Ka Paigham, Part 3' (A Message From Karbala), *Rashtriya Sahara*, Delhi, 29 January, 2007. These special editorials of Aziz Burney are available on the website of the *RS* under the category of 'Aziz Burney Ki Khususi Tahriren'.

50. Arshad Amanullah, *Media Aur Musalmaan* (Media And Muslims) (New Delhi: Al Kitab International, 2003), p. 150.

51. Interview with Aziz Burney on 25 November 2006 in Noida, UP.

52. Interview with Asad Mirza on 23 November 2006 in New Delhi.

53. Interview with Aziz Burney on 25 November 2006 in Noida, UP.

54. Sukumar Muralidharan, 'The Times of India's final frontier', *Himal*, August 2006.

55. Like *Qaumi Tanzim* (Patna and Ranchi) and *Inquilab* (Mumbai and Kolkata). Maulana Abdul Waheed Siddiqui, editor of the daily *Nai Duniya*, Delhi, made such an effort, launching its Kanpur edition in 1954.

56. Interview with Aziz Burney on 25 November 2006 in Noida, UP.

57. He passed away on 2 December 2006. He used to be one of the core members of the editorial team of the *RS*. He joined the *HE* as the executive editor. See his obituary by Ahmad Jawed, the news editor of the newspaper in the 3 December issue of the *HE*.

58. Interview with Khalid Anwar on 21 November 2006 in Delhi.

59. Special editorial, *Hindustan Express*, Delhi, 10 May 2006.

60. Anjum, *Media Roop Aur Bahroop*, p. 206.

61. Rizwanullah himself has published the book in 2006 from New Delhi.

62. It would be interesting to know that Urdu is one of the three languages in which MI5, the UK Security Service, maintains its official website. Its URL is: http://www.mi5.gov.uk/output/Page323.html.

63. See Shahid Lakhmanyavi's write-up in the daily *Urdu Times*, Mumbai, on 4 June 2006. The *Milli Gazette* (16–30 November 2006), a fortnightly from New Delhi, has published its English version.

64. *Aag*, Lucknow, 26 January 2007, p. 6.

65. *Aag*, Lucknow, 25 January 2007, p. 5.

66. Wasima Zaidi in her letter to the editor on 25 January 2007.

67. Interview with Aziz Burney on 25 November 2006 in Noida, UP.

PART IV
POPULAR IMAGES AND THE STORY OF STEREOTYPES

18

Bollywood Films with Special Reference to Urdu Politics and Muslims

Moinuddin Jinabade

This paper is apparently concerned with the media images of minorities in general in respect to Bollywood films, but in its essence it directly touches the sensibilities of the Muslim minority whom these films stereotypically depict. In view of this it is necessary to emphasize some basic themes that are generally overlooked or taken for granted.

We all know that the Muslim minority is not a single entity in India. Apart from social classification, it is divided into many linguistic identities. Surprisingly, only the north Indian Muslims are victims of Urdu politics. The communal politics of the aalim has deliberately branded Urdu as the language of the Muslims extending it as a language of all Muslims that inhabit India. But of course, the common knowledge of the demographic tongue is varied with no cohesive force that can be claimed as one entity, the Muslims of different parts of India speak the languages of the regions they inhabit. For example, a Muslim from Punjab speaks Punjabi, whereas a Muslim from Bihar speaks Magahi, or Bhojpuri. In Bengal, Bengali Muslims speak Bengali, but in urban pockets in and around Kolkata Urdu/Hindi is the mother tongue of a considerable number of Muslims, and they are called Bihari Muslims irrespective of the place of their origin.

To call any language a dialect or a folk language is nothing but a kind of imperialist agenda in the name of linguistic discourse. For me all languages that are spoken—major or minor—are languages steeped in their own essence of regional identity, and perhaps for this reason no language has so far been declared as the national language in the Indian Constitution. The founding fathers of the Indian Constitution considered all regional languages included in the Eighth Schedule as national languages. Today more and more regional languages are demanding their inclusion in the Eighth Schedule and the size of the Eighth Schedule is continuously increasing, which is a good sign for all Indian languages. After all what is India but unity in diversity?

The post-Partition politics of north India is hell-bent on spreading communal venom in the name of languages. The result was that the Urdu–Hindi controversy of the nineteenth century became more relevant after the partition of the country. Post-1947 the graveness of this language imbroglio has manifested itself in glaring forms, like an ever-present wall built upon by images that decry the Muslim community as medieval. That this controversy is felt everywhere is not an understatement—the extent of it is such that one can rightly say that the Urdu–Hindi politics has been sponsored by the state itself.

Conspicuously, Hindi chauvinism in India crossed all limits after Partition. This chauvinism took a dangerous turn in the north when it got converted into fascism. A fresh clause, Article 351, was incorporated in the Indian Constitution, declaring all north Indian languages as *a style of Hindi*. The most unfortunate part was that of the inclusion of Hindustani in this list. We must not forget that there was a consensus before Partition that Hindustani in both Urdu and Devanagari scripts will be the national language of India. This was around the time when Urdu speakers had abandoned the term 'Persian script' and started using the term 'Urdu script'. This change of term was justified because the sounds available in Urdu are available neither in Persian nor in Arabic, and the whole grammatical structure of Urdu is the same as that of all north Indian languages. Thus they called it the Urdu script. This positive change in the minds of the Urdu speakers was perhaps due to the destructive politics of the Muslim League. The resultant destruction too was not the result of Partition alone but the obvious outcome of an open-ended ethnic war in Pakistan.

Today in India only people of the communal mindset label the Urdu script as 'Persian' or 'Arabic'. If this parochial and uncompromising attitude persists, it will surely percolate to the regions where, maybe, chauvinist Bengalis will claim Assamese, Manipuri, and Oriya as dialects of Bengali, or the Marathas will claim Konkani or the Tamils will claim Telugu, Kannada, and Malayalam. This type of an attitude spawned by communal forces undermines the collective identities of people belonging to different regions by subtly spreading discord throughout the nation in the name of the cohesive force of the language identity. Forgetting the fact that Hindi is also a Persian word, the unnecessary insistence of political forces was aimed to destroy the impact of the spoken language of Bombay films.

Today the common complaint of Urdu speakers is that even pure Urdu films are blatantly called Hindi films. One could argue that Bombay films are not Sanskritized Hindi films and their language is a common spoken dialect, popularly known as Hindustani. But Urdu speakers will say that if Hindustani is also a style of Hindi, then by implication of the constitutional sanction (Article 351) Hindustani is also Hindi. I always find Hindi protagonists speechless when this argument of the misnomer of 'Hindi' films is forwarded by an Urdu speaker, not necessarily in agreement with the Muslims or those politicians dabbling in politics in the name of Urdu. But since Muslim politics is very complicated for the simple reason that most of our intellectuals deal with Muslims only with rhetoric, they do not even have the basic facts in order to counter and rightly claim the language of Bollywood films as Urdu.

My question is: who can understand the so-called Urdu dialogue of films like *Pakeezah*? The fact remains that the mindset and the attitude of the Urdu politicians too is not much different. I do not think that such dialogues, and such *Mufarras* and *Moarrab* (polished Persianized and Arabicized Urdu) can ever be understood by anyone except madrasa products. This argument, by corollary, has a decisive impact on media images of the Indian Muslims depicted in Bombay films, where Muslims are nothing but Urdu speakers of the north. As such, it can safely be concluded that going by the image projected by the media, a Muslim is only a Muslim of north India, and an Urdu speaker—and the Urdu knowing Muslim is a *shair* (poet), a caricature. The best example of the distortion of the image of Muslims and the Urdu shair is exhibited in *In Custody*, a novel by Anita Desai based on the story of which Ismail Merchant later produced a movie with the same name; its Urdu version is called *Muhafiz*.

Now coming to the regular potboiler churned by the Bombay tinsel town, the image that they depict of Muslims is crude, cartoon-like, spiced with religion that to the common man seems excessive catering to the Muslim audience. Similarly, this stereotyping extends to other minorities as well. Bollywood has invariably stereotyped the depiction of Indian Christian characters as cigarette-smoking call girls, raving drunkards, church padres, and your everyday anti-Indian smuggler in league with the Muslim gangster. In the same manner, Parsis are always depicted as the silly lot of Bombay, wearing a vest and fez and the men being bullied by their wives. In the Muslim context I will elaborate on this point by giving examples of blockbusters that have been seen by most Indians.

Take the case of *Sholay*: its setting is a Western-movie type of village called Ramgarh where 99.9 per cent of the populace was Hindu. The scriptwriter thought it prudent to place one family of Muslims in the village, that too two males, one old blind Maulana and his son Salim. And in the beginning the movie showed one comic character called Surma Bhopali, who dons a cap and constantly chews paan. The Maulana is shown as a pious Muslim who goes for namaz even when the dead body of his son is brought before him. Surma Bhopali, on the other hand, is a tale-telling, talkative dingbat, spitting red paan spittle.

For the benefit of their jingling purses, the Bombay tinsel town merchants inevitably include one or two Muslims in their movies. This is obviously done in order to satisfy the Muslims' sensibilities, as they come to view movies in which the protagonist and all his cronies are Hindus. You may have noticed that in these movies the poor Muslim *bakra* is either shown as pious, swearing by the Koran, or as some paan-chewing, *sherwani* wearing mouther of popular Urdu couplets, or as a mechanic, or some sort of menial—and, of course, the inevitable gangster, big or small. In the movie *Amar Akbar Anthony*, Akbar a Hindu-born child brought up by a caring Muslim couple is shown as a *qawaal*. In *Pakeezah*, the entire cast is shown as a remnant of some forgotten past of *nawabi* nature. Now, if the story is based on that type of a background, one can understand, but I fail to understand why of all the professions in this world the scriptwriter decided to make Akbar a qawaal decked in shiny kurta-pajamas, clapping his bandana-decked hands to the songs he sings.

Even good movies never fail to bring in this depiction of the typical Muslim stereotype. *Maqbool* is a very well-made film, with a strong script and cast. It is a wonderful adaptation of Shakespeare's *Macbeth* set against the crime-infested world of Bombay. The primary protagonists in the movie are mostly Muslims and they are gangsters. Fine, but was it absolutely necessary to make those gangster characters Muslims? Is it not like stretching the preconceived images that the media has over the years depicted of the Muslim community a little more, a lot more? Creative freedom is very good and is absolutely necessary, but if that freedom subtly and almost always has a negative display, then how good is it for society? Not every Muslim that you come across the street is a Dawood crony, or an Urdu poet, or a mechanic, or an aalim.

Not that these films are badly made or anything like that—my argument here questions why the media always depicts the Muslim community in a *'shady out of the way almost always appearing as an appeasement for the Muslim audience'* manner? A few great movies that depict Muslims accurately do exist, but they are too few and are not watched by the mainstream audience. It is the mainstream audience whose opinion matters to the community and not some intellectuals with the power of great understanding—after all, the common people are the majority and have the power to influence government policies. Ironically, Bollywood has Muslim actors and actresses in numbers out of proportion to their Hindu counterparts, and yet it is they who without a thought indulge in creating stereotypes of their own community and propagate it to the rest of the nation. The negative images of Muslims have been ingrained so deep in the subconscious that, without a hitch, stereotyped roles are created on Muslim personalities, and now appear normal even to the Muslim audience.

Even on TV, no wailing soap operas are made based on Muslim families, or drama series made depicting Muslims leading lives as company executives, government employee, or progressive writers, etc. I remember there was once a serial telecast by Doordarshan called *Gul Gulshan Gulfam*, which was based on a family of Kashmiri Muslims. That was many years ago, and no one from that family was a terrorist or a gangster or a qawwal or a mechanic. Even the commercial advertisements that sponsor these programmes never show a Muslim family smiling happy with the product that is being advertised by them. In today's world images are worth their measure in gold, and the mainstream media has monopolized this to a great extent. For the proper incorporation of the minorities with the rest of the country it is optimum that the images of the minorities, particularly Muslims, be positive. And it is the task of the media to be honest and do just that, because the harm that they have already done is helping to create distorted images of the Muslims in the minds of the Hindus. Through the depiction of negative images, a non-conforming person who is neutral to religio-political manipulation can be easily influenced by being converted to a minority-hating chauvinist, even without his conscious knowledge. This subtlety in brainwashing the populace through the repeated depiction of negative images of the Muslims helps breed a phobia that becomes instinctive and that is not natural.

19

Indian Muslims and Indian Films
Some Observations of Contemporary Indian Art Cinema

John W. Hood

Although India produces an exceptionally high number of films—on average well in excess of seven hundred a year—the Muslim community is intentionally represented in cinema to a considerably lesser degree than its proportion of the population or, less easily quantifiable, its contribution to the cultural history of the nation might warrant. Muslim contribution to Indian literature and languages, to music, to the fine arts and crafts, and to architecture has been immense. In cinema, however, the Islamic presence, to say nothing of influence, has been minimal. This essay aims to substantiate this observation as well as to discuss the ways in which Muslims and Muslim interests have indeed been treated in some of the better Indian films. Although the focus of the essay is on the work of independent filmmakers, I have offered some discussion of two well-known commercial films for the value of the contrast that they offer.

It may be that cinema, the most modern of all the arts, reached its significant stage of development in India roughly contemporaneously with the distinct decline in Muslim political influence after 1947. In that year India attained independence from foreign rule at the price of the truncation of its territory with the partition of the country. With the migration of many formerly Indian Muslims to the new state of Pakistan, the Muslim population of India decreased considerably (although India continues to accommodate, after Indonesia, the second largest Muslim community in the world). Moreover, those Muslims who elected to remain Indians were regarded with suspicion and often blamed for the diminution of the nation and the horrors that were its consequence. Thus, a few years before the emergence of what came to be known as the art cinema[1] the brightness of the Muslim star over India had dimmed considerably.

The brutal communal conflicts that bloodied the last months of pre-independent India did not come to an end with Independence and Partition but have continued for various reasons in different parts of the country right up to the present. The potential for such conflicts can be discerned, at least to some extent, in the way in which the Muslims of India are perceived by the majority Hindus. The Muslim community in India is relatively backward, most evidently in economic terms, but noticeably in political and social conditions as well. Of course, it is easy to assert a causal connection between the economic condition of the Indian Muslims and their political and social circumstances. While their external emanations of depression might often be used to define them as a significant minority community, imbued with the properties of Otherness that include an unconcealed dissatisfaction with their lot, so painting them to the majority community as a perceived (though not necessarily genuine) threat and a cause for suspicion, discomfort, and feelings of vulnerability are prevalent. Thus, there is the potential, and for obvious reasons often a risky one, for an essentially political dimension to be given to any significant treatment of Muslim interests in cinema.

The basic structural realities of Indian society are rooted in diversity and inequality, and resentment prevails among various communities throughout the society for inequities and injustices suffered at the hands of one or more of the Others at various times in their history. In interpreting such grievances time can be very elastic, such as when Hindus substantiate their insistence on the threat posed to their community by Muslims by appeal to alleged temple destruction by some Muslim ruler or other many centuries back. While imperialists such as Macaulay poured contempt on Indian ideas of history which, it was claimed, reflect a regrettable unconcern for the past, it is nevertheless arguable that, in the minds of many Indians, the past—recent or remote—does have a hold over the Indian present, and the effects of deeds or policies or laws originating in times long gone may be felt acutely now and be perceived as germane to the lingering resentment that they may be alleged to have engendered. The web of physical, emotional, and moral destruction emanating out of the designed confrontation at Ayodhya in 1992 and the even more barbaric Godhra carnage and riots that shamed the state of Gujarat in February and March, 2002 are two prominent examples of what is often claimed to be the product of a long history of antagonism and incompatibility. Otherness is not only perceived in Indian society, it is often endowed with horrendous potential and, as has been seen in recent times, can be used politically to contrive menace.

Many nationalists whose vision is determined by an idealism founded in secularism, humanism, and modernism—and such advanced beings do exist—would want to assert that all this is a misinterpretation or, at best, an exaggeration. It perhaps arises out of a seeming inability to sympathize with the particular difficulties pertinent to a newly independent country still coming to terms with the ramifications of an extraordinarily complex colonialist past along with the various claims and counter-claims to possess the future. Here, of course, the idealist is allowing the envisioned potential to obscure the actual. The facts of this coming to terms, however, are often not encouraging, and we only have to look at the forensic and succinct account of communal violence given in Sudhir Kakar's work[2] to gauge something of the depth of mutual suspicion and resentment, together with the strength and persistence of the irrational, that thrive among some elements in Indian society.

Although it is easy to envision and believe in potentials long before they are realized to any extent, one must not cynically underrate the possibility of shared social advancement by the various communities of India, especially the two largest ones. While history often has been a story of mistrust and destructive conflict, it also bears witness to some remarkable expressions of harmony. Even though Islam and Hinduism may be in so many ways mutually exclusive, their co-existence in India has for long given rise to a process of mutual cultural enrichment and significant and substantial festive sharing, for so much that is abiding and endearing in folk and village culture represents a melding of Muslim and Hindu experiences. Much of the development of some of India's modern languages has been nurtured by communal co-existence. Indian architecture has been enhanced not only by the visual prominence of both mosque and temple but by many emblematic and stylistic fusions of the Islamic and Hindu traditions. The Bhakti and Sufi movements served to create elements of a humanitarianism that would happily dispel sectarian difference, while poet saints such as Kabir and Tukaram have immensely appealed to the hearts of men and women of diverse communities. Despite the particular zeal of Hindu revivalists such as Bankim Chandra Chattopadhyay and Bal Gangadhar Tilak, there have been notable expressions of nationalism that eclipsed exclusivist communal terms with the inclusive term 'Indian', while the Congress platform in the freedom movement cultivated to a significant extent an idealism that saw India's destiny as following a path of Hindu–Muslim cooperation and shared beliefs in common national ideals and social values. Sadly the voices of men like Maulana Azad could not drown out the voices of Jinnah and his supporters, so preventing us from playing down the ultimate reality of sectarianism in India, the Partition and all its appallingly tragic human consequences. Nevertheless, that catastrophe must not prevent us from overlooking those countless Muslims who consciously elected to remain in India, to call it their native land and to live and work for its good.

Thus the Hindu–Muslim experience in India has been and continues to be fraught with some amazing contradictions: harmony and hostility, cultural enrichment and bigoted mistrust, lofty idealism and petty self-interest, religious quietism and social violence. In various ways, similar contradictions in diverse shapes and forms exist in the history of many societies; it is when their identities arise out of seemingly indelible perceptions of a permanent Other that they take on the destructive potential that characterizes communalism in India.

All of this may well suggest that the Muslim experience in India is not so negligible to be ignored by creative artists, especially writers and filmmakers. Islam in India reaches back more than a millennium, and the contemporary Indian landscape is enriched, both obviously and subtly, by its cultural contributions. It is impossible to think of Indian culture devoid of its Muslim influence. And yet there have been those who would seek to cleanse Hindu India of this Muslim influence and deny its contributions to Indian culture. Filtering down from this blind bigotry is an attitude that creates communal tensions, sometimes emanating into outbreaks of serious violence. Bigotry and prejudice and irrational hatred are given nurture. In all of this, from the culturally sublime to perversity and human frailty, there is the vast maelstrom of the human condition in its humdrum and riches, its joys and nightmares, all offering an endless source of material to writers and filmmakers. Social realist filmmakers seeking to faithfully depict their society as it is can hardly ignore the realities of social tension emanating out of communalism, while those of idealist bent can just as hardly ignore the opportunity to creatively condemn confrontation and hostility in order to propagate ideals of social cohesion based on mutual respect and trust. Social idealism aside, the Hindu–Muslim experience provides a mine of human interest resources, endless in its diversity and fascination. Even more simply, the Muslim community in itself offers a vast well-spring of subject potential for fine cinema.

While literature in English and in the vernacular languages, has responded extensively to the communal realities of the country, largely in works related to the Partition, serious cinema has, generally, shied away from any conscious examination of the tensions between the two major communities. A number of reasons might be offered for this, perhaps the main one being that the issues are exceptionally sensitive and, no matter how carefully treated, are always vulnerable to an element of audience misinterpretation that might, in fact, exacerbate existing tensions rather than mollify them, particularly among people with strong prejudices. The risk of failing to get a Censor Board classification is largely based on this possibility. There can be no advance certainty of what form audience reaction to a film will take, so where communal tensions are involved the Censor Board is more likely to play safe than to be daring. M.S. Sathyu's film, *Garam Hawa* ('Hot Wind', 1974), about the effects of the Partition on ordinary people, received very positive public acclaim, but in the first instance it was, nevertheless, denied a censors' certificate; the Board was eventually overruled after an appeal to the prime minister. That the issue is such a volatile one might be illustrated by the public response and reaction to Mani Ratnam's film *Bombay* (1995). While many thought that the film was a genuine and worthy endeavour to dispel communal antagonisms, others went so far as to advocate its being banned, while the irrational fanatics who sought to defend the indefensible simply resorted to violence and destruction.

(One reason that might be offered for the difference between literature and cinema in regard to depictions of communal subjects is that literature is a less public art than cinema. One reads in private, when and where one likes. Retail outlets for books are infinitely more numerous than cinema halls showing a certain film at a certain time, though of course bookshops might occasionally be vulnerable to censorious thugs with a sectarian agenda; however, even the most categorical of fatwas could not stop Salman Rushdie from writing or his books from being sold. If one sees one's films on video-cassette or CD, the experience is similar to the literary one. However, most people see their films in the cinema—places that are, indeed, vulnerable to the extravagances of sectarian thugs, and it is understandable that the proprietors of cinema halls will simply not show a film rather than risk their halls being burnt down. And if there is the slightest chance that a film—always costly to make—might be therefore rejected, a filmmaker is not likely to run the risk of making it in the first place. The public nature of fine arts might also be noted in this connection as we remind ourselves of the damage done to some of M.F. Hussein's work at exhibitions disapproved of by the Hindu right.)

The partition of India, which came as the cost of Independence in 1947, may be described as the greatest trauma in Indian history and one of the most far-reaching tragedies in the history of humankind. There are many Indians who blame Muslims for this truncation of the nation, the devastation that it wrought in human life and the consequent strife that has marked the relations between India and Pakistan, especially over the question of the Muslim-majority state of Kashmir. Such levelling of blame is hardly rational. Although the Jinnah-led Muslim League may well have a lot to answer for before the court of history, those quick to assert blame all too easily forget that the majority of India's Muslims elected not to follow the Muslim League into Pakistan but to remain in what they saw and felt as their homeland.

Although many good films have been made in the context of the Partition, or with Partition in the background, it may be surprising that so few fine films have been made on the Partition itself. Perhaps one reason may be that people do not like to see representations of their national history denuded of pride and greatness (although such disinclination has not seemed to be a stumbling-block to writers). Nevertheless, Govind Nihalani's *Tamas* ('Darkness', 1986) directly confronts the Partition and also stands as a superb film in its own right. Like M.S. Sathyu's *Garam Hawa, Tamas* had to struggle to reach the public screens. As soon as it was first shown it was the subject of intense controversy and injunctions were brought against it, first in the Bombay High Court and then in the Supreme Court in Delhi. Fortunately it survived these injunctions.

Tamas runs for nearly five hours and it was Nihalani's intention that it be seen in its entirety in one sitting; eventually, however, it was arranged to be shown as a six-part television series. The film is set in north-west India a short time before Partition, in a town and its surrounding villages that give home to the region's three major communities: Hindus, Muslims, and Sikhs. It is Nihalani's great achievement that he has been able to show first of all how, despite living side by side for hundreds of years, the distrust that the members of one community might have for another would, under certain circumstances, transcend reason and intelligence and aspire to savagery in horribly misplaced notions of honour. It is the petty though wicked mischief makers who, perversely, are successful: Nihalani makes it plain to see how the simple slaughter of a pig and the dumping of it on the steps of a mosque can immediately bring about the slaughter of a cow in front of a temple which, in turn, will lead to a frenzy of unimagined, sustained violence. He also makes plain the blindness of those leaders who might have had it in their power to stop the barbarity. The leaders of the various communal and political groups are shown, however, to have particular agendas of their own which do not allow for any degree of compromise or even an attempt to see things in broader perspective. We are also shown how diaphanously thin is the veneer of civilization that keeps us elevated above the brutes. During his training, Ranvir—the son of the leader of the Hindu Mahasabha—is ordered to kill a chicken to overcome his fear of violence. It is a very trying and sickening experience for him, but it is not long after that he shows off his 'manliness' to his comrades of the Hindu youth brigade by ruthlessly stabbing to death a helpless and innocent elderly Muslim man.

Tamas is really a very restrained film, despite the necessarily graphic representation of its various horrors. The point is, given the nature of the subject, it could have been much more shocking without even warranting the criticism of sensationalizing. It is also a strongly moral film, despite the utterly immoral enormities that it depicts. Its morality is simply based in a faith in the invincibility of human decency. Nihalani might well have established the point that civilization is never really very far from savagery, but once this point is established, the reverse is also true, and we see so many moving examples of people going to amazing extremes to do good for others—even those of a different community. Particularly important is the film's essentially apolitical stance which sustains its strictly balanced view. There is the depiction of interest groups familiarly throwing around random accusations of blame, which they find convenient to generalize; hence, the Muslims blame the Hindus, and the Sikhs blame the Muslims, and the Hindus blame the communists, and so on. Nihalani lets his characters do the blaming, while leaving his audience in no doubt about the credentials of those characters. His concern for individuals emphasizes the simplest of truisms: there are good people in every community as there are wicked people in every community. Hope is based in the belief that the good outnumber the wicked, and even though a good man occasionally will be led to do something he will forever regret, his moral salvation lies in that very capacity for regret.

As the Partition has not given rise to so many first-class films, communalism in India has also been prudently avoided. It is true that the majority of the serious filmmakers of India are non-Muslim; it is also true that sensitivity to potential communalist ramifications is widespread and filmmakers, both Hindu and Muslim, would seem to be more comfortable pursuing less provocative themes. Many, indeed, would argue that such a pursuit is more modern and forward-looking. Even when a film does deal with sectarianism, the director may find it politic to handle the theme with velvet gloves. For example, M.S. Sathyu's film, *Galige* ('Moments', 1995), is a strongly anti-sectarian film, establishing right from the opening titles the view that religious emblems and insignia can only serve to divide and minimize a society and can never promote its cohesion and enhance its potential for advancement; hence, before the story starts, this widely held thesis—though a potentially inflammable one among some interest groups—is made clear. The film goes on to develop a somewhat hackneyed love story about a boy and a girl from categorically different backgrounds whose union in love is symbolic of the joy society might experience if it pursues love to unite itself rather than sectarianism to divide and destroy and to make its future precarious.

It is, perhaps, doubtful that such a story could be told of a Hindu and Muslim without exacerbating the prejudices of many in either community, and so Sathyu gives the girl a strongly secular background: without inherent religious or community values (or prejudices), he has her brought up in an orphanage where truly humanist ideals prevail. As a young adult she is shackled by no religious commitment, enjoys considerable personal freedom, has a good job, and is economically self-sufficient. As such she is an emblem of an ideal, a model of joy and contentment that can exist only, it would seem, without sectarian trappings. (We might also note, incidentally, her distinction from the generality of her sex.) The boy is still a bird of passage, heading toward the ideal plane on which the girl lives, yet in the process of coming to terms with his past, and herein lies the fundamental stumbling block, for the boy's past is indelibly stained with the worst of sectarian identity and commitment. After the two have established their relationship, it transpires that the boy was once a Sikh terrorist who had blown up a bus. He had genuinely believed the bus to be empty and that it would remain empty, but when a party of school children is seen to board the vehicle he realizes the enormity of what he has done. He struggles to break free from his comrades in order to defuse the device, but they will not let him go. The bus is blown up with horrific loss of life, leading the young man to flee the Punjab and deny his cultural roots by shaving his face and cutting his hair. The law, of course, does not forget him and pursues him relentlessly until he surrenders to the police when he learns that he is to become a father.

An aunt and uncle of the girl come and stay with her for a while, their presence being employed by Sathyu to expose the bigotries and superstition common to so many caste observing Hindus, while in the substantial sequences set in Ferozepur, he aims to depict something of the tightness of the Sikh community and the militancy of some of its younger men. The Muslim community is alluded to specifically early in the film when a group of elderly gentlemen get down from a train at a station and proceed to offer their prayers, much to the amusement of several young people on the train. One of the young men is the boy of our love story; by no means sharing the amusement of his friends, he leaps out and helps the Muslim men to re-board just as the train starts to leave the station. At that stage we might well suspect that he too is a Muslim, realizing later that human decency does not have to be enclosed within sectarian borders.

While *Galige* represents Muslims as such in a positive though inconsequential manner, yet only indirectly and by extension, the film is pertinent to Muslims as much as to anyone else in its overriding concern with sectarianism, and is very easy to read in Hindu–Muslim terms beyond its secular Sikh actuality. However, the representation of Muslims in many films is merely nominal and sometimes mildly patronizing. For example, in a film that is to all intents and purposes secular, a director might include a Muslim character, obvious by name or dress, who is overtly kind or decent or even patriotic, in order to demonstrate some attitude of political correctness on his own part. In illustrating this practice, Sara Dickey[3] cites the example of a Tamil film, *Patikkaatavan*, in which the Muslim adoptive father is portrayed as a paragon of kindness and generosity. Such characters in various films may advance the plot significantly or even not at all, but in most cases their being Muslim is in no way material—the narrative dynamics would in no way be affected by their being of any other community.

Of course, cinema does not have to be an instrument of social criticism or a platform for social reform. Many filmmakers would quite justifiably reject any claim that their art ought to have any kind of prescribed purpose. However, there are many other filmmakers who do consciously opt to make films of social import, and having made such a choice are committed, one might fairly assume, to a faithful representation of their world and its particular problems. Cinema does, in fact, have great potential as a social influence in any country. Cinematic images are immediate and realistic, and even blatant fantasy images are imbued with a pronounced and often overwhelming sense of actuality. Because of this immediacy and verisimilitude, cinema has a forceful persuasive power and a cogent ability to elicit a variety of emotions ranging from the incidental to the profound. However, while it is easy to see how an audience may be made to laugh or cry, it is not easy to determine the extent to which a film might inspire individuals, continue to encourage them, or to strengthen their resolve or belief in certain matters; the same difficulty, of course, applies to discerning the negative, the extent to which a film might inspire anger, hatred, revenge, or violence. Most modern arguments against censorship assert strongly the view that there is no scientifically demonstrated causal connection between the experience of something on the screen and a person's subsequent behaviour. There is, however, a great deal of anecdotal evidence to suggest that while a movie may not actually cause a person to act in a certain way, it can, conceivably, strengthen already existing beliefs or attitudes, and out of this strengthening there might emanate some specific behaviour related to the material earlier seen on the screen.

While cinema may educate and inform, while it may even occasionally modify a person's beliefs or ways of thinking, it is just as likely to simply strengthen the attitudes a person already has. However, serious cinema often sets out to challenge convention, traditional values, or popular opinion, while popular cinema, for perfectly good commercial reasons, is usually content to support the social and political *status quo*. Commercial cinema tends to be socially conservative and so avoids challenging issues like dowry, the evils of the caste system, or—no matter how Gandhian it could be portrayed to be—communal harmony, for fear of upsetting vested interest groups that might be instrumental in initiating a decline in attendances or even a boycott of the film. The cinema of social advancement is not necessarily good business.

However, despite the obvious power of many films whose makers have been brave enough to rock the social boat,[4] art filmmakers do feel the need to be cautious on certain issues. Saeed Mirza, right from his first film, *Arvind Desai Ki Ajeeb Dastan* ('The Strange Fate of Arvind Desai', 1978), has shown himself to be an intense and incisive social thinker. His 1989 film, *Salim Langde Pe Mat Ro* ('Don't Cry for Lame Salim') confronts communal violence by feuding gangs on the streets of Bombay. The film is graphic, candid, and objective, but it would seem that it is this very objectivity that prevents the film from being much more than a moving human interest story, its viewers going away sadly wishing that *other* people would start to behave themselves. One can very easily sympathize with a director's wish not to polarize his audience, to truthfully reflect in his film the way he sees things to be without seeking causes or levelling blame or responsibility. Controversial films are occasionally, not generally, popular.

Saeed Mirza's *Naseem* (1995) concentrates on a Muslim family in Bombay, central to which is a bed-ridden grandfather and his young granddaughter, Naseem. On one level the film is successful in telling another human interest story, but Mirza, with the use of chronological titles and intermittent flashes of television news bulletins, quite deliberately gives his film a definite historical context, that of the period when the hordes of *kar sevak*s and their supporters were marching towards Ayodhya in order to destroy the Babri Masjid.

We learn quite a lot about the family, especially the grandfather's memories and the girl's education, both social and formal. From the flashbacks depicting old man's reminiscences we get a glimpse into what India has been since Independence. The first of the flashbacks demonstrates with delightfully self-effacing humour the historical fact that independent India is the product of both Hindu and Muslim endeavour and sacrifice. The sequences relating to Naseem's education serve quite clearly to make the point that secularism and modernity are by no means alien to the Muslim community. The fact that Naseem, a girl, is pursuing a secondary education at all is a notable one in India, for any community. Her study of English Literature sees her looking outward to the rest of the world; her study of science sees her looking rationally at the realities of the present and the possibilities of the future; and her study of history depicts an effort to relate to her country's past and the tradition and historical legacy she has inherited from people like her grandfather. The world she shares with her friends is seen to be one imbued with optimism and hope.

What Mirza is particularly successful in establishing, quite without artifice, is the fact that Naseem's family are good, decent people who hold no malice to anyone, and whose one real wish is to love one another and pursue their lives responsibly and in peace. In other words, religious differences notwithstanding, they are very much like most of us who sit watching the film. There is something warming and heartening in this, and one should not underestimate Mirza's ability to create such empathy.

The underlying thrust of the film, however, is in its treatment of the Babri Masjid theme. We learn quite incidentally of the concern of other members of the family about the imminence of the vandalism at Ayodhya. Although there are relatively frequent allusions to television reports or individuals' voicing of concerns, the presentation of these is incidental in that it is not clearly connected to what is transpiring in the rest of the film. It is obvious that the grandfather dies in an India that has regressed, at least in communal terms. It is also obvious that Naseem's future, even her present safety, is threatened by the bigotry and irrational passions that would in no time obscure the rationality and humanism of her education.

Naseem does indeed serve to depict Indian Muslims in a positive, realistic light, enhancing their image in society and, perhaps, strengthening their own view of themselves. If the prejudicial view of Muslims as some kind of threatening Other is to be diluted and eventually obviated, this kind of approach certainly is to be welcomed.

Especially noteworthy in the positive portrayal of Muslims is Shyam Benegal's beautiful film, *Mammo* (1994). Mammo and her husband had been among those who left India for Pakistan at the time of the Partition. Although she survived the tragedies that were part of the massive dislocation, she was not able to survive life with her in-laws after the death of her husband; even more telling was the irrepressible urge to return to India, the land of her roots. After a brief prologue which anticipates the ending of the film, the narrative opens with Mammo in Bombay on the doorstep of the sister with whom she had lost contact for so many years. The sister lives with her grandson, a boy virtually orphaned in that his mother died when he was very young and his father, wanting to start life again with a new wife, did not want the encumbrance of a child from a previous marriage. Mammo moves in with her sister and young nephew, and the three of them adjust to the changed circumstances entailed by the sudden expansion of a household.

Of course, it is not just the sudden expansion of the household that causes change but more the nature of the guest—a buoyant, high-spirited, loving, worldly, compassionate woman with an enormous heart. When such a character as Mammo breezes into a small suburban flat, the winds of change blow strong. Yet nothing really dramatic takes place in the film other than what the individual family members might consider to be dramatic. Apart from domestic tensions and disruptions and petty conflicts—all of which are warm, amusing, and endearing in their essential humanity—the drama of the film evolves outside the family in the offices of those bureaucrats whose lives seem to be dedicated to making the lives of unimportant people like Mammo and her family unhappy. Mammo's visa runs out, and in her desperation to stay in the land of her birth with her only relatives, she agrees to pursue a course through the back door of officialdom. Her bribes are duly offered and received, although she does not bank on the corruption of the officials being so rank as to accept the bribe and renege on their part of the deal. Mammo is arrested and deported to Pakistan.

The film is inescapably Muslim in its social context, its essential historical circumstances, and Mammo's unshakeable faith in Islam (she gives lessons to girls on the Koran, and when, after a domestic misunderstanding, she leaves the house, her sister and nephew trudge from mosque to mosque to find her). Yet none of the film's Muslim 'dress' is a bar to Shyam's very skilful universalizing of his drama's fundamentally human nature, the characters being portrayed as people with whom we can all identify. It is a film that succeeds marvellously in bringing together the people in the audience, of whatever social background, with the people on the screen.

Much the same can indeed be said of Nabyendu Chatterjee's film, *Mansur Mianer Ghora* ('Mansur Mian's Horse', 1999), set in Calcutta. Like Mammo's Bombay, Mansur's Calcutta is home to a substantial Muslim population. (Prior to 1947, Calcutta was the capital of undivided Bengal, a state with a Muslim majority. With Partition, many Muslims went to the eastern wing of the state, then named East Pakistan and, a quarter of a century later, Bangladesh. A good many, however, remained in West Bengal, especially in the vast metropolis of Calcutta.) As is the case in Benegal's film, here too the Muslim ambience does nothing to exclude a more universal interest. The dress of the characters, much of the architecture and the Muslim cemetery give the film its particular visual definition, which is given deeper root by such things as Mansur at his prayers and the grand Id party.

The film is structured largely on juxtapositions of distinction: the old and the new, the living and the dead, wealth and poverty, and the essentially human as distinct from the materialistic. Chatterjee skilfully directs these dialectics through seeming conflict to synthesis. The old need not be overwhelmed by the new but can be successfully blended with it, as the notion of collectors' items and museums might suggest; the dead do indeed live on in the hearts of those whose love for them is undying; and the poor Mansur and his family can celebrate Id in the home of an exceptionally wealthy family. Mansur is content to walk humbly with his God, and while we admire him for this we also spare some sympathy for Mansur's son who struggles to support his small family, seeking a more secure basis for their lives.

The appeal of *Mansur Mianer Ghora* lies, like that of *Mammo,* with its characters, especially its central one. Mansur Mian is a much unsophisticated character, almost two-dimensional in his simplicity. Rather than make for diminution of interest, however, his lack of complexity serves well to emphasize the bonds that make his life what it is and the warm, humane values that drive it. He has nothing like the vivaciousness of Mammo, but he has a powerful presence, even in the scenes where he lies dying. Thus, we take away from the film, as we do from *Mammo*, a marked feeling for what is irrepressibly good in mankind. There are some characters in *Mammo* who are memorable for their meanness and who threaten our optimism, but they have no counterpart in *Mansur Mianer Ghora*, where even Mansur's son's petty materialist boss and his family dissolve quickly into irrelevance once Mansur's spirit is released by his death. It is a film remarkable for its concern with the loveliness and the melancholy of human hopes and dreams, set in the context of the life of a very ordinary, poor, and humble man. Mansur Mian's ordinariness is significant, for through it his community, far from being in any way at all idealized in the film, comes across for what it actually is: people—nothing more, nothing less.

After *Mammo* Benegal's next film was *Sardari Begum* (1996), the main interest of which is the central character, the *thumri* singer who gives her name to the film. Although there is an underlying Muslim element in the atmospherics of the film, Muslim interest is largely incidental. There are, however, some interesting references. The opening titles are set against a comment on the mindlessness of communalism. We see a *Holi* procession wending its way through the predominantly Muslim locality of Chandni Chowk in Old Delhi. As it approaches a mosque, the revelry gets out of hand, perverse passions prevail, and in the course of the fracas that develops, some impetuous nobody in the crowd hurls a stone; the elderly lady whose head it strikes, killing her, is in fact the great singer, Sardari Begum. The superb irony in this is that the would-be champion of Hinduism who threw the stone would probably never know the identity or the fate of whoever it hit. This is characteristic of the mindlessness of communal violence. There is also a significant irony in the fact that the feisty and self-reliant Muslim woman, Sardari Begum, is famous for singing thumri, essentially a Hindu form of music. In the light of this it is interesting that the singer acts as a match-maker in inter-communal marriages—Benegal's gentle, passing reference to the notion of social integration. As Sardari Begum is a free spirit, Muslim orthodoxy comes in for some critical references throughout the film, just as Hindu orthodoxy had in an earlier Benegal film of a somewhat similar kind, *Bhumika* ('The Role', 1977).

The relative neglect of Muslims in the serious cinema does need to be underlined. The most important regional contribution to Indian art cinema has undoubtedly come from Bengal, a state with a special experience of communalism given its truncation by the Partition. Indeed, many of the early art films from Bengal do have a Partition context to them, such as Nemai Ghosh's *Chinnamul* ('Uprooted', 1951). Of course, the most notable of these films are those of Ritwik Ghatak, born in Dhaka in Muslim-dominated East Bengal. Ritwik's films are characterized by their sentiment of nostalgia for a once-united Bengal without making any attempt to suggest, let alone attribute, blame for its division; hence, his most important films—*Meghe Dhaka Tara* ('Cloud Covered Stars', 1960), *Komal Gandhar* ('E Flat', 1961), and *Subarnarekha* (1962)—as well as the much earlier *Nagarik* ('The Citizen', 1953) are essentially films about the displaced Hindu middle-class community, refugees in what was once their own land. *Titash Ekti Nadir Nam* ('A River Called Titash', 1973) is set in a village in East Bengal yet focuses, as does Advaita Malla Barman's novel on which it is based, on a Hindu fishing community. Thus, the Partition, which affected and altered the lives of Muslims as much as Hindus, is the unavoidable context to Ritwik's most important work, yet the Partition as such—and much less the Muslim community—is beyond his interest. The disaffected with whom he sympathizes are generally middle-class Hindus and his vision lies in the cultural idealism of a united Bengal.

India's most celebrated filmmaker, Satyajit Ray, also had little more than a superficial interest in representing the Muslim community in his films. There are, however, two films in which Muslims and their community are given significance: minimally in the film set in the Swadeshi period in Bengal and based on the novel of Tagore, *Ghare Baire* ('The Home and the World', 1984), which quite clearly reflects the confusion of Indian nationalism with the Hindu revivalism that was flourishing at the time; and substantially in *Shatranj Ke Khilari* ('The Chess Players', 1977), a delightful period piece with whose aristocratic quaintness and decadence of the court of Lucknow modern Muslims would have great difficulty in identifying. (Similarly, Shyam Benegal's film set during the Mutiny, *Junoon* ['Possessed', 1978], while dealing with a Muslim hero in an essentially proactive role, also gets lost in period romance and has no obvious relevance to the Muslim community of today. It is, nevertheless, a telling reminder of the direct role played by Muslims in what is often referred to as the first Indian Freedom Movement, just as Ray's film reminds us of the perfidiousness of the imperial power in extending its hold over Indian states.)

One notably fine film in which the major character is a Muslim is Adoor Gopalakrishnan's *Mathilukal* ('The Walls', 1990), which recreates the autobiographical story of Vaikom Muhammad Basheer, the immensely popular Muslim Malayalam novelist and short-story writer, and his experience of jail life as a political prisoner under the British. Apart from one or two Islamic reflections, such as Basheer's philosophical reaction to a man about to be hanged, it is by no means an overtly Muslim film, Adoor's direction aiming as much at secularism as does so much of Basheer's writing. The main point of the film is to examine the counterpoint notions of incarceration and freedom and the admissibility of joy into a prison environment. Despite Basheer's reason for imprisonment, the film offers no nationalist or social polemic. Nevertheless, the film is a significant reminder that Muslims fought for the freedom of India in cooperation with Hindus under the Congress banner, sympathetic to the Gandhian ideal of national brotherhood.

Goutam Ghose's *Padma Nadir Majhi* ('Boatman of the Padma', 1993), a joint West Bengal–Bangladesh production, is based on the classic novel by Manik Bandyopadhyay. The film is set among a fishing community on the banks of the Padma river in East Bengal. The central character, Kuver, and his family are Hindus, as are the majority of the community, although the film offers ample evidence of Hindu–Muslim integration. The mingling of the two communities is handled naturally and with ease, the director seeing no reason to underline any indication of political correctness. Besides the fisherman, Kuver, the other main character is the Muslim landlord and island developer, Hossain Mian.

Although Muslims are evidently the minority community in the film, there are signs that in terms of wealth and influence Muslims also happen to be the leading members of this rural society. The most influential and respected of these leaders is Hossain Mian, indiscriminately paternalistic to both communities and revered, even loved, by most of the people. Although he makes little outward show of his business acumen, we may fairly assume that he is a shrewd and able dealer, while Kuver's discovery that he is involved in opium smuggling elicits from Hossain a plausible defence that does not quite whitewash him but is adequate, nevertheless, to make do. He is a man of sustained dignity and ready compassion, maintaining an acute sense of justice tempered with mercy. He conducts his affairs and those of the village with a notable element of humane idealism and develops his island community with a vision of a harmonious common good, reflected in his refusal to build a mosque there as that would incline the Hindus to demand a temple; hence tension would militate against his dream of genuine integration.

In reading Manik's novel it is possible to attribute to Hossain Mian ulterior motives of personal advancement and prosperity, to see in him a shrewd and cunning businessman with not necessarily more than a superficial concern for the people from whose labours he seeks to profit. Ghose's film, however, would seem to minimize this possibility of equivocation. The late Utpal Dutt brings to the role of Hossain Mian a consistency of warmth and sincerity, the discovery of the opium bundle and the plausible excuse comprising the only reason for suspicion in his good nature. The significance of this treatment of Hossain Mian is that it is made without idealizing the character or making any note—other than the immediate signs of name and appearance—of his religious community. Any social message to be derived in addition to the intrinsic worth of Manik's story must lie in the fact of the dependence of Kuver on Mian, Mian's dependence on people like Kuver, and the respect that each has for the other's needs. Muslim respectability and social influence come across very naturally in this film and with no trace of any kind of patronizing or tokenism.

Particularly interesting is some of the later work of Buddhadeb Dasgupta. His films too are predominantly secular, the only noticeable Muslim in his first nine feature films being the bizarre Abdullah the Magician in *Tahader Katha* ('Their Story', 1992). Yet even in this there is an interesting deception, for Abdullah is in fact a Hindu—a Brahman, no less—who has, it would seem, adopted a Muslim persona to add credibility to his weird act with a touch of the exotic. The innocent Hindu rustics on whom he preys with his second-rate sorcery apparently see an element of mystery in the Muslim showman, something they would not see, presumably, if Abdullah's sacred thread were visible to them. In a film in which a lofty-minded idealist is held to be mad, the sanity of the Brahman sorcerer, posing as a Muslim, ought to be critically questioned.

Two films later, in *Lal Darja* ('The Red Doors', 1996) Dasgupta made a major character a Muslim. Dinu diddles his boss, Nabin, for petty cash and petrol from the car which he is employed to drive. He lacks grace in that he not only sleeps across the front seat while waiting for Nabin, but protrudes his feet from the window. He drinks, sometimes to excess. He also keeps two wives and, by the end of the film, a third has come onto the scene. It would be easy to conclude that this incorrigible rogue does no credit to the Muslim community at all, yet Dasgupta uses this readily loveable character to be something of a guiding beacon for Nabin in seeking a way out of his moribund existence. His diddling can be explained by the fact that he is probably underpaid, like most Indian menials, and he does after all have to support two wives and a daughter; his gracelessness is merely a consequence of being tired and bored; and while his bigamy is much harder to justify, it can certainly be said that his women are aware of each other and still love him implicitly, as does his daughter. What is most important about Dinu is that he has an enormous capacity to love, to nurture and protect; the respectable Nabin lacks these simple virtues, and his life is the duller and the sorrier for it.

In 2000 Dasgupta's *Uttara* ('The Wrestlers') was released. The only Muslim in this film is in a very minor role, that of a postman who is, in the scheme of things, a mere functionary. However, what is of interest here is the reason why the film was made. While a major strand of the narrative is prompted by a short story, *Uratia* by Samaresh Basu, the general concept of the film is inspired by an appalling act of bigoted extremism in the burning to death in their car of an Australian Christian medical missionary and his two young sons in 1999 in rural Orissa. By that time the Hindu nationalist BJP had established itself as the government of India, and various lunatic groups noted for their extremist bigotry against minorities had for some years been making their voices heard more and more—at least since the destruction of the Babri Masjid, an act of vandalism led by the man who would become the deputy prime minister in the BJP government, among others. As the largest minority in India, Muslims were the prime target of their venom. But for a little while before the horrible murder in Orissa, right wing extremists along with leaders of the ruling party in Delhi and in some of the states had started to serve notice on converts to Christianity, which meant that anti-Muslim venom was now being spread to embrace Christians and Dalits as well. The notion of Otherness had been enhanced. One major effect of *Uttara* is to warn of the mindlessness of thugs who appoint themselves guardians of orthodoxy, while another is to assert the power of decency and goodness in ordinary, little people, humbler even than the Graham Staines who was incinerated along with his two little boys.

Dasgupta presented a major character as a Muslim, this time a woman, in *Swapner Din* ('Chased by a Dream', 2004). By the time this film was conceived, Indian intolerance had sunk to its lowest in the state of Gujarat. The first act of barbarity was the incineration in a train of a party of kar sevaks returning home from 'devotional work' at Ayodhya. In self-righteous revenge a wholesale programme of rape, burning alive of people including women, the elderly and small children, arson, looting, shooting, bashing, and hacking was let loose against Muslims indiscriminately. The police stood by and watched and the government, both state and central, was nothing less than provocative in its venomous rhetoric. Given the utter mindlessness of this holocaust, Buddhadeb Dasgupta was no longer content to speak in safe, general terms, but decided to be specific in making his Amina, one of the three main characters in *Swapner Din,* a terrorized fugitive from these savage riots in which her husband, a good and loving man—like most of the myriad innocent victims of bigotry throughout history—was senselessly murdered by men whose basic urge in life is to hate.

Amina's nightmare of extreme horror and her dreams for her as yet unborn child are set in a context of absurdity of which violence is a prominent element. Maybe because she has survived a horrible ordeal, maybe in anticipation of the child to whom she will soon give birth, maybe because, simply, of what she is, Amina comes across as exceptionally positive, determined, and far from easily intimidated. She is a woman of immense personal resource—after all, she has managed to get herself with little or no money from one side of India to the other in her endeavour to return to her home in Bangladesh. It is in trying to extra-legally infiltrate the border (Amina has no papers and therefore no proof of her nationality) that her equanimity is put to the supreme test, for here her own countrymen, for want of a bribe, reject her out of hand. Her two travelling companions—Bengali Hindus—who had picked her up on the road somewhere near the border in West Bengal also try to get across with her; one of them is shot while making a run for it while the other, in a superb irony in the light of Amina's failure to re-enter her homeland, makes it to safety. Amina, who did not have the necessary papers to return to her home after her nightmare abroad, now is forced to return to that same land of nightmare without the necessary documents that would make her at least legal there.

Swapner Din, it must be stressed, is not a film about communalism or sectarianism, nor is it one that seeks to laud Muslims for one reason or another. However, when making sense of little people's getting entangled in the net of irrationality that the strong so often throw over this or that part of the world, certain groups necessarily become identified. There is nothing political in this: reasons are not given for the Gujarat riots, blame is not attributed to anyone, nor is hatred expressed against the anonymous perpetrators. Ultimately it is a film about ordinary people in which simple dreams are made to stand up to the machinations of bullies.

The Indian serious cinema is in many ways more dynamic than commercial cinema. The formulary demands of the Bombay product are not part of the alternative cinema, which is indelibly pervaded by individualism and where the artistic, intellectual, and moral integrity of the filmmaker are enduring and indefeasible. Here it is possible to make films challenging the sacred cows of society, and although such films far from make up the major part of the independent cinema, many of them are very highly regarded and have not resulted in the burning of cinema halls or the stoning of directors. Indeed, there are a number of artistically excellent films that have proven to be of social significance as well as having achieved considerable popular acclaim. Commercial films, however, are produced according to a tried and true formula—'true' at least as far as desired popular response is concerned—involving, in established narrative structures, the classic conflict model of protagonist versus antagonist, the process into complication and at least threatened disorder or even chaos, and the final resolution of the conflict in favour of the protagonist. The leaders of the commercial film industry claim to be giving the public simply what the public wants, and given the communal nature of Indian society this appeal to the majority is of more than passing significance; one must bear in mind commercial cinema's contribution to the enforcement of established social values and mores as well as established social prejudices and fears. For example, gender equality is far from fully realized in Indian society and is notably absent in commercial cinema. It is indeed possible that if commercial cinema were to push its best films into stimulating popular thought and acceptance of female equality, something of a valuable social revolution might be engendered in India—at least, it might be talked about. However, female servility and men raping and otherwise physically abusing women makes good box office, so a revolution of social conscience in the commercial cinema is as fantastic a notion as the plot of a Bombay movie. Despite their statistical actuality, women are treated cinematically and socially as a minority. Moreover, cinematically and socially, especially domestically, they are seen by men as an Other. In appreciating this attitude it is not difficult to perceive, quite logically, how the minimal treatment or occasional negative treatment of a minority community in cinema might aid in the strengthening of majority community prejudices and perceived grievances and fears.

Two films might well illustrate some of the generally perceived features of the popular cinema in regard to the depiction of the Muslim community. (The contrast to the films of the serious cinema might be noted, though it is not intended that it be seen as categorical.) *Amar, Akbar, Anthony* was made in 1977 under the direction of Manmohan Desai and is a classic of the narrative-confusion model of popular cinema which emanates out of the phenomenon of characters being swapped or abducted or going missing at birth or very early in life. *Amar, Akbar, Anthony* might purport to be a movie of social integration, offering as it does the highly unlikely story of three infant brothers separated from their parents and each other and being brought up in three different communities: Amar is brought up as a Hindu, Akbar as a Muslim, and Anthony as a Christian. We might also note the simple significance in the date of their sundering—15 August—as the date of both the Independence and the partition of India.

As the film proceeds from one improbability to the next, various elements of social harmony are expressed such as Anthony's energetic support of Akbar at his Qawali recital, Akbar's declared non-violence (he wants to win his beloved's father over by love and not by force, and at the end of the film he declares that his hands have only ever been raised in prayer—right before royally punching the villain out of the frame), the ecumenical nature of the Sacred Man of Shirdi sequence, and Amar's line, 'Amar Lal and his brothers—all are my brothers: Hindu, Muslim, Sikh and Christian, all are brothers!'

But despite these lofty sentiments, there is no obvious equality among the three unknown-to-each-other brothers, nor are laughter and respect equally demanded. The image that each of the three young men presents is quite significant to an assessment of the film's sincerity. Amar, the Hindu, is a police inspector, tempted earlier in the piece by the lures of a prostitute, but nevertheless an incorruptible, impartial, extraordinarily tough upholder of the law. Akbar is a

Qawali singer, for no pertinently narrative reason other than the opportunities such a profession gives for easily introducing the mandatory songs and dances into the film. Anthony is the proprietor of a country liquor bar, a confrère of the social dregs and not always averse to indulgence in petty felony. Hence we might note a hierarchy amongst the three: the mildly disreputable Christian is at the bottom, the pleasant enough though somewhat inconsequential Muslim is in the middle, while the upholder of the law, the guardian of society, the respectable and awesome Hindu, is at the top. While Anthony's church and Akbar's Muslim locality are shown as self-contained characteristic spaces, there is no characteristically Hindu space with which Amar identifies; presumably the Hindu world pervades all.

The movie relies greatly on its comedy, and it is interesting that while Anthony is responsible for some very funny moments, much of the humour actually takes as its butt the Muslim elements in the film. Tayyab Ali, the father of Salma, Akbar's intended, is an absurd character, a four-and-a-half feet tall caricature of a Muslim gentleman; the comic scene in the streets of the Muslim locality depends for its laughs simply on the humiliation meted out to Tayyab. A laugh is extracted out of Anthony's line when, disguised as a priest, he declares that he has married off Akbar four times already. And there is a degree of ironic humour in the writing of a secret note in Urdu 'because nobody here understands it'.

Twenty-two years earlier the brothers and their parents by some twist of fate had been separated from one another, and each of the boys since has wandered through life in modern India via the path of one of its major communities. Ultimately, when the film reaches its climax, the grand reunion of former criminal father, formerly blind mother and formerly Hindu, Muslim, and Christian brothers is effected. And of course, the real significance of this noble encompassing is a victory for the majority community, for the father's name is Kishan Lal (make what you will of his straight-cut beard without a moustache), mother is Bharati, and Inspector Amar Khanna, it is revealed, was originally known to the world as Raju. Akbar and Anthony are merely brought back into the Hindu fold. Indeed, the characteristic improbability of the film is its surest safeguard against feasibility and the serious acceptance of its ultimately incidental deference to social integration.

Shekhar Kapoor's film, *Mr India,* is an example of interest in the notion of the Other extending to movies with an element of appeal to children. The film is a simple and more than usually improbable story about the conflict between the arch-enemy of India, Mugambo, and Mr India, the representative of the average Indian citizen. Mugambo's aim is to spread chaos and destruction throughout India in order to bring the country to its knees and facilitate his takeover, and his means of weakening India is in the exploitation of arms smuggling, adulteration of grain and the deliberate creation of food shortages, drug pushing, and the spread of gambling dens and bars, particularly with the aim of increasing crime. There could be little dispute that the majority of Indians, if asked who is India's number one enemy and who is responsible for the pushing of drugs in India or the smuggling of arms, would offer the same answer to both questions. Thus, for all its childish and fanciful improbability, based as it is on a man who can make himself invisible, *Mr India* is a simply nationalistic film based on notions of siege mentality with the thinly veiled implication of Pakistan as the reality behind the Mugambo fantasy.

The film is structured to a large extent on the basic contrast between Mugambo and India. Mugambo—the ever-present and actual Other—bears insidious responsibility for all India's ills (conveniently absolving India's own leaders of responsibility for civil unrest and communal violence, food shortages, high prices and adulteration of grain staples, drug addiction, vice and crime). India, represented by a simple music teacher, Arun, orphaned as a child by the very agents of Mugambo, and the orphan children whom he has adopted as his own family, bear the onslaught with courage, forbearance, and faith in the dictum that good will always prevail, an attitude that might also be described as a euphemism for burying one's head in the sand. Indians sing and dance and love one another, especially children, while the followers of Mugambo live in totalitarian straits in a world governed by military technology and the constant fear of baths of boiling acid, under an emperor with no qualms about making children the objects of his appalling cruelty. Indians live lives of gentle peacefulness, while the followers of Mugambo look up to a crazed megalomaniac. Of course, India is not perfect, for as Mugambo points out, they are a divided people who 'fight in the name of religion, language and caste. Let them! I will provide them with arms to continue, and India will be at my feet and every Indian will be my slave.' But again, responsibility for India's domestic dissensions is placed at the feet of the menacing external Other. Moreover, to add a sense of actuality to the nature of Mugambo, it is not presented as an independent, self-sufficient power, but one aided by at least one other nation which supplies it with arms and technology and which has representatives working for Mugambo by the names of Watson and Walcott. Does one wonder who that other power might be?

Part of Mr India's task in saving his country from the threat of Mugambo is to save Hinduism, for the foreigner, Walcott, wishes to steal a golden idol from a temple and sell it abroad. The god he attempts to purloin is Hanuman, the faithful servant of Ram, and the implications of this particularity in contemporary India are quite obvious. Mr India maintains Hanuman in power, forcing the agents of the enemies of Hinduism to the ground chanting 'Long live Bajrangbali!', an allusion also to the chauvinistic right-wing organization, the Bajrang Dal.

To put Mr India's defence of Hinduism into sharper relief, the film is notable for its lack of Muslims. It is all too easy—and, one might think, dangerously so—to identify Muslims with the Mugambo menace. Mr India, who describes himself to Mugambo, before bringing him down, as merely an everyday, ordinary Indian, overtly defends Hinduism, or more specifically the major stalwart in the notion of Ram Rajya, but not Indian Islam or even Indian secularism. Apart from the suggested association of Muslims with Mugambo, Muslims are, as far as Mr India or the ordinary everyday Indian is concerned, merely irrelevant.

Given its perceived need to appeal to the majority in the interests of optimum box office turnover, it is hardly likely that we will ever see the commercial cinema giving substantial and fair representation to the Muslim community. When we look to the independent cinema, the outlook is less bleak, but it has to be admitted that for various reasons the Muslim community, the Muslim contribution to India, and Muslim human interests are, relatively speaking, very much under-represented even here. Nevertheless, of those Muslim-interest films that have been made—whether by Muslim or non-Muslim filmmakers is immaterial—many are exceptionally fine works as cinema and none has provoked a communal riot or the burning of a cinema hall.

One might imagine that films such as *Mammo* or *Naseem* or *Mansur Miar Ghora,* or even films that are less Muslim-specific, such as *Swapner Din* or *Sardari Begum* or *Lal Darja* must have some effect in enhancing the Muslim image in India, for as long as significant elements in the majority community continue to see the Muslim community as the constant Other, it is important for Indian society in general that the Muslim image be enhanced. To capitalize on common interests, shared concerns, jointly cherished ideals, and the everlasting universals of love and joy and grief and pain—something cinema is wonderfully well equipped to do—is to stress quite unselectively the fundamental humanity that pervades society. Films that can do that can make a lofty contribution to national integration in showing to sceptics that the one country can be loved and lived in by a variety of people who can, if they simply look to basics, find more to unite than to divide them. It is also important that cinema reflect the fact that the Muslim community is simply not a mere agglutinate component of Indian society but an integral part of it, a natural legatee of so much of India's vast and diverse cultural tradition, and a continuing contributor to India's cultural growth and development. Hence, 'Indianness' in cinema needs to be broadened in scope and made more inclusive in nature. Genuine social integration can never be imposed but can be achieved only by a process, for which sound public opinion must be developed. Cinema's potential in this cannot be understated.

NOTES

1. The term is loosely applied. Some prefer 'parallel' cinema, 'alternative' cinema, 'independent' cinema.
2. Sudhir Kakar, *The Colours of Violence* (New Delhi: Viking, 1995).
3. Sara Dickey, *Cinema and the Urban Poor in South India* (New Delhi: Cambridge University Press, 1993), p. 95.
4. There was a furore over the release of Mani Ratnam's *Bombay.* Deepa Mehta's films have also been greeted aggressively by social conservatives.

Appendix I
Medium is the Image[1]

Vinod Mehta

Indian Muslims face multiple problems, possibly more than any other major religious group in our secular republic. Some of the baggage they carry is a leftover from history. One would have thought Partition is an old story, dead and buried along with the generation that saw its horrors, but I am alarmed when a generation which has no first-hand experience of Partition still claims to have 'living memory' of the division of India. Clearly, the prejudices and the occasionally exaggerated tales of slaughter and carnage have been passed on. No doubt, the influence of this cycle diminishes with every passing decade; I only emphasize that the truism about the past being forgotten and forgiven is only half-correct. It takes a long time to disremember the past.

The most acute problem facing Indian Muslims is the problem of perception. Clearly, the angle at which the majority community views them is the basis of the Hindu perception of Muslims en bloc. That this view is negative, inaccurate, and retrogressive, made up of half-truths, propaganda, and sometimes outright lies, does not help solve the problem. A perception is a perception—right or wrong is another matter. Politicians in India have shrewdly realized the criticality of perception and are obsessively concerned about their 'image'. The fact that the image has little or no relation with reality is irrelevant. Finally, in the voter's mind it is not the reality which counts but the perception.

Occasionally, perception and reality merge: there is no disconnect. We have a very good example in the case of Manmohan Singh. The gulf between who he is and how he is seen is non-existent. Manmohan Singh is a rare and lucky man.

But, at the best of times, perception and reality are in conflict. The difficulty is compounded when there is a systematic attempt to malign the image of an individual or a group of individuals. One can argue that this whole image business is complete nonsense, a media myth. It does not matter. The late British prime minister Harold Wilson once said that the only image he believes in is the one he sees while shaving every morning. I wish that were true. In an ideal world, truth would win but, as is obvious, we live in an imperfect world. To bury one's head in the hope that truth will triumph is dangerously optimistic.

In the high-tech age we live in, it is not merely coffee which is instant; communication too is instant. Not only do we inhabit a global village, but we are also being bombarded by images. Our sensibility is under assault. The principal medium for image construction is the media.

Whether one speaks English or Hindi or Urdu, the medium is the image. It will not go away, it will follow you. To argue that a community consciously work towards improving community perception is merely common sense.

Few will seriously disagree that Indian Muslims have failed to come to terms with the media. There is a small, educated, articulate middle-class which recognizes the salience of the media, but the bulk of India's 160-million Muslims are either 'missing' from our media or, alternately, those who claim to speak for them are not just media-illiterate but more crucially convey entirely the wrong message on behalf of Indian Muslims. They feed and fortify prevailing prejudices.

The core prejudice is that the bulk of Indian Muslims are held prisoner by an extremely powerful religious leadership, which seems to have a vested interest in ensuring their backwardness. This leadership is geriatric, ultra-conservative, chauvinistic, gender-insensitive, and looks to the holy Koran for resolving every challenge posed by India 2004. Of course, this conclusion is an oversimplification verging on falsehood. Alas, however oversimplified, Indian Muslims have to accept this negative perception. To live in a state of denial is to run away from the problem.

If you accept that Hindu–Muslim relations will depend largely on how the former perceives the latter, and if you accept that there is a perception mismatch, the corrective for which must be launched by the minority community, one can proceed further. I do not pretend to know all the answers to this complex puzzle, but I am sure if a new generation in the Muslim community addresses it, an agenda could be drawn up. The Muslim 'problem' in India will not be solved by merely correcting image distortions; that would be an extremely naive view of a multilayered historical problem. But it would go a long way in creating a positive background in which issues of Muslim economic and social backwardness can be addressed. Finally, the community itself will have to shoulder the burden of bringing Muslims into the mainstream. However, that task will be considerably eased if image distortions are corrected.

I have only one suggestion to make. Most Hindus make up their mind about Muslims on the basis of the Muslim faces they see and the Muslim voices they hear. Some of this interaction comes through personal contact but much of it comes courtesy the media. Unfortunately, the faces the average Hindu sees and the voices he hears whenever there is a Muslim 'question' are invariably of 90-year-old men insisting on preserving the status quo. These men (you never see women) seem to come from another age; when it comes to change, say, in family planning, they even denounce practices in Muslim countries like Bangladesh and Egypt.

The All India Muslim Personal Law Board is one such body. It has emerged as the sole spokesman for the community. These are wise and venerable men but their physical appearance on television and in newspapers only confirm the worst prejudices of the majority community. An urgent need exists for new, younger faces and voices to represent the views and aspirations of Indian Muslims. What they have to say may come as a big and pleasant surprise.

NOTE

1. This article appeared in *Outlook*, 1 November 2004.

Appendix II
Who's the Real Muslim?[1]

Ather Farouqui

In his piece,[2] Vinod Mehta simplistically holds Indian Muslims responsible for the way Hindus perceive them. Surely, Indian Muslims have two identities: one as members of the wider Indian society, sharing all that is good and bad with other Indians of their region and class; and the other as members of the pan-Islamic community that includes other global Muslim societies. Mehta ignores the second part entirely.

The pan-Islamic aspect is more relevant in the case of north Indian Muslims and to some extent to Muslims residing in the larger Indian cities. South Indian rural Muslims and non-Bihari Bengali Muslims of West Bengal, for example, have little to do with the broader Islamic brotherhood. Again, rural India is host to a number of social ills encompassing both the Hindu and Muslim communities, and for this reason Hindus too bear a highly distorted image in the media the world over.

There is a newly emergent trend driven by the business interests of some sections of the English media, which have a ready prescription for the ills suffered by Muslims in India, and it squarely puts the onus of transformation on the Muslim middle-class alone. In doing so, the media is choosing to ignore the social and economic complexities of Indian Muslim society, that is, the extreme educational and economic deprivation of most Indian Muslims. In all this, the role played by Indo-Pakistani Muslims in the Gulf and Saudi Arabia—which has affected the psyche of beneficiary Muslims of their petro-dollars in India—cannot be ignored, for it is this psyche which lends support to Muslim fundamentalism and colludes with the government (which has its own vested interests) in not attending to the urgent need for modern educational institutions for Muslim children, thereby allowing the madrasas to flourish. Thus the trauma of partition is still a raw wound for both Muslims and Hindus: the former still suffering the consequences and the latter not ready to believe that it was an accident of history for which no one community is to blame. Mehta presumably does not subscribe to the RSS view about Muslims, but for all practical purposes, his thinking is no different from that of the RSS.

The reference by Mehta to Manmohan Singh (in the image context) is also quite blinkered. President A.P.J. Abdul Kalam is someone who does not carry the baggage of his community. This is because there is a threshold beyond which individuals are seen autonomously, without the image of their community dogging them. Manmohan Singh's media image does not in any way represent the media image of Sikhs. It has been suggested that had the media representation of the Sikhs not been negative, the 1984 Sikh riots would not have taken place. Nor is there any guarantee that something similar will not happen to them again or to the Muslims as in Gujarat in 2002.

On the issue of media representation, there is a need to examine seriously whether, as is Mehta's view, the Muslim leadership is really unaware of its impact, and not only in India but also in the so-called Islamic countries. My own belief is that the 'Muslim leadership' in India is as shrewd as its RSS counterpart and recognizes fully the reach of the media. It can hardly be that a senior ulema's outcry against family planning was based on sheer ignorance. After all, their funding fathers who have dozens of wives—and who do not even remember the names of their children—need to be kept in good humour too.

While illiteracy and poverty can be blamed for Muslim behaviour and the resultant negative media images, it would not be the whole truth. Even in places where Muslims are educated and gainfully employed—for example, immigrant Muslims in Western Europe and the US—they are more or less ghettoized.

Moreover, Mehta's views suffer from the common error of regarding Muslims as a monolithic, homogeneous community. Leaving aside regional and linguistic diversity, there is the broad Shia–Sunni divide, and, within each schism, hundreds of sects. So, defining a true Muslim remains a perennial problem.

While Mehta's assessment of the role of language in the process of image formation is pertinent, the question is what one can do about the sectarian politics played out in the name of Urdu by political parties. Sectarian Urdu newspapers and magazine further emotionalize the issue.

The unfortunate baggage of our colonial past and the inescapable reality of globalization is that only English-speaking people are perceived as modern, as a recent issue of *Outlook* (5 October 2004) implied in its cover story. Most Indian Muslims do not even fall under the category of literates, leave alone among the tiny minority of elite Indians who speak English. If English is a criterion of modernity—as per most recent prescriptions for Muslim upliftment—the unfortunate thing is that there are not more than one million Muslims in the whole of India who can speak English fluently, and this number is perhaps an overestimation.

In Delhi alone, the dropout rate of school-going Muslim children is as high as 98 per cent. The number of Muslim students in good English medium schools is almost negligible. There is a pressing need for the media to cover these issues and people like Vinod Mehta should perhaps turn their attention to it instead of providing facile prescriptions that free them of all responsibility in the matter.

It has become fashionable in media circles to talk of the Jawaharlal Nehru University (JNU) as a bastion of left politics. But it is the large number of Muslim students (mainly studying Arabic, Urdu, and Persian) that give the left student organizations a decisive say in student union elections, thus giving them a hold over all secular student organizations. Left-wing organizations were in fact the most active in wooing them. These Muslim students have made all left-wing organizations their captive; left organizations have kept their organizations shut from all populist and ghettoized mentality. All right-wing Muslim organizations who are known to be close to Muslim countries, getting funds and fanning Muslim fundamentalism, have a strong hold in JNU. I wonder if the media is aware of this; if so, why does it choose to ignore this Islamicization of a secular institution, or does it not find it important enough? One feels as helpless in front of the English media as in front of the mullahs and doctrinaire Marxists: only they seem to know the real truth!

And what of Mehta's take on the All India Muslim Personal Law Board? Since its inception, it has been no more than an exclusive club of opportunistic mullahs and self-appointed 'traders' of Muslim politics, shrewd enough to recognize that it is their reactionary statements that induce the media to seek them out on Muslim issues. The Board is a Frankenstien's monster created by the media. But Mehta would have us believe otherwise by giving it the legitimacy it neither deserves nor commands. The Supreme Court judgement in the Shah Bano case was unacceptable to 99 per cent of Muslims and resisted with unprecedented vigour till Parliament was forced to reconsider it and bypass the judgement. This kind of psyche will never allow the trauma of Partition to become a thing of the past.

Nor are we willing to come to terms with the future vis-à-vis the situation in Kashmir, which has increasingly become an issue of Muslim separatism fuelled by pan-Islamic proclivities. This is the reality that cannot be altered by rhetoric. Abusing imperialism and America will not alter the truth that Islam does not provide any space for democracy, and only a *Momin* may be head of state. The pan-Islamic version of Islamic society at best tries to present faith as the vehicle of civil life, to show that there can be no substitute for the Islamic faith, and, therefore, the first duty of every Muslim is to convert all non-believers to the Islamic fold. Even today, Muslim civil life is facing all kind of problems due to this mental bankruptcy, and distorted media images of Muslims are the obvious result of this attitude. Those to be blamed are Muslim societies; their intellectuals, and institutions, whose very existences are based on hypocrisy.

Way back in 1956, when the Sunni–Qadiyani riots (Qadyanis are also known as Ahmadis or non-Muslims, or *Kafirs*) erupted in a part of Punjab in Pakistan, a commission headed by Justice Munir was instituted to enquire into the reasons for the trouble. A number of leading ulema were invited to decide whether or not Qadiyanis could be called Muslims. This led to the question of the definition of 'Muslim'. Surprisingly, there were no two ulema who would agree on any one definition.

Syed Shahabuddin, a most articulate and shrewd Muslim politician—one who is aware of the importance of the media in these times, was once considered the most potential radical Muslim threat, and was in the forefront of the Shah Bano agitation and after that the Babri Masjid demolition—talks with a forked tongue. On the one hand he talks about modernization, and on the other he categorically denies the need for *ijtihad* (juridical conclusion according to the need of the times) in civil life, saying,

Let the Muslim Indians develop their own strategy for survival, and for equality, justice and dignity .... The real issue, therefore, is to find a national solution to the national problem of providing equitable space in the fields of education, information and administration to minority languages in the country as a whole as well as at the state level .... The real battle for Muslim Indians is also the battle of all religious, racial and ethnic minorities anywhere in the world .... In political terms, the essence of the problem is to find a balance between change and conservation, between rejection and assimilation, and between alienation and participation. This is imperative so that a Muslim, wherever he is, is not an alien to the nation state of which he is an inextricable part but a creative contributor to its productivity as well as its welfare. If the national communities accept them, trust them and respect them in all parts of the world at large, Muslims will not carry the image of being the group of fanatical subversives or terrorists, ever anxious to restore Muslim rule or establish Islamic power! The priority for Muslim Indians should therefore be to find peace and dignity in their own motherland rather than to undertake the national project for the reconstruction of religious thought of Islam for the sake of *Ummah*.[3]

And also:

To me, the interpretation of the shariat—a common task for the Islamic world, as a whole—does not appear to be a top priority for Muslim Indians ... this is nothing but an echo of our historically constructed ego.[4]

Shahabuddin clearly wants Muslims to not only remain backward but also divided from the rest of society. It is this negative image (which somehow most Muslims too appear to subscribe to, for whatever reason) that allows the present Muslim leadership to remain leaders and the dangerously ignorant English-speaking Muslim intellectuals the opportunity to pose as Muslim spokespersons. Of course the media is only too ready to provide space to these people, whose reactionary utterances make for good copy. Since the Muslim religious leadership, which is solely responsible for destroying the image of Muslims in media, and the intellectuals are not directly concerned with votes, one cannot expect them to be as careful and shrewd as Laloo Yadav.

The fact remains that despite the media, the common Hindu realizes he has to live with the Muslims, who, for various historical and social reasons, are still the most backward and ghettoized community in India. Whether it be the Babri Masjid demolition or the question of a life of dignity for Muslims, the Hindus have played their role responsibly—let us not forget how they recently threw out the BJP by democratic franchise. The so-called Muslim leadership, on the other hand, was and is always out to manipulate and mismanage affairs. Sooner or later Indian Muslims will have to come to terms with a uniform lifestyle in conformity with their economic and regional compulsions. The minority rhetoric of left-wing intellectuals to counter the madness of the atavistic RSS is no solution. Left parties everywhere have become victims of electoral politics; exercising populist policies vis-à-vis Muslim affairs and not taking a firm stand against Muslim fundamentalism will not work. On the contrary it may make things worse! To abuse America will not justify 9/11 and will only encourage Muslim militancy and non-Muslim retaliation.

So the pressing need is to make Muslims understand that modernization and reform are the only answer to their problems.

Notes

1. Excerpts were published in *Outlook,* 6 December 2004.
2. Vinod Mehta, 'Medium is the Image', *Outlook*, 1 November 2004. See Appendix I this volume.
3. *The Pioneer*, 11 July 2002.
4. *The Pioneer*, 16 September 2002.

Contributors

ARSHAD AMANULLAH is a documentary filmmaker and writer based in New Delhi.

CHARLES J. BORGES is Associate Professor in History, Loyola College, Maryland.

HOWARD BRASTED is Associate Professor in Indian and Islamic History, University of New England, Armidale.

ATHER FAROUQUI is Director, Delhi Public School, Jeddah and Riyadh, Saudi Arabia.

SABYA SACHI is a freelance writer and artist based in Kolkata.

JOHN W. HOOD is with a law firm in Minnetonka, Minnesota.

ROBIN JEFFREY is Director, Research School of Pacific and Asian Studies (RSPAS), Australian National University.

MOINUDDIN JINABADE is Professor, Centre of Indian Languages, Jawaharlal Nehru University, New Delhi.

WAHIDUDDIN KHAN is President, The Islamic Centre, New Delhi.

RAJNI KOTHARI is Chair Professor in Democracy, Centre for the Study of Developing Societies, Delhi.

SUSAN B. MAITRA is Senior Editor, *Foreign Service Journal*, Washington, DC.

DAGMAR MARKOVA is with the Oriental Institute of the Academy of Sciences, Prague.

CHANDAN MITRA is Managing Director and Editor, *The Pioneer*, New Delhi, and an independently elected Member of Parliament.

VINOD MEHTA is Editor-in-Chief, *Outlook*, New Delhi.

K.M.A. MUNIM (1920–2004) was Chief Editor of *Bangladesh Observer.*

KULDIP NAYAR is a prominent journalist, columnist, and author; he is also former Indian High Commissioner to the United Kingdom.

MRINAL PANDE is Chief Editor of *Hindustan.*

SIDDHARTH VARADARAJAN is Associate Editor, *The Hindu*, New Delhi.

Index